The Hidden Life of Otto Frank

The Hidden Life of Otto Frank

CAROL ANN LEE

VIKING
an imprint of
PENGUIN BOOKS

VIKING

Published by the Penguin Group
Penguin Books Ltd, 80 Strand, London WC2R ORL, England
Penguin Putnam Inc., 375 Hudson Street, New York, New York 10014, USA
Penguin Books Australia Ltd, 250 Camberwell Road,
Camberwell, Victoria 3124, Australia
Penguin Books Canada Ltd, 10 Alcorn Avenue, Toronto, Ontario, Canada M4V 3B2
Penguin Books India (P) Ltd, 11 Community Centre,
Panchsheel Park, New Delhi – 110 017, India
Penguin Books (NZ) Ltd, Cnr Rosedale and Airborne Roads,
Albany, Auckland, New Zealand
Penguin Books (South Africa) (Pty) Ltd, 24 Sturdee Avenue,
Rosebank 2196, South Africa

Penguin Books Ltd, Registered Offices: 80 Strand, London WC2R ORL, England

www.penguin.com

First published 2002
1

Set in 11/13pt Monotype Bembo
Typeset by Rowland Phototypesetting Ltd, Bury St Edmunds, Suffolk
Printed in Great Britain by Clays Ltd, St Ives plc

A CIP catalogue record for this book is available from the British Library

ISBN 0-670-91331-6

In memory of my father, Raymond Lee

Contents

PART TWO
Publish Without a Doubt 1945–1980

Acknowledgements

Many people gave generously of their time and knowledge during the writing of this book. I must first of all thank Yt Stoker, whose patient and expert guidance through the archives of the Anne Frank Stichting, and in other areas of research, was invaluable and contributed much to the final form of the book. I would also like to thank Teresien da Silva, Jan Erik Dubbelman and Dienke Hondius of the Stichting. Dienke's loan of the English translation of *Terugkeer* ('The Return' – her intelligent and scrupulous study of Jewish concentration camp survivors who returned to the Netherlands) is gratefully acknowledged, and this illuminated a particularly dark era in Otto Frank's life for me.

I received help from a number of other archives and institutions, and wish to single out for particular thanks Sierk Plantinga at the Rijksarchief Den Haag, Johannes van der Vos, Hubert Berkhout and David Barnouw at NIOD, Verola de Weert at the Amsterdam Bevolkingregister, the staff of the Algemeen Archief Amsterdam, the Jewish Historical Museum Amsterdam, the Koninklijke Bibliotheek in Den Haag, the Auschwitz-Birkenau Museum, the United States Holocaust Museum, the Simon Wiesenthal Center in Los Angeles, and Gillian Walnes of the Anne Frank Educational Trust for providing advice and contacts.

I received excellent ideas for further research from Susan Massotty, Simone Schroth and Elma Verhey. Francoise Gaarlandt-Kist provided expert guidance on how to improve an initially unwieldy manuscript and Jan Michael helped me not to despair about the work that entailed, but to see it as a surmountable challenge. I also thank Pauline Micheels for putting me in touch with Dola de Jong, and Marion Nietfeld for setting me on a trail which had never been followed before. I am indebted to Paul van Maaren for material which helped light the way.

Grateful acknowledgement is made to all those authors and publishers who allowed me to quote from their works, and to those people named below who permitted me to quote from their private letters (the citations within the text are all traceable to the references for each individual chapter found at the back of the book). Quotations from Anne's diary, and the personal correspondence of the Frank and Elias families – used by the kind permission of Buddy Elias – are under copyright of the Anne Frank-Fonds, Basel.

I offer my heartfelt gratitude to those who shared personal and often deeply painful memories with me: Ilse Blitz, Angus Cameron, Annette Duke, Barbara Epstein, Vincent Frank-Steiner, Jack Furth, Hilde Goldberg (many thanks to her sister-in-law, Bea, for providing the initial contact), Edith Gordon, Stephan van Hoeve, Dola de Jong, Bee Klug, Gabriel Levin, Rose and Sal de Liema, Lillian Marks, Barbara Mooyart-Doubleday, Father John Neiman, Laureen Nussbaum, Katja Olszewska, Hanneli Pick-Goslar, Alfred Radley, Tony van Renterghem, Judith and Henk Salomon, Jacqueline Sanders-van Maarsen, Eva and Zvi Schloss, Rabbi David Soetendorp, Franzi Spronz, Anneke Steenmeijer, Cor Suijk and Thesy Nebel. I regret that it was not possible to speak to Miep Gies, who no longer grants interviews after enduring a bout of severe ill health. The questions I would have liked to ask Mrs Gies were answered on her behalf by Cor Suijk.

Gusta Krusemeyer and Henri Beerman translated scores of documents from German and Dutch into English for me, even though they had their own work to do. I thank them deeply for that, and for their kindness, generosity and amiability, which made working with them such a pleasure. Thanks too to Maarten Fagh for putting me in touch with them, and to Hendrikus Wilhelm Reiters for additional help with German translations.

The following group of people have supported my work in ways too numerous to mention, and are very close to my heart: Buddy and Gerti Elias, Jan Michael and Paul Clark, and Alison Davies. My love and respect goes out to all of them, and to my mother, brother and his wife, and my husband's sister, who have all been instrumental in the completion of this book.

Finally, as any writer who also happens to be a mother knows, the most basic necessity before settling down to write is not only a room of one's own, but the certainty that one's child is in the safest possible hands. For this, and for countless other things, I thank my beloved husband Ronnie and my parents-in-law Dick and Truus Cornelisz. They shared the care of my son, River, during the often peculiar writing hours I kept, and I want to dedicate this book to them.

Preface

The idea to write this book came from Swiss publisher Thomas Meyer. He suggested it to me after a talk I gave in Basel about my biography of Anne Frank, *Roses from the Earth*. I thought about it at length, remembering how captivated I had been by Otto Frank's letters from the Western Front, which I had not been able to include in my book about his daughter, and by his determination to have the diary published in an era when the Holocaust (not referred to then as such) was a subject on which there was little available literature. I was also fascinated by the dichotomy between Otto Frank fighting for his country in the First World War and his persecution by his country in the Second, and how he reconciled himself to the appalling contrast in his circumstances. His life was divided in two in another way: after 1945 and the loss of his first wife and children in the Holocaust, Otto Frank embarked upon a mission to bring Anne's diary to as wide a public as possible. Her book became one of his primary reasons for living.

Generally speaking, only the most basic details of his existence have been public knowledge. Otto Frank was famous for the last thirty years of his life but, even then, few interviewers thought to ask him about himself. He wrote thousands of replies to readers of his daughter's diary who wished for some communication with him, but rarely deviated from a set response. When he did, with a remark seemingly thrown in as an afterthought – 'I was liberated from Auschwitz at the end of January, two days after I had faced an execution squad. I returned to Amsterdam . . .' – it raised many questions, most of which remained unanswered.

Otto Frank was ninety-one years old when he died in 1980. By any standards, it is a long life to study in depth. During the winter of 1999, I examined some of my old notes, read Otto Frank's intriguing letters, spoke to a few of his relatives and friends, and walked through the streets in Amsterdam, close to my own home, where Otto's life had at first come good and then come undone. I realized how much I wanted to write about this hidden, haunted life.

Looking back now, I see that I had no idea quite how hidden and haunted his life really was.

★

It was never my intention to raise the matter of the betrayal of Otto Frank and his family again. I felt there had been too much speculation on the subject already and, although I wrote at length about the case against Wilhelm van Maaren (the main suspect) in *Roses from the Earth*, ultimately I concluded that there was no decisive evidence.

Then, late last year, I was given a letter written by Otto Frank which has never been published before. It told an incredible story that has been kept secret for decades. By chance, two months later, I was given a second letter written by a person named in the first, who was a member of the NSB (Dutch Nazi Party). It contained facts about the hiding period which at the time were unknown to anyone else outside the small circle of the eight fugitives and their helpers. Deeply unpleasant in tone, it heavily contradicted some of the statements made in the first letter and made several accusations which I doubted to be true. The writer referred to other letters he had written in defence of Silberbauer, the man who arrested the Frank family and with whom he had corresponded. In the archives of the *Nederlandse Instituut voor Oorlogsdocumentatie* (Netherlands Institute for War Documentation – NIOD), I found two more of his letters, a summary about his wartime activities by a member of the SD (Security Service), and a report by the authorities investigating Silberbauer in 1963/64. The obvious question was why had this person not been interrogated in regard to the betrayal? It took months of research, tracing names, and sifting through layer upon layer of documentation before I found the answer.

In the meantime, I set out to discover what had happened to the letter writer. I learned that he had been imprisoned after the war – for betraying people to the SD. I found small strands of information, such as dates and addresses, and followed the paths where they led. Sometimes I came up against a wall but, occasionally, a gap in the wall allowed me a glimpse of something relevant and I would keep going. A breakthrough came when I was able to consult the letter writer's collaborator files in The Hague; amongst the papers was an attestation by Otto Frank, and further references to the relationship between the two. I knew by then that the letter writer was no longer alive; he had died six weeks before I first heard of him. But I spoke twice, briefly, to his wife, the results of which are documented here.

My search continued in archives which have never been consulted in reference to the betrayal at 263 Prinsengracht, yet contain material relating directly to it. When all the strands were untangled, a disturbing chain of events emerged. But at least I understood why the story had remained hidden and, perhaps, why the informant was never brought to justice. I also came to understand just how easily one very ordinary, not particularly intelligent, young man with anti-Semitic leanings could be drawn into the colossal Nazi machine, alienating him from his family and impacting profoundly upon the lives of everyone around him. With regard to this, the Dutch publication of *The Hidden Life of Otto Frank* had surprising consequences; these are discussed in the Afterword.

I hope that these discoveries will be seen in context. They are just one facet of the extraordinary life of Otto Frank – a life which was remarkable, inspirational and ultimately dedicated to the advancement of world peace and the elimination of prejudice.

NOTE: A number of Otto Frank's letters quoted in this book are gramatically incorrect; this occurred when he was writing in English, and no changes have been made to his original text.

Prologue: The Jew Hunters of Amsterdam

Jan van Eyckstraat in Amsterdam-Zuid is a short, narrow street typical of the pleasant neighbourhood in which it lies. Nearby is a monument to the Dutch resistance: a pair of clasped stone hands rise dramatically from a small pool. Several young families live in the spacious, elegant houses that line the street, at the end of which there is a school. Across the main road, on Gerrit van der Veenstraat, stands another school whose dark history, despite now being shrouded in secrecy, will not be forgotten.

In the summer of 1944, Jan van Eyckstraat was very different.

Superficially it looked the same, but the school at the end of the street was an older building, whose large windows and bright mosaics would only remain for another few months; in November 1944 it was destroyed by an Allied bomb. There were no children injured because the building had ceased to exist as a school; in 1941 it became the Zentralstelle für Jüdische Auswanderung (Central Agency for Jewish Emigration), based on the office of the same name in Vienna. During the Nazi persecution of the Jews, under the auspices of re-housing, the apparatus of the deportations functioned from the Zentralstelle with an implacable efficiency. It was 'a conveyor belt . . . a Jew is fed in, with all he possesses, at one end, pushed through the entire building, from counter to counter, from office to office, and comes out at the other end deprived of all his rights, robbed of all his money, and bearing only a scrap of paper telling him to leave the country within fourteen days, lest he be sent to a concentration camp'.

The Zentralstelle was directly responsible to the Sicherheitsdienst (the Security and Intelligence Service of the German SS – the SD) whose headquarters were located across the road. The clock tower of the requisitioned school dominated the immediate skyline and cast long shadows down the Euterpestraat.★

On Jan van Eyckstraat itself, numbers 15, 19 and 21 had a similarly sinister reputation: the Expositur department of the Joodse Raad voor Amsterdam (Jewish Council of Amsterdam) had its offices there. Jews who had been seized in round-ups waited in the courtyard of the Zentralstelle while their

★ Euterpestraat was the original name for Gerrit van der Veenstraat; it was renamed in 1945 after the Dutch resistance fighter.

papers were checked by the staff of the Expositur to determine whether they were eligible for exemption from deportation. Few were excused; many then made the short journey from the Zentralstelle to the Hollandse Schouwburg (Dutch Theatre) on Plantage Middenlaan to await tram number nine, which would take them to the train station, and thence to 'the deadly east'.* The employees of the Expositor were also charged with maintaining contact between the Joodse Raad and the German authorities.

On the same side of the street, at Jan van Eyckstraat 31, lived Karel Wolters with his wife and three children. A lawyer and prosecutor in Amsterdam, and head of a successful legal practice, Wolters moved to the area in May 1941, having then been a member of the Nationaal-Socialistische Beweging (Dutch Nazi Party or NSB) for nine years. Several months later, he was appointed Verwalter by the Wirtschaftsprüfstelle (Bureau of Economic Investigation) and given the responsibility of liquidating nineteen Jewish businesses. One of them was a spice company on the Prinsengracht called Pectacon.

Immediately across the street from Wolters were numbers 20 and 22. The former was occupied by Kurt Döring, Emil Rühl and Friedrich Christian Viebahn. They had adjacent rooms at the SD headquarters on the Euterpestraat, where their reputation for being 'amongst the most feared' men of the Grüne Polizei arose from the vicious interrogations they conducted in the cellars. All three were later accused and convicted of multiple crimes committed during the war, including several counts of murder. The magistrate at the shared trial of Rühl and Viebahn addressed them sternly with the rhetorical question, 'You know very well, don't you, that the first thing a German interrogates with are his hands?'

Rühl, Viebahn and Döring were close friends, and liked to socialize with their neighbour at number 22, Maarten Kuiper, a Dutch policeman who joined the ranks of the SD at the end of 1942. Kuiper launched himself on a career in which he 'murdered and tortured like a medieval executioner', and participated in an array of reprisal killings against members of the Dutch resistance with Rühl. A witness to Kuiper's prosecution after the war observed with revulsion, 'One is reminded of a pike, which can still bite resolutely into a finger even after having been on dry land for hours.' Kuiper was on good terms with the other resident of the house, Herman

---

* The Hollandse Schouwburg was also known as the Joodsche Schouwburg. A former theatre, it was used by the Germans for collecting Jews until they could be deported to Westerbork, the first stop on the journey to the concentration camps of the east.

Rouwendaal, who worked as a spy for the Abwehr (Wehrmacht counter-intelligence organization), informing on resistance workers and infiltrating their groups to such effect that a reporter at his trial was moved to remark, 'Either Rouwendaal played his role like a genius, or the resistance showed an incredible trustfulness.'

The former landlord of the house which Rouwendaal and Kuiper shared was twenty-six-year-old Tonny Ahlers. A violent, unstable anti-Semite whose entire family – apart from his father – had disowned him because of his pro-German proclivities, Ahlers was regarded by many as a dangerous, unfathomable young man. He threatened anyone who displeased him with a spell in the cells on the Euterpestraat, where he made daily reports to Kurt Döring, who employed him as an informant, having noticed Ahlers's ability to exert 'a certain influence' over people. Ahlers called in regularly on his friend Peters who worked at the Zentralstelle, and he kept vigil over the Expositur, bragging to others that he was 'protected by rich Jews, for example, Asscher from the Joodse Raad'. Occasionally he assisted Karel Wolters in his liquidation duties, although they were no longer neighbours since Ahlers's move to Amstelveen with his wife and young son in April 1944.

Despite a stinging argument with Rouwendaal, Ahlers must have been a frequent visitor to his old house, because Emil Rühl was under the impression that he still lived there. Ahlers was, in any case, so impressed by his friend Maarten Kuiper that he liked to boast he was the older man's son-in-law. Kuiper hated Jews and gained pleasure from his work as a paid informant of Jews in hiding. He often attended their arrests. In the summer of 1944, one of these was with Willem Grootendorst and Gezinus Gringhuis, both of whom worked with Ahlers's friend Peters at the Zentralstelle. The arrest, led by SS Oberscharführer Karl Josef Silberbauer, took place in the annexe of the spice company whose liquidation Karel Wolters had overseen three years earlier; it included the director of the company, Otto Frank, and his family.

'It was *the* enemy citadel in Amsterdam; the crater from which calamity poured upon them [the Jews].' Historian Jacob Presser was referring specifically to the Zentralstelle, but he could have been alluding to the nearby Jan van Eyckstraat and its inhabitants. From this one street, calamity had spread across the life of Otto Frank like a sheet of flame, and the embers still burned many years later.

For Tonny Ahlers knew Otto Frank; they had a history together.

PART ONE

A Thousand Old, Treasured Things
1889–1945

1. Very German

Before the Holocaust, Otto Frank had little interest in his Jewish heritage. He was neither proud nor ashamed of being born a Jew; it was a matter of indifference to him. During the Great War, when he was serving in the German army, he made a rare comment in a letter home: 'I often get the feeling that mothers, brothers and sisters are the only trustworthy people. At least, that's how it is in Jewish families like ours.' His attitude was characteristic of the Liberal German Jewish bourgeoisie, particularly in Frankfurt where he grew up. He declared that at the time, 'Assimilation was very, very strong. Many turned to baptism just to get higher positions. My grandmother never went to synagogue, except once, to be married. And in all her life she never set foot in a synagogue again.'

For many Jews, this approach was the only way in which they felt they could be accepted into wider German society. The 'Jewish Problem' was the most hotly debated of all German political topics in the latter half of the nineteenth century. Nine years before Otto's birth, the campaign to strip Jews of their rights received enough votes to have two days devoted to it in the Reichstag. In the 1890s the issue of what was to be done with Jewish citizens took a new and dangerous turn. Instead of being regarded as a religious group, Jews began to be seen as a race, and one which had no place in Germany. In 1899, the Hamburg division of the united anti-Semitic parties took the debate on to yet another level, foreseeing the ends to which industrialization and science could be applied: 'Thanks to the development of our modern means of communication, the Jewish Problem would become in the course of the twentieth century a global problem and, as such, it would be jointly and decisively solved by the other nations through total segregation and (if self-defence should demand it) finally through the annihilation of the Jewish people.'

Looking back on his youth, Otto Frank refused to concede that German nationalism had deliberately excluded him: 'There was at this time some anti-Semitism in certain circles, but it was not aggressive and one did not suffer from it.' He had always felt 'quite consciously German. Otherwise, I would never have become an officer during World War I, nor would I have fought for Germany. But later on, as we know, this made not the slightest difference in the eyes of our persecutors.' Sal de

Liema, who knew Otto from Westerbork and Auschwitz, explained that this caused problems between them: 'I am Dutch, Otto Frank was German, and Dutch people are different to German people. A German Jew is a different person to a Dutch Jew. We had other ideas . . . I told him, "Don't talk German to me," because I hated the German language. Of course it was his language. He was a German. He was a Jew, but he was a German first.'

'Extremely well brought up,' was Anne Frank's succinct observation on what she knew of her father's childhood. It was rather more than that; the sons and daughter of Michael and Alice Frank were given a childhood that belongs to a distinctly bygone era. They were close in age: Robert was born in 1886, Otto Heinrich on 12 May 1889, Herbert in 1891 and Helene (Leni) in 1893. While Michael Frank pursued a career in banking, the family rented a neo-classical style villa at Gärtnerweg 40, Frankfurt-am-Main. Michael had left Landau, the town of his birth, in 1879 at the age of twenty-eight, and settled in Frankfurt. In 1885 he married twenty-year-old Alice Stern, whose prosperous Liberal Jewish family had lived in the city for over four hundred years. As the nineteenth century drew to a close, Michael moved into stockbroking and embarked upon a number of successful independent ventures, including investments in two health farms and a company producing cough and cold lozenges. In 1901 he established a bank business under his name, specializing in foreign currency exchange. The Franks moved into their own home the following year: a luxurious, new semi-detached house at Mertonstrasse 4 in the city's Westend. The house, with its three front-facing balconies, centre tower and landscaped garden, had a separate entrance for the Franks' small staff.

Exquisitely dressed, young Otto and his siblings visited a riding school on a regular basis until they were proficient on horseback, called upon neighbours at the correct hour in the afternoon, had private music lessons, and accompanied their parents on outings to the opera where they had their own box. Alice Frank's cousin, Karl Stern, and his wife Else lived on the nearby Beethovenstrasse; their granddaughter, Edith Oppenheimer, recalls that Else was Christian by birth 'but religion was never an issue. My mother and Otto used to tell of the wonderful family parties that were held often, some costume balls. There were special parties for children.' Michael and Alice Frank were not remote parents by any means, despite the emphasis on manners and comportment; judging from the surviving letters of Otto and his older brother Robert, the house on Mertonstrasse rang regularly with laughter, stories, poetry and singing.

After attending a private prep school, Otto was sent to the Lessing Gymnasium not far from home. He entered into the spirit of the school's principle: tolerance. His nature ('aware and curious, warm and friendly') made him popular and no one in his class paid any attention to the fact that he was the only Jewish pupil among them. In his old age, however, Otto received a letter from a former classmate who wanted his opinion on a book he had written about the Lessing Gymnasium. Otto's response was glacial: 'I received the book that you co-edited and I can imagine how much work you had, doing research on the lives of all the graduates. I was unpleasantly struck by your apparently knowing nothing about the concentration camps and gas chambers, since there is no mention of my Jewish comrades dying in the gas chambers. Since I am the only member of my family who survived Auschwitz, as you may know from my daughter Anne's diary, you should understand my feelings.'

There were no Hebrew lessons for the Frank children, and like most assimilated German Jews of the time, the family opposed Zionism, feeling that Germany was their homeland. 'We were very, very liberal,' Otto recalled, 'I was not barmitzvahed.' His cousin Edith elaborates, 'The formal exercise of the Jewish religion was not important to Otto. It was not an issue in middle-class Germany before the Great War. Otto was very outgoing, and a lot of fun. Everyone in the family thought he had a great future.' Otto's love of classical German literature began at the Lessing Gymnasium, and he enjoyed writing for the school newspaper. During the holidays, he became restless: 'I could not bear staying at home very long after school.' In Frankfurt, life was too rigorously organized and the 'parties every week, balls, festivities, beautiful girls, waltzing, dinners . . . etc.,' had begun to bore him. When his parents sent him to Spain for the 1907 Easter break to recuperate, it sparked an interest in foreign travel. Like his future daughter Anne, Otto collected postcards sent to him by relatives from around the world, and after the success of Anne's published diary travel to exotic locations became his one occasional extravagance. In June 1908 Otto received his Abitur and enrolled in an economics course at Heidelberg University. He then left for a long vacation in England.

University education in Germany in the early years of the twentieth century did not come cheaply, and was seen as 'a chancy speculation' even for those who could afford it. Most were graduates of the humanistic Gymnasium like Otto Frank, or wealthy students from abroad like Charles Webster Straus, who arrived in Heidelberg to complete a year's foreign study as part of his course at Princeton University in America. Charles, or Charlie as Otto was soon calling him, was born in the same month and year as Otto. In a 1957 letter he recalled how his friendship with Otto began:

> I was a student at Heidelberg University in 1908 and 1909. While there, through members of my mother's family living in Mannheim who knew the Frank family intimately, I met Otto . . . Over the following months, Otto and I became close friends. He had matriculated at the same time as I had at Heidelberg University and we not only attended many courses together, but he spent many evenings with my parents and me at our hotel, as I spent many evenings and, indeed, many weekends with his family who owned a country place near Frankfurt. Otto was not only my closest friend during the three semesters we both studied at the university but he was the one that my parents liked best.

Having decided that his economics course contained too much theory, Otto left Heidelberg and returned to Frankfurt, where he started a year's training with a bank. Straus had also cut short his studies, and upon his arrival home, 'My father asked me to invite Otto to come with me and have a year's experience working at Macy's, of which my father at that time was half owner. My father added that, if Otto decided on the basis of that experience to remain at Macy's, a good future awaited him. I urged Otto to accept this invitation – which he did. He started working at Macy's in 1909 along with me.' Otto's family were divided about the move to New York; his father encouraged him to see it as an opportunity to learn about commerce and to improve his English, but his sister Leni was upset, especially so because Otto would miss her sixteenth birthday. There was someone else, too, who did not want Otto to leave: his fiancée.

Only Michael Frank accompanied Otto to Hamburg where the luxury German liner, *Kaiser Wilhelm Der Grosse*, awaited him in September 1909. It was raining when father and son said farewell, and by the time the ship had reached the open sea, the weather had worsened, leaving most of the neo-baroque public rooms empty as passengers took to their cabins. Otto headed for the deserted writing room and amidst 'this endless rolling from side to side', composed a brief letter to Leni: 'As I don't want to write a postcard for such an important event as your birthday, I decided to write this, and to send the card on later. A sixteenth birthday is not an easy thing and it only comes once in a lifetime. So celebrate it accordingly, and don't let my absence spoil it for you, be really happy.' He had little to say about himself, other than,

I'm still feeling fine here, touch wood (I'm knocking three times underneath the table now). The boat is magnificently appointed and offers all one can dream of – really luxurious. I can't tell you a lot because as you can imagine since I left father, not much has happened. I haven't made any friends yet, but I'm not bothered. My companion must be coming aboard later, which is agreeable to me, because I have my peace and quiet to arrange the cabin. Just now, 5.30, it's pouring cats and dogs, but that doesn't affect me here in the writing room.

Otto had received a number of good-luck telegrams from family and friends before boarding the ship, but within days of arriving in New York he was frantically booking a passage home: his father was dead, and his engagement had been broken off in dramatic fashion.

Michael Frank's sudden death, on 17 September 1909, brought his widow's strength of will, which she kept hidden under an outward show of serenity, to the fore. Alice immediately took over the management of the bank while her sons pursued their own concerns.* Otto's younger brother, Herbert, continued with his studies, while his older brother Robert, whom everyone regarded as the intellectual of the family, remained deputy manager of Ricard, a fine arts dealership in which his father had invested. Otto was unsure of his own future, having been further diverted from his career path in New York by the dissolution of his marriage engagement.

Otto's youthful love affair was the subject of much speculation eighty years later following the discovery of five pages from Anne's diary which he had apparently deliberately withheld.† There Anne had written, 'I know a few things about Daddy's past, and what I don't know, I've made up . . . It can't be easy for a loving wife to know she'll never be first in her husband's affections, and Mummy did know that . . . [Daddy's] ideals had been shattered.'

On 11 May 1944 Anne shed further light on the facts. She writes that she wants to publish a book based on her diary after the war and adds: '*Cady's Life* must also be finished.' She then outlines how this novel will develop. The two protagonists, Hans and Cady, 'draw apart' after their romance ends, but meet by chance while they are on holiday in the same hotel. Hans is married by then, as he explains to Cady. She hears no more from him, but 'years later' finds out that he 'had finished up in England where he was in

---

* Buddy Elias thinks Michael Frank probably died of a heart attack.
† These pages are discussed fully in Appendix 1.

poor health. When Cady was twenty-seven, she married a well-to-do farmer [and] had two daughters and a son . . . Hans always remained in the back of Cady's mind, until one night she took her leave of him in a dream.' Anne notes defensively: 'It isn't sentimental nonsense for it's modelled on the story of Daddy's life.'

In the published diary edited by Otto, these lines are omitted. Instead, after the section about *Het Achterhuis* (the original Dutch title for the diary★), there follows two lines: 'I have other ideas as well, besides *Het Achterhuis*. But I will write more fully about them some other time, when they have taken a clearer form in my mind.' The footnote points out, 'The last two sentences in this letter were published in Dutch but do not appear in the diary.' There is, in the same way, the case of an earlier entry in the diary, the original of which reads: 'I find myself thinking all the time about Pim [Otto's nickname], and what he told me last year . . . Poor Pim, he can't make me think that he has forgotten her. He will never forget. He has become very tolerant, for he too sees Mummy's faults.' The version Otto edited contains two curious changes: 'I find myself thinking all the time about Pim, and what he told me about the love of his youth . . . Poor Pim, he can't make *me* think that he has forgotten everything. He will never forget this. He has become very tolerant.' Assuming these variations on the original text were made by Otto, he seems to have been at once impelled to reveal and conceal the meaning behind Anne's words, on the one hand adding 'the love of his youth' while on the other substituting 'forgotten everything' for 'forgotten her'.

In a 1994 letter written by Otto's cousin Milly Stanfield, the truth is unveiled at last, although she does not name the woman involved: 'Actually [Otto] was engaged to her when he was about eighteen, just before he went to the States for a year and was very serious about her, but when he got back found she had not waited for him and married someone else. He was very upset, of course, but years later (1922, I think) met her and her husband at the same hotel on holiday. He told me it didn't worry him and rather amused him.' Milly was not only Otto's cousin, she was also part of Otto's circle at that time and a close confidante. Otto's cousin Edith also heard the story: 'Otto was due to come to America to apprentice in business, and he asked his love to wait for him. According to Milly, she promised but she did not. In any case, Milly said he took the break-up very hard.' In her diary Anne, or rather Otto, makes it clear that the affair happened during his youth, and Otto himself told his friend Jean Schick Grossman about 'the

★ This means literally 'The Back House', but is usually translated as 'The Secret Annexe'.

young love he had experienced when he was nineteen', which Anne 'actually wrote a novel about'. In Anne's intended romance *Cady's Life*, Otto becomes Cady, and Hans represents his lost love. There is a sense of closure in both novel and fact; Cady resigns herself to her loss after a dream, and Otto apparently did the same after the encounter in the hotel. The diary as edited by him hints that he never attained the same sexual passion again, but whether he ever loved as deeply is unclear, since Otto changed the line to read 'the love of his youth', rather than 'the love of his life'.

Nevertheless, when one reads what Milly has written, Anne's plans for her novel, 'modelled on the story of Daddy's life', make complete sense.

Otto resolved to return to America quickly in an effort to put the emotional upheaval of autumn 1909 behind him. On 19 December he wrote to his sister from New York, where he was lodging with family acquaintances: 'You cannot imagine how often I think of you and how I feel here. It seems I don't know how lucky I am, to live in this house and feel so at home. Marly is very kind, and I get along with Eugenie B too. She is a nice girl, not very clever, but pretty.' In a reference perhaps to his broken engagement, Otto confessed wryly, 'You know how I get along with girls: good, but apparently not very good.' He warned Leni not to read too many 'forbidden' novels because 'it's too exciting. You have to be sensible and know your limitations.' He advised her to read Mörike ('an excellent writer. I have all his works in my cupboard'), concluding with an older brother's admonition not 'to dirty [the books], because they're bound in white, and keep them in order'.

The rather glamorous world Otto inhabited in New York was more exclusively Jewish than the one he had known in Frankfurt, but it was not without tension. In 1870 there were approximately eighty thousand Jews in New York, less than nine per cent of the population; by 1909 there were almost a million Jews in residence and ninety thousand Russian and Polish Jews arriving each year. The German Jews resident in New York accused the recent immigrants of being an embarrassment, 'the dregs of Europe', and attempted to 're-mould' them. When Otto moved to New York, there were huge programmes of philanthropy underway, led by the Strauses among others. His evenings were often spent at charity balls in the Strauses' home at 27 West 72nd Street, held in the lavishly decorated front parlour known as the Pompeian or Egyptian Room. Otto's friend Charles Straus, aged twenty-one, was then running for political office and had changed his name to Nathan Straus Jnr, giving everyone three months to get used to his new moniker. His sister-in-law insisted on calling him Charlie to annoy him; Otto also did so, and Straus seems to have found it endearing.

Otto socialized in a particular group which included the Strauses, the Abrahams and the 'Brooklyn Branch' of the Rothschilds from Frankfurt. Eventually there was a breach between those families 'who evolved from storekeeping into banking and such families as the Strauses of Macy's who had "stayed behind" in retailing', but Otto moved freely from one spectrum to the other. To understand how the organization of a large corporation operated, he worked in Macy's different departments, and then transferred to a city bank. The Franks were still very wealthy then; Otto returned to Frankfurt on a number of occasions and travel by liner was expensive. Sometimes he stopped briefly in London, where his brother Herbert was living at 40 Threadneedle Street while working in a bank, and he visited his cousin Milly Stanfield in Hampstead when he could.

Milly was ten years younger than Otto. She grew up to become a talented teacher, writer and musician. She recalled vividly the first time she saw Otto. It was at the family home in Hampstead in 1908: 'Otto played the cello in his youth and the first time he visited us in London I had just started on my three-quarter baby instrument and he took it up and played a solo on it.' Milly came to regard Otto as 'a big brother: he talked to me very freely and felt I knew him well'. Later that same year, Milly and her parents visited the Continent and travelled to Frankfurt where she met Otto's family. She was impressed by their home and lifestyle: 'The Franks had a big luncheon with an enormous ice-cream gateau decorated with fairytale figures, and Tanti Toni invited us all to the circus.'

Otto returned to this life in Frankfurt during early 1910, but by the summer he was again in New York. He remained there until 1911, when he embarked upon a full-time administrative position with a metal engineering company in Dusseldorf. He travelled to Frankfurt regularly and enjoyed a holiday in Switzerland in 1912 with his family, Milly, and her parents. The Stanfields accompanied their relatives back to Frankfurt for an extended break. They were there again in July 1914, shortly before war broke out in Europe. The Franks told them they were mad to travel when 'Alsace was practically under siege'. Other relatives from Paris joined them in the house on Mertonstrasse: Otto's Uncle Leon and Aunt Nanette and their three sons, Oscar, Georges and Jean-Michel. Unlike their German relatives, the French branch of the Frank family suffered extreme anti-Semitism in Paris, where they lived on the avenue Kléber, and none more so than Jean-Michel, who was disliked by his contemporaries for being Jewish, extremely intelligent, and for his 'oriental doll look'. These highly strung guests created a stir, which Milly missed but heard about later: 'The Paris Franks were sure there would be war and were almost hysterical. They had sons of military age and remembered the Franco-Prussian War of 1870 . . . their two elder sons [were] both brilliant young men.'

At the beginning of August the Stanfields were advised by the British Consulate to go back to England. They found Frankfurt's Hauptbahnhof in uproar and their train was delayed for two hours: 'The Franks and several of mother's cousins came to the station in relays, bringing us goodies, keeping us company.' At home in London, fifteen-year-old Milly felt her loyalties torn as she worried about Otto and his family in Frankfurt: 'It seemed as if a wall of fire separated Germany from the Allies of the West.'

Until 1914 German military academies made enrolment by Jews extremely difficult and excluded them from certain regiments. In the national crisis of the Great War, the need to find a scapegoat for Germany's problems increased, and Jewish men were accused of shirking war service and profiting from the black market. The attitude towards them was clarified by Franz Oppenheimer: 'Don't fool yourselves, you are and will remain Germany's pariahs.'

One hundred thousand Jews fought for Germany in the Great War, 12,000 died in battle, 30,000 were decorated, 19,000 promoted and 2,000 became officers. The Union of Jewish Soldiers Serving at the Front had a membership of 40,000, and a rabbi in German uniform led their prayers. The first member of the German Parliament killed in action was Jewish: Dr Ludwig Haas, member for Mannheim. One of the few diaries of German soldiers published in English was that of a Jewish man from Frankfurt, Herbert Sulzbach. Many of the entries illustrate his patriotism: 'You still feel it is something wonderful to be one of the millions who are able to join in the fighting and you feel it is really necessary.'

These sentiments were echoed by Otto Frank when he was drafted into the military. In 1914 his Dusseldorf employer loaned him out to a company which did important war work and he stayed with them until August 1915, when both he and Robert were called up. Milly remembered, 'Robert fared better [than Otto]. He had volunteered as a stretcher-bearer, in the German equivalent of our Royal Army Medical Corps. As dangerous as fighting, it was a most essential service and far better suited to Robert's personal beliefs. Herbert, the youngest of the brothers, was not robust enough to join the army and was given a desk job.' On 7 August 1915 – one month after their Parisian cousin Oscar was killed in action at Neuville-Saint-Vaast – 'Kanonier Otto Frank' wrote to his family from the training depot in Mainz:

After a good meal at the station, we drove here and I climbed into my straw-bed at 11 o'clock. Nineteen men in a room designed for eight! Today we've been ordered into our units and given clothes. Afterwards, there was a big clean-up of the mess. I had to clean the windows, polish my boots, etc. All in all, I think I've got it good. In contrast to what Robert said, here they're almost all elderly, fat people – surely not how the army should be! Still, the Unteroffizier is very quiet and nice. Everything is in the best of order now. In two weeks, I'll probably be living out of doors! The food is pretty good, but maybe you could send something – eggs, cigars or cigarettes. No clothes just yet, except a pair of socks perhaps.

I've rarely spent a more amusing and comfortable train journey than the one yesterday. Some of the officers shared my compartment and they drank like fish! I met people I knew from Puttenberg. No one from Frankfurt as yet, though quite a few are here. I'm quite content, although the prospect of my straw-bed this evening is not a pleasant one. I'm happy to be here, since this was apparently the last transport, everything else was cancelled. Everyone wants to join in the victory!

A week later, Otto wrote again, delighted with the mail his family had sent him and the promise of a visit they planned to make to his unit. He told them not to worry about whether he was getting enough food and rest: 'I'm not hungry . . . The work is easy and I'm not even tired. My muscles ache but that doesn't trouble me. I'm looking forward to your visit of course . . . I don't even know myself where we are because I haven't been to town, but I know you'll find it. If anything comes up which means I can't make it, I'll write.'

Otto was sent to the Western Front shortly after writing the letter. His unit contained mostly surveyors and mathematicians; he was a range-finder attached to the infantry. Although his early letters were hopeful, he was reminded of the peril that he now faced when he learned that Oscar's brother, Georges, had also been killed in action. It was precisely what their parents, Leon and Nanette, had feared most. The deaths of two of their three sons sent them both mad. Leon killed himself in November 1915 by jumping from a window, unable to cope with the loss of his children as well as the daily barrage of anti-Semitism they faced in Paris. Nanette was committed to a mental hospital, leaving Jean-Michel, then twenty, alone in the family home. In 1916 Herbert went to stay with him.

Otto was to maintain his optimism, and in February 1916 he wrote to Leni in whimsical mood:

Your letter pleased me so much. You write that you're different now, but in what way? If you stay unmarried, then I'll stay unmarried too, and we'll head a wonderful household together, what? Silly boy. Why do I think about such things now? I believe my life here is better than yours at home. I miss nothing here and the danger I am in is only in your imagination. It's really not that bad.

A few days later he wrote to Leni again, hoping to mend a quarrel that had broken out on paper between her and Robert:

You know how important it is to me that we're all on the best of terms and how I like to act as mediator if it helps to clear up misunderstandings between us. The two of us rarely have misunderstandings, do we? It's because our natures are so similar, and I'm always happy to see that you still trust your brother Otto, and that we can talk to each other as ever . . . It's only a matter of temperament that you can't be with Robert the way you are with me. But where there is a will to understand, an understanding is possible.

He ended his letter with another gentle reprimand not to worry about him: 'You do not have to be afraid for me – really. It would be sheer accident if anything happened, although accidents do occur.'

Five months later, he must have wondered at his own words. On 1 July 1916 the Battle of the Somme began. At 6.30 a.m. the guns of thirteen British divisions opened over the German trenches. An hour later, German troops responded, 'condemning that quiet country region to the misery and ravages of some of the most ferocious fighting in the world's history'. Otto was in the thick of it, yet escaped injury 'by a miracle'. The First World War records of the German army were destroyed by bombing in the Second, and Otto's surviving letters from the period are almost entirely without reference to his experiences; he clearly wished to save his mother and sister from the true horrors of the front line. On 24 December 1916 he wrote only that he was happy to hear that Robert and Leni had resolved their differences, and that there was no point in dwelling on the past: 'It doesn't help in these bitter and serious times . . . I hope we can see each other at home again when peace prevails. This cannot last much longer, surely.'

When the Somme offensive was over, hundreds of thousands of troops on both sides were dead, maimed, or suffering shell-shock. Morale, especially among German troops, deteriorated towards the end of 1917 and officers were charged with the task of mustering enthusiasm among their men. That year, Otto was proposed as an officer candidate by his chief, whom he regarded as 'a decent, enlightened man who handled his unit with the utmost fairness [and] a democratic man who would have no officers' mess or officers' orderlies in his unit'. In February 1918 Otto became an officer after demonstrating his bravery in a reconnaissance action and resolved to treat his men in the same liberal way as his chief.

Otto continued to write frequently to his mother and sister, who worked together as volunteer nurses in a Red Cross military hospital. To Leni, who enjoyed the attention it brought her from the soldiers recuperating under her care, Otto patiently answered questions about love while ruminating on his own future:

> The language of the heart and the emotions it makes are the most important of all . . . You're the kind of person who acts on emotion, needs love in order to flourish, and is able to give love. I am very similar in this respect. You must understand, child, that now your father has gone, we aren't able to give you the advice he would have done. We can only do our best and try to instil in you the feeling that your brothers are always near and that you can trust us implicitly . . . It's always better to think things through than to do something hastily which could bring you disappointment later. We call them 'ideals' because they're unreachable.

He wrote frequently to his brothers, pleased with the way in which Bitz (Herbert) was beginning to show initiative with the family bank business, which was in difficulty, and happy that Robert was going to be stationed nearby, close enough for them to meet. He admitted to his mother that he was finding the war 'debilitating', but 'we're not living in an ideal world'. He was concerned about their dwindling funds and felt that the sale of a number of paintings from their home on Mertonstrasse was necessary: 'In these times you have to be happy with any cash because you don't know what's around the corner.'

On 20 November 1917 Otto's unit moved up to Cambrai, just as the British launched their tank attack on the Hindenburg Line, and became the first range-finding unit to deal with this new kind of warfare. The British success was short-lived; ten days later they were forced back to where they began. Despite the apparent stalemate, Otto was cheerful about the coming months: 'I'm salivating at the newspapers and hoping that the Russians get bushed, because Russia can't survive another winter again and so I'm still optimistic.'

In June 1918, after his promotion to lieutenant, Otto wrote to Leni that he was 'in a good mood. I have some small roses in front of where I sit and the weather is fine. When will the easy life start again, I often think now, and am longing for it to happen in reality. A man alone is incomplete. My thoughts wander. I don't focus on anything in particular. I think about the past and I think about the future. A useless game of thoughts.' When he wrote again a couple of weeks later, he was despondent:

> You can't imagine the feelings that our loneliness and isolation from culture and women awaken in us out here. We think of a thousand, old, treasured things and are only too happy to lose ourselves in dreams. We all have it so good at home that we aren't especially eager to have homes of our own, strong as the impulse to do so may be in us ... It is not just immediate happiness but the future that one's thoughts return to time and again, and the moments when one does not think of the future are few indeed.

Another week passed and he began to wonder whether the end really was in sight: 'It's raining a bit and that relieves us from the pressing heat of the day. My hope that this year we will force an ending to all this conflict prevails even though I find it difficult to believe peace will come this year. The pre-conditions for it still need to be set.' When he wrote on 31 July, it was to announce that they were being transferred to the city of St Quentin. Otto was billeted with a large French farming family there. His cousin Milly recalled that they 'all loved him and nicknamed him "Le Grand Brun". He went back – I think with Edith in the late 1920s – and they treated him as a long lost son.'

When the war ended in November 1918, Alice and Leni Frank wept with joy; none of their menfolk had been harmed. They began to prepare excitedly for Robert and Otto's homecoming, but only Robert returned. For a full month the family in Frankfurt agonized over what could have happened to Otto, from whom they had not heard since Christmas. It was a dark afternoon in January 1919 when he finally stepped through the door at Mertonstrasse, thin and seemingly taller than ever. His black hair was thin on the crown, and his pale eyes were tinged with tiredness, but he smiled at his overjoyed family. When they had all composed themselves, and were sitting together around the dining-room table with cups of tea, Otto explained why he was so late. His unit had borrowed two horses from a Belgian farmer, who was distraught to see them go. Otto promised he would bring both horses back personally, and, as a German officer, his word was his honour. When fighting ceased, he returned the horses and the farmer received them with amazed gratitude. Otto then told them about his excruciating journey home. Milly remembered that he told her family the same story: 'Otto had had to walk the whole way back from France after

Germany capitulated. It took him three weeks; he arrived looking like a ghost.'

When Otto stopped talking, Alice started to shout. She was incensed at her son for prolonging his homecoming over a couple of mangy horses, and was not to be placated, even when Otto insisted that he had sent her a letter which must have gone astray. She drew herself up regally to her full height, although she was only small, and threw the china teapot straight at her astonished son.

In the aftermath of the Great War, approximately 490,000 Jews lived in Germany. During the 1918 Revolution, Jews were attacked by angry crowds who blamed them for the shortage of food, inflation, and all that was deplorable in Weimar's early years. There were frenzied fights on the streets of Berlin, witnessed by a correspondent for the London *Times*. On 14 August 1919 he noted cautiously that 'indications of growing anti-Semitism are becoming frequent'.

The Franks had more pressing problems; their bank business was plainly in trouble, primarily as a result of Alice's investment in war loans, which proved utterly worthless. A large portion of their wealth had been lost, and, in 1919, Otto took over the running of the bank in an attempt to salvage what was left. He was reluctant to assume his new role, and did so 'more from necessity than by choice', assuming management of the business in cough and cold lozenges at the same time. He confided in Milly that the task was not close to his heart, but 'as his older brother Robert was interested in Fine Arts and their father had died when they were in their teens, it fell to Otto to manage the family bank in the period of chaos that marked the first year after Peace was signed, when the Mark plummeted for about three years. His younger brother, Herbert, was devoted to him, but he was never a leader.' Milly and her mother visited Frankfurt in October 1920 and found many of their relatives (though not the Franks) poor and hungry: 'The morning after our arrival Alice and Leni fetched us to go to Otto's bank to get some money. After one look at us, they took us straight to a good delicatessen for morning snacks . . . They made a habit of taking us out every morning to stock up a little.' Milly spoke to Otto about the political situation: 'He pointed out the weakness of the government in power and the existence of two fringe parties, the Nationalists and the Communists. Both were potentially dangerous, especially those of the Right. Otto, a middle-of-the-road Liberal, was worried.'

During his work for the bank, Otto became friendly with Erich Elias at the Frankfurt Stock Exchange. Erich, born in Zweibrücken in 1890 to a grain merchant and his wife, was the eldest of three children. He was very close to his brother, Paul, but his sister committed suicide at the age of eighteen after becoming pregnant by an officer who would not contemplate marrying a Jewish girl. Erich worked for the Heichelheim Bank as an agent and stockbroker, but left at the end of 1920 and joined the Michael Frank bank as a full partner on 3 February 1921. Two months before, Leni had written to him, 'I am not afraid to put my life in your hands,' and, on 16 February 1921, she and Erich married in a romantic ceremony in Frankfurt. They lived in the house on Mertonstrasse, where their first child, Stephan, was born on 20 December 1921.

There were two more weddings in the family the following year. On 12 April 1922 Herbert married American Hortense Schott, who lived in Aachen. The marriage was turbulent and not expected to last. On 11 July 1922 Robert married Charlotte (Lottie) Witt, a policeman's daughter and a gentile. Lottie wanted to convert to Judaism, but Robert told her it was not necessary. Alice was against the wedding initially: Lottie was Robert's secretary at Ricard, and Alice felt that she was not good enough for him. Robert ignored his mother and eventually Alice overcame her misgivings, accepting Lottie into the family. Her one remaining wish was that Otto would find himself a suitable wife.

Police reports from the early 1920s recorded escalating anti-Semitism in Germany: 'The mood for Jewish pogroms is spreading systematically in all parts of the country,' said one, while another concluded: 'The fact cannot be denied that the anti-Semitic idea has penetrated the widest levels of the middle class, even far into the working class.' Although aware of the growing menace, Otto Frank hoped it was a transitory affliction; his anxiety over the predicament of the Michael Frank bank was far greater. Herbert had resigned in autumn 1921, finding the work too dull, but at Otto's request he resumed his position on the board in 1923. Despite the unstable German economy, and the stern licensing laws on dealing in foreign currency, Otto and Erich decided to open a branch of the bank in Amsterdam, then the centre of foreign currency trading. It was an option taken by other ailing German banks, many of which subsequently found themselves in difficulties, since their Amsterdam subsidiaries were forbidden to entice Dutch clients and had to concentrate solely on German flight capital.

Having worked abroad before, Otto was nominated for the task of establishing the bank in Amsterdam and, in late 1923, Michael M. Frank & Sons, 'banking and trading in foreign currency', opened at Keizersgracht 604. In May 1924 two proxies of the bank were registered with the Amsterdam

Chamber of Commerce: Jacques Heuskin and Johannes Kleiman. Belgian-born Heuskin had lived most of his life in Luxembourg, where he probably met Otto's uncle, Armand Geiershofer, a glove manufacturer, who then introduced him to Otto. Kleiman, born in Koog aan de Zaan on 17 August 1896, met Otto in spring 1923, when Otto was travelling between Amsterdam, Berlin and Frankfurt in order to establish the business. Kleiman's rather bird-like features were accentuated by the large glasses he was obliged to wear. He liked Otto from the moment they met. Their long, unreserved friendship, however, did not begin until 1933, when Otto and his family emigrated to Amsterdam.

The attempted rescue failed. On 15 December 1924 the Amsterdam branch of Michael M. Frank & Sons went into liquidation, presumably as a result of 'speculative activity, perhaps involving the French franc, a currency that was being traded with considerable losses in Amsterdam in the summer of 1925'. The business moved to Kleiman's address in the city and he was then granted full powers, remaining 'Otto's confidant and mainstay in Amsterdam until the dissolution of the business'. The liquidation process lasted over four years and the German creditors were told they would be paid in instalments. Heuskin was dismissed and Kleiman left to work for his brother's business.

Otto returned to Frankfurt in early 1925. He was almost thirty-six years old and had to find some method of expurgating the family's spreading debts. On a personal level, he desperately wanted a home of his own and children, as he had confessed in a letter to Leni seven years before: 'We can't wait too long after the war if we want to be young for the children we hope to have. For children are, after all, the be-all and end-all of a healthy marriage.' There was only one way to resolve all these problems simultaneously, and on 5 April 1925 Otto Frank became engaged to Edith Holländer of Aachen, whose dowry included a substantial sum of money. They married a month later in the city synagogue.

To family and friends, the announcement came like a bombshell. His cousin Edith Oppenheimer recalls, 'No one knew her. She lived far away, and she was much more religious than Otto.' To his immediate family at the time, and then later to his second wife and her daughter, Otto admitted that his marriage to Edith Holländer was, plainly put, 'a business arrangement'.

'I have the impression that Daddy married Mummy because he felt she would be a suitable wife. I have to admit I admire Mummy for the way she assumed the role of his wife and has never, as far as I know, complained or been jealous . . . Daddy certainly admired Mummy's attitude and thought she had an excellent character . . . What kind of marriage has it turned out to be? No quarrels or differences of opinion – but hardly an ideal marriage. Daddy respects Mummy and loves her, but not with the kind of love I envision for a marriage . . . Daddy's not in love. He kisses her the way he kisses us . . . one day Daddy is bound to realize that while, on the outside, she has never demanded his total love, on the inside, she has slowly but surely been crumbling away. She loves him more than anyone, and it's hard to see this kind of love not being returned.'

Anne's observation of her parents' marriage (see Appendix 1), hidden away for more than fifty years, was unforgiving, incisive – and truthful. Otto confessed to his second wife and her daughter that he had never loved Edith, but had great respect for her intelligence and skills as a mother. He said little about his first marriage apart from that, although he told a number of people that it was an arranged union which appeared to suit them both. Today, some members of the Holländer family believe that Otto benefited the most, using Edith's considerable dowry to 'clean up long-standing debts . . . Edith was known to be a clever person, faithful to the family tradition which believed in true values . . . Otto Frank was obviously the master of that household.' This view extends to the diary; one member asserts that the Holländers were

grossly neglected in all editions of Anne's books . . . after corrections, editions and self-serving additions by Anne's father who was by then the one living family member, Otto had become Anne's mentor, role model and undisputed influence in her life. This may sound like sour grapes now, but it is common family knowledge – of a family who has by now no voice in this world any more.

Nonetheless, arranged marriages among Jewish families at that time were the norm; in certain circles they were held in more esteem than actual romances. Edith's parents were aware that their daughter's suitor was far from wealthy, and that a large dowry was viewed as a definite advantage. Their greatest misgiving was probably their future son-in-law's apathy towards his religion. The Holländers were prominent in Aachen's Jewish community, observed the Sabbath and festivals, and Edith's mother kept a kosher household. Otto later recalled that Edith was 'very religious. Not orthodox, but she was kosher . . . Of course, when my mother-in-law came we never had anything from a pig. We adjusted.'

The Holländer family fortune originated from Edith's grandfather, Benjamin Holländer, who started an industrial supplies and scrap metal business in 1858 under his own name. Edith's father, Abraham, was born in Eschweiler in 1860, one of nine children. After marriage to Rosa Stern of Langenschwalbach, and the birth of their first child, Julius, in 1894, Abraham took his wife, son and parents to Aachen where he expanded the family business. Abraham gained control of the firm and quickly made his fortune. Three more children were born in the beautiful Holländer home on Liebfrauenstrasse: Walter (1897), Bettina (1898), and Edith, born on 16 January 1900.

Edith was described as being a shy girl, family-orientated and academic. In 1906 she began her studies at the Evangelische Victoriaschule, a private Protestant school for girls which also accepted pupils of other religions. She learned English, French and Hebrew alongside the five cousins with whom she was good friends: Meta, Frieda, Irma, Ilse and Elsbeth. In her diary Anne marvelled at her mother's privileged upbringing: 'We listen open-mouthed to the stories of engagement parties of two hundred and fifty people, private balls and dinners.' This happy existence suddenly fragmented with the coming of the Great War. Edith's sister Betti, only sixteen, was struck down with appendicitis. She died on 22 September 1914. Edith honoured her memory by naming her first child Margot Betti after her. Edith's uncle Karl died on 28 December 1915 serving in the German army. Her eldest brother, Julius, who was also a soldier by then, was shot in the arm, leaving him with a permanent handicap. In the midst of all this, in 1916, Edith graduated from school and was given a book about Frederick the Great by one of her teachers 'in recognition of your effort and good behaviour'.

After completing their education at the Aachen Gymnasium, both Julius and Walter took a course in business with a professor from the Institute of Technology in preparation for positions within their father's firm. Unfortunately, things did not go according to plan; Abraham Holländer dominated them and 'permitted them only filial rights, not equal to his own, in the running of the firm'. They compensated for this rejection by enrolling in various charities, joining football and gymnastic clubs and volunteering for Jewish causes. By contrast Edith had a good relationship with her mother and adored her brothers. She overcame her shyness once she got to know people, and had many friends with whom she played tennis and went dancing. She drove part way to the East Frisian islands to go swimming with her cousin Irene, one of the first women in Germany to own a car. Edith was stylish in her clothes, wearing 'flapper' dresses and pearls, and had her hair cut in a neat bob. She learned to do the Charleston and bought herself a gramophone player and a selection of records which the Elias family still have, with Edith's distinctive handwriting upon the inventory.

Edith was the only one of Abraham and Rosa's children who married. Her introduction to Otto Frank may have occurred through the bank business, or through Herbert's wife, Hortense, who had once lived in Aachen. Edith's cousins were envious of the marriage, which took place on 12 May 1925, the day that Otto turned thirty-six. Edith wore a fashionable white gown embroidered with flowers and a long, diaphanous train. Otto dressed in a dark suit and bow tie. After the wedding there was a celebration at the Grosser Monarch Hotel in Aachen and then the couple departed to tour Italy, accompanied on their honeymoon by Edith's parents.

Anne's lines about her parents' marriage imply that Otto told Edith he had been deeply in love with another woman when he was younger, but Edith had apparently never experienced the emotions she felt for Otto before, and hoped at first that he would reciprocate. It was not to be, however, and Edith had to settle, unhappily, for a passionless though stalwart union. Her husband cannot have been satisfied either; his letters from the Western Front portray him as a romantic and an idealist. 'The longing for love is human nature,' he had written in 1918, and he believed then that marrying someone for reasons other than love resulted in 'half a life'. His marriage to Edith Holländer, according to their perceptive daughter, occurred when 'his ideals had been shattered and his youth was over', but whether or not Anne's observations were based on her own interpretations of her parents' relationship, or upon her father's confiding in her, there can be little doubt that neither he nor Edith found in each other the soulmate for whom they both evidently longed.

Fourteen years later, to mark their anniversary, Otto wrote a reflective letter to Edith which clearly outlines how their relationship evolved:

> Our marriage hasn't been lacking in any whims of fate and, looking back at the time from San Remo until now, only then do you actually realize how much everything has changed. Yet, the most difficult situations haven't disrupted the harmony between us. From the beginning you have shown spirit, such as one seldom sees, a solidarity which gave you the strength to carry on through thick and thin. Apart from having a talent for this, upbringing and the parental home also play a constant role in this and we have to be thankful for that which we have received from home. Thus we should also strive to pass on to our children this feeling of solidarity, tolerance and of dedication to the other. What is still to come, nobody knows, but that we will not make life miserable for each other through little arguments and fights, that we do know. May the coming years of our marriage be as harmonious as the previous ones.

As Edith cannot have failed to notice in his sermon-like portrait of their marriage, her husband talked at length about equanimity and forbearance, but said nothing about love.

For the first year of their married life, Otto and Edith lived with his mother in Frankfurt. One month after their wedding Edith became pregnant, while her sister-in-law, Leni, gave birth to her second child, Bernhard (Buddy), on 2 June 1925. With a toddler and a baby in the house already, Otto and Edith had some idea of what to expect when, on 16 February 1926, their daughter Margot Betti was born. The Holländers immediately visited the new arrival; as soon as she was out of hospital, Edith began to keep notes of this and other events in her daughter's life. (In May, when Edith travelled alone on the sleeper-train to Aachen with Margot, she was pleased by her daughter's good behaviour.) There were many visits to Aachen for Margot, ensuring that both the Holländers and Alice were given equal amounts of time with their granddaughter. On 21 December Leni accompanied Margot to Aachen again so that Otto and Edith could take a holiday alone together in Switzerland. Julius brought Margot home to Frankfurt in his car on 17 January 1927, and two days later Abraham Holländer died at the age of sixty-six. Edith recorded in Margot's baby book: 'I am going home for fourteen days. Margot has given her grandfather much sunshine and happiness.'

Edith now only ate kosher food when at her parents' home, but she attended the Westend synagogue regularly whilst living on Mertonstrasse and continued to do so after October 1927, when she, Otto and Margot moved into a home of their own at Marbachweg 307, in a neighbourhood where there were few Jewish families. Although the area was not particularly attractive, the Franks' apartment in one half of a large yellow house with green shutters was spacious; Margot had her own bedroom and there was a guest room with a balcony overlooking the garden at the rear. Gertrud Naumann, who lived next door, was ten years old but mature for her age and often popped in to baby-sit for Margot. Below the Franks, in the other half of the house, lived their landlord, Otto Könitzer, and his family. Otto and Edith had little to do with him; they knew that he was a Nazi Party supporter.

In June Otto and Edith enjoyed a holiday with Nathan Straus and his family in Sils-Maria where Olga Spitzer, Otto's cousin, had a luxury home, Villa Larêt. Returning to Frankfurt, Otto and Edith engaged a new domestic help, Kathi Stilgenbauer, a young woman whom Margot adored. At the end of the year, the family travelled by train to Aachen and celebrated

Hanukkah with Edith's mother and brothers. Edith was pregnant and gave birth on 12 June 1929. The child was again a girl, as Otto told Kathi over the telephone from the hospital where he had remained the entire night during his wife's complicated labour. Annelies Marie was born at 7.30 a.m. and recorded by the exhausted nurse in charge as a male child. Edith started a new book for this second daughter and recorded that 'Mother and Margot visit the baby sister on 14 June. Margot is completely delighted.'

Otto Frank loved both his children, but from the very beginning he had a special bond with his youngest daughter. Her boldness made him laugh and brought him out of himself in a way that Margot's tranquillity did not. It was on her father that Anne bestowed her first smiles, it was Otto to whom she ran when she was hurt or uncertain, and it was he who tucked her into bed at night and then sat with her until she fell asleep. (In turn, after Anne's birth, Margot was to draw closer to her mother.) Otto later admitted that Anne was 'a little rebel with a will of her own.' He continued, 'She was often wakeful at night,' and recalled 'going in to her many times, petting her and singing nursery songs to quiet her'. Anne also became the favourite of her uncle Julius, who had been a tempestuous child himself and recognized something of his own character in Anne, as did Edith's mother, Rosa. Julius and Walter had already been to Frankfurt once during Anne's first year, and in August the Franks travelled to Aachen, where Julius, suffering from the depression that always threatened to engulf him, managed to wake early each day to clown around for Anne.

In the middle of the hot summer of 1929, Erich Elias left Frankfurt for Switzerland, where he had been invited to open a branch of Opekta (of which he was a founder member), a subsidiary of Pomosin-Werke, Frankfurt. Pomosin manufactured pectin, a gelling agent most commonly used in jam preparation. Leni and four-year-old Buddy remained part of the Mertonstrasse household for another year, and seven-year-old Stephan stayed behind until 1931. The Eliases lived in a pension until they could afford their own home in Basel.

Otto, Edith and the children returned to Frankfurt in September, and Edith gave up trying to breastfeed Anne, who immediately began to gain weight normally – something which had worried them before. Margot also experienced health problems, and was made to sit under a sun-lamp every week in an attempt to improve her constitution. Edith cared lovingly for the girls through the day, but in the evening, when he had finished work, Otto would bath and play with them, reading them stories he had invented himself about two sisters, one good and one bad: the two Paulas. Both

Margot and Anne loved his tales, and Anne used the character of Bad Paula in a story of her own years.

In October the bank's profits took a sudden terrifying plunge in the wake of the Wall Street Crash. The trade in throat lozenges dipped sharply as well, and with Edith's dowry money gone Otto saw no alternative but to incorporate both businesses into one office in a much cheaper building. The address, Bockenheimer Anlage, was close to where Michael Frank had begun his business more than forty years earlier and was shared with another firm to keep costs down. It was not the only difficulty in their lives that year; Otto's cousin Milly visited them and found 'conditions in Germany just impossible . . . I remember talking to Otto about politics. He said, "I don't like it. I don't know what's going to happen. I'm scared of the Right." He saw it coming – at a time when I don't think many of the Jews were particularly worried.' Shortly before her marriage and subsequent leaving of the Franks' employ in 1929, Kathi Stilgenbauer asked Otto who the Brownshirts were: 'Mr Frank just laughed and tried to make a joke of the whole thing . . . But Mrs Frank looked up from her plate and she fixed her eyes on us and said, "We'll find out soon enough who they are, Kathi."' In March 1931 matters came to a head when Otto Könitzer decided he could no longer stomach Jews living in his house and gave the Franks their notice. They moved into a five-room apartment at Ganghoferstrasse 24 where the interior dimensions were much smaller, but this was partially compensated for by having a garden and pleasanter surroundings for the children. Their old friends from Marbachweg called almost daily, unaffected by Könitzer's reaction, and the new neighbours were generally welcoming.

The bank business continued to deteriorate, damaged by the closure of the Frankfurt Stock Exchange in the summer of 1931 and the stricter laws imposed upon companies dealing in foreign currency. In April 1932 it suffered another blow and one from which it never recovered; Herbert Frank was arrested by income tax officials on grounds of breaching the 1931 Bestimmung über den Effektenhandel mit dem Ausland (Regulation Governing the Trade in Securities with Foreign Countries Act). A few months earlier, a stockbroker from Karlsruhe had made him an offer: over one million Reichmarks of foreign shares in German industrial companies for which Herbert would act as agent. The transaction was illegal, but Herbert accepted the offer in good faith and sold the shares, earning the usual commission. In Herbert's favour was the fact that he had kept a record of the transactions he made. The affair reached the pages of the *Frankfurter Zeitung*, to whom Otto granted an interview in which he stated that his brother, the proprietor with the controlling interest in the bank, had been unaware that the securities had been issued abroad and had trusted the man from Karlsruhe, who had since disappeared. Herbert was jailed and the family lodged an appeal against his arrest. Otto wrote to Leni, 'Herbert spoke to me this morning and seemed well enough. He has a lot of courage and won't be bought out. I'm convinced that from the whole situation not much will change . . . Business is poor. You can't see straight when nothing seems to be going right. Only the children are enjoying themselves, as no doubt your children are too.' Herbert was released on 14 May and given a date for his trial in October 1933. Robert was out of the country, travelling backwards and forwards between Frankfurt, Paris and London in an effort to establish better connections in the world of art dealership, hoping to find his own solution to the family's financial problems. The situation was more serious than ever; it seemed that the house on Mertonstrasse would have to be relinquished, an eventuality none of them wanted to consider.

In June Otto's mother Alice took the train to Paris, aiming to borrow money from her nephew Jean-Michel, who had been left a significant sum by his mother following her death in the asylum. Part of his inheritance had been used to set up a partnership in furniture design. He had workshops in rue Montauban where he collaborated with artists such as Alberto and Diego Giacometti, and Salvador Dali. His clinical style was already highly collectable, though Coco Chanel commented it made her feel as if she were 'passing a cemetery'. To outsiders and society Jean-Michel was a flamboyant Communist homosexual who dabbled in drugs 'to disturb his friends' and always dressed in the same grey London suit. His family knew him as he really was: witty and compassionate. He worshipped Leni, in whom he found a kindred spirit. Otto described the family crisis to him over the telephone, as he explained in a letter to his mother:

The break-down into ongoing expenses, outstanding debts and mortgage payments speak for themselves . . . I can't believe that Jean couldn't understand and only saw how the situation really is through my letter to Leni . . . My last letter to her wasn't meant to be forwarded, but it shows a clear picture of the situation, which has become impossible. If Soden [the business in cough and cold lozenges] wouldn't go as bad as never before, we could have gained a bit, but this way we lack the most basic means . . .

My pessimism and worries of the last few months were only too well-founded but I have to ask whether it still makes sense to hold on to the house on Mertonstrasse. I'm speaking from an economic and political point of view. Herbie will try to get away from Frankfurt and find a job elsewhere. There isn't much he can do here but he needs something to live on even if it's not substantial. Erich has work. We have no idea where we will end up, but the main thing is that we stay healthy and that you have an income. We're younger and better able to deal with adversity. It is important to see things as they are and to act accordingly. We'll try to hold on to the business as long as we can. We'll have to discuss later what the solution should be. Apart from H, we have no customers who can keep us from sinking. But to dissolve the firm seems pointless at this time . . . We keep our courage up as always.

Later that day, Alice sent Otto a telegram: Jean-Michel had given her the money needed to meet the July mortgage payments on the house on Mertonstrasse. Otto wrote to her jubilantly the next day:

I hardly need tell you how great my relief is, since it would have been impossible to keep the house otherwise. Jean has behaved admirably, and we cannot thank him enough. I spoke briefly to Robert. He's still so overwrought that you can hardly hold a conversation with him . . .

I don't know quite how everything can be arranged. But it's obvious that everyone is keen to keep the house and optimistic, so I glean courage from that. Hopefully the possibility to earn more will improve soon, at the moment there's no way forward . . .

I always tried to sweep problems under the carpet but that's no longer viable, and the sooner and more openly we discuss the situation the better. I can imagine that you're not enjoying your stay in Paris any more. But you must be satisfied with what you've achieved, and especially with Jean, who cares for you . . .

Not much to add about us. Margot is an angel, she had a school outing today. She was thrilled . . .

I'm anxious to hear more and hope you're not too over-excited.

On 1 October Herbert resigned from the bank and headed for Paris where he had several relatives, including Jean-Michel, and many friends. His wife, Hortense, had left him in September 1930 and in August 1932 they were divorced. She moved to Zurich and the Franks never saw her again. Herbert refused to attend his trial in Frankfurt, claiming material and mental injury and sent Otto to represent him. Otto told the court that the bank had trusted the stockbroker because he was German and therefore assumed he understood the German law on the issue of dealing in foreign currency. Herbert won his appeal and avoided a fine, but the incident had upset him and he decided against returning to Frankfurt. Despite the fortuitous outcome of the trial and the money from Jean-Michel, the bank business had not recovered, and at the end of December 1932 Otto gave in their notice at the apartment on Ganghoferstrasse 'as a result of changes in the economic situation'. They moved in with Alice again in March 1933, but, even then, Otto knew it was only a temporary measure until the difficulties with paying the mortgage on the Mertonstrasse house resurfaced.

The rise of the Nazi Party added to the Franks' already manifold problems, and Otto began to consider leaving the country of which he was so proud. On 31 July 1932 almost fourteen million Germans had voted for Hitler in the national elections, gaining the Nazis two hundred and thirty seats in the Reichstag.

In January 1933 Otto and Edith were visiting friends when they heard on the wireless that Hitler had been made Chancellor. As the cheers mounted in the background, Otto glanced across at Edith and saw her sitting 'as if turned to stone'. He himself was unable to muster a reply when their host said cheerfully, 'Well, let's see what the man can do!' The heat of loathing which had been seething for decades was about to burst forth, as Otto knew:

> As early as 1932, groups of Stormtroopers (Brownshirts) came marching by singing: 'When Jewish blood splatters off the knife.' That made it more than clear to everyone. I immediately discussed it with my wife: 'How can we leave here?', but eventually there is of course the question: How will you be able to support yourself if you go away and give up more or less everything?

Otto's cousin Edith Oppenheimer relates how life changed that year:

My parents and Otto exchanged visits in Frankfurt. My mother was ten years younger than Otto, but they were good friends (I think my father was jealous of this. Mother would have liked to have seen Otto more, after the war, but father didn't allow it.) It was a happy time until 1933. My father always told us that one weekend in 1933 he and mother were invited to visit relatives. The male friend handed my father a book and said, 'I think you should read this.' It was *Mein Kampf*. Father stayed up all night reading, and the next morning announced that we were going to America. There was a family conference, and he tried to persuade the other members of the family that it was dangerous to stay, but [my grandfather] Opa Stern, who managed the Meyer and Sohn leather factory, felt an obligation to stay. He was later arrested and tortured, and committed suicide in prison.

Edith Oppenheimer's grandmother, her parents and her other grand-parents left Germany for America, 'with great bewilderment that their Germany could have turned against them in this way'.

Otto's efforts in establishing a business with which he was familiar in a country elsewhere had failed before; to make another attempt with a wife and two children depending on him he had to be as certain as he could be that this time it would have some measure of success. He vacillated only until a decree was promulgated towards the forced segregation of Jewish and non-Jewish children in schools. At first Margot had attended the Ludwig Richter School. Although she was only one of five Jewish children in a class of forty-two, and received twice-weekly instruction in the Jewish religion as her mother desired, Margot had never been made to feel apart from her fellow pupils. Her first report card praised her diligence and natural aptitude. In the wake of the new decree, Margot's head teacher and form tutor were dismissed from their posts by Nazi officials as political opponents of the New Order. After moving to Mertonstrasse Margot had begun at the Varrentrapp School, closer to her grandmother's home, but since Easter she had been forced to sit away from her non-Jewish classmates with all the other Jewish children.

Following the segregation decree Otto turned to his brother-in-law, Erich Elias in Switzerland, to ask for advice and assistance, refusing to 'bring up children like horses with blinkers, ignorant of the social landscape outside their small group'. Erich was eager to help; he told him that the Opekta company in Cologne was hoping to 'expand the international market for pectin', and through him Otto was appointed manager of Pomosin Utrecht, supplier of pectin to jam factories since 1928. Unfortunately, the position collapsed before Otto had the chance to do anything with it. The managing director of Pomosin-Utrecht, F. J. M. van Angeren, caused so many diffi-culties for him that Otto asked Erich if he could find him another post. Erich suggested that Otto set up independently, opening a branch in Amsterdam, a city with which Otto already had connections. Otto liked the idea, and Erich, who was now the manager of the Swiss concern, provided him with the venture capital: an interest-free loan of fl.15,000 repayable over ten years. Shares of Opekta, Amsterdam, served as security against the loan, which meant Otto could repay the debt at any time by surrendering his shares. Probably hoping to appease the disagreeable van Angeren, Otto declared that he would only sell to housewives, leaving the factory-market free to Pomosin Utrecht.

Having long felt that banking was not for him, Otto told those friends who had remained loyal that his family would be emigrating to the

Netherlands. 'My family had lived in Germany for centuries and we had many friends and acquaintances, not only Jewish but also Christian ones, but by and by many of the latter deserted us, incited by the National Socialistic propaganda.' Gertrud Naumann was one of the few friends who stood by them; she recalled that the last time she visited the Franks, Otto was uncharacteristically subdued: 'Mr Frank never spoke about anything that troubled him. But . . . you could see the way it was worrying him and working inside him.' The last photograph of the family in Frankfurt was taken by Otto on his favourite Leica camera in March 1933: Edith holds the hands of her daughters on the Hauptwache square in the city centre, both young girls wear serious expressions, and Edith's own smile has an understandable melancholy to it. They had already made plans to stay in Aachen while Otto established himself in Amsterdam.

On 1 April 1933, three weeks after the photograph was taken, there was a nationwide boycott of all Jewish businesses in Germany. Thereafter, numerous laws expelling Jews from business and social life were implemented in quick succession. Since Hitler's seizure of the Reich Chancellorship on 30 January, the democratic state had been systematically destroyed, leaving the path clear for the elimination of all opposition. The Communist Party was almost wiped out along with every other political group until only the Nazi Party remained. Mass arrests, incarceration in prisons and concentration camps, and the elimination of those who spoke out against the NSDAP became commonplace.

At the beginning of August Otto Frank departed from the city of his affluent youth: 'The world around me had collapsed. When most of the people of my country turned into hordes of nationalist, cruel anti-Semitic criminals, I had to face the consequences, and though this hurt me deeply I realized that Germany was not the world and I left for ever.'

2. The Eyes of Our Persecutors

'One must not lose courage,' Edith Frank wrote to Gertrud Naumann a few days after her arrival in Amsterdam. Until December 1933 Edith and the children remained in Aachen with her mother and brothers at Monheim-sallee 42–44, the large town house the Holländers had begun renting the year before. Anne's lively personality made Oma Holländer both laugh and despair; when they were out together one day and boarded a busy tram, the three-year-old Anne looked this way and that before asking loudly, 'Won't someone offer a seat to this old lady?'

Edith travelled repeatedly to Amsterdam between August and December 1933 to view apartments with her husband. On 16 November Otto sent a postcard to Gertrud: 'We'll soon have a place to live. Winter will pass and perhaps we'll see you here sometime next year. I have a lot of work and am tired and nervous but otherwise, thank God, in good health.' Although Otto had recorded himself and Edith as residents of Amsterdam in the municipal registry on 16 August as required, it was not until 5 December that they officially moved into an apartment: Merwedeplein 37 in Amsterdam-Zuid's Rivierenbuurt. The flat was large and light, with a spacious room on the floor above which they could rent out for extra income. A wide balcony at the rear overlooked their neighbours' gardens. Hundreds of Jews in flight were settling into the area; their German, Austrian and Polish voices reson-ated in the air. One Dutch newspaper, irritated by their presence, issued them with a warning on how to behave: 'Do not speak German on the street. Do not attract attention by speaking loudly and dressing loudly. Study and follow the ways of the land.' Other admonitions would follow.

Edith wrote to Gertrud a few days after her official immigration:

> We have so much to do. You are right: how well I could use your help with unpacking and clearing up. Tante Hedi has been here for a week, without her I would not finish at all. Tomorrow both uncles will bring Margot here and will stay for Christmas. Anne also wants to come. Rosa will have a hard time to keep the child there for another couple of weeks.

When the apartment was furnished with their belongings shipped over from Germany, Edith's brothers Julius and Walter brought Margot by car to

Amsterdam and stayed until the New Year. Anne remained in Aachen with Oma Holländer so that Margot could settle into the unfamiliar surroundings in peace. On 4 January 1934 Margot began her new school on nearby Jeker-straat and Anne arrived in Amsterdam a month later, on Margot's birthday.

The break with the past, and with Germany, was now superficially complete. Robert Frank and his wife, Lottie, emigrated from Frankfurt to London in mid 1933 and opened their own art dealership in a basement on St James Street. They entered London life with ebullience: Robert bought himself a bowler hat and umbrella, and Lottie liked to hold court over afternoon tea at Fortnum & Mason. Their house in Kensington became a popular meeting place for people in the art world. Alice Frank, somewhat less enthusiastically, moved to Switzerland. She admitted defeat over the mortgage repayments for her home on Mertonstrasse, surrendering the property in October 1933. She journeyed by train to Basel, taking with her a list of the Nazi-approved items in her possession. Leni and Erich, together with their sons Stephan and Buddy, escorted her to the four-room apartment she would rent until they found a larger home where she could join them. Alice found it difficult to adjust, although the area in which she lived was agreeably quiet, and she had trouble understanding Swiss German. Edith confided to Gertrud the real problem: 'Omi still suffers from homesickness in Basel and from being separated from her children.' The former was a hardship Edith could understand only too well.

During the first months of his residency in Amsterdam, while his wife and children were in Aachen, Otto had rented a room at Stadionkade 24II and travelled to work by tram, which stopped just short of the Opekta office at Nieuwe Zijds Voorburgwal 120–126. Although the offices were in a tall, modern building, the premises leased to Opekta were small: two rooms and a claustrophobic kitchen. Otto's brief was to convince housewives to use pectin in their jam-making. Pectin was not processed by Otto's company; they merely prepared, received and despatched orders. Sales occurred mainly through pharmacists, although there were also some transactions to whole-salers.

Some of the groundwork for the company had already been laid by Victor Gustav Kugler, who had previously worked for Pomosin-Utrecht. Kugler was born in June 1900 in the (then) Austro-Hungarian town of Hohenelbe. His mother was single when she gave birth to him, and relied on support from her parents. Kugler was baptized a Catholic and attended a Catholic school. In 1917 he joined the Austrian navy, but an injury led to his exemption from active duty. After the Great War he worked for the

Deutsche Maschinenfabrik as an electrician and was transferred to Utrecht where he married a local woman. By 1923 he was assistant to the director of Pomosin-Utrecht. When Opekta Frankfurt decided to expand their sales techniques, Kugler was placed in charge of the operation in Amsterdam. He was deemed too slow, however, and Otto took over the task. Kugler became 'more or less Otto's right-hand man' and made the sixteen-mile trip from his home in Hilversum on his motorized bike every day. Otto said that he admired his no-nonsense approach to work, and sensed the compassion and integrity beneath his serious bearing.

Apart from a junior clerk whose main duty was packaging the products, Otto employed only one other full-time member of staff. When this secretary fell ill, another Austrian-born worker was recommended to him: Hermine (Miep) Santrouschitz, born in 1909 in Vienna. Miep arrived in the Netherlands as a starving child, sent by a welfare organization to live with a Dutch family until she recovered. She settled in so well with her foster family, the Nieuwenhuises, who called her Miep, that she never returned to Austria. She moved with the Nieuwenhuises from Leiden to Amsterdam's Rivierenbuurt in 1922. In late 1933 a friend told her about the position with Opekta and she applied for it, not knowing what it entailed. Her first two weeks were spent in the tiny office kitchen making jam. Once she had perfected that, Otto promoted her to dealing with customer complaints and giving out information, along with typing and bookkeeping.

Miep's attraction to Otto was instant:

In a shy but gentlemanly way this slim, smiling man introduced himself . . . His dark eyes held my eyes to him, and I felt immediately his kind and gentle nature, stiffened somewhat by shyness and a slightly nervous demeanour . . . He apologized for his poor Dutch . . . I gladly spoke German . . . He wore a moustache and when he smiled, which was often, he revealed quite uneven teeth.

They shared the same passionate political views and promptly became close friends:

I called him Mr Frank and he called me Miss Santrouschitz, as Northern Europeans of our generation did not use first names with each other. Feeling at ease with him quite quickly, I threw formality aside and demanded, 'Please call me Miep.' Mr Frank did as I asked.

Otto developed a flair for advertising the Opekta business. Together with Miep, he spent hours thinking up new means of enticing housewives into buying their product. They placed scores of adverts in newspapers and magazines, and produced an *Opekta Journal*. Otto experimented with various recipes, including jam for diabetics, tomato jam and even chocolate jam. Although their first year was not lucrative – the company was established 'just too late to be able to profit from the 1933 harvest (and hence from the preserving season)' – it did provide Otto with a small income. This was even more welcome in January 1934, when the Michael Frank bank ceased all trading. On 26 September 1938 the business was officially eliminated from the Frankfurt register.

By 1933 few people could be in doubt that Jews in Germany were in grave danger, yet little aid was offered. In the Netherlands, the population swung between concern and indifference; a 1933 meeting held in Amsterdam's RAI centre in response to the anti-Jewish boycott in Germany was well-attended by Jews and gentiles, but protests were few in number and rarely vociferous. Three waves of German Jewish refugees, approximately 30,000 in total, entered the Netherlands: in 1933, after Hitler came to power; in 1935, following the Nuremberg Laws; and in 1938, in the wake of Kristallnacht. The majority settled in Amsterdam. Reactions from Dutch Jews and gentiles ranged from negativity to expressions of solidarity. After 1934 and again in 1938 the Dutch government placed restrictions on the number of refugees permitted entry to the Netherlands. The justice minister, Goseling, referred to these desperate, beleaguered people as 'undesirable aliens' who would do better to return to Germany and Austria.

The relief committees of the 1930s encouraged the newcomers to go further afield, and promoted Britain and America as desirable locations. Many refugees were sent straight back to Germany, where they ended their days in concentration camps and prisons. Those who did gain entrance to the Netherlands were often placed in refugee camps since the Dutch government felt no responsibility towards their well-being and were of the opinion that the refugees could and should receive aid solely from private Dutch Jewish organizations. The government's first choice for a sizeable refugee camp was adjacent to Elspeet, not far from the residence of Queen Wilhelmina, who protested against it. In 1939 construction began at another site: Drenthe in the north-east of the Netherlands, far away from the main cities and towns. Strict instructions were given for the building of Kamp Westerbork: it was imperative that it did not exceed the comfort and attractiveness of the housing occupied by local, impoverished residents. Freedom of movement within the camp, even then, was limited.

Solvent German Jews who settled in the Netherlands found prejudice from the Dutch population arose more from their nationality than the fact that they were Jewish. Hilde Goldberg (her married name), who emigrated from Berlin to Amsterdam in 1929 with her parents Walter and Betty Jacobsthal, and her brother Joachim, remembers:

The Rivierenbuurt was then completely Dutch. There really were only Dutch people living there, no refugees from elsewhere. It was hard for my parents at first, of course, but we adapted easily, my brother and I. I understood perfectly from the age of about four both Dutch and German. Later we wouldn't speak German at all, not even at home because of what the Nazis had come to represent, and we wouldn't dream of speaking German on the streets. That would have caused us great trouble.

Laureen Nussbaum (née Klein), whose parents had known Otto and Edith in Frankfurt before emigrating to the Rivierenbuurt in 1936, remembers,

It was not about anti-Semitism then. There was a lot of anger and dislike towards us because we were German. It didn't matter that we were Jewish Germans arriving in the country in fear of our lives; we were simply Germans to the Dutch. We asked our parents to refrain from conversing in their own language in public for that reason.

Most of the German Jewish refugees found their homes in the Rivierenbuurt and in the area around Beethovenstraat. Their appearance in these pleasant neighbourhoods caused economic jealousy, as Laureen recalls:

The Franks and my family, and most of the other German Jews, rented apartments in the south which the Dutch Jews, and many of the non-Jewish Dutch, could not afford to do. These houses were very lovely: large, modern, and expensive. They had central heating – an absolute luxury then. So it was more envy than anything else. The Dutch Jews covered the whole spectrum of social status, from the very poor to the very wealthy, but in the main the German Jews were affluent, which bred resentment.

Many Dutch Jews and non-Jews found the refugees arrogant and bestowed upon them the sarcastic diminutive *chez nous*.

Dutch Jews were also fearful that anti-Semitism would erupt in the Netherlands as it had in Germany, with so many refugees choosing to go no further in their flight from prejudice. There had been some racism towards Jews in the Netherlands before the 1930s, but it was seldom openly aggressive:

Mild forms of anti-Semitism increased from the end of the nineteenth century, but never gave rise to pogroms as in Eastern Europe. It was, for instance, not possible for a Jew to advance to a high post in the civil service; in this Holland was not different from other European countries. Some restaurants and dance-halls made it plain that Jews were not welcome on their premises, a form of exclusion also applicable to black Dutchmen from Surinam.

Among those Jewish refugees who desperately missed Germany was Edith Frank. Miep recalls that Edith longed for her homeland 'much more than Mr Frank. Very often in conversation she would refer with melancholy to their life in Frankfurt, the superiority of some kinds of German sweets and the quality of German clothing'. Hilde Goldberg agrees:

We got to know Otto when he was in the process of setting up Opekta and he would experiment with jam recipes in our kitchen. He got on with life in Amsterdam, but Edith found the adjustment very hard. She came from a very protective, very middle-class background and here it was more 'make-do-and-mend'. She had a real flair for fashion, was always beautifully dressed and with her hair set just so, and she dressed her children beautifully too – their dresses, although casual enough to play in, were always well-made. She was a good mother, very conscientious, but she never really made friends with people because she had such reserve. I think the problems between her and Anne before they went into hiding were due to her reticence to mix with people. The neighbourhood was very friendly and everyone knew each other but she held herself back, and I think that irritated Anne. My mother always felt that Edith looked down on her because she was not so neat and tidy – Edith was always immaculate.

Having told Gertrud, 'one must not lose courage', Edith tried to find positive factors to the various elements in her new life: 'Our home is similar to that in Ganghoferstrasse, only much smaller. In our bedrooms there is room only for the beds. There is no cellar, no pantry, but everything is light, comfortable and warm, so I can manage without a help.' She had great difficulty learning the Dutch language, and asked a neighbour to give her private lessons, but was so discouraged by her early attempts that she abandoned the classes and endeavoured to learn it purely by ear. Otto and the children came into constant contact with the language and picked it up quickly, conversing with each other before long in a mixture of German and Dutch, alienating Edith further. Edith's weekly visit to the Liberal synagogue became even more important to her in these circumstances. Otto grew slightly more interested in Judaism following the move from Frankfurt to Amsterdam, but for him it was a social rather than a spiritual focus. He later admitted, 'The feeling of being regarded as a foreign substance in the German nation made those Jews who had not attached much value to their Jewish identity again aware of it.' In his ignorance, however, Otto tried to register his family with the Orthodox community. He was astonished to be told that he would 'have to have a new marriage ceremony' because the Orthodox rabbinate did not recognize Liberal Jewish marriages. There was then no Liberal Jewish congregation in Amsterdam, only an Orthodox one.

Hilde Goldberg, whose father Walter helped to found the Liberal Jewish movement in Amsterdam, recalls,

There was no synagogue in which the Liberal German Jews could worship. Otto and my father got together a committee in order to establish somewhere for the Liberal Jewish congregation to go. It wasn't anything much at first – just a hall – but later it became a proper organization.

Services were held in the hall of the Apollopaviljoen and other temporary locations until 1937, when a large synagogue in Lekstraat was built, bringing 'modernization to Judaism and offering a link to the non-Jewish environment without giving Judaism up entirely'.

Throughout the summer of 1934 Otto's uncle, Armand Geiershofer of Luxembourg, sent him large amounts of money which went directly into the Opekta account. Otto wrote each time to thank him, adding on 9 July that Edith and Anne had gone to Aachen for a few days. Margot stayed behind in Amsterdam; she was finding the adjustment more problematic than Anne, who enjoyed attending the local Montessori school. Edith informed Gertrud, 'Both children speak Dutch well and have nice friends.' In autumn 1934 Otto wrote to Armand, 'Though my income remains fairly modest, one must be satisfied to have found some way of earning a living and getting on.' In a more open letter to Gertrud he confessed, 'I am travelling almost every day, and only get home in the evening. It's not like in Frankfurt, where one eats at home at lunchtime – and where one can relax a little too. It goes on all day . . .' The business was slow in establishing itself, but towards the end of the year Otto rented new premises with more floor space. The offices were at Singel 400, three storeys above a warehouse and overlooking the canal. Otto had to work harder than ever to promote his product, since two other companies were promoting a product similar to his own. Otto was unable to afford the expense of several sales representatives and had to act as such himself on occasion, visiting housewives and wholesalers across the country. He was habitually absent from home for a week or more, and Edith conceded to Gertrud, 'Mr Frank doesn't relax at all and looks thin and tired.' The children were faring much better: 'During the holidays I was by the sea with the girls, because Anne has not fully recovered [from a recent illness], but she will go to stay in a small children's home and will miss school for another three weeks. Margot is tall, tanned and strong, and has great joy in learning.'

Business improved for Otto slightly in 1935 when he managed to persuade a number of small wholesalers to stock pectin, but his profits still depended upon the success of the strawberry harvest and it was not until the war that the company began to show a satisfactory revenue. Through the transactions to wholesalers, Otto was able to employ more staff. In January a thirty-four-year-old Amsterdam lawyer, Anton Dunselman, was appointed supervisory director of the company. A young man named Henk van Beusekom worked in the warehouse, Otto's friend Isa Cauvern was given secretarial tasks, and there were at least two demonstrators, one of whom was a Jewish refugee from Frankfurt, Renee Wolfe Manola. She was employed by Opekta for six months before emigrating to America. At some point in 1935, probably after Renee departed, the Jansen family began to work for Otto.

Jetje Jansen was engaged at Opekta throughout 1935 and 1936 as a full-time demonstrator while her husband, Joseph (a professional theatre actor who once had aspirations to become a Roman Catholic priest), worked for Otto on a casual basis building display stands for trade exhibitions. Their son helped with the packing and despatch duties in the warehouse. The Jansens were a deeply unhappy family: Jetje was Jewish and since 1932 she and her husband had begun to draw inextricably away from each other; in that year Joseph Jansen had joined the NSB. Later he claimed to have become a member because, 'I was convinced that democracy needed to be renewed and that . . . the socio-economic structure with regard to the working class needed improvement . . . because of the actions of my wife she gave me a feeling of inferiority and if our relationship had been good, it would never have come so far with me and I would never have resorted to the NSB.' He later became a member of the Weerafdeling (WA) and eventually joined the Schutzstaffel (SS), leaving Jetje for a baker's widow who supported the NSB. In 1935, however, he was a jealous husband and over the course of his wife's employment at Opekta he convinced himself that she and Otto were having an affair. There were no apparent grounds for his suspicion, but it sparked in Joseph Jansen a deep and lasting hatred of Otto Frank. Otto's uncomplicated decision in 1935 to employ the Jansens would lead him into a maze of blackmail, terror and despair.

It was through Jansen that Tonny Ahlers was to enter the life of Otto Frank.

In early summer 1935 Otto's mother, Alice, arrived in Amsterdam for an extensive holiday. Anne accompanied her on the return journey to Basel; she had been pestering her parents for some time to be allowed to visit her cousins Stephan and Buddy. In December Otto and Margot travelled by train to Basel, leaving Anne at home with her mother, and then with Oma Holländer in nearby Aachen, to recuperate from a viral infection she had been suffering from since October. In Switzerland, under Buddy's expert tuition, Margot learned to skate; when she heard about this, Anne immediately wanted lessons too. Otto later recalled the differences in his two daughters:

Anne was a normal, lively child who needed much tenderness and attention, and who delighted us and frequently upset us. When she entered a room, there was always a fuss. Anne never stopped asking questions. When we had visitors, she was so interested in them that it was hard to get rid of her. At school she was never a particularly brilliant pupil. She hated arithmetic, and I used to practise her multiplication tables with her. She did well only in the subjects she was interested in . . . Margot was the bright one. Everybody admired her. She got along with everybody . . . She was a wonderful person.

The Franks' social circle was beginning to extend; Otto and Edith had become close friends with their neighbours Hans and Ruth Goslar, German Jewish refugees like themselves. Hans Goslar had been director of the press office in Berlin from 1919 until the Nazis' rise to power, when he was dismissed from his influential post. For several months, he and his wife Ruth Judith Klee, a scholar, tried to settle in England, where Hans had been offered a job. Problems arose when the company would not allow Hans to abstain from work on the Sabbath. Hans left the business, and took his wife and daughter Hanneli to Amsterdam, intending eventually to move to Palestine. He began a business in his own home, advising Jewish refugees on legal and financial matters. Through the Goslars, Edith was able to enjoy a more religious life than she had previously in Amsterdam: Hans, a founder member of the German Zionist group Mizrachi, invited them for the Friday night celebration, and Edith and Ruth often attended the synagogue together. Margot was growing increasingly interested in Judaism and enjoyed her Hebrew classes. Hanneli Goslar, who was Anne's best friend at the time, recalls,

Margot always said that after the war she wanted to be a nurse in Palestine. Otto had no interest in attending the synagogue for worship. Anne was like him in that sense. He influenced her decision perhaps, but he was such a wonderful father. I loved him. Every night I would be at the Franks' house and every night Otto would have a beer and Anne and I would sit nearby. He would tip the glass up and up and up – and we would sit, open-mouthed, waiting for him to spill it – but he never did and night after night he did it to tease us!

In the summer of 1936 Edith took the children to Otto's cousin's villa in Sils-Maria. In September Alice and Stephan arrived in Amsterdam; Edith's mother was also visiting them. Stephan sent home a postcard complaining that the weather was

... dreadful. We drove here with the car. I [Alice's nickname, pronounced 'ee'] has a cold and is in bed. If she isn't better by Saturday then she will come home with me ... I'm glad we left Zandvoort – it was stormy, no fun ... I'm sightseeing in Amsterdam with great interest and have already been to the Rijksmuseum ... I'll be sorry when these wonderful days are over but glad to come home to Basel too. I sends greetings from her bed.

He sent a second card, which gives a small glimpse of family life:

Yesterday I was with Ottel [another of Otto's nicknames] in his office. There wasn't much to see of Opekta. I ate a Dutch breakfast and went to the cinema. I know all of Amsterdam now. I was in the Koloniaal Instituut [now the Tropen Museum] too. Today I'm going on a canal boat. I sleep very well in my fold-up bed. Anne is already up at six o'clock every morning and then we sit and chat. Otto crawls into her bed and then Margot jumps down from the top bunk.

When their visitors had gone, Edith holidayed alone in Aachen and travelled briefly to Frankfurt. She wrote to Gertrud in October, 'I found the children in good spirits and they are happy to have me back again. Papi left on Monday again for a week ... We have at least seen each other and had a chance to talk. Let's hope we'll have another chance soon.' The following year they received a letter from Kathi Stilgenbauer, their former housekeeper in Frankfurt, informing them that her husband had been arrested and imprisoned by the Nazis. Edith wrote: 'We think often of you and your grief.' Later that year, Otto visited Germany on business; it was the last time he was in the country before the war. Meeting Gertrud, he told her, 'If they saw us together now they would arrest us.' When Edith wrote to Gertrud again, she did so in a mood of dejection: 'My husband is hardly ever at home. Work is getting harder and harder.'

Otto's friend Johannes Kleiman had joined Opekta as bookkeeper, but the Jansens had gone and new representatives were taken on, together with another full-time typist, Bep Voskuijl. Bep was Dutch, born in 1919, the eldest child in a large family, tall and rather shy. After finishing school, she worked briefly as a domestic help and in a sewing workshop before taking evening courses to qualify as a secretary. In the summer of 1937 she began working for Opekta: 'I was under Isa Cauvern. Miep, who was ten years older, was more or less my boss . . . The relationship between Frank and Kleiman was not just business, but also friendship; they used to play cards every week, I believe. Otto Frank and Ab Cauvern [Isa's husband] were also good friends.' She remembered Otto as 'affectionate, unsparing with himself and keenly sensitive . . . a soft word always made far more impression than any shouting'. Bep obtained a position for her father at Opekta; Johan Voskuijl was a trained bookkeeper, but worked for Otto as warehouse manager. He and Otto became close friends, and he confided in Otto his diagnosis with stomach cancer. Despite the painful treatments, he continued to work at his own insistence.

By 1937 Miep was a regular visitor to the Franks' home, together with her future husband, Jan Gies. Jan, then thirty-two, worked for the Social Services Authority and lived on Rijnstraat, also in the Rivierenbuurt. Miep saw many similarities between Jan and Otto, not only in their appearance (both men were tall, slim and dark) but also in their character: 'Men of few words with high principles and ironic senses of humour.' They had dinner with the Franks on an almost weekly basis, and enjoyed discussing politics with them; they shared the same views about the Nazi Party and spoke vigorously about events in Germany where Jews had lost all their rights and were subject to stringent, escalating laws. It was impossible to maintain a livelihood under all the sanctions. In 1935 Hitler had denounced the Versailles Treaty, and introduced conscription for all non-Jewish males in Germany as the country began to rearm. In September that same year, the far-reaching Nuremberg Laws came into effect, stripping Jews of their nationality and banning them from sexual relationships with or marriages to Aryans.

On 29 October 1937 Otto began two months of frequent travelling in connection with the business. He had plans for 'something in England', as Edith wrote to friends, adding, 'whether it will turn out is uncertain. Unfortunately we are not satisfied with how the business is going and need to supplement it somehow.' Otto visited Basel first, then Paris, London and Bristol. There was only a brief respite at home before he left again, with Anne, on 17 December, for Luxembourg and took the train to Basel where he remained in discussions with Erich Elias, and stayed with his family there until 25 December. Edith wrote to Gertrud:

> Last week my husband had to go to Basel and took Anne with him, to her great pleasure. For two years she had hoped for a trip with her Papi. Whether Omi will bring her back, I do not know yet. Since Uncle Robert and Uncle Herbert are also there at the moment she was very fortunate indeed. Margot travelled to Oma today, where I hope she has a good time . . . My husband is overly tired and really needs a few days off. The business is tough, apart from that we live quietly. I manage my work quite well.

By 1938 Edith was worried about their safety in the Netherlands. Since Hitler's occupation of the Rhineland in 1936, the possibility of invasion had hung over the Dutch, but the government was eager to maintain relations with both Germany and Britain, needing the support of Germany for the economy and Britain for security. Hitler used the 1936–1939 Spanish Civil War to test out his plans for attack, and signed the Rome-Berlin Axis with Mussolini and the Anti-Comintern Pact with Japan, giving him two valuable allies. In 1938 his domination of Europe began; on 12 March German troops overran Vienna, and Austria was incorporated into the Reich. Miep recalls how 'the whole [Opekta] office stood together listening to Mr Frank's wireless, as the dramatic voice announced Hitler's triumphant entry into the city of his youth, Vienna'. The humiliations and restrictions that had befallen Germany's Jews now swept through Austria.

A former neighbour of the Franks from Merwedeplein whose family had settled in America, recalled that her parents urged the family to join them there: 'Mrs Frank wrote that she wanted to emigrate, but Mr Frank saw no need to leave Holland. He trusted in man's basic goodness, rather than focusing on the darker, irrational side of human nature.' Otto regarded Amsterdam as a haven: 'In the Netherlands, after those experiences in Germany, it was as if our life was restored to us. Our children went to school and at least in the beginning our lives proceeded normally. In those days it was possible for us to start over and feel free.' Edith's apprehension and Otto's optimism was something Miep had also noticed in their conversations about Germany: 'Mrs Frank was particularly vocal in her bitter response . . . Mr Frank, with his usual nervous, quiet manner, kept shaking his head, expressing hope.' Although Edith was distressed and anxious about the current situation in Germany, she brooded about the past there, confiding to Gertrud that 'for us the years at Marbachweg were also amongst the best . . . That I cannot travel home more often annoys me.' Edith still regarded Germany as home, even after five years of living in Amsterdam.

Otto's cousin Milly visited the family in Amsterdam in 1938. Her hotel was in the neighbourhood, and she took frequent walks with Otto, who had instructed his daughters to only speak Dutch in public. Milly recalled that Margot and Anne were 'entirely different. Margot was serious for her age, brilliant at school, and gave the impression of having great depth of character. Anne was vivid, mischievous, very affectionate and like quicksilver. There was something appealing about her. I had a lovely weekend with them. There was such a feeling of warmth in their home.'

On 1 June Johannes Kleiman made an application at the Amsterdam Trade Registration Office for Handelsmaatschappij Pectacon N.V. This was Otto's new brainchild, a business he hoped would cover the loss of profits during the winter months, when fruit was scarcer. For the first five months of its existence, Pectacon operated from Kleiman's apartment. The main products were spices and seasonings, imported from Hungary and Belgium and then exported. Goods were sold to butchers throughout the Netherlands, and three sales representatives travelled the country, activating new trade and taking orders.

Since it was a new venture for Otto, and one in which he had little experience as far as seasonings and recipes were concerned, he employed a German Jewish refugee as his adviser: Hermann van Pels, who was an expert in the field. Van Pels was born in Germany in 1890, the son of Dutch parents. In December 1925 he married Auguste (Gusti) Röttgen, ten years his junior. They rented a flat in Osnabrück where their son Peter was born in November 1926. Both Hermann and Gusti were quick-thinking, boisterous, sociable people who were extremely temperamental. Their son was just the opposite: introverted, not gifted academically, although excellent at carpentry, and modest to a fault. As the persecutions in Germany escalated, the van Pelses fled to Amsterdam, renting an apartment at Zuider Amstellaan 34, directly behind the Frank family.

After joining Pectacon, Hermann van Pels and his wife became part of Otto and Edith's social circle. Although Otto liked them both, he was very critical of their parenting skills: 'Peter's parents were absolutely no good for him. They hit him and threw him out. Peter didn't have the backing of his parents at all and you see that also in his answers to Anne [when they were in hiding together].' Nonetheless, Hermann van Pels was a valuable addition to Otto's staff. He invented recipes which were then ground and mixed at Pectacon, schooled Kugler in combining seasonings and reviewed the recipes with him after taking orders from the sales representatives. Kugler eventually became something of an expert himself on spices, and acted as the main link between the management and the warehouse staff who milled and packed the goods. In November Pectacon was officially registered with the Amsterdam Chamber of Commerce as sharing the Opekta premises on the Singel.

When a young Jewish Polish student shot the Third Secretary of the German Embassy in Paris, Ernst von Rath, in protest at his parents' expulsion from Germany, the Nazis used the incident as a spring-board for unleashing a pogrom. During the nights of 9 and 10 November 1938 (Kristallnacht), the Nazis and their followers attacked Jewish communities throughout Germany, destroying thousands of synagogues, businesses and homes, killing almost a hundred Jews, and arresting thousands. Seven thousand Jews gained entry to the Netherlands in the aftermath of the pogrom; they were the last refugees to cross the Dutch border legally before the war. On 12 November Walter and Julius Holländer were arrested. Julius was freed because of his war wound, but Walter was sent to Sachsenhausen concentration camp, not far from Berlin. If he could prove he had the means to leave Germany, then he would be released. He and Julius had already considered emigrating to America, but required an affidavit from a relative already resident in the country before they could leave. Julius applied to the Dutch Embassy immediately, thinking that he might have more of a chance there, since Edith lived in Amsterdam. On 1 December Walter was released and transferred to the Dutch refugee camp at Zeeburg in Amsterdam, where the internees were not permitted to have any contact with the outside world and were under constant police supervision. Although they were not allowed to earn an income, the internees had to pay for their stay. Walter was able to leave on several occasions, but always after having obtained written permission, and usually only to visit the Huize Oosteinde, a popular meeting place for refugees. While Walter was in Zeeburg, his mother and brother remained at home in Aachen. The Holländer business had been liquidated under new Nazi laws.

At the end of 1938 another newly arrived Jewish refugee from Berlin, Fritz Pfeffer, and his gentile girlfriend Lotte Kaletta, became part of the Saturday afternoon crowd who met every week at the Franks' apartment. Pfeffer was born in 1889, in the German town of Giessen where his father owned a clothing store. After completing his education, Pfeffer trained as a dentist and went into business in Berlin. In 1921 he married Vera Bythiner, many years his junior, with whom he had a son, Werner Peter, born in 1927. The marriage ended in divorce six years later and, somewhat unusually, Pfeffer was granted custody of his son, on whom he doted. In 1936 at the age of thirty-seven, he met Martha Charlotte (Lotte) Kaletta, who was then nineteen and had come to him as a patient. Lotte's first marriage to another Jewish dentist had fallen apart after the birth of her son, who was also in the custody of his father. Lotte soon moved into Pfeffer's home and lavished all the love she was unable to give daily to her own son on to Werner Peter. Kristallnacht tore their lives apart; Pfeffer sent his son to live in London with his own brother Ernst, deciding against accompanying him there because his professional papers were worthless in England and he had neither the funds nor a grasp of the English language. In December 1938 Pfeffer and Lotte emigrated to Amsterdam, leaving Lotte's son behind with his father. Both were later killed by the Nazis, as was Pfeffer's first wife.

Pfeffer found work in a friend's surgery in the Rivierenbuurt and rented a third-floor apartment at Daniel Willinkplein 23. He and Lotte hoped to wed in the Netherlands or Belgium, but Pfeffer's status as a German Jew, even before the implementation of the Nuremberg Laws that followed the invasion of the Low Countries, created insurmountable difficulties. To avoid confrontation with officials, in 1940 the couple registered themselves as living in separate houses. Hilde Goldberg's family already knew Pfeffer from Berlin, where he and Hilde's father had been members of the same rowing club. She recalls:

In the last difficult days before the occupation Fritz Pfeffer would come to our house every evening. He would always ring the bell, then come in and say, 'Well, what's new?' And when we heard the bell go in the evening, we would all cry, 'Well, what's new!' He was a good man, and very intelligent. Lotte was beautiful, kind and thoughtful. She was also very hospitable and had a great sense of humour.

When Pfeffer and Lotte became acquainted with the Franks and their friends, their recounted experiences from Germany met with incomprehension; only Edith seemed to believe their stories about the extent of the brutality in their former homeland. Amongst the other guests at the Franks' home were the Baschwitz family, refugees from Germany who arrived in the Netherlands in 1933. The relationship with Otto was of some years standing, as Isa Baschwitz recalls:

In Frankfurt, my father [Kurt Baschwitz] was a schoolfriend of the older, intellectual brother of Otto, Robert Frank. In Amsterdam, Otto made contact. The family used to visit each other for morning coffee. I used to go around mainly with Margot who was three years younger than I. Anne was a very vivacious girl who, because she had a heart condition, was rather pampered and spoilt and always got her own way.

Despite all the tensions, at the end of the year, Otto sent a spirited letter to his mother: 'What can one say in a birthday letter in times like these? We have to be grateful for what we still have – and not give up hope! It is miserably cold here, too, and we think constantly of those who, unlike ourselves, have no warm place to stay.'

In the Netherlands prior to 1940, there were few instances of organized anti-Semitic violence. Jews were seen as 'different' and anti-Semitic literature was a regular feature in Amsterdam cafés, but real danger was minimal. Prejudice was more likely to be expressed verbally than physically. For instance, following a large Zionist meeting in Zandvoort a woman stood up and asked loudly, 'Gentlemen, once you have all left for Palestine, may we have Zandvoort back?' Incidents such as the 1938 attack on Jews in Amsterdam's Bijenkorf department store were rare.

In the wake of that particular episode, a youth who had participated in the riot was sentenced to eight months in the Leeuwarden prison. Tonny Ahlers, whom the authorities recorded as '1.82m tall, lean, with dark-blond hair and a snub nose', had been in trouble on a number of previous occasions for anti-Semitic behaviour. At twenty-one years old, he was a drifter and unemployed for most of the time. Ahlers's mother, who had divorced his father and remarried, described her son as having 'always been a misfit' with 'a naturally bad character', dishonest but capable of smooth-talking his way out of any situation. His brothers and sisters avoided him as much as possible; his father was the only member of the family who put up with his contemptuous manner, bragging, and petty thievery. Indeed, he seemed to find it all rather amusing.

In the late 1930s Tonny Ahlers's hatred of Jews was manifesting itself in an increasingly aggressive form. What began in his teenage years as mindless acts of vandalism were beginning to turn into something far more insidious. The breaking of synagogue windows and defiling the statue of the Jewish playwright Herman Heijermans were indications of the iniquitous path he was soon to take. As Nazi violence against Jews in Germany reached a fever pitch, and the power of the SS breached all ordinary societal limits, Tonny

Ahlers let his family know that his interest in the Third Reich was not just puerile curiosity; it was the map of his future.

At the beginning of 1939 Julius Holländer received an affidavit from his cousin Ernst Holländer, guaranteeing work and support in America. Rosa Holländer would join Edith and the family in Amsterdam. In March she arrived, and her luggage consisted only of some cutlery and food. In a 1954 interview Otto recalled, 'My wife's mother always paid more attention to Anne's character, as Margot was very easy to handle. Oma spoiled the girls, but not unreasonably.' The interviewer, Otto's friend Jean Schick Grossman, continued the theme:

To other members of the family, Edith Frank's gentle mother sometimes had to defend her soft treatment of Anne. She had a son, Anne's uncle [Julius], who as a child was also highly strung and stormy, and who was considered a 'rather peculiar person' in later years. The grandmother often said, 'If we had known more of the psychology of children when my son was Anne's age, he might have developed differently.'

In April, alone in Aachen, Julius packed some items of antique furniture which had sentimental value for Edith and despatched them to Amsterdam. Everything else was left behind in their apartment and what remained of the business was later sold at auction. He then took the boat from Rotterdam to New York and travelled from there to Massachusetts. Walter was freed from Zeeburg on 14 December 1939 and departed for America two days later. For over a year, both brothers were unable to find employment and had to rely on their cousin's aid.

Edith was in need of a break after all the worry she had endured and, in spring 1939, she and Margot took the train to Luxembourg where they stayed with some relatives of Otto. In May, when Otto was absent from home on a business trip, he sent a loving letter to Anne, who kept it to serve 'as a support to me all my life'. In it he reminded her gently,

I have often told you that you must educate yourself. We have agreed the controls with each other and you yourself are doing a great deal to swallow the 'buts'. And yet you like to spoil yourself and like even more to be spoiled by others. All that isn't bad, if deep in your little heart you remain as loveable as you always have been. I have told you that as a child, I, too, often rushed into things without thinking twice and made many mistakes. But the main thing is to reflect a little bit and then to find one's way back to the right path.

He signed the letter 'Pim', the nickname Anne and Margot had given him. Asked later how it originated, Otto laughed, 'I don't know. Père – father – Pim?' His friend Jean Schick Grossman wrote about the relationship between the girls and their parents, and made it clear that Edith was as substantive to their upbringing as Otto had been:

In his courteous, quiet voice, Otto told me of the education of his daughters. Books and sources of knowledge were always accessible to them. When he could not answer their questions himself, he went with them to find out . . . I was keenly aware of Otto's own feeling for the wonders of the universe, his awareness of how much life is enriched by the knowledge of the world and its peoples past and present, their literature and art and what lies behind their actions . . . As for discipline: 'The system is patience,' Anne's father said. Anne was sometimes difficult. Her parents tried to be fair and reasonable, and their reproofs were always gentle: a mild deprivation of privilege and occasionally, when she was little, a quick spank. They were not afraid to be firm, to say, 'This you cannot do,' and hold to it. They held to their word in promises too, earning their children's trust and reliance . . . Edith and Otto understood the differences between their two daughters and their individual needs. They chose different schools for the girls . . . everyone helped with the housework, and they rented out rooms. Edith went about the city with her daughters, to the shops, to concerts, to museums.

While Edith took pleasure in familiarizing her children with the cultural aspects of Amsterdam now that they were both of an age where they could appreciate her efforts, Otto was exhausted, working every hour he could to ensure the success of Pectacon and Opekta. Edith told Gertrud in a letter dated July 1939, 'My husband is very tired and in desperate need of a few days' rest. The business is a constant struggle but otherwise things are going smoothly for us.' In November there was an unnerving incident at the offices on the Singel. Kugler recalled, 'We had a visit from a real Nazi. He had a cigarette in his mouth and when I told him I had been in the Austrian navy, he took it out and said, "Oh. That's all for today."' Kugler did not explain – if indeed he knew – why the Nazi had appeared or if he ever returned.

On 23 August 1939 Germany and Russia signed a non-aggression pact agreeing to the eventual partition of Poland between them. On 1 September 1939 Germany invaded Poland. Two days later France and Great Britain declared war on Germany. Russian troops stormed Poland's eastern territories on 17 September and two weeks later were in control of seven cities. Poland surrendered and was divided between Germany and Russia. Hitler's

Einsatzgruppen began a systematic programme of murder in the country in 1941, killing thousands of intellectuals, officials and priests. The occupying forces in Poland issued crippling anti-Semitic decrees through the Judenräte (Jewish Councils), composed of prominent Jewish citizens. In Austria, Jews were made to wear an identifying yellow star and enter ghettos. In Poland they were forced to emigrate if they could afford to do so; in 1941 the borders closed. Many of those who wanted to emigrate to Palestine had their dreams shattered by opposition from the Arabs and from the British, who were reluctant to do anything to upset the oil trade. On 9 April 1940 Denmark and Norway fell to the German army. Suddenly Dutch neutrality, which had saved the country from the Great War, was under threat. Most Dutch were startled and perplexed, and many still believed they would remain on the sidelines of another world war. The German author Konrad Merz said of the Netherlands during the 1930s that 'often it seems to me that a flight to Holland is like a flight into past decades'.

Otto was finally facing the truth of their situation, but it was too late. His cousin Milly recalled:

During the first months of the war, Otto was virtually our only link to the Continent. We couldn't write to relations in Germany for England was at war with Germany. But Otto could write to Germany because he was doing so from neutral Holland. I got a letter from him saying how terribly unhappy he was because he was sure that Germany was going to attack. He said, 'I don't know what to do about the children. I can't talk to Edith about it. There's no use worrying her before she has to be worried. Forgive me, but I just had to write it.'

Milly suggested that they send the children to her in England. Otto wrote back, 'Edith and I discussed your letter. We both feel we simply can't do it. We couldn't bear to part with the girls. They mean too much to us. But if it's any comfort to you, you are the people we would have trusted.'

In the early hours of 10 May 1940 Germany invaded the Netherlands, Belgium, Luxembourg and France. The next day, Miep remembers, 'The mood in the office was forlorn and shocked. Mr Frank's face was white. We crowded around the wireless in Mr Frank's office and listened through the day for developments.' The country was in the grip of hysteria, which worsened with the announcement that the Dutch royal family and the prime minister and his Cabinet had escaped to London. In the midst of large-scale battles to defend the country, the Germans called for surrender, threatening to bomb Rotterdam. Before the deadline had expired, the Germans attacked the port. The Netherlands capitulated on 14 May (Belgium followed on 28 May). Austrian-born Arthur Seyss-Inquart, Reich Commissioner, now presided over the country. His direct staff were all Austrian or German SS officers, men who regarded the persecution of the Jews as 'an important task'.

The Germans entered Amsterdam aglow with victory, watched grimly by some and greeted as heroes by others. There were 140,000 Jews then resident in the country; sixty per cent of these lived in Amsterdam. When night fell, bonfires were lit throughout the city as people burned English and anti-Nazi literature. Jewish families laden down with belongings hurried to the harbour to see if they could board boats to England. The evening wore on, and the streets kept filling up; people ran from house to house, asking advice, making plans, building more fires in neighbourhood squares. There were rumours that convoys of ships waited in the harbour for Jews, and that people pushing through the tearful, screaming crowds in their haste to embark on their journey had fallen and drowned. And there were those Jews who closed their front doors, then went into the kitchen for knives or to the washroom for pills, and did not wake up to a second day of Nazi occupation.

The Dutch NSB, formed in 1931 by Anton Mussert, was at first free of anti-Semitic policy. Its introduction led to an initial decrease in membership, and in 1933 the party had only 1,000 members. On the eve of invasion, this had leapt to 32,000. After the occupation, anti-Semitism became a driving force, acting like a magnet for young men like Tonny Ahlers, who joined them in the summer of 1940. Ahlers's mother confirmed, 'Before the war, he was already anti-Semitic . . . After the capitulation of the Netherlands this trait showed itself more clearly.' Ahlers also joined the more extreme Nationaal Socialistische Nederlandse Arbeiders Partij (NSNAP) in October 1940, on the invitation of two of his neighbours who were party leaders. The organization quickly gained a reputation for violence against Jews and acts of robbery in general. Ahlers became a familiar face at the Herengracht headquarters of the Sicherheitspolizei (the Sipo, or security police who later employed people to hunt down Jews), where he spent much of his time in the company of three officials: Brückner, Grimm and Schieffer, all of whom were tried after the war and imprisoned for their crimes. Ahlers and his friend Peters, who later worked for the Zentralstelle für Jüdische Auswanderung (Central Agency for Jewish Emigration) delivered 'progress reports about the situation in the city to Schieffer for him to forward to the German commander in The Hague'. Ahlers was eager to display aspects of this new life to people whom he knew, and his brother recalled how, 'After the May days of 1940 he wore a swastika armband right away. The few times he came home he always paraded contacts and papers of the SD . . . He also used these papers to commit various frauds.'

Within a few weeks of the invasion, NSBers had taken over the press and clerical positions vacated by Jews who were forced from their posts. The paramilitary section of the NSB, the WA, caused friction with vicious, impromptu attacks on Jews in the streets. Apart from this, the first few months of the occupation were relatively subdued. The only incident Otto noticed that whole summer was in his neighbourhood:

It was very quiet in Amsterdam. But at the beginning of June, I once saw a German army car coming down Scheldestraat and into Noorder-Amstellaan. At the corner it stopped and the driver asked the flower seller, who had his stand there, some question. Then they drove on. But at the next corner the car turned around, returned, stopped again at the Scheldestraat corner, and a soldier jumped out and slapped the flower-seller's face. That was how it began.

In the summer of 1940 Robert Frank was among those Germans living in Britain who were arrested 'in the interests of national security'. It took Lottie weeks to find out what was happening to him; she knew only that an 'R. Frank' was listed for deportation, in a shipment of those considered dangerous, to Australia. Eventually, Lottie was notified that it was not her husband on the list, and she was able to visit him at the refugee camp on the Isle of Man where he had been interned. After a few months Robert was released and returned to work in London. In America, Walter and Julius had found employment with the E. F. Dodge Paper Box Company in Leominster, Massachusetts and became close to their employer, who told Julius he was willing to sign an affidavit so that Edith and the family could negotiate a passage to America. But, as Otto recalled, 'time was too short and after Hitler had invaded Holland in May 1940 it was not possible anymore to leave the country'. France signed armistices with Germany and Italy on 22 June, and the French government, partially in control of the country and led by Marshal Pétain, cooperated with the German invaders.

On 22 October 1940 the Verordnung über die Anmeldung von Unternehmen (Decree Concerning the Registration of Companies) was issued whereby, 'All industrial or commercial firms owned by Jews or having Jewish partners are to be reported. Failure to report will be punishable by up to five years' imprisonment or fines of up to fl.100,000.' This also included all firms with Jewish capital and Jewish shareholders; every company had to report to the Wirtschaftsprüfstelle (Bureau of Economic Investigation or

BEI). The day after the decree was issued, Otto had a new company, La Synthèse N.V., registered in Hilversum. This was a cover for Pectacon, which Otto hoped to prevent from falling into German hands. Shares in the company had been issued to Jan Gies, the supervisory director, and Victor Kugler, the managing director. Although Otto was the actual owner, he made it appear that the business was one hundred per cent 'Aryan'.

On 27 November 1940 Otto registered Opekta under the terms of the 22 October decree, naming himself as sole proprietor and declaring his investment of fl.10,000 capital. Regarding Pectacon, he admitted to owning fl.2,000 of the company's fl.10,000 total share capital and claimed that the remaining shares had not been issued. On 2 December Otto contacted the BEI to apologize for the delay in further particulars about his businesses, explaining that the reason behind this was a move to larger premises. The new offices of Opekta and Pectacon were at 263 Prinsengracht. The building consisted of a seventeenth-century front-house and an eighteenth-century annexe. It had stood empty for a year when Otto began renting it from the owner, M. A. Wessel. There was a large warehouse on the ground floor, and Otto had the open-plan first floor of the annexe divided into two rooms where he could have his own office and an adjacent kitchen. The other offices, where Kleiman, Miep, Bep, Kugler and van Pels worked, were on the first floor of the front-house. Goods were stored on the second floor of the front-house, while spices were kept in a dark room overlooking the annexe at the rear on the same floor. The rest of the building remained empty. Six people worked for Opekta and five for Pectacon, including the sales representatives but not the temporary staff who came and went on a regular basis.

In the midst of Otto's business concerns, on 16 February 1941, Margot Frank turned fifteen. In the family tradition, Otto wrote 'Mutz' a poem, and he and Edith bought her as much as they could afford. In addition to her Hebrew classes, Margot also enrolled in a Zionist youth organization. Otto tried to interest Margot in German literature, hiring a friend of his, Anneliese Schütz, a Berlin journalist who could find no work in Amsterdam, to give weekly classes hosted each week by a different family. Anneliese started them off with Goethe and Schiller, Otto's own favourites. Laureen Nussbaum also attended the classes:

The fact that Anneliese Schütz was given this job, teaching us older children German literature, speaks for the sense of community which existed then. The younger children had other activities to keep them busy. Looking back, those classes were very good for us, but it was strange because we hadn't sorted out our feelings about

Germany yet. We hated what had happened to us there and what was happening still, of course, but our parents were still tied to the country and talked about it in a nostalgic way for how it had been before Hitler. The Dutch simply hated all things German.

On 12 March a decree was issued concerning the 'Treatment of Businesses Subject to Registration', clarifying in strangulated terms the settlement of the 22 October decree: 'This Economic Dejudification Decree stipulated *inter alia* that any changes in a business that might obviate the obligation to report that business as laid down in October 1940 must have (German) approval (Article 2) and that all relevant changes made between 9 May 1940 and the day that the decree came into operation (12 March 1941) were subject to retroactive German approval (Article 3). Such approval had to be applied for within a month of the proclamation of the new decree (that is, before 12 April).' At Pectacon, it was decided to 'request approval for changes that had already been made' and Otto informed the BEI that a meeting had been held on 13 February 1941 during which the remaining shares of fl.8,000 had been issued to Kleiman and Dunselman. Otto resigned his position which was taken over by Kleiman, and told the BEI that he was retaining his permitted shares of fl.2,000. Thus the business was wholly 'Aryan'. The meeting, in reality, had never taken place.

In early March Otto heard that his cousin, Jean-Michel Frank, had committed suicide. Jean-Michel had left Paris in winter 1940, having heard 'accounts from refugees in Paris about the persecution of homosexuals and Jews'. He emigrated to Buenos Aires, where he impressed the director of the Museum of Decorative Arts who found for him 'a whole circle of rich clients'. He moved on to New York where he gave lectures at the School of Fine and Applied Arts and was fêted by society. Then on 8 March 1941, in imitation of his father's own suicide, he threw himself from the window of his Manhattan apartment. He was forty-six years old. His friend Jean Cocteau mourned, 'His death was the prologue of the play, the final curtain rundown between a world of light and a world of darkness.'

The measures against the Jews in the Netherlands were slow to surface at first – a deliberate tactic on the part of the occupying forces – but gradually, law upon law was executed, each new decree being harsher and quicker to take effect than the last. In time they were all issued through the Jewish weekly newspaper, the *Joodse Weekblad*. The Germans appealed to the Amsterdam Bevolkingsregister for a map indicating where Jews lived and how many of them there were by means of dots ('one dot = ten Jews').

From October, everyone had to observe the curfew which ran from midnight through to four o'clock in the morning. There was no travel beyond the Dutch border and various goods became impossible to find. The Dutch government, headed by Professor Gerbrandy of the anti-Revolutionary Party, and the royal family in exile began making wireless broadcasts; these, and the speeches of Britain's prime minister Winston Churchill, helped maintain morale amongst the anti-German Dutch.

On 11 and 12 February 1941 fights broke out in the Jewish market on Waterlooplein and the market on Amstelveld, initiated by the WA. A member of the WA, Hendrik Koot, was fatally injured, and Höhere SS and Polizeiführer Hans Rauter ordered the Jewish quarter to be closed off. The Joodse Raad voor Amsterdam (Jewish Council of Amsterdam) was formed to keep order in the area and to give instructions to the Jewish community. Much has been written about the culpability or otherwise of the Joodse Raad, but it has been adequately labelled as both instrument and victim, cooperating with the Germans but in the expectation that resistance would only lead to further reprisals. Hendrik Koot died three days after the confrontations. The Dutch Nazi weekly newspaper, *Volk en Vaderland*, announced in reaction to his death, 'Judah has dropped its mask at last. Murdered? No, cut down with sadistic lust. Crushed under the heel by a nomadic race of alien blood.' On 17 February 1941 Koot's funeral took place in Amsterdam's Zorgvlied cemetery. In the photograph of the ceremony which appeared in *De Telegraaf* newspaper the following day, a young man appears, prominent in a white raincoat and standing next to Mussert: Tonny Ahlers.

Ahlers was present, too, at another landmark event in the history of the German occupation of the Netherlands. Koco was an *ijssalon* (café) on Amsterdam's Van Woustraat run by two German Jewish refugees, Kohn and Cahn. After a number of disruptions from the Nazis, some of the clientele had provided the owners with an array of crudely made weapons, including a flask of ammonia which hung on a wall in the café. On 19 February 1941 members of the Grüne Polizei and the NSB – among them Tonny Ahlers – entered the establishment. They were attacked and sprayed with ammonia, but recovered quickly enough to start shooting. The owners, together with the customers who had instigated the assault, were arrested. Cahn was killed by a firing squad after torture and became the first person to be executed during the occupation. The Koco affair led to further reprisals: 'The Germans had only been waiting for a pretext and now they had it. On February 22 and 23 they descended on the Jewish quarter *en masse*.' What followed were scenes of unmitigated horror as four hundred and twenty-five Jewish men and boys were dragged from their homes and from the streets, steered under blows on to the Jonas Daniel Meijerplein and then despatched, beaten and bloody, to the concentration camps of Buchenwald and Mauthausen. The Dutch responded to these measures with a strike, mainly organized by the Communist Party, on 25 February. Businesses throughout Amsterdam, Hilversum and Zaandam, as well as all means of public transport, came to a standstill for three days, until martial law and the threat of severe repercussions brought the action to an end.

During the strike, Ahlers and his friend Peters used their knowledge of the city (and special passes allowing them to circumvent the curfew) to help the WA root out and arrest those involved. Immediately afterward, Ahlers began working at the Fokker factory as an inspector. The assignment was given to him by Untersturmführer Kurt Döring of the SD, who employed him as an informant, with special instructions to watch out for the distribution of communist pamphlets among the Fokker workforce. Döring recalled, 'When I was sent to Amsterdam in 1940 Ahlers was already a regular visitor to the SD office on the Herengracht. Originally he was not in the active service of the SD but he kept pressing me for active employment.' Apart from his work at Fokker, Ahlers had a lucrative sideline photographing brawls that broke out between Nazis and Jews and selling the pictures on to the SS; post-war witnesses confirmed that he often instigated the fights in order to photograph them. Ahlers was then still living in a small room on the Haarlemmerweg, but his landlady hoped to get rid of him: 'I discovered that Ahlers was definitely pro-German. I did not completely trust him and when I glanced into one of his cupboards I saw a uniform hanging in there with the insignia of the SS. He also had a flag with the swastika upon it in his room.' When Ahlers bragged to her about the work he was doing for the SD, she was appalled: 'I said, "Really, son, how can you do that? It's spying." He said, "Yeah, it might be, but Germany is going to win this war and we've all got our part to play in the reconstruction that will follow."' She gave her tenant notice to quit shortly after their conversation.

Ahlers moved on to the Baarsjesweg and came into contact with the disreputable Dutchman Josef van Poppel, who worked for the Reichssicherheitshauptamt (Reich Security Main Office) in Berlin and the Abwehr in Scheveningen. Van Poppel also published the anti-Semitic weekly, *Doodsklok*, which referred often to Jews living on the Prinsengracht, and in one issue ridiculed the father of Otto's closest friend, Nathan Straus.★ He and

---

★ Poppel's girlfriend, the Jewish woman Helena Lam, worked as an agent for the German Abwehr in Belgium and betrayed many people there. She was later sentenced to ten years' imprisonment. Poppel ended his days in an insane asylum.

Ahlers met through their local NSNAP group. Van Poppel had already heard of him: 'I knew that Ahlers was working for the SD. The German Döring was his direct superior. In those days there was a Café Trip on Rembrandtplein owned by the former *souteneur* van den Brink. He had his own SD . . .' Ahlers worked for van den Brink and paraded his SD permit before van Poppel, telling him that one of his tasks was to incite young men into joining anti-German groups in order to betray them to the SD. Van Poppel recalled that Ahlers's work as an *agent provocateur* was lucrative: 'He operated mainly in cafés such as Ruttens and Heck. For the same purpose, he frequented a café on Kalverstraat. I think it was called the Storchnest. He was very well off back then and spent entire days in Café Trip.' Eventually, Ahlers became a secret agent himself, working within van Poppel's network. Van Poppel admitted after the war that Tonny Ahlers was the most anti-Semitic of his men and 'had everybody arrested whom he wanted to be arrested, because his superior, Döring, covered him completely'.

Van Poppel added one final, damning remark in his verification of his former friend's wartime past: 'With a lot of Jewish arrests, Tonny Ahlers was the instigator.'

It was at this point that Ahlers and Otto Frank met.

In her diary, on 7 May 1944, Anne writes, 'I have never been in such a state as Daddy, who once ran out on to the street with a knife in his hand to put an end to it all.' The line was from Anne's original version, and Otto did not include it in the edition he sanctioned for publication. The date of his uncharacteristic impulse to commit suicide is not known, and neither are the circumstances that led up to it, or those which followed it. But, clearly, before the Frank family went into hiding at the Prinsengracht, Otto Frank had been so deeply traumatized by something that he had considered killing himself.

In March and April 1941 Otto's life fell into crisis. In a letter sent to the Bureau Nationale Veiligheid (Bureau of National Security or BNV) in Scheveningen on 21 August 1945 he recounted one version of events:

In March 1941 I was on the Rokin when I met a certain Mr Jansen, the husband of one of my demonstrators who worked earlier in my firm N.V. Nederlandse Opekta, Prinsengracht 263, Amsterdam. The son of the gentleman Jansen also worked in my warehouse. Mr Jansen helped to build exhibition stands for my company, and thus the family was well known to me and of good conduct.

In March when we met, Mr Jansen and I had a short conversation, and

Mr Jansen asked me if I still got any goods from Germany because I was Jewish. I said that I did and that I had no difficulties and after we spoke about other things, Jansen said, 'The war will be over soon,' to which I answered that I was convinced that it wouldn't, and that the Germans were still having a tough time of it. Then we split up.

The man to whom he referred was of course Joseph Jansen, the husband of his former Opekta sales representative Jetje, with whom Jansen believed Otto had enjoyed an affair. In another account, Otto added, 'I did not like him very much.'

Otto gave several descriptions of the unnerving incident that followed his conversation with Jansen; most are official declarations given to the Dutch police in the late 1940s, and the other is a hazy anecdote given to Anne's first biographer, Ernst Schnabel, in 1957. All deviate from each other in minor instances, which is understandable given the scale of events unfolding at that time, but all fail ultimately to tell the startling story of what really happened.

18 April 1941 was a quiet day at the Prinsengracht. The doorbell rang, and one of the office staff buzzed it open. There were footsteps on the stairs and then the door to the front office opened. A young man entered, in his early twenties, tall, slender and dark-haired, with pronounced cheekbones and light-coloured, friendly eyes. One of the secretaries asked what they could do for him. 'I want to see Otto Frank,' he said, 'in private.' When asked what his business was, he answered with a sneer: 'I'm a member of the NSB.'

In his office on the first floor of the annexe, Otto glanced up from his desk as the diamond-patterned double doors opened. The young man entered, and closed the doors behind him so that no one else could hear what he was about to say. Only then did he introduce himself: 'Tonny Ahlers.'

In his declaration to the BNV in Scheveningen, Otto recounted:

[Ahlers] asked me if I knew a certain man named Jansen, to which I answered that there were a lot of Jansens and I didn't know which one he meant. He showed me a signature on a letter in which I read, 'Hou-zee, Jansen' ['Hou-zee' was the greeting used by the NSB] and then: 'member 29992'. I recognized the handwriting and said I knew who it was and asked for the letter to read. He gave it to me and I read it and saw that it was addressed to the leaders of the NSB and they had to pass it on to the SS. In this letter, it was announced that Mr Jansen had met me, the director of Opekta, and that I was saying insulting things against the German Wehrmacht and other accusatory things.

At this stage, Otto's various accounts of the meeting with Ahlers begin to diverge. In his letter to the BNV, Otto writes: '[Ahlers] said that he was working as a courier between the NSB and the SS and that he had intercepted the letter. He did not ask for a reward but anyway I voluntarily gave him ten guilders. I asked him to come back again . . . he came back, so I gave him another five or ten guilders . . .' In his 1946 evidence against Jansen, Otto stated something similar, but he told Ernst Schnabel in 1957 that Ahlers demanded twenty guilders from him there and then.

Although it is perfectly possible that Otto was genuinely confused over whether money was demanded or offered, and how much (if anything) changed hands, there are a number of factors which simply do not make sense – unless one is also aware of what transpired after this first meeting. But to take matters at face value, one would have to ask the following: if Otto met Ahlers on only one occasion, before his horrific experiences in the camps, how was he able, in 1945, to recall with such precision Ahlers's full name, his initials and his 1941 address? It seems improbable that Ahlers would have volunteered that information if they had only met once; indeed, why would he? Curiously, Otto could not remember Jansen's forename, despite having known him for a much longer period. In his letter to the BNV, Otto continues, 'I asked him to come back again but he made it clear it was not the money for him, although he didn't earn much.' According to that account (but not Otto's 1957 interview and another statement he gave in late 1945), Ahlers handed him Jansen's letter, thereby saving him from the clutches of the Gestapo and then walked out of his life for ever. Given our previous knowledge of Ahlers, one has to say that this does not have the ring of truth. Why would the anti-Semitic Ahlers save the Jewish Otto Frank? They did not know each other after all.

There are further surprises in Otto's 1945 account: 'I didn't know what kind of other things the young man did. But I do remember that he showed me some other letters. One of them was about a maid who wrote that the people for whom she worked listened to the English wireless, I can't remember to whom this letter was addressed.' No one else has ever come forward to declare that, like Otto Frank, he was saved from the Gestapo by Ahlers's intervention, which raises the question: what was Ahlers going to do with these other letters? In this instance, we have the answer. Ahlers's former landlady from the Haarlemmerweg declared in 1946 that her ex-tenant had told her that he was unemployed but receiving benefits.

However, in the conversation that led to her dismissing Ahlers from her home one month before his meeting with Otto Frank, Ahlers informed her that he had found a job that paid fifty guilders per week: 'He said he had to confiscate the wirelesses of people who listened to the forbidden broadcasts from England. He would also receive five guilders commission for every wireless he handed in.'

Ahlers was not about to play guardian angel to someone else with the other letter he showed to Otto that day. And although in all his versions of the events of 18 April 1941 Otto is firm that after one or possibly two encounters with Ahlers, he 'did not see or speak to the young man again', in truth, he was prevaricating. According to Ahlers and other witnesses, that first meeting in Otto's private office was the start of regular visits. Otto's 1945 engagements diary features the name Ahlers on several occasions, and in a letter dated 27 November 1945, Otto writes that he and Ahlers met again that summer.

From all the available documents, it would appear that, for one reason or another, their purpose was to come to an agreement on their story.

3. Fac et Spera (Work and Hope)

When Tonny Ahlers closed the doors to Otto's private office that April day in 1941 he left by the long corridor in which the stairs to the upper floors of the annexe were clearly visible. 'The Jew Frank' was probably not what Ahlers had expected. In his elegant office on the Prinsengracht, Otto was taller than the younger man, well-dressed, courteous, and spoke Dutch in the voice of an affluent and educated German. Ahlers, always on the lookout for an easy means of making money and with a need to dominate people, knew an opportunity when he saw one.

Initially Ahlers received cash from Otto Frank in return for his silence over Jansen's letter. Even though he apparently allowed Otto to keep the letter, he knew what it had contained and could have used that information against Otto at any point. By Ahlers's own admission, after that first meeting, he began to watch Otto Frank and took a keen interest in his business affairs. He soon discovered, for instance, that Otto was delivering to the Wehrmacht (German Army). In a 1966 letter, Ahlers writes that Otto was 'selling Pectin products to the German-Wehrmacht'. There is steadfast evidence to confirm Ahlers's claims about the deliveries. In an unpublished interview with the Netherlands Institute for War Documentation, Miep Gies admitted that during the war they had sold to the Wehrmacht and that a 'trusted Wehrmacht cook' came into the business with Kleiman. In another unpublished interview with the Dutch authorities in 1964, Otto acknowledged that his company had done business with the German occupying forces, and a 1945 letter written by the former warehouseman at 263 Prinsengracht during the war divulges: 'The company supplied a lot of goods to the Wehrmacht during the occupation, by way of brokers.' One of these was, 'Mr van Keulen from Haarlem, a supplier of canned goods and buyer of goods for the Germans . . . A lot of people visited the business, among others van Keulen.' Miep Gies later insisted that she had never heard of him but, in fact, van Keulen *was* one of the buyers and suppliers to the business during the war, and some time after the liberation Otto called upon him in Haarlem.

In his 1966 letter Ahlers continues: 'This pectin was a conserve product which was used in the German war industry. There were many other Dutch businesses doing this as well.' Pectin was a preservative that could be put to many uses, depending upon the type of pectin it was. All pectin was useful for food production, but certain kinds could be applied as a balm for wounds and a thickener for raising blood volume in blood transfusions. Other types of pectin were used in the steel industry as a hardener and in the oil industry as an emulsifier. Therefore, it is possible that the Wehrmacht used the pectin they bought from Otto Frank's company for the war industry, but it is highly unlikely that, even if this was the case, Otto would have known for what purpose the supplies were intended.

The matter goes further, however. In that same letter Ahlers writes, '[Otto Frank] had no problems in getting his raw materials. In my opinion Frank got his raw materials straight from Berlin . . . he felt completely sure and safe in the situation [that the materials would keep coming]. The only way he could feel safe, surely, is because he was delivering to the Wehrmacht.' Ahlers was correct about the business with Berlin. Immediately after the invasion of May 1940, Otto had been delivering to, and receiving goods from, intermediaries of the Armee Oberkommando (German Army High Command), headed by Hitler himself and based in Berlin. One such order in the Opekta/ Pectacon delivery book reads: '5 June 1940. Sold to S-, The Hague, by order of the Armee Oberkommando, Berlin. Various goods. 5 June 1940. From S-, The Hague. Bought. By order of the Armee Oberkommando, Berlin. The buyer safeguards the seller against all objections, by whatever authority, which might endanger the execution of this contract.' The deliveries to the Wehrmacht (via brokers) and to the Army High Command ensured the survival of Otto's business. More than eighty per cent of Dutch firms delivered to the Wehrmacht during the war, and one can hardly be shocked by the statistics or the fact that Otto did the same; the Nazis were in supreme control of the country, and it would have been almost impossible to avoid this sort of contact. Refusal to do so would have resulted in disaster for Otto Frank; merely speaking ill of the Germans could result in arrest, as he was aware.

Ahlers clearly knew a great deal about Otto's business affairs, and for one very good reason: Ahlers himself was involved in these transactions. After being dismissed from the Fokker factory he established his own company, Petoma, in spring 1942 to manufacture surrogates. By then Ahlers had responsibilities: in early 1941 he began dating a Dutch girl named Martha who was four years younger than he was, and in June she told him she was pregnant. They married on 23 July 1941 and their son was born the following year. Petoma was based on the Jan van Galenstraat, a few minutes' walk from the Prinsengracht. Martha, who was divorced from her husband in 1985, told the author that Tony Ahlers and Otto Frank 'did business together. My husband had his own company during the war and Otto Frank made deliveries to him.' Other family members confirm this. Ahlers's son remembers his father explaining that pectin was sold in bottles, but during the war they sometimes had to use special paper: 'The type that holds in water. My father sold this paper to Otto Frank and he got a nice profit from it because he got the price of the contents along with their packaging.' The arrangement between Otto and Ahlers must have begun before the hiding period, but how long it lasted is not clear. In 1943 (when the Franks were already in hiding), Ahlers began a second company, PTM, which was a buying agency for the Wehrmacht; Ahlers also manufactured products on their behalf. The head of another business which worked with Ahlers's company declared, 'My goal was to become a supplier for the Wehrmacht, with all the attendant advantages like Arbeitseinsatz, allocation of raw materials, etc.' In the same way, through his association with the Wehrmacht, Otto was able to receive commodities for longer than usual, and then good quality substitutes. At the offices on the Prinsengracht, 'a marked business revival' took place after the occupation.

Otto Frank had made a pact with the devil, but the price can scarcely be imagined. In working with the enemy, Otto hoped to protect not only his company, but also himself and his family, for by then most Jewish people realized something of the immense danger that faced them. Throughout the war years, Otto was to all intents and purposes leading a double life. It was not just the business associations but the ever-present spectre of Ahlers that haunted him – a man less than half his age who had saved his life, but whose hold over him was profound; Jansen's terrible letter ensured that Otto remained in Ahlers's debt. Ten years after the end of the war, in an unrelated matter, Otto wrote to his lawyer Myer Mermin that 'no good comes from giving way to blackmail'. Mermin could not have guessed the depth to which Otto knew it to be true.

When the doors finally closed behind Tonny Ahlers on 18 April 1941, Otto Frank was left alone in his office with Jansen's poisonous letter in his hands. After a moment's thought, Otto went through to the front offices where Kugler and Miep were working. He showed them the letter. They were shocked and horrified; Miep was already familiar with the meeting with Jansen on the Rokin, and after the war told the police investigating the matter:

Mr Frank read me the said letter and I remember, still today, that it was written in the letter that the Jew Frank was still tied to his company and had expressed himself in an anti-German fashion during a conversation. I do not know any more who signed the letter in question, but I deduced from the content of the letter that it had been written by the Jansen I knew.

Kugler added in his statement to the police, 'As far as I can tell, there was not a single motive for Jansen wanting to expose Mr Frank to prosecution.'

Otto told two other people about the letter: his friend Gerard Oeverhaus, a Dutch detective with the Foreign Police to whom he had spoken often about the anti-Jewish decrees, and his lawyer, Anton Dunselman, who had been involved in Otto's business ventures since the 1920s. Dunselman read the letter at his office on the Keizersgracht, took some notes from it and locked it away. He later destroyed it, fearing that his own safety would be in danger 'during a possible arrest of Mr Frank'. Otto mentioned nothing about the letter at home: 'I did not want to tell my wife about the incident and frighten her. Because of Jansen's letter I have been afraid for months that if I met him in the street, Jansen would file a new complaint against me.' The damage Jansen intended to cause Otto had not been stopped, however; it had only been diverted.

Shortly after his first meeting with Tonny Ahlers, Otto spoke to Kleiman about the possibility of going into hiding. Jan Gies recalled, 'The initiative to go into hiding, to find a hiding place, to organize everything for it, came from Otto Frank. He had thought it all out . . . and he had already divided certain different tasks for his staff members when he asked them to help him and his family.' Kleiman was the first to be taken into Otto's confidence; Kugler and then Miep, Jan and Bep were each asked whether they would, in Otto's words, 'be willing to take full responsibility for everything connected with our hiding'. After they had given their assent, Otto outlined precisely how he envisaged their individual responsibilities. Questioned recently if she had understood what this entailed, Miep said simply, 'The shopping, yes. I did not ask any further. At that time you did not ask questions. You would not ask so many things. You just did what was asked from you and nothing more.' Miep and Bep viewed it as an extension to their work: 'We were the office ladies. We would get instructions, and we understood very well that that was the way it should be. There was no other way. We did not feel wronged or restricted by that . . . That was normal, wasn't it? That was very normal. It was just like it was with your work.' To refuse would have been unthinkable in that context. Kugler, too, felt that he had only one option: 'I didn't think about the dangers it would have for me. Thousands of Dutch people hid others. After the liberation I saw so many people that I knew were Jews who had been hidden by friends . . . We knew that if we didn't hide them, it would be like committing them to death. So we had very little choice.'

Hermann van Pels was brought into the discussion between Kleiman and

Otto, and he and his family were invited to share the Franks' ill-fated hiding place, rather than the Goslars, who had a year-old baby and would soon be expecting a third child. Otto quickly realized 'that the best solution would be to hide in the annexe of our office building, Prinsengracht 263'. An employee of Kleiman's brother (who was also informed about the plan to hide) cleared and cleaned the annexe prior to belongings and supplies being installed. Under the pretence of specialist cleaning or repair, large items of furniture were conveyed first to Kleiman's home in Biesboschstraat and then to the annexe in his brother's van. Dried and canned food, linen, clothing and utensils were easier to move without suspicion over a long period. Although these clandestine visits were always made after office hours or at the weekend, as a future precaution the windows of the front-house which overlooked the annexe were painted blue, and those in the corridor linking both parts of the building were pasted over with semi-transparent paper (glassine). Such prudence was essential to prevent outsiders from calculating what was happening at 263 Prinsengracht. But, without being aware of it, Otto Frank was already under surveillance: in post-war letters to Silberbauer (the Gestapo officer who eventually arrested the Franks), Ahlers writes that he knew the truth about the secret annexe and who was hidden there.

In April 1941 Greece surrendered to Italy and Germany took control of Yugoslavia. On 22 June Hitler's army invaded Russia, prompting Britain to offer aid to the Russians. As the year wore on, the appalling weather stilled the German advance and killed thousands of German soldiers.

In May, La Synthèse N.V., the company Otto Frank had registered as a cover for Pectacon, was renamed Gies & Co. There were no further changes to the company, over which Otto remained director. On 16 July Miep and Jan Gies were married, although they had been living together since 1940. Otto and Anne, Kleiman, Kugler, Bep and Hermann and Gusti van Pels were amongst the guests. Margot and Oma Holländer were unable to attend due to illness and Edith stayed at home to care for them. The sun shone before and after the ceremony, and a surprise reception, hosted by Otto, was held at the Prinsengracht offices the next day. Present on both occasions was an attractive young woman named Esther, who was then working for Otto as a secretary. He later had to dismiss her under new regulations regarding Jews in employment. Miep remembers,

That's the way things were. She did not come back, I think. She did not survive the war . . . She was the only one in the office who was Jewish. She said goodbye, and we wished her the best. She stayed in Amsterdam, but could not find work anywhere else . . . It was all so painful, you see. You heard about her dismissal but did not talk about it further. You did not know what was going to happen. You gave into that. Had to accept it. The Germans were the boss and you were scared – frightened to death.

Otto also employed two men who were members of the NSB. Miep recalls a conversation she had with Otto about one of them, a sales rep named Daatselaar:

Mr Frank had been aware of his membership of the Dutch Nazi Party before he'd gone into hiding, because the man had worn his NSB pin on his lapel. I remembered that Mr Frank had commented, 'This man you can trust. I know he's not a Nazi at heart. He must have joined the NSB because he was hanging around with a bunch of young men who joined. Being a bachelor and needing a social life, that's why he joined too.'

Although he trusted Daatselaar, Otto did not tell him about the hiding plan, but he did use the man as an example to Anne when she became upset that the mother of one of her friends was a staunch supporter of the NSB. Otto's close relationship with his youngest daughter was still strong, despite Anne's early adolescent turmoil. When she and her friend Sanne Ledermann left Amsterdam for a holiday with Sanne's aunt in Beekbergen, she wrote to her father often, addressing him as 'My most beloved Hunny Kungha',★ and confessed that she missed him terribly and longed for the day when he, Edith and Margot would arrive. The one consolation was the stillness in Beekbergen; there were no air raids and Anne told her grandmother in Switzerland that, evening storms notwithstanding, 'We sleep a lot better at night here than in Amsterdam. There's nothing at all to disturb us.'

When the Franks returned home, they did so to a fresh rash of anti-Jewish edicts. The laws passed in 1941 resulted in the loss of Jewish participation in almost all areas of public entertainment, sport and education in the Netherlands. In his memoir, Otto wrote:

When I think back to the time when a lot of laws were introduced in Holland, due to the occupying power, which made our lives much harder, I have to say that my wife and I did everything we could to stop the children noticing the trouble we would go to, to make sure this was still a trouble-free time for them.

★ One of several nonsense names Anne used for her father.

He recalled how, following the expulsion of all Jewish children from their normal schools into Special High Schools for Jewish Children, it became difficult for his daughters to 'keep up their friendships with non-Jewish children, particularly now that it was also forbidden for Christians to visit Jewish families and vice versa'. After the war, Otto confided to a friend how important Edith's presence had been for the children . . .

as the anti-Jewish regulations narrowed their world . . . she continued to make their friends welcome, to give parties for them. She and Oma Holländer set the children daily examples of generosity and concern for others. When war brought privation to Amsterdam, no poor person who came to their door went away empty-handed. Edith used to send Margot and Anne down the steep stairs with food and gifts, to save the old or enfeebled the difficult climb.

Otto was aware that his youngest daughter was developing more quickly than normal under the pressures of the occupation: 'Through Margot, Anne got to know pupils in the higher classes of the new school. Soon boys started to notice her. She was rather attractive and knew how to use her charms.' Anne became fascinated with sexuality, something her mother refused to discuss with her. Otto was rather more open, though he kept information to a minimum, as Anne's new best friend at the Jewish Lyceum, Jacqueline van Maarsen, recalls: 'She was extremely curious about sexual relations between men and women and pumped her father constantly for information. He invented all sorts of subterfuge, which she then told me and which really made me laugh.'

In September, when Otto decided he needed a break from Amsterdam, it was Anne who accompanied him to the hotel in Arnhem he had booked. Edith, again, stayed at home with her mother and Margot. In a postcard to his own mother in Switzerland, Otto explained, 'We're not staying long, I just wanted to have a bit more peace and quiet, but didn't want to go off completely on my own. Anne is always good, dear company and she was able to have a few days off school. Everything is well.' Upon his return to work, Otto learned that everything was far from well: Pectacon had been earmarked for liquidation. The BEI had received a German report which accurately described the changes made to the business by Otto as 'intended to create the impression that most of the capital as well as the directorship of the business are in Aryan hands'. The report condemned 'the decisions taken at the annual general meeting on 13 February 1941, which according to VO 48/41 are subject to retrospective approval, are not approved and therefore have no legal validity'. On the basis of these findings, the Generalkommissar für Finanz und Wirtschaft, Abteilung Wirtschaftsprüfstelle (General Commissioner for Finance and Economic Affairs, Division for Economic Investigation) appointed Karel Wolters, a Nazi-approved lawyer, as 'trustee of the company under 48/41' and charged him with the liquidation of Pectacon. On 22 September 1941 Otto Frank and Johannes Kleiman visited Wolters at his offices on Rokin.

Karel Wolters was born in Venlo in 1909. A successful lawyer and public prosecutor, he had joined the NSB in 1933 and during the occupation became a member of the Rechtsfront, the Economisch Front and the Nederlandsch-Duitsche Kultuurgemeenschap. As previously mentioned, since May 1941 Wolters, together with his wife and three children, had been living on Jan van Eyckstraat. Questioned specifically about Pectacon after the war, Wolters replied, 'I know that I acted as liquidator of N.V. Pectacon, but I cannot remember any more details. Possibly the business was sold through me. I do not know the salary.' The documents relating to Wolters' dealings with Otto Frank make for curious reading. It was a known fact that the men working as Verwalters were mostly crooks, but the statements made about Wolters by the Jewish businessmen and their personnel who came under his control describe him as being protective towards them. His attitude towards Otto was extraordinary; he wanted Pectacon to continue as usual, according to Kleiman's declaration. Kleiman refused:

We were not in favour, because it was very well possible that a member of the NSB or a German would take charge of the business and that is why I proposed to Wolters to liquidate the business. I asked for a period of eight to ten days' time. Wolters agreed to this. In practice, we were in charge of the liquidation. I started by cashing outstanding accounts and paying the debts.

In his declaration, Otto outlined how they were able, through the meditation of a broker,

to transfer the entire store of goods and the machinery to the firm Gies & Co., at that time still established in Hilversum. I also owned shares in this firm, which I never reported and still own at present. This created the possibility that all machinery and so forth could be saved. The firm Gies & Co. then established itself at our address 263 Prinsengracht and the N.V. Pectacon at the office of Wolters, Rokin 6. The amount of the liquidation was fl.18,000 of which, as non-Jewish capital, an amount of fl.5,000 was paid to Kleiman and to Dunselman fl.3,000. The remaining amount of fl.10,000 after deduction of fl.2,300 for the benefit of Wirtschaftsprüfstelle was deposited at the Bank of Lippmann, Rosenthal in Amsterdam.*

Pectacon's books from 1940 are missing, but those available reveal irregularities between the entries previous to the invasion and those from the period of liquidation, leading one to speculate that there were extensive negotiations between Kleiman and Wolters. The Deutsche Revisions- und Treuhand AG (whose final report is also missing), referred to the proceedings as 'very unfavourable' and found Kleiman's explanation of the poor revenue from supplies sold 'unsatisfactory'. Wolters finished his dealings with Pectacon on 15 April 1942. He evidently did his best, under the circumstances, to help Otto Frank maintain the company, giving credence to the claim made by other Jewish businessmen that his attitude towards them was more protective than antagonistic.†

Aside from Otto, his staff, and Karel Wolters, one other person was aware that Gies & Co. was a smokescreen. In his 1966 letter to a Dutch journalist, Tonny Ahlers wrote darkly, 'I knew about [Otto Frank's] little game with Gies.' Whether or not he informed Otto that he knew is no longer possible to determine. What is certain, however, is that this was just the latest fragment in an increasingly dangerous arsenal of knowledge that Ahlers was building up against Otto Frank.

More problems arose at the Prinsengracht offices in October 1941, during the ongoing liquidation of Pectacon. The loan that Erich Elias had made to Otto in 1933, enabling him to set up the business in Amsterdam, had been taken over by the new manager of Rovag, a Swiss subsidiary of Pomosin-Werke and the firm for which Erich had worked in 1933. The new manager wanted to know what was happening with the repayments. Otto explained that he had already paid back fl.5,000 of the original fl.15,000 loaned to him; the remainder had, 'at the request of the gentlemen in Frankfurt' (officials from Pomosin-Werke headquarters) been taken over by the non-Jewish Dunselman. The implication was that the company was

---

* In August 1941 Jewish-owned finances were placed under the supervision of the bankers Lippmann, Rosenthal & Co., puppets of the Nazi government. The bank was used by the Nazis as a well for dipping into when they came up with new schemes that needed financing.
† Wolters enlisted in the Waffen SS in February 1943 and was deployed on 30 September 1944 to the Eastern Front, attached to the legal staff. Towards the end of the war he was wounded and returned to the Netherlands. In 1945 he was imprisoned in Scheveningen. On 16 June 1948, he was sentenced to eight years in prison and forbidden to hold office or serve in the military for the remainder of his life.

now fully 'Aryan'. This smokescreen was given further credence during a meeting held on 12 December, at which Otto and Dunselman were the only people present apart from a stenographer. Otto handed in his resignation as company director on the understanding that the 'Aryan' Kleiman would fill his position. It was also noted that Dunselman had spoken to the two men from Pomosin-Werke, Frankfurt who had 'taken the steps needed to Aryanize the company'. The Frankfurt officials had written to the BEI, stating that due to the agreement made in 1933 about the Rovag loan, Pomosin-Werke were the true owners of the Opekta-Amsterdam shares. Whilst awaiting the BEI's decision, the two men suggested depositing Otto's shares with the Handelstrust West N.V. in Amsterdam, a Dutch branch of the Dresdner Bank, often used by the German administrators of Jewish businesses undergoing Aryanization.

Although Otto was worried that Pomosin-Werke might pursue their claim to his business after the war, the actions of the 'two gentlemen from Frankfurt' helped to save the company. When the BEI decided to 'Aryanize' Opekta fully by giving it to one of the company's competitors, the judgement was never executed – presumably because of an appeal by Pomosin. Whatever the reason behind it, Pomosin's early intervention, together with the help of Dunselman, Kleiman and Wolters, meant that Otto was able to stay in employment. Miep recalls how this worked in practice:

Mr Frank would remain in the capacity of adviser, but in reality would continue to run the business as usual. The only real change would be from the legal standpoint . . . Mr Frank came to work every day. He sat at his desk in his private office and made all the decisions and gave all the orders. Nothing changed except when a cheque had been made out, or a letter had been typed. Mr Frank would then pass whatever it was that needed signing over to Kleiman or Kugler for a totally Christian signature.

Given all the problems Otto was encountering at that time, it was hardly surprising that Anne wrote to her relatives in Basel that her father was suffering rheumatism in his back. He maintained a normal demeanour at the office, Miep remembers: 'He was always himself, never missed work, never complained, and kept his private life at home.' In November, along with all German Jews in occupied territories, the Franks were divested of their nationality and had to report to the Zentralstelle with a list of their possessions. Otto recalled: 'We tried our best to keep these things from obtruding on the children . . . The children were scarcely aware of it when we had to register. I went alone. The Dutch official who was in charge of the list did not say a word when he saw me.' On 5 December all non-Dutch Jews had to file with the Zentralstelle for 'voluntary emigration'.

Four days later, China declared war on Japan and Germany and on 11 December, following the bombing of Pearl Harbor by the Japanese, America entered the war. For many of the Jews of Europe, the news provided a glimmer of hope in a distressing year, but for others it meant that their one possible means of escape had now closed to them.

On 29 January 1942, after months of pain and an operation in late 1941, Rosa Holländer died of cancer. Otto and Edith had not told Anne the true nature of her grandmother's illness, and she was deeply upset by her death. She writes about Oma Holländer from time to time in her diary, and confides to 'Kitty': 'No one will ever know how much she is in my thoughts and how much I love her still.' The death was announced in the pages of the *Joodse Weekblad* and Rosa Holländer was buried in the Jewish cemetery Gan Hashalom in Hoofddorp.

Edith's sorrow was aggravated by the lack of communication with Julius and Walter; there had been no postal service to Europe from America since its entry into the war. Her only contact with her brothers was via her mother-in-law in Switzerland. On 12 April Alice Frank sent Otto and Edith a food parcel and a letter explaining the situation: 'Julius is longing for news, which one can very well understand. I write to him as often as possible and hope for an answer, but you have to be very patient.' Erich added a business note:

Dear Otto

I have to disappointment you – goods made by us cannot be delivered. The situation being what it is, we do not have the right to export. That's the government for you, they have this highly valuable merchandise as compensation. I will see what develops. Didn't you hear anything from Frankfurt? You can imagine how sorry I am, but we are resigned to it.

Erich eventually lost his job with the company in Switzerland; although the country kept its neutrality, there were plenty of Nazi sympathizers. On 27 April Erich 'Israel' Elias was ordered by the German Consulate in Basel to hand in his passport after having been deprived of his German citizenship. His son Buddy remembers entering the Consulate with him that day. Erich had dressed in his best suit and hat, and stalked furiously up to the desk where he flung his passport at the bewildered official without a word before marching out again.

On 2 June 1942, together with the rest of the family, Otto wrote to congratulate Buddy on his seventeenth birthday. His letter was distinctly melancholy in tone: 'We can see from our children how time has gone by and sometimes I feel to a certain extent that I am a grandfather – when I think of my grown-up daughters. Well, let's hope that we will be able to see each other again soon, peacetime must come again, after all.' Ten days later, on 12 June, Anne celebrated her thirteenth birthday. Amongst the gifts from her parents was the diary she had chosen from the local bookstore a few days before. Around this time, Otto told his daughters that preparations had been made for them to go into hiding, and tried to soften the blow by reassuring Anne, 'Don't you worry about it, we shall arrange everything. Make the most of your carefree young life while you can.'

On 4 July Otto wrote to his family in Switzerland. His letter is couched in terms which hint that the plan to go into hiding would be implemented in the near future:

> Everything is fine here too, although we all know that day by day, life is getting harder. Please don't be in any way concerned, even if you hear little from us. When I'm not at the office there's still a lot to do and a lot to think about, and one has to come to terms with decisions that are very difficult to take on board . . . We haven't forgotten you and know that you're thinking of us constantly, but you can't change anything and you know you have to look after yourselves.

A brief letter written for Julius and Walter, but sent to Otto's mother, implies further that the disappearance was about to take place: 'Everything is difficult for us these days, but we have to take things as they come. I hope peace will come this year and that we will be able to see each other once again. I regret that we're unable to correspond with I [Alice] and her family but there's nothing we can do. I'm sure she will understand.'

Ultimately, the Franks did not go into hiding on the date they had intended. On Sunday 5 July 1942 sixteen-year-old Margot Frank was ordered to report to the SS for deportation to a German labour camp.

Although concentration camps had been in existence since 1933, they were not used specifically for extermination purposes, although inmates died frequently from the treatment meted out to them by the guards, and the slave labour they were forced to perform. Only after the Wannsee Conference in Berlin in January 1942 did all the agencies involved meet and finalize their plans for the destruction of the Jews. Adolf Eichmann, as Head of Section IVB4 in Berlin, led the operation to annihilate the Jews. By then the camp

– whether concentration camp, work camp, transit camp or ghetto – had become part of life in occupied territory. Poland was transformed 'into a vast slave plantation' with almost six thousand camps spread across it. In Germany the camps were more visible and more numerous yet. In the region of Hessen over six hundred camps existed and Berlin had the distinction of possessing a similar quantity purely for forced labour.

In preparation for the deportations from the Netherlands, the German administration had taken over Westerbork, surrounding it with barbed wire and installing armed SS men throughout the camp. In return for exemptions, a number of German Jews remained in charge of the actual administration, causing resentment from Dutch Jews who accused them of being better Nazis than the SS. Westerbork was used as a holding camp for Jews awaiting deportation from the Netherlands and it became, as Abel Herzberg wrote,

> another word for purgatory. There was nothing to sustain one, materially or spiritually. Each was thrown on his own resources, utterly alone. Desperation, total and absolute, seized everyone. People sought help but seldom found it, and, if they did, knew that it could not possibly prevail. Deportation to Poland might at best be postponed – for a week, perhaps, or for a few weeks at most. Husbands were powerless to protect their wives, parents had to watch helplessly while their children were torn away from them for ever. The sick, the blind, the hurt, the mentally disturbed, pregnant women, the dying, orphans, new-born babies – none was spared on the Tuesdays when the cattle trucks were being loaded with human freight for Poland. Tuesdays, week in, week out, for two interminable years.

In Amsterdam, the offices of the Joodse Raad teemed as people fought for 'Bolle' exemption stamps which offered, quite literally, a stay of execution. Few of those eligible for the stamps actually received them and, in the end, they too were deported, first to Westerbork and then on to the concentration camps of Auschwitz or Sobibor. Trains left Westerbork every month between July 1942 and September 1944; passenger numbers peaked in October 1942 (11,965), and in May (8,006) and June 1943 (8,420). Regarding the smooth operation of the trains, the responsibility for such ruthless efficiency lay with the Reichsbahn, part of the transport ministry, where 500,000 clerical and 900,000 operating staff performed their duties without murmur. For the purposes of the Reichsbahn's budget, deported Jews were categorized as normal passengers, with children under four years of age travelling free.

The Dutch, by and large, considered the rumours about the concentration camps as unpleasant propaganda and ignored the tales of horror: 'Dance-halls were full, cinema attendances were higher than ever, the beaches were as popular as always. Sports events in general, soccer in particular, drew large crowds to the stadiums.' The official line was that the Jews were being sent to work camps, but only the foolish or deluded could have believed that was the case when each day saw groups of handicapped, elderly, sick and infant Jews taken away. Jacob Presser fumed to a university colleague: 'It is not the villain who is our problem, but the "common man" who demeans himself in the execution of atrocious acts.' In full view of the local Dutch population, families wearing the yellow star and carrying rucksacks walked in long rows through Amsterdam's streets, and trams loaded with devastated Jews trundled along to Muiderpoort Station and Centraal Station.

The Netherlands has the worst record of Jewish deaths during the Holocaust in Western Europe. In Belgium, 60 per cent of Jews survived, in France the figure stands at around 75 per cent. In the Netherlands, the percentage of survival is shocking, even more so in comparison; only 25 per cent of Jews survived. Several factors have been identified as contributing to this appalling catalogue. By the 1930s, Jews were fully integrated into Dutch society, unlike Eastern European Jews who were familiar with pogroms and aggressive anti-Semitism. The German administration of the Netherlands was largely Austrian, which perhaps led to easier working relationships with the authorities (mostly Austrian themselves) in Berlin. The geography of the Netherlands did little to help the Jews, since there were few natural hiding places and little chance of escape over borders which led into occupied territory, or the North Sea. Furthermore, unlike France and Belgium where the trains came to a halt, more or less, between March and July 1943, there was never any point at which the deportations from the Netherlands slowed down.

Most damaging of all was a Dutch bureaucracy that insisted on quality and efficiency, registering Jews and non-Jews and thus equipping the Germans with valuable information. In her book, *One by One by One*, Judith Miller explains:

The Germans ruled Holland through a brutally efficient civilian occupation of barely one thousand men and women, administration that would have been impossible without the active cooperation of thousands of Dutch civil servants from the country's well-disciplined bureaucracy. Westerbork and the other Dutch concentration camps were run mainly by the Dutch SS not by Germans. And the brutality of the indigenous Dutch SS was such that at Amersfoort Camp, for example, the German-sponsored Dutch Jewish Council once officially protested to the Germans the ill-treatment of Jews by Dutch Gestapo.

There were never more than two hundred German policemen operating in Amsterdam, but the occupying forces were able to perform their duties without wide-scale interference. The Dutch underground press gave relatively little coverage to the plight of the Jews, an oversight which *Vrij Nederland* admitted: 'Unnoticed, the poison of propaganda has affected us, and its after-effects will be felt for a long time, especially in our children, who have been used to it and do not know any better. For them, being a Jew means being a constant exception.'

During that first weekend in July 1942, Margot Frank was among thousands of German Jews between the ages of fifteen and sixteen targeted by the Germans for the first of the systematic deportations to the camps. The aim was to send 4,000 Jews to 'Germany' during three days in mid July. The lists of deportees were drawn up by the Central Agency for Jewish Emigration (Zentralstelle). Among the staff was a man named Peters, the closest friend of Tonny Ahlers, who was himself often seen at the Zentralstelle.

Margot's friend Laureen Nussbaum recalls,

It was agony. Some of my friends wanted to go when the call-up came because they did not expect anything too bad, but their parents begged them to stay and hide, while the parents of other friends made them obey the call-up in order to save the rest of the family. During the first round, my sister Susi was also sent a card, but, in the end, she didn't have to go because of a loophole in the laws which my mother discovered. That period was hell, nevertheless. It was the beginning of summer vacation and when we went back to our Jewish schools, the classes had thinned out considerably. I became one of six in a class; my sister was the only child in her class. The pupils, the teachers, all disappeared.

In her diary, Anne explicitly and emotionally described the events of 5 July: the shock, the fear and the panic. The decision to go into hiding the following day was taken immediately. Otto recalled,

It was said that life in the camps, even in the camps in Poland, was not so bad; that the work was hard but there was food enough, and the persecutions stopped, which was the main thing. I told a great many people what I suspected. I also told them what I had heard on the British wireless, but a good many still thought these were atrocity stories . . .

By evening, all those who had pledged to help them, together with the van Pels family, were aware that the building on the Prinsengracht was about to hold a perilous secret. Otto sent a final coded postcard to Switzerland, wishing his sister a happy birthday months in advance:

> We wanted to be sure that you received our thoughts for you on the right day, as later we'll have no opportunity. We wish you all the best from the bottom of our hearts. We are well and together, that's the main thing. Everything is difficult these days, but you just have to take some things with a pinch of salt. I hope we'll find peace this year already so that we can see each other again. It's a pity that we can no longer correspond with you, but that's how it is. You must understand.
>
>   As always, I send you all my best wishes,
>   Otto.

Following the first deportation from the Netherlands, a protest leaflet distributed in Amsterdam issued a warning which was eerily prophetic:

> During the night of 15 July 1942, around 1.50 a.m., the first group [of called-up Jews] had to report at Amsterdam's Centraal Station. Thereafter, every day, 1,200 Jews will have to do likewise. From Westerbork in Drenthe where the unfortunate people are being screened, approximately 4,000 Jews altogether are being deported each time. The trains for this purpose stand ready. Specialists from Prague well versed as executioners have gone there in order to expedite the deportations as much as possible. In this manner, a total of approximately 120,000 Jewish Dutch citizens will be taken away.
>
> Such are the sober facts. They compare in brutality and matter-of-factness only with the instructions of the Egyptian Pharaoh who had all Jewish male children killed, and with Herod, that anti-Semite who had all infants in Bethlehem killed in order to kill Jesus. Now, several thousand years later, Hitler and his henchmen have found their place in this company. Official Polish reports name the figure of 700,000 Jews who have already perished in the clutches of the Germans. Our Jewish fellow citizens will suffer a similar fate . . . we are dealing with the realization of threats which the Nazis have hurled at the Jews again and again – their destruction and annihilation.
>
> The Dutch people have taken note of the anti-Jewish measure with disgust and outrage. To be sure, our people must pay heavily for the fact that they did not refuse to sign the Declaration on Jews so ingenuously presented to them. It is our joint guilt – that of the Jewish Council not excepted – that our enemies now dispose of a complete Jewish administration.
>
> All prior German measures had aimed at isolating the Jews from the rest of the Dutch, to make contact impossible, and to kill our sentiments concerning living

side by side and in solidarity. They have succeeded much better than we know ourselves or are probably willing to admit. The Jews have to be killed in secrecy and we, the witnesses, must remain deaf, blind, and silent . . . God and history will condemn us and hold us partly responsible for this mass murder if we now remain silent and simply look on . . .

The Frank family entered their hiding place on 6 July 1942; they were joined by Hermann, Gusti and Peter van Pels on 13 July 1942, and on 16 November, after having asked Miep if she knew of somewhere safe, Fritz Pfeffer arrived. For two years, eight people lived in the strict confinement of five rooms, remaining behind the grey door of the annexe (itself concealed by a specially constructed moveable bookcase) exclusively through the day and only ever venturing as far as the offices at night. Apart from their protective friends, no one was supposed to know they were there. Neighbours from the Merwedeplein believed a story begun by a deliberately misleading letter left behind by Otto that they had escaped to Switzerland via his old army friend Crampe. Otto's family in Switzerland did not know where they were, but began to realize, through inferences made by Kleiman in business letters to Erich, that they were being cared for.

Their survival was dependent upon abiding by a certain set of rules regarding security, upon retaining their sanity and a belief that they would eventually regain their freedom, but, most of all, upon their helpers. Miep and Jan, Bep and her father, Kleiman and his wife Johanna, and Kugler (who did not confide in his wife) provided them with food and the necessary articles of day-to-day living, kept up their spirits, and generally shielded them in every sense. In a letter to Yad Vashem, Otto described their duties:

Miep and Bep had the extremely difficult task to provide food. To nourish eight people while most of the food-stuff was rationed, was a hard job. They had to buy in different shops, so that it would not raise suspicion if they bought big quantities in one. Mr Gies and Mr Kleiman bought ration cards on the black market for us, and after some time we became short of money, they sold parts of our jewellery. Besides Mr Kugler sold spices without booking sales to help finance our needs. All these activities were risky and they always had to be careful not to be trapped by collaborators of the Germans or by *agents provocateurs*. Apart from food there were lots of other items which we needed in the course of the twenty-five months of our hiding, such as toilet-articles, medicine, clothes for the growing children, etc, as well as books and other materials to keep us busy.

Miep later admitted that she enjoyed the challenge of shopping for her hidden friends: 'I would go to all the shops, and you would try things out a little with the man in the shop. How far you could go. How much you could ask. To what extent you could pretend to be in such a terrible situation. Yes, that was like playing in a theatre.' Miep called on a friend of van Pels who had a butcher's shop on the Rozengracht for meat and bought groceries from a shop on the nearby Leliegracht owned by Hendrik van Hoeve, a resistance worker who was himself hiding a Jewish couple in his home. Kleiman's friend Siemons, who had a bakery on the Raamgracht, provided them with bread. Bep had the responsibility for setting aside bottles of milk from the office staff's allowance and Jan Gies was able to purchase ration cards through his work in a resistance group, the National Relief Fund. As time wore on, the advantage of hoarding dried and canned food, stashed in the attic of the annexe, became increasingly clear.

The helpers' aid went beyond such practicalities, however. In his memoir, Otto explained:

Nobody could imagine what it meant for us that my four employees proved to be sacrificial helpers and genuine friends, in a time when bad powers had the upper hand. They demonstrated a true example of humane cooperation, whilst taking a huge personal risk in looking after us. As time went by, this became more and more difficult. Their daily visits gave us an enormous lift.

In a radio interview granted after the war, Kleiman said: 'The reason I offered to help Otto Frank and his family during the hiding period is because I knew him as a sincere businessman and a very decent and helpful person, qualities for which he is generally respected.' Kugler's attitude was much the same:

What else could I do? I had to help them; they were my friends. Life changed utterly for the people in hiding. They had to remain completely silent, especially during the day. But it was also a tense and frightening time for us, the helpers. Our greatest fear was that the hiding place would be discovered. I had to put on an act for Otto Frank's former business associates, for clients and for the neighbours. Yet day-to-day life inside the secret annexe, as well as life outside, just continued along. Their only chance for a better future was the secret annexe, where they attempted to survive the storm.

It was difficult for the helpers to keep their double lives a secret. Willy, one of Bep Voskuijl's sisters, recalled: 'We knew nothing about the Frank family being in hiding. What we did notice is that after dinner Bep and father often sat together talking very quietly.' Jan Gies recalled: 'People who looked after those in hiding also had and suffered from a particular kind of life. They might have become somewhat withdrawn. They weren't as free to express themselves . . . Because it is, well, actually a terrible life in such a small community. Having to be silent about those things, and cope with them, and keep everyone at arm's length – while acting as if everything is normal.' In contrast to her reply about the dismissal of her Jewish co-worker Esther, Miep said she had no fear when taking the risk of hiding the Franks and their friends:

That was not a word in our vocabulary: scared. Especially not at first, in the beginning. Yes, later, you were worried sometimes. You would think, 'How can this go on?' . . . But the care for these people – and, really, the compassion for what these people went through – that was stronger. That won out.

The need to go into hiding changed the balance of the relationship between Miep and Otto, however, and Miep was aware that Otto himself altered as a result: 'He didn't like that. Because, after all, he was the director, and in normal life whatever he said would happen. But now he depended upon us. Well, just imagine the situation. That change. He had to wait to see whether we agreed with everything. Whether we approved. Whether we did everything according to his requests.' Miep and Jan also had a fugitive hidden in their home, something they deliberately did not tell Otto. Miep explains why: 'Otto would never have approved of that. I know just what he would have said: "Miep, if anything happens to you . . ." You lived in separate worlds. Also towards our friends. They knew nothing about it. That was the rule: don't tell.' Jan confirmed: 'We knew, for example, those people on the other side of the street, they are good. Why? That is hard for us to say. You see things . . . you hear things. You hear people talking, and this is how you figure out the value of certain individuals. That is not a 100 per cent rule but in general it worked for me. I was lucky.'

Since the helpers were also Otto's employees, they kept the business running on his behalf and Kleiman and Kugler conferred with him every day. There were some difficulties now that Kugler had more responsibility; Anne writes of van Pels working himself 'into a rage again because of some blunder on Mr Kugler's part', and on 20 October 1942 she records, 'a big row here . . . Mr van Pels and Pim were so angry that both of them slept badly. Kugler is really being silly. Now he wants to employ a girl but obviously he can't for our sake and for his own as well.' Nonetheless, Kugler used money from the business to aid those in hiding. Gies & Co. showed a small profit during the war. After the invasion, Otto and Kleiman had purchased devices with which to make substitute spices, as goods from the Dutch East Indies were no longer available due to the worldwide conflict. There was demand enough for the products manufactured by Otto's business. Opekta was left alone by the Germans; on 1 July 1944 the BEI informed the company that they had approved the resignation of the 'Jewish director Otto Frank' in December 1941, and that 'Jews no longer exert any personal or financial influence on this company'. Consequently Opekta was no longer 'liable to registration in terms of VO 189/1940'.

The eight in hiding were not ignorant about the fate of the Jews in the Netherlands. They had a wireless, which they listened to daily, and heard reports from England that Jews were being 'regularly killed by machine-gun fire, hand-grenades – and even poisoned by gas'. Although the news disturbed them deeply, they continued to listen to the broadcasts for, as Otto later wrote, 'through the wireless we could feel connected with the outside world'. The news and their own confinement took their toll on each of them. There were frequent arguments, as each of them despaired and grew depressed, retreated and lost their faith in the future at some point. Yet there was also humour during the hiding period, a strong sense of community, and celebrations of birthdays and holidays. Otto swiftly realized that boredom would be amongst the worst of their personal demons: 'Only with a certain time allocation laid down from the start and with each one having his own duties, could we have hoped to live through the situation. Above all the children had to have enough books to read and to learn. None of us wanted to think how long this voluntary imprisonment would last.' Through the day, they followed a timetable of reading, writing, and studying languages. In the evening, when absolute silence was no longer a necessity, they listened to classical music on the wireless, played board games, recited poetry and discussed politics. They were all enthusiastic readers and in the evening Otto read aloud to his family from the favourites of his youth: Heine, Goethe, Schiller and Körner. Religion was also a part of their lives in hiding: on Friday nights they observed the Sabbath, led by Edith and Fritz Pfeffer's example. They also cooked from Jewish recipes and honoured the High Holy days. They celebrated Christmas, but the festivities were simply a means of having fun, without any actual religious feeling behind the giving of presents.

After the war, Otto revealed one of the ways the inhabitants of 263 Prinsengracht avoided sinking too far into despondency: 'I remember to have once read a sentence: "If the end of the world would be imminent, I still would plant a tree today." When we lived in the secret annexe we had the device "fac et spera", which means "work and hope."'

★

While the Frank family and their friends were cut off from the rest of the world, Tonny Ahlers enjoyed a period of prosperity. How long the deliveries from Otto's company to his own went on during this period, and how this was organized (possibly through Kleiman), is unclear. Presumably, Ahlers had hoped the agreement would continue; that surely can be the only explanation as to why, as he wrote to former SS Oberscharführer Silberbauer in 1964, he 'permitted' Otto and his family to go into hiding for a length of time. Aside from the agency, Ahlers kept himself busy in other ways. He took part regularly in skirmishes, and reported Jews and people breaking the laws of the land (as they now stood under German occupation) to Untersturmführer Kurt Döring. He tried to betray the spy for whom he worked, Josef van Poppel, for reasons known only to himself. Van Poppel had been unexpectedly thrown out of the NSNAP, which he believed was due to the activities of Ahlers. In 1942, van Poppel began to suspect that the SD had asked Ahlers to keep an eye on him: 'I constantly had people come to my home asking trick questions. For instance they would say the SD was looking for them and could I help?' He recalled that sometime in 1942 Ahlers banged on his door and shouted that he was under orders to arrest him:

I asked [Ahlers] for proof, but the only thing he could show me was a document which stated he was an agent for the SD. I told him that I would throw him down the stairs if he didn't go away. Ahlers said he was arresting me because he knew that I was hiding someone who was wanted by the SD. This was just a piece of gossip he had picked up at Café Trip. Ahlers went away with the two men in WA uniforms who had remained at the bottom of the stairs during our altercation. He came back about three hours later and apologized for his behaviour. And actually, I *did* have someone in my home, a man called Geri . . . Through Ahlers, Geri was arrested that same afternoon and received a three-year prison sentence.

Van Poppel also confirmed Ahlers's involvement in the arrest and execution of two men he knew.

In February 1943 Ahlers did something for which his family never forgave him. A man named Aloserij was visiting Ahlers's mother and stepfather, as he often did, to play cards. Ahlers was also present, and he and Aloserij started to argue about the Russian advance. Aloserij remembered:

The next day I was arrested. They took me to the Doelenstraat police station and kept me there for four days before releasing me . . . Undoubtedly, Ahlers informed the SD about the debate and betrayed me – and his stepfather – to the SD. Exactly a year later I was arrested again . . . after they informed me that my arrest was due to my 'attitude' at Ahlers's stepfather's home, I was sent to Vught concentration camp.

The Aloserij affair had other repercussions: Ahlers's stepfather was also deported to Vught and Ahlers's brother had his house searched by the SD for communist propaganda before being placed under observation by the German police. Ahlers attempted to betray another family friend, but the man was able to escape through a window as the Gestapo entered his apartment. The man's wife recalled, 'Ahlers was known around here as a member of the NSB and as an SD man.' 'Here' was the Jordaan district of Amsterdam, and specifically the area around the secret annexe.

At the start of 1943 two young men went into hiding in Ahlers's apartment on the Haarlemmerweg, which Ahlers rented from a painter who later gave evidence against him. After the war, one of the hidden men admitted, 'Very soon we noticed that we were anything but safe in Ahlers's home. He had a buying agency for the Wehrmacht and strong ties with the SD. He was, among others, very close with a certain Döring . . . we soon left for another address.' Ahlers himself moved on in November 1943, to a spacious apartment at Jan van Eyckstraat 22, where he lived with his wife and baby son. The house became available when the Jewish owners were deported; a document from the Amsterdam Telephone Service shows that Ahlers was given permission from the SS to occupy the house. With his contacts at the Zentralstelle, Ahlers was able to furnish the apartment with beautiful belongings pilfered from other deported Jewish families. Two of Ahlers's employees at Petoma visited him in his new home. He showed them 'photographs in which he appeared in his black [NSB] uniform during parties. In his living room there was a large portrait of him next to Mussert. On his door there was a sign with the text: "When absent, call at the Sicherheitsdienst, Euterpestraat" . . . When we wanted to quit [Petoma] he did not accept this and told us that if we did not go to work he would fetch the Grüne Polizei.'

Following the move to Jan van Eyckstraat, Ahlers's life took a yet more pernicious turn. His association with the SD became stronger, unsurprisingly so, since his luxurious apartment was located in the dark heart of Nazi Amsterdam, a stone's throw from the SD headquarters. The street on which he lived was bordered at one end by the Zentralstelle and at the other by the Expositur department of the Joodse Raad, and almost all his neighbours were members of the SD. Next door lived his boss Kurt Döring (post-war witnesses recalled that Döring rarely mistreated the prisoners brought to him after their arrests – unless they were Jewish. One witness confirmed his 'hateful' behaviour during which he would scream *'Saujude'* and *'Schwein-*

hunde' at them), together with the German officials Friedrich Christian Viebahn and Emil Rühl.* Ahlers rented a room to the Nazi spy Herman Rouwendaal who specialized in infiltrating resistance groups, providing the Abwehr with weapons, and betraying Allied pilots. It was probably through Rouwendaal that Ahlers first came into contact with Maarten Kuiper, a detective with the SD. Kuiper had known Rouwendaal since August 1943, when they worked for the same police bureau in Amsterdam-East. On 27 January 1944, Kuiper visited Rouwendaal in Ahlers's apartment.

Kuiper, born in The Hague in November 1898, enlisted in the Dutch army at the age of seventeen and served four years before leaving to join the Royal Dutch Steamboat Company as a foreman. In 1924 he travelled to the Belgian Congo as a pantry servant. There was a brief period working as a docker before he found work in the Amsterdam Municipal Police in 1925, conducting himself with 'a fixed, almost exaggerated professional zeal'. In 1941 Kuiper became a member of the NSB, and was given the task of pursuing Communists. He joined the SD headquarters on the Euterpestraat 'at his own request' and within a short time he was executing members of the resistance and other enemies of the Reich in cold blood. He also established a formidable reputation as an anti-Semite, 'hunting down Jews as industriously as he had at first hunted Communists'. By the mid war years, he was one of the most prolific betrayers of Jews in hiding, estimating 'the number of arrests he made during the first years of the war minimally at 250 persons. In the following years he lost count.' Tonny Ahlers seems to have idolized Maarten Kuiper. They became friends, moving in the same corrupt circles, united by their hatred of Communists and Jews. Ahlers even began to tell people that Kuiper, the notorious Jew-hunter, was his father-in-law.

Throughout his 'evil career', Kuiper received a bonus for every Jew he arrested. And among those arrests was one that took place in the summer of 1944, in the annexe of a spice company on the Prinsengracht.

In his memoir – the only commentary by another member of the group in hiding in the annexe at 263 Prinsengracht – Otto discloses nothing of his emotional response to that period, instead choosing to focus on one of the very few positive aspects:

---

* At his trial, having successfully argued that he only acted under the orders of his superior Lages, Döring was eventually sentenced to three years' imprisonment with time in remand to be taken into account. Rühl and Viebahn received prison sentences of fifteen years. The Court decided that having served so long under the strict discipline of the German police, their sense of responsibility must have been worn down. They were released from jail in Breda in April 1956 and handed over to the German authorities.

I have to say that in a certain way it was a happy time. I think of all the good that we experienced, whilst all discomfort, longing, conflicts and fears disappear. How fine it was to live in such close contact with the ones I loved, to speak to my wife about the children and about future plans, to help the girls with their studies, to read classics with them and to speak about all kinds of problems and all views about life. I also found time to read. All this would not have been possible in a normal life, when all day long you are at work. I remember very well that I once said, 'When the Allies win, and we survive, we will later look back with gratitude on the time that we have spent here together.'

On his role as peacemaker among the individual members of the annexe he remarked: 'We had thought that communal life hiding with the family of my partner would make life less monotonous. My main task was to ensure as happy a communal life as possible, and when I compromised, Anne reproached me for being too yielding.' Although it was a mantle he took on willingly in order to maintain the status quo, he confided to Miep that he felt overwhelmed by the responsibility, and worried too about the danger his friends were in, caring for them.

From the first day, it was Otto who oversaw the minutiae of life in the hiding place. He and Anne tacked strips of material to the windows to frustrate prying eyes across the courtyard while Margot and Edith gave in to their shock and after that, it was he who decided the rules regarding safety and personal space. In other areas too, it was Otto who took charge: he suggested subjects to study and books to read, conducted the children's lessons, decided how they would manage their rations and resources, determined what new security measures they should take following the occasional burglaries at the offices, joined in with all the games and, outwardly at least, maintained a positive perspective on their situation. Miep describes Otto as 'the most logical, the one that balanced everyone out. He was the leader, the one in charge. When a decision needed to be made, all eyes turned to Mr Frank'. He was quite different to the Otto they had known before. Miep recalls, 'I noticed a new composure, a new calm about Mr Frank. Always a nervous man before, he now displayed a veneer of total control, a feeling of safety and calm emanated from him. I could see that he was setting a calm example for the others.' Sometimes his nerves were bad, though Miep may not have seen it; Anne occasionally comments on his bad moods, during which he kept whatever was troubling him to himself. On 17 October 1943 she comments, 'Daddy goes about with his lips tightly pursed, when anyone speaks to him, he looks startled, as if he is afraid he will have to patch up some tricky relationship again.' His one means of escape was reading, either 'serious, rather dry descriptions of people and places', German classics or, most commonly of all, Dickens.

'The one person who visibly meant something to Anne was her father. That was always apparent.' Miep's first-hand observation of the relationship between Otto and Anne is one that strikes all readers of the diary, and after the diary's publication it was often cited by young people as one of their primary reasons for writing to Otto. In her revised diary, Anne opens her biographical sketch of life up to that point by describing him as 'the dearest darling of a father I have ever seen . . .' Otto removed this reference from the published version, whether from modesty or for aesthetics is not known. Initially, Otto worried that his youngest daughter would find the adjustment to life in hiding merciless: 'From the start it was clear to us that a life in total seclusion would be much harder for the lively Anne to put up with than for us. We knew that she would miss greatly her many friends and school. Margot, who was more mature, would come to terms with our situation.'

From the start, Otto bolstered Anne's morale. Soon after their arrival in the annexe Anne wrote in her diary: 'it is as if the whole world had turned upside down, but I am still alive, Kitty, and that is the main thing, Daddy says'. He told her that the Dutch people were not to blame for their predicament, declaring that 'you could fill a whole diary saying how fantastic the Dutch are'. Usually, when Anne's fears overcame her, he was the one to comfort her. His friend Jean Schick Grossman recalled how, after the war, 'Otto told me how inadequate he felt to meet all of Anne's emotional needs in hiding. Cut off from friends her own age, often she tried to find in him a substitute for the normal companionship she missed.' In an attempt to combat Anne's loneliness, he tried to keep her as occupied as possible. Otto remonstrated with Anne when her behaviour seemed unreasonable, and occasionally lost his temper, although not often.

Otto urged Anne on in her search for self-discovery and perfection, and when she was thirteen told her the facts of life, going further than most parents of his generation, although still not completely satisfying her curiosity: 'Daddy told me about prostitutes, etc, but all in all there are still a lot of questions that haven't been answered yet.' Otto was the only one who noticed Anne's retreat into solitude when Anne later withdrew into herself during the period of confusion prior to her infatuation with Peter: 'I desperately want to be alone. Daddy has noticed that I'm not quite my usual self, but I really can't tell him everything.' Otto was reluctant to say anything to either Anne or Peter, despite the discomfort and amusement their romance aroused among the other fugitives. In his memoir, Otto explained how the relationship 'brought a few problems, but because I had trust in both Anne and Peter I could speak openly with the two of them. I was clear of the fact that this friendship would make life easier for Anne in the annexe.' Peter was extremely fond of Otto, and would later prove to be a brave and thoughtful friend to him.

Otto told Anne, during her adolescent struggle to establish her independence, that 'All children must look after their own upbringing.' Otto published Anne's penultimate entry in the diary, where she considers how she has distanced herself from him, almost intact, but several sections where she criticized him personally, for instance, his indifference to her idea that each person in the annexe should give a talk on a given subject, and his apparently lavatorial sense of humour, were cut from the published version. Gone too, was the entry:

I used to be jealous of Margot's relationship with Daddy before, there is no longer any trace of that now; I still feel hurt when Daddy treats me unreasonably because of his nerves, but then I think: 'I can't really blame you people for being like that, you talk so much about children – and the thoughts of young people – but you don't know the first thing about them!' I long for more than Daddy's kisses, for more than his caresses. Isn't it terrible of me to keep thinking about this all the time?

Anne herself removed this from her rewritten diary, and Otto chose not to reinstate it. Anne retained the comment on their relationship in her second version concerning how she had realized that 'Daddy would never become my confidant'. In the published diary, this was changed to 'my confidant over everything', a subtle but meaningful difference.

Otto's tranquil relationship with his eldest daughter appears to have been unmarred by confrontation. Otto's post-war recollections about Margot only ever referred to her innate goodness. Margot also kept a diary during the period in hiding but it has never been found; it would have been intriguing to read, since her personality in Anne's diary, and from Otto's comments, is one-dimensional. Otto admitted to one of his closest and most trusted friends during the 1970s, Father John Neiman, that he was not even aware that Margot, like Anne, was recording her thoughts:

Otto never spoke much about Margot, but he did say that one of the most surprising things to come out of his reading of Anne's diary was the discovery that Margot had also been keeping a diary. The two girls sometimes read parts of their journals to each other. He had had no idea about Margot's need to confide in someone, or rather, something. She was always so reserved. None of them, apart from Anne, had known about it. And I think, of course, that he was very disappointed Margot's diary had not been preserved.

Whether Margot was ever plagued by insecurities, depressions and jealousies as her young sister was will probably never be known. Otto told Margot that Anne wanted to confide in her but found it difficult. He had devised a way in which the two sisters could become closer: 'Have some secret with Anne. Something you do not tell your mother or me.' Margot suggested to Anne that they send each other little notes, which Anne kept in her diary. Through them, a fraction of Margot's emotions are revealed. She writes that Anne and Peter should enjoy their friendship, commenting,

I only feel a bit sorry that I haven't found anyone yet, and am not likely to for the time being, with whom I can discuss my thoughts and feelings . . . one misses enough here, things that other people just take for granted . . . I have the feeling that if I wished to discuss a lot with anyone, I should want to be on rather intimate terms with him. I would want to have the feeling that he understood me through and through without my having to say much, but for that reason it would have to be someone whom I felt to be my superior intellectually.

In a second letter she writes wistfully: 'In my heart of hearts I feel I have the right to share mutual confidences with someone . . .' Margot did confide to some extent in her mother, with whom her relationship was always exemplary, in contrast to the conflict between Anne and Edith.

Otto was disturbed by the discord between his wife and youngest daughter. In her diary on 3 October 1942 Anne writes,

I told Daddy that I'm much more fond of him than Mummy, to which he replied that I'd get over that . . . Daddy said that I should sometimes volunteer to help Mummy, when she doesn't feel well or has a headache; but I shan't since I don't like her and I don't feel like it. I would certainly do it for Daddy, I noticed that when he was ill. Also it's easy for me to picture Mummy dying one day, but Daddy dying one day seems inconceivable to me.

Otto cut this entry considerably. In his memoir, he recalled,

I was concerned that there was no particularly good understanding between my wife and Anne, and I believe my wife suffered more from this than Anne. In reality she was an excellent mother, who went to all lengths for her children. She often complained that Anne was against everything that she did, but it was a consolation for her to know that Anne trusted me. It was often hard for me to mediate between Anne and her mother. On one hand, I didn't want to hurt my wife, but it was often difficult for me to point Anne in the right direction when she was cheeky and naughty to her mother. Usually I would wait until after such a scene, would take Anne aside, and would speak to her as if she were an adult. I explained to her, that in the situation we were in, each one of us had to control himself, even when there were grounds to complain. That often helped for a while.

Edith was often upset by Anne's attitude towards her, and confided to her husband, 'I know how she feels about me, but I'm glad she has you.'

The recently discovered pages from Anne's diary are interesting in that they show how, over time, Anne began to consider her mother's feelings more, but her closing paragraph indicates the gulf that still existed: 'What do we know of one another's thoughts? I can't talk to her, I can't look lovingly into those cold eyes, I can't. Not ever! – If she had even one quality an understanding mother is supposed to have, gentleness or friendliness or patience or something, I'd keep trying to get closer to her. But as for loving this insensitive person, this mocking creature – it's becoming more and more impossible every day!' Nonetheless, Edith was often supportive to Anne when Otto was not. She understood her daughter's fear of discovery when they were listening to the wireless in the private office and returned to the annexe with her while Otto stayed below, uncomprehending. It was Edith too who sympathized with Anne at night when she wanted a light switched on during the shooting from German and Allied aircraft: Anne had

begged Daddy to light the candle again. He was relentless, the light remained off. Suddenly there was a burst of machine-gun fire, and that is ten times worse than guns, Mummy jumped out of bed and to Pim's great annoyance lit the candle. When he complained her answer was firm: 'After all, Anne's not exactly a veteran soldier,' and that was the end of it.

Anne herself remarked that 'Mummy and Daddy are always on my side', and changed her entry of 27 September 1942 from: 'Daddy at least defends me, without him I would honestly be almost unable to stand it here,' to: 'Mummy and Daddy always defend me stoutly, I'd have to give up if it weren't for them.'

The relationship between Otto and Edith during the time spent in hiding has not been given a great deal of attention. Otto never spoke of it, and Anne's diary gives only brief insights, though the newly discovered pages have focused attention upon it. For those outside the family, the relationship seemed admirable. Anne records Mrs van Pels taunting her husband by remarking often, 'Mr Frank always answers his wife, doesn't he?' In addition to those comments already quoted from the missing pages, Anne also noted that the marriage had always been presented to her as ideal:

never a quarrel, no angry faces, perfect harmony, etc . . . Daddy accepts Mummy as she is, is often annoyed, but says as little as possible, because he knows the sacrifices Mummy has had to make. Daddy doesn't always ask her opinion – about the business, about other matters, about people, about all kinds of things. He doesn't tell her everything, because he knows she's far too emotional, far too critical, and often far too biased . . . He looks at her teasingly, or mockingly, but never lovingly.

Anne's judgement is harshly phrased, but behind it lay the truth. It was Edith who ultimately found the enforced seclusion harder than any of them, a possibility Otto had not considered. Previous to her marriage to Otto, she showed signs of being an emancipated woman, but afterwards she took on the 'precisely defined role' of wife and mother, which was what she had been brought up to expect from life, drawing her 'sense of her own value from performing such duties'. In hiding, this was no longer feasible; her role was shared with Mrs van Pels which diminished her standing, and because she and Otto shared their room with Margot after Pfeffer's arrival it was obvious that she and her husband were not intimate. As the first year in hiding drew to a close, Edith's demeanour was becoming perceptibly 'dismal', so Miep recalls; she 'began to act oddly'. Otto would in all probability have tried to buoy up his wife's spirits, and, apparently realizing this, Edith chose to confide in Miep instead, who simply listened to her confessions that she was 'suffering under a great weight of despair . . . she was deeply ashamed of the fact that she felt the end would never come'.

The end did come, in the summer of 1944. And it was Edith's forebodings, rather than Otto's confidence, which proved to be the grim and terrible truth. The Allied invasion of 6 June 1944 had given Otto new purpose in his declarations of optimism. Kleiman sent a postcard to the Eliases in Switzerland on 22 June 1944, alluding to the fact that Otto and his family were still in safe hands. Otto himself had been convinced that 1944 would bring them freedom. His calm encouragement that the outcome would be positive was given expression in a poem he wrote for Edith's birthday on 16 January 1943. A copy of it was found amongst Otto's possessions after his death; it has never been published before:

> No flowers, and no eel,
> No cake, and no scarf,
> No stockings, no purses,
> No, not even something to munch on,

No sweets, no chocolate,
Not even a confection from Verkade,
Nothing to wear, nothing to read,
How did it used to be?
If only we had something.
Stop! Two packets of cigarettes.
That's all, there's nothing else
Because the shops, they are empty.
Furthermore, you wished
Not to celebrate, to keep it completely quiet
And that's what will happen,
And everybody will understand.
The former friends, the old acquaintances,
The brothers, those in faraway places,
I am sure they are thinking of you.
But there is no letter on the birthday table,
No telephone can reach you.
There has never been anything like it,
And still, even though secluded in the annexe,
We celebrate your birthday today
Without as much as a bouquet of flowers
To be seen in our room,
But we are not alone, to the contrary,
Money and good words cannot buy
The love and loyalty that we are shown here.
Nobody can measure what it means,
How always again, every morning,
Those good friends look after us,
Bring us news, give us food,
Always ready with head and hands.
What more can you want in life
Than friends who give you everything,
That you have the children with you
– and also Pim – who want to help you
Carry the burden as best they can.
We four are together from early to late,
And if we survive this difficult period in good health,
Then everything else will be fine.
We hope that there will be peace soon,
And that we can spend your next birthday

> Free, and without worries.
> We hope so – and we *will* succeed.★

On 1 August 1944 Anne wrote in her diary before placing it inside Otto's briefcase, where she always kept it, for the last time.

There had been many causes for worry about discovery over the two years in hiding. In 1943 and 1944 there were a spate of burglaries at the offices and in the warehouse. Each time the danger seemed greater than before; during the last break-in, on the evening of 8 April 1944, Otto, Peter and Hermann van Pels were seen by the thieves and their secret annexe was almost exposed. The hole left in the warehouse door on that occasion was seen by the man who provided them with groceries, Hendrik van Hoeve. When van Hoeve saw Jan Gies the day after the break-in, he told him he had not informed the police: 'Because with you, I didn't think it was the thing to do. I don't know anything, but I guess a lot.' The following month, May 1944, van Hoeve was arrested; the NSB had discovered he was hiding a Jewish couple in his home and raided the building. This gave the eight in hiding at the Prinsengracht a great deal about which to worry: their food supplies would lessen as a result, and they were terrified that van Hoeve would break under torture and confess their own hiding place. Fortunately for them, van Hoeve withstood his ill-treatment at the Gestapo headquarters without a word about any of the people whom he knew to be in hiding; he was then sent to several concentration camps, including Dora, an underground factory where inmates were regularly worked and beaten to death.

During that same break-in at the Prinsengracht, on 8 April 1944, Martin Sleegers, the nightwatchman in the area, had also noticed the hole in the warehouse door. He called a policeman, and they inspected the building that night; it was these two men whom the fugitives in the annexe heard rattling at the bookcase in front of the secret door. Jan Gies spoke to Sleegers after the event and asked him to keep a special watch on their building. Anne writes in her diary, 'Now everyone is going on about whether Sleegers is reliable.' Among the papers seized in 1945 from the home of Gezinus Gringhuis (one of the men who arrested the Frank family), was a small notebook containing names and addresses of Jews, informants and details of Jewish possessions he had stolen. The author found this book in Gringhuis's file in NIOD. In the middle of the book appears: 'Sleegers, Herengracht

---

★ The poem has been translated from German; in the original language it was written in rhyme.

100'. It was definitely the same Sleegers; Otto's voluminous papers included a list of all those mentioned in the diary and alongside it he filled in their real names and addresses. Sleegers was on that list. Furthermore, one of the other men present at the Franks' arrest, Willem Grootendorst, recalled a raid on the evening of 8 April 1944 just a few doors down from where the Franks and their friends were hiding; it is possible that either he or Gringhuis was the policeman who accompanied Sleegers as far as the bookcase door that night. Nobody was aware of Sleegers' connection to Gringhuis, and perhaps Grootendorst; he should also have been questioned about the betrayal.

There were two other factors which troubled the eight in hiding: Bep's sister was apparently involved with a German soldier, and the owner of 263 Prinsengracht sold the building without their knowledge in February 1943 to a member of the NSB. The new owner, a man named Pieron, arrived at the offices one day to inspect the property, and Kleiman had to stall his interest in the annexe by pretending he had lost the key to the communicating door. Anne mentions the incident in her diary, but does not record whether or not Pieron questioned Kleiman further.

Shortly after Pieron bought the building, a new head warehouseman was hired to take over from Bep's father, Johan Voskuijl, whose cancer now prevented him from working. Wilhelm van Maaren, born in Amsterdam on 10 August 1895, was married with three children. By the time he began working at the Prinsengracht warehouses, he had a trail of failed business ventures behind him and was regarded by many as untrustworthy. Throughout the war, he also harboured a fugitive in his home: his son was avoiding deportation to a German labour camp. Soon after his initial employment, van Maaren began asking pointed questions about the annexe, and about Otto. He set small traps in the warehouse, such as potato meal scattered on the floor to show footprints. When Kugler and Kleiman asked him what he was doing, he replied that he wanted to catch whoever had been thieving from the stores. One of his two assistants in the warehouse, J. de Kok, later admitted to selling these goods – which van Maaren himself had stolen. The people in hiding were frightened of van Maaren (Anne refers to him several times in her diary), and the helpers were equally wary of him. He was the first person they suspected of betraying them. Certainly van Maaren passed on his suspicions about what was happening in the annexe to his assistants, but he was not the only one who had heard the rumour that there were Jews hiding there.

In his letter to the Dutch authorities about the betrayal in 1945, Kleiman writes, 'Our accountant van Erp visited a homoeopath (Dr Bangert) after the raid and told him that a number of Jews were arrested at one of his business relations (van Erp), without telling Dr Bangert the name or address.

Dr Bangert then asked van Erp whether this case concerned the premises at Prinsengracht 263. Full of surprise, van Erp had to assent to this and when he asked how Dr Bangert knew this, Dr Bangert replied that he already knew a year ago that Jews were hidden at that address.' Who told Dr Bangert about the annexe? Van Maaren's wife was a patient of his, but had only begun consulting him after the arrest. Unfortunately, this was one of several leads that the police failed to follow up, but clearly, people had their suspicions and were talking about them.*

* In *Anne Frank: The Biography* (New York: Henry Holt, 1998), the author, Melissa Muller, claims that Lena van Bladeren-Hartog, who apparently cleaned the offices at 263 Prinsengracht around the time of the arrest, betrayed the eight fugitives. In July 1944, Lena told another woman, Anna Genot, that she had heard the rumour that there were Jews in hiding where she worked. Lena later insisted she had said this after the arrest. Anna Genot's husband told Kleiman about the conversation and, during the first investigation into the betrayal, Kleiman brought the matter to the attention of the police. Curiously, he did not appear to consider Lena a suspect; rather, he wanted to know who had told her about the hidden Jews. Muller claims that Lena also confronted Bep Voskuijl with the rumour about the hidden Jews, adding that she could 'no longer just sit by' and allow the situation to continue, if it were true. According to Muller, Bep told the other helpers about the conversation, yet incredibly, none of them thought to mention it to the police during either of the investigations, despite being asked specifically about the Hartogs. During the second investigation into the betrayal, Kugler wrote privately to Otto about the conversation between Lena and Anna Genot, but failed to proclaim another more urgent encounter Bep had with Lena. Similarly, there is no mention of Lena or her apparent threats in Miep Gies's autobiography.

Muller further asserts that on the morning of the arrest Lena's husband, Lammert Hartog, had pulled on his jacket and disappeared at 'the first opportunity'. This information she must have from Kleiman's letter to the Dutch authorities in 1945, for he writes that Hartog was panicked by the arrival of the Gestapo but explains this as being due to the fact that Hartog was avoiding a summons for labour in Germany and worked for Otto's company 'illegally'. Furthermore, Hartog could not have disappeared immediately, because one of the Dutch Nazis was stationed in the warehouse and when Otto left the building at gun-point, he recalled seeing both warehouse clerks standing by the front entrance, as did Kugler. In her published memoirs Miep Gies recalls Hartog working until the end of the day. According to Muller, Lena and her husband 'never went back to work at the building after the Jews' arrest', implying that the Hartogs did not return to work because they had some part in the betrayal. In fact, the head warehouseman van Maaren dismissed Hartog shortly after the arrest, in keeping with the perception of him acting then 'at times as if he were the head of the business'.

As to the motive(s): Muller claims that Lena was afraid that her husband would be in danger when the hiding place was discovered. Why then would she have blown the whistle when her husband – who was himself wanted by the Gestapo – was in the building? Surely it would have been wiser to do so when her husband was not there. Having no other income, Lammert Hartog needed his job in the warehouse, which Lena had obtained for him. Muller claims that Lena had a second motive in the betrayal: she had lost her only son in the German navy and wanted to revenge his death in some way. This too, seems highly improbable: any

The detectives in charge of the 1963/64 investigation into the betrayal confessed that they had no idea who had turned traitor against the Franks and their friends, but ended their report: 'After studying several files . . . it was discovered that two days before the arrest of the Frank family, two Jews were arrested, also at Prinsengracht, in the immediate surroundings of the annexe, after the two had been betrayed by the Jewish betrayers Branca Simons and Ans van Dijk who were executed after the war.'* Van Dijk worked for a man named Pieter Schaap, who led the arrest of Hendrik van Hoeve, the supplier of groceries to the eight in hiding. Among Schaap's colleagues were Herman Rouwendaal and Maarten Kuiper.

In the summer of 1944 everything began to go wrong for Tonny Ahlers. After a significant period of prosperity in 1943, suddenly he found himself in debt and in trouble on a number of counts. His criminal files give few clues as to how this occurred. What is clear is that Ahlers's businesses were floundering, and he was unable to pay his suppliers, or the various authorities to whom he owed money. He was desperate for sugar for a particular product he was making for the Wehrmacht; that summer and winter, a large supply of sugar went missing from the Prinsengracht warehouses. Van

---

parent knows that in losing a child, grief is the over-riding emotion, unless that child has been deliberately put to death. None of the people in hiding or their helpers could be blamed for the death of Lena's son in the Kriegsmarine. Muller apparently received this information from a relative of the Hartogs. Yet a careful check of the Dutch and German archives reveals a fact that renders the proposed motive untenable. Klaas Hartog, Lena's son, died in May 1945, nine months *after* the betrayal; more surprising still, it was not until 1952 that a comrade came forward to confirm it.

Regarding the Hartogs, Father John Neiman, a close and trusted friend not only of Otto Frank, but also of Miep Gies for many years (she flew to the United States especially for his ordination to the priesthood) has one final comment to add: 'I read Melissa Muller's book and the story that she had constructed around Lena van Bladeren-Hartog. Then in November 2000 I travelled to Amsterdam and stayed with Miep. I told her I had read the book by Melissa Muller. And then I asked, "Miep, was it Lena? Was it Lena who betrayed them?" And she looked straight at me and said, "No. It was not."'

In the ABC television dramatization *Anne Frank: The Whole Story* (2001), based on Muller's book, 'Lena' is actually depicted making the call to the Gestapo and is shown cleaning the Opekta office when Pfeffer, plainly wearing the yellow star, arrives to enter the hiding place. While the former is based on no firm evidence whatsoever, the latter is blatant invention. In reality, Pfeffer went into hiding in 1942, long before Lena van Bladeren-Hartog was employed at the offices. One American newspaper reported, 'ABC concedes that facts aren't everything.'

* One of Ans van Dijk's circle of friends was the woman who betrayed Otto's second wife, Fritzi Geiringer, and her family.

Maaren was blamed but maintained his innocence and later, when other goods were stolen and his home was searched, police found nothing. Perhaps Ahlers was the thief; certainly he had a record of petty thefts, robberies and break-ins behind him. Ahlers moved out of the house on Jan van Eyckstraat and into another in Amstelveen. He and his tenant, the Abwehr spy Herman Rouwendaal, had argued about rent, and Ahlers, although furious himself, feared that Rouwendaal would kill him. He told his neighbour, SD official Emil Rühl, about the argument and asked if the Gestapo could provide him with protection against the enraged spy. Shortly after the quarrel, Rouwendaal's wife was anonymously betrayed for anti-German behaviour and sent to a concentration camp.*

In early 1944, Ahlers delivered a business associate to the SD for possession of illegal wirelesses. The man was aware of Ahlers's sympathies with the Nazis, having seen 'documents that showed he was a confidential agent of the SD'. The man explained that, after his arrest, his son-in-law approached Ahlers for help: 'Ahlers then went to visit my wife and told her that he could do something, but only if he had fl.200 to bribe the SD with brandy. My wife gave him the money, but never heard from him again.' The man had known Ahlers for some time, but considered him to be 'a very dangerous person for that particular period of the occupation . . . he did not mind hanging somebody if it suited him'.

The summer of 1944 was thus a nightmare for Ahlers. He wanted money and he needed to prove himself again in the eyes of those whom he respected. His business concerns were sinking fast and by the end of the year he would be declared bankrupt (money was then high – fl.40 per Jewish head – for betrayals). He needed to demonstrate that he was worthy of the Gestapo's protection against Rouwendaal. He had moved from his luxury apartment in the centre of Nazi Amsterdam to another, plainer house in a quiet suburb. He still venerated his Nazi superiors, particularly Maarten Kuiper, but with the move and the loss of his business he was no longer able to back up the 'big talk' with which they had always associated him. The man over whom he had wielded such power, Otto Frank, was of no use to him now that his own companies were in the process of folding. Ahlers's post-war, vituperative letters disclose how he hated Otto Frank, as he hated all Jews. Those same letters reveal that Ahlers apparently knew where Otto and his family were hiding. After the war, Ahlers declared his motto was always: 'There are different ways that lead to one and the same goal.'

* Rouwendaal was sentenced to life imprisonment and died on 15 July 1964 in Gossel. His wife survived, but divorced her husband after the war.

Maarten Kuiper eventually took over Ahlers's old home on Jan van Eyck-straat. Kuiper, the SD detective with a penchant for hunting down Jews, who 'had a hand in hundreds of arrests' and received a premium for the betrayals he made of Jews in hiding, acting on tip-offs given to him by anonymous informants, colleagues and friends. Kuiper, who liked to attend the arrests of the Jews he betrayed. At this juncture, the words of Josef van Poppel, whom Ahlers attempted to deliver up to the Gestapo, echo through the years that have passed since then: 'With a lot of Jewish arrests, Ahlers was the instigator.'

Kuiper moved into Ahlers's old house on Jan van Eyckstraat on 3 August 1944.

On the sunlit morning of 4 August 1944, following a telephone call to Julius Dettman at the SD headquarters, the annexe was raided by the Gestapo and three members of the NSB. The assault was led by thirty-three year old SS Oberscharführer Karl Josef Silberbauer. Three of his accomplices were identified by Otto from photographs in 1945: Gezinus Gringhuis, then fifty-one years old and resident at Marathonweg, and Willem Grootendorst, born the same month and year as Otto Frank and resident at Corantijnstraat. Until now, the other man present at the arrest on the Prinsengracht has remained publicly anonymous, although in a letter to the Dutch authorities Kleiman queried why he was never investigated after the war in relation to their case, despite being identified by them. As Kugler explained to Otto privately years later, the man had been sentenced to death in 1947. His name was Maarten Kuiper.

Julius Dettman hung himself on 25 July 1945 before he could be questioned about the case, but both Silberbauer and his Gestapo chief, Willi Lages, were interrogated in 1964. Silberbauer and Lages contradicted each other frequently in their interviews, but agreed unequivocally on one aspect of the affair.

In Lages' words, because the denunciation was made directly to Julius Dettman and the police had gone straight to the hidden address, the call was not made anonymously at all, but 'came from somebody who was known by our organization ... the tip giver was known and in the past his information was always based on truth'.★

In the summer of 1945, Maarten Kuiper and Tonny Ahlers were arrested and convicted of betraying people to the SD.

★ Contrary to Melissa Muller's assertion in her biography of Anne Frank, the police records categorically show that it was not known whether the caller was German or Dutch and there is no evidence that it was a woman's voice on the telephone.

4. Unforgettable Marks on My Soul

Throughout 1942 and 1943, thousands of Jews in Amsterdam were arrested in mass raids and sent to Westerbork to await deportation to the east. A report from the German authorities in The Hague, dated 25 June 1943, reveals how successful the attempt to rid the Netherlands of its Jewish citizens had been:

Of those 140,000 *Volljuden* [Jews with two Jewish parents] originally registered with the police in the Netherlands, 100,000 Jews have now been removed from the body of the nation (the exact figure is 102,000). Of these, 72,000 have been deported to do labour in the east. An additional 10,000 have left the country in other ways (deportation to concentration camps in Germany proper, internment camps, resettlement in Theresienstadt, emigration, fleeing the country). Nearly 20,000 Jews are presently concentrated in the camps at Westerbork, Vught and Barneveld. Thus, within eleven months the Netherlands have been cleared of nearly three-quarters of the original number of Jews.

The last great increase of Jews to be deported was achieved on Sunday, 20 June 1943 by means of a second mammoth operation in Amsterdam. All of Amsterdam's city districts in the south, including the Transvaal district (approximately ⅓ of Amsterdam's total area), were sealed off, and security police together with general police searched apartment after apartment. The Jews found (except for mixed marriages, Jews of foreign nationality, those able to prove that they were not fully Jewish, and a few special cases) were prepared for departure and transported to Westerbork the same night. Although, in view of the hitherto obviously unsatisfactory results of ridding Amsterdam of Jews, the lot of them might have expected such an operation to occur again soon, success was this time secured because the preparations for this huge operation could be kept secret until the last moment. Despite many rumours, the Jewish lot was taken completely by surprise and is now depressed, one reason why only few Jews are presently showing their faces in public. There were no incidents. The Dutch population is thoroughly opposed to the deportations but outwardly displays for the most part an air of impassivity. Large numbers of people were angry because they could only leave the sealed off districts with difficulty. Jewish auxiliary police from Camp Westerbork were used to help with the carting off process.

In the course of the operation we also succeeded in catching and carting off the core of the former Jewish Council. Those Jews already in Westerbork, especially emigrants from Germany, reacted to this circumstance by gloating openly. They voiced their general regret, though, that the top echelon, in particular the Jews Asscher and Cohen and their retinue had not been brought in as well.

By this time the Jews have also been removed from all armament plants (except for those involved in diamond processing). The transfer of a portion of skilled workers to Camp Vught is in progress . . .

The telephone call to the Gestapo headquarters in Amsterdam was made early on the warm morning of 4 August 1944. It went straight through to Julius Dettman, telling him that there were Jews hiding in the back premises of an office building at 263 Prinsengracht. Dettman notified Abraham Kaper, head of IVB4, the unit assigned to picking up Jews, and told him to send several of his men straight to the address; he had just had a sure tip from a known informer. The details were not as precise as we have been led to believe – the betrayer knew that the Jews were in hiding at the Opekta offices, but he did not know exactly where, or how many of them there were. That did not trouble the Gestapo; it was rare enough to hear about hidden Jews and the informant was a trustworthy source.

In the summer of 1944, when it became known that the payment for hidden Jews had escalated, more betrayals were made:

People gave information to the police to settle old scores with those in hiding, or with those who helped them. Some made a lot of money . . . In the later years of the occupation, when all remaining Jews were in hiding and information from the population registers were effectively worthless, the local knowledge offered by these men [paid informers] was often of great value to the Germans, as was the information offered by the public.

Betrayals stemmed from many different drives: anti-Semitism, personal dislike, adherence to the Nazi doctrine. Of the 25,000 Jews who had gone into hiding, around 9,000 were caught, and more Jews were captured by the Dutch police than by Germans.

Who betrayed the eight in hiding at 263 Prinsengracht? The author believes that Maarten Kuiper probably made an internal call to Julius Dettman's direct line at the SD headquarters. Kuiper had betrayed hundreds of Jews in hiding and was well known to both Lages and Dettman for that reason. Whenever he could he attended the arrests of the Jews he had betrayed. But the person standing behind Kuiper, or whoever made the fatal telephone call, and the person who provided the information that there were Jews hiding at 263 Prinsengracht, was Tonny Ahlers. He had several incentives to deliver the Franks to their enemy: he needed money, he hated Jews, he had to prove himself to the Gestapo so that they would protect him against Rouwendaal, he may have wanted Otto Frank out of the way now that the tide of war was turning and, above all, he was vicious and spiteful enough to want to send people to their deaths.

But that was not the end of the affair, or the relationship between Otto and Ahlers. There were several twists and turns to come, all of which have remained secret; covered up out of Ahlers's desperation, Otto's confusion, and an inability on the part of the post-war authorities to approach the circumstances of 4 August 1944 with an open mind.

Asked about his arrest during an interview on French television in the 1960s, Otto said softly, 'When the Gestapo came in with their guns, that was the end of everything.' Unlike the dramatized versions of the events of that morning, the episode occurred without histrionics from either the per-secutors or their victims.

The Gestapo and the NSB moved quietly through the building, giving orders to Miep, Bep and Kleiman to remain seated, before compelling Kugler to reveal the secret door to the hiding place. Otto relived the moment when they reached him:

It was around ten-thirty. I was upstairs by the van Pelses in Peter's room and I was helping him with his schoolwork, I didn't hear anything. And when I did hear something I didn't pay any attention to it. Peter had just finished an English dictation and I had just said, 'But, Peter, in English double is spelled with only one b!' I was showing him the mistake in dictation when suddenly someone came running up the stairs. The stairs were squeaking. I stood up, because it was still early in the morning and everyone was supposed to be quiet – then the door opened and a man was standing right in front of us with a gun in his hand and it was pointed at us. The man was in plain clothes. Peter and I put up our hands. The man made us walk in front of him and ordered us to go downstairs, and he walked behind us with the pistol. Downstairs everyone was gathered. My wife, the children, the van Pelses stood there with their hands in the air. Then Pfeffer came in, and behind him were still more strangers. In the middle of the room there was someone from the Grüne Polizei [Silberbauer]. He was studying our faces. They then asked us where we kept our valuables. I pointed to the closet by the wall, where I had stored a small wooden chest. The man from the Grüne Polizei took the box, looked all around him and grabbed Otto's briefcase. He turned it upside down and shook everything inside it out; there were papers lying all over the wooden floor – notebooks and loose pages. He proceeded to put all the valuable things in the briefcase and shut it. Then he said: 'Get ready. Everyone must be back here in five minutes.' The van Pelses went upstairs to get their knapsacks, Anne and Pfeffer went to their room, and I took my knapsack which was hanging on the wall. Suddenly the man from the Grüne Polizei was standing fixated by my wife's bed, staring at a locker that was between the bed and the window and he said loudly, 'Where did you get this?' He was referring to a grey footlocker with metal strips, like all of us had during World War I, and on the lid was written: Reserve Lieutenant Otto Frank. I answered: 'It belongs to me.' 'What do you mean?' 'I was an officer.' That really confused him. He stared at me and asked, 'Why didn't you come forward?' I bit my lip. 'They certainly would have taken that into consideration, man. You would have been sent to Theresienstadt.' I was silent. I just looked at him. Then he said, 'Take your time . . .'

Theresienstadt, a so-called privileged camp for Jewish war veterans and the elderly, was no less lethal for its inmates than the other camps; the Nazis merely used it as a showcase for public relations purposes. As for Anne's diary, which lay scattered on the floor, Otto remembered that Anne did not even glance at it. 'Perhaps she had a premonition that all was lost now.'

An hour later, the fugitives were taken from their hiding place to the offices below, where Kugler and Kleiman were waiting to be examined by Silberbauer. Bep had managed to escape, while Miep sat alone in the front office, having alerted Jan to the danger and taken the keys to the building from Kleiman. Silberbauer had already questioned her aggressively, but decided not to arrest her after discovering that she, like him, was originally from Vienna. However, after hurling questions at Kleiman and Kugler, and receiving the singular answer that there was nothing they wished to say, Silberbauer announced that they were also under arrest. The ten prisoners were led down the staircase and out into the street, where a closed police van was parked in front of the warehouse doors. They climbed in and the doors banged shut behind them.

The journey away from the Prinsengracht took place in silence. It was midday, and in Amsterdam-Zuid the sun glimmered through the trees lining the Euterpestraat. In the past, children would have been spilling out into the playground of the school at the end of Jan van Eyckstraat, but the requisitioned building was silent. In contrast, the SD headquarters at Euterpestraat 99 seethed with activity; German officials and Dutch Nazis gathered on the steps, the street and the courtyard at the back. The black and white SS flag snapped on its tall pole above them. Inside, the former school was even busier as reports were filed, phone calls were made and taken, meetings held, lunches eaten, and in the cellars, prisoners were interrogated and tortured.

The new arrivals from the Prinsengracht were shown into a room and locked up. As they sat there in numb shock, Otto tried to apologize to Kleiman for the situation, but his friend interrupted him, 'Don't give it another thought. If it was up to me, I wouldn't have done it any differently.' Later Kleiman and Kugler were removed from the room. Kugler recalled, 'At a distance, in the corridor outside Silberbauer's office, we saw the Franks, the van Pelses and Pfeffer. All eight looked serious and troubled, not knowing what the future would bring. We waved to each other and that was goodbye.'

After a quick interview, during which Otto stated quite honestly that he did not know where other Jews might be hiding, Silberbauer sent them to the basement cells for the night. The following day they were transferred to the prison on the Weteringschans and remained there for two days in filthy, overcrowded conditions. On 7 August they were taken as part of a large group of people to Centraal Station. The sun shone brightly again, but over the platform hung a heavy, fearful silence as the agitated prisoners waited for the train. Amongst the crowd were two sisters, Lin and Janny Brilleslijper, whose resistance activities had resulted in their arrests and removal from their husbands and children.* Janny noticed the Franks instantly: 'A very worried father and a nervous mother and two children wearing sports-type clothes and backpacks.' She did not speak to them then because no one was talking: 'The houses of the city were bathed in gold and all these people had a sort of silent melancholy about them.'

The train to Westerbork was not composed of the dreaded cattle cars, but was a normal train, albeit with bolted doors. In an interview, Otto described their mood as surprisingly hopeful:

We were together again, and had been given a little food for the journey. We knew where we were bound, but in spite of that it was almost as if we were once more going travelling, or having an outing, and we were actually cheerful. Cheerful, at least, when I compare this journey with our next. In our hearts, of course, we were already anticipating the possibility that we might not remain in Westerbork to the end. We knew about deportation to Poland, after all. And we also knew what was happening in Auschwitz, Treblinka and Madjanek. But then, were not the Russians already deep in Poland? The war was so far advanced that we could begin to place a little hope in luck. As we rode toward Westerbork we were hoping that our luck would hold.

---

* Brilleslijper was their maiden name. To avoid confusion, I have used that name throughout.

It was late afternoon when they disembarked in Westerbork, eighty miles from Amsterdam. The flatness of the land, which was like a great plain, caused the summer winds to drive sand and dirt into every eye, every crevice. Flies settled on everything, and especially on the very young children and the babies. In the winter the area became a swamp under rainfall. Within the barbed-wire perimeter fence were over a hundred barracks, each containing wooden bunks, and although there was electricity, the lights seldom worked. At night men and women were housed separately, but could meet during the day at work. Like other detention camps, it was a city within itself, offering inmates the possibility of gardening, sports and theatre before they were shipped off to 'the undiscovered country'. The commandant, Albert Gemmeker, lived in a house with a chicken farm attached at the edge of the camp and could be benevolent to the people in his charge, but not to the extent of stopping the transports. Life in the camp revolved around the schedule of the departures. Everyone tried to avoid the trains by any means available, but few succeeded.

As Otto queued with his family at the registration desks in the main square, Vera Cohn, who took down their details, was struck by his bearing:

Mr Frank was a pleasant looking man, courteous and cultured. He stood before me tall and erect. He answered my routine questions quietly . . . None of the Franks showed any signs of despair over their plight. Their composure, as they grouped around my typing desk in the receiving room, was one of quiet dignity. However bitter and fearful the emotions that welled in him, Mr Frank refused to compromise his dignity as a person. His wife and daughters, as though taking a cue from him, acted precisely the same.

Rootje de Winter had also noticed the family. She and her husband Manuel and daughter Judith had been in the camp for a month, having been denounced in their hiding place by a Nazi spy. She pointed out Anne to Judith, hoping that the two of them could become acquainted. Judith recalls,

The new transport from Amsterdam came rolling in and we watched the people getting down from the train. There among them was Otto, and beside him, Anne. My mother wanted me to go over to her and make friends because we were about the same age. And I did speak to Anne, and to Margot, but I did not want to become real friends. That was a form of self-preservation which I had learnt – you never knew what was coming next.

After a visit to the quarantine barracks, where an employee of Lippmann, Rosenthal & Co divested them of any remaining possessions, the Franks and their friends were told that because they had been in hiding they were assigned to the Punishment Block, No. 67. Their freedom would be limited further even than the other inmates, they had to wear a uniform and clogs instead of their own clothes and shoes, the men had their heads shaved, the women's hair was shorn painfully short, and their rations were lower than the rest while their work was harder. Unpaid employment began at 5 a.m. in Westerbork's Industrial Department, where they had to chop up old batteries, then sort the tar, the metal caps and the carbon bars into baskets. It was dirty work, as Rootje confirmed: 'We looked like coalminers.' Otto wanted to find something else for Anne to do, and approached Rachel van Amerongen-Frankfoorder, a former resistance fighter who was housed in the Punishment Compound but cleaned toilets and handed out clothes to new arrivals. She remembers, 'Otto Frank came up to me with Anne and asked if Anne could help me. Anne was very nice and also asked me if she could help me.' The decision was not Rachel's to make, but she saw how desperate Otto was to save Anne from the battery shed: 'That's the reason he came to me with Anne – not with his wife and not with Margot. I think that Anne was the apple of his eye. Otto Frank was an especially nice and friendly man. You sensed that he had known better times.'

Through their work, the Franks met other families who had experiences similar to theirs. Lenie de Jong-van Naarden and her husband Philip de Jong had also been in hiding and ended up in Westerbork where, Lenie remembers, 'My husband quickly made contact with Otto Frank and got along with him very well. They had profound conversations and we had a very good relationship with Mrs Frank, whom I always addressed as Mrs Frank. I never called her by her first name; she was really a very special woman. I had less difficulty saying "Otto". She worried a lot about her children.'

Edith and Anne had left their differences behind them when the annexe was raided, everyone without exception remembers them – together with Margot – clinging to each other in the camps. Another woman who met the family, Ronnie Goldstein-van Cleef, found the Franks often 'pretty depressed. They had had the feeling that nothing could happen to them. They were very close to each other. They always walked together.' Edith was sometimes accompanied on her way to work by Lin Brilleslijper, who recalled, 'We spoke much about Jewish art, in which she was very interested. She was a friendly, intelligent person of warm feelings, from a middle-class, German–Jewish family. Her open character, her warm-heartedness and her goodness attracted me very much.' To others, Edith spoke little; Rootje described her as being almost mute while Otto 'was quiet . . . but it was a reassuring quietness that helped Anne and helped the rest of us too. He lived in the men's barracks, but once, when Anne was sick, he came over to visit her every evening and would stand beside her bed for hours, telling her stories.' She remembered Anne comforting a young Orthodox Jewish boy in the same manner. Rootje's daughter Judith retains only one clear memory of Otto at that time: 'I was lying on my bunk in Westerbork below Anne's bunk. She was sitting up in bed and talking to Otto. They talked on and on. I wanted to go out, and jumped up and tore my finger on a nail that was sticking out from the wood. I still have the scar, it's very clear.'

Sal de Liema remembers meeting Otto in the Industrial Department while they were 'knocking the black stuff out of batteries . . . We were sitting on top of a huge pile of old batteries and we were working there. Otto Frank was there too and the whole family.' Sal and his wife Rose went into hiding in early 1942, moving from place to place until they were caught on 5 August 1944. In Westerbork, Sal slept in the same barracks as Otto and they became close friends: 'I was with [Otto] all the time, all the time we were together, we clicked together. We had nothing . . . And that's why we held on to each other . . . We really didn't know in the morning if we would live at night.' Rose de Liema reflects on how they tried to keep up their spirits: 'We had long discussions about our experiences. But mainly we tried to encourage each other and hope that the war would soon be over. If we could only hold out long enough. While in hiding we always listened in secret to the English radio and we knew that the invasion had been a success. But every day we feared transportation to an extermination camp.'

In a speech recorded for schoolchildren many years later, Otto fleetingly recalled his time in Westerbork: 'Conditions were not too bad as the people in charge and the guards were Dutch, of course. The men and the women were living in separate barracks. We could meet in the evening after work . . . At this time the Allied armies advanced steadily and so we hoped that we would not be deported to the concentration camps in Poland. But fate had decided differently . . .' On the balmy evening of 2 September 1944 the announcement was made for the following day's transportation from Westerbork. There were 1,019 people named on the list. Among them were Otto, his family, the van Pelses and Pfeffer. It was to be the final deportation to the east.

That night the camp was in uproar. Janny Brilleslijper recalls, 'Everyone was running around. I knew that Otto Frank went all over the place. He had the illusion he could go to Theresienstadt.' Otto's exertions were in vain. The 498 women, 442 men and 79 children listed – Otto and his family included – would be deported the very next day. It was agony for everyone, but the anguish was even worse for parents, helpless to protect their children from the unimaginable future. Author Primo Levi gave an account of the night before his transportation to Auschwitz, turning his attention in particular to the mothers, like Edith Frank, who were already almost demented by their inability to prevent their children being led to their murders:

All took leave from life in the manner which most suited them. Some praying, some deliberately drunk, others lustfully intoxicated for the last time. But the mothers stayed up to prepare the food for the journey with tender care, and washed their children and packed their luggage; and at dawn the barbed wire was full of children's washing hung out in the wind to dry. Nor did they forget the diapers, the toys, the cushions and the hundred other small things which mothers remember and which children always need. Would you not do the same? If you and your child were going to be killed tomorrow, would you not give him to eat today?

For three days and two nights, the nightmare train carrying the Westerbork passengers travelled through the Netherlands, Germany and Poland. This time they were in sealed cattle cars, apart from the odd gap in the wood or a missing plank, without light or sanitation and with hardly any food or water. Through the day, before they reached Poland, the carriages were unbearably hot; after passing the Polish border, especially at night, they rocked endlessly in a bitter wind. There were many casualties on board the train, but no opportunity to move the corpses from where they lay on the straw-covered floor. The stink of death and bodily waste could not be extinguished.

   Otto and his family sat squeezed into a carriage of more than sixty people with the van Pelses, Pfeffer, the de Winters, Ronnie Goldstein-van Cleef, Lenie and Philip de Jong, and the Brilleslijper sisters. Before they left the Netherlands, an incident occurred that shook them all even further. Lin remembered,

The train stopped. Six prisoners had sawn a hole in the floor of their truck, and dropped out on to the tracks from the moving train. One was killed but five managed to save their lives, though one man lost a hand and a girl lost both hands. They still live today; they were helped to safety by the Dutch. The others who had been in the escape truck were crushed into our truck. We could scarcely sit, and the smell was terrible.

When the train stopped at a siding, Rootje recalled, they were unable to shout to ask anyone where they were, 'because SS guards were patrolling up and down outside the train'. They all felt, instinctively, that they were headed for Auschwitz and the edge of the world. Otto left no record of the journey, except to remark that 'each of us tried to be as courageous as possible and not to let our heads drop'. Primo Levi, however, wrote of his own deportation to Poland: 'We felt ourselves by now "on the other side". There was a long halt in open country. The train started up with extreme slowness, and the convoy stopped for the last time, in the dead of night, in the middle of a dark and silent plain.'

When the Westerbork train eventually reached 'the other side' and stood there, the steam hissing from it, sounds began to penetrate the silence. From beyond the darkness came shouts, screams, the creaking of machinery and the sharp howling of dogs. Red and white lights illuminated the track on either side of the train.

Rose de Liema recalls with unending horror the moment when the doors were dragged apart: 'We stumbled out and I had the feeling I had arrived in hell. It was night, chimneys were burning with huge bright flames. The SS beat everybody with sticks and guns.

'Then the selection started.'

Historians cannot agree on the exact number of people who were killed at Auschwitz because the relevant records were destroyed by the SS, but the majority of the victims were Jews. The camp was 'a world unlike any other because it was created and governed according to the principles of absolute evil. Its only function was death.'

In spring 1940 SS Reichsführer Heinrich Himmler placed Rudolf Höss in charge of building a large camp from the remains of an old army barracks in the industrial Polish village of Oświęcim. Himmler called Höss into a secret meeting in summer 1941, the purpose of which was to brief him on the Final Solution and to impart the news that 'Auschwitz would serve as the centre of destruction'. Before the meeting was over, Himmler explained that 'Every Jew that we can lay our hands on is to be destroyed now . . .' On 12 May 1942 the first transportation of Jews was killed upon arrival in the gas chamber of the camp, which had now been named Auschwitz.

There were continued extensions to the camp, and by the end of its life it had been transformed from a large area of uninhabited, marshy ground into a prison empire of twenty-five square miles of barracks, gas chambers, crematoria, sub-camps and factories. The satellite camps numbered thirty-eight, and the complex boasted a soccer stadium, library, photographic lab, a symphony orchestra and a brothel known as 'the puff'. Most gassings took place in Birkenau, where the majority of female prisoners were housed. Two thousand armed guards kept discipline in the camp (compared to the 200 German soldiers in Amsterdam), while 800 Jews, given the collective name of Sonderkommando, toiled to guarantee the smooth working of the gas chambers. Every three months the Sonderkommando were sent to the chambers themselves. The cost of killing one person in Auschwitz was 0.25 marks.

Many trains arriving at the camp did so by night, a deliberate means of adding to the prisoners' disorientation. Once the men and women had been separated, a selection determined who would be put to work and who would be gassed before sunrise. It was a rare thing indeed for people aged over fifty, babies, children under fifteen years of age, mothers who refused to be parted from their children, the sick and the disabled to be spared instant death. In his early days as camp commandant, Höss stood outside a gas chamber to learn how the process unfolded when the doors had been secured:

Those who were standing nearest to the induction vents were killed at once. It can be said that about one third died straightaway. The remainder staggered about and began to scream and struggle for air. The screaming, however, soon changed to the death rattle and in a few minutes all lay still . . . The door was opened half an hour after the induction of the gas, and the ventilation switched on . . . The special detachment now set about removing the gold teeth and cutting the hair from the women. After this, the bodies were taken up by elevator and laid in front of the ovens, which had meanwhile been stoked up. Depending on the size of the bodies, up to three corpses could be put into one oven at the same time. The time required for cremation . . . took twenty minutes.

A former member of the Sonderkommando, Sigmund Bendel, told a British military court about the next stage: 'One hour later, everything is back in order. The men remove the ashes from the pit and make a heap of them. The next convoy is delivered to Crematorium IV.'

After a short break from his work, Höss returned to the camp in May 1944, delegating the actual running of Auschwitz to Richard Baer, and that of Birkenau to Josef Kramer. By the summer of 1944 the crematoria had been restored to prime condition and the railway track lengthened to within two hundred yards of the crematoria in preparation for the pinnacle of the Final Solution. Four hundred thousand Hungarian Jews arrived in the camp over a period of two months and the level of destruction (9,000 Hungarian

Jews were gassed in one day alone) was such that the crematoria could not cope. Nine mammoth pits were dug in the fields behind the building and the bodies were cremated there. The Nazis calculated that by placing a corpulent man alongside a woman or a child, the man's fat would run over his dead companions, making the thinner bodies burn faster and more easily. The sky was scorched red and black and the fires were visible from thirty miles away. On the night of 2 August, two days before Otto and his family were betrayed, an entire gypsy camp of 4,000 people were gassed.

As early as 1942 the governments of Britain and America had been informed that mass murder was taking place in Europe. In spring 1942 two men who had managed the miracle of escaping from Auschwitz drafted a report on the gassings in the camp. Their sixty-page summary was read in the White House and the Vatican and reached the Red Cross, as well as Jewish community leaders in Budapest. On 4 April 1944 'US reconnaissance planes flying over Auschwitz took some remarkably clear photographs that show all the essential evidence – the gas chambers and crematoria, the prisoners standing in line – yet even the experts trained to interpret such photographic evidence apparently saw nothing here but a large prison camp . . .' By July 1944 the Allied armies were in a position to obliterate Auschwitz, and Churchill wrote to Anthony Eden that same month about the Final Solution: 'There is no doubt that this is probably the greatest and most horrible single crime ever committed in the whole history of the world.' But the Allies did nothing and the gassings went on all summer.

As the men and women of the Westerbork transportation were separated, Otto turned for a last glimpse of his family over the heads of the terrified crowd. He saw Margot, and later told his surviving relatives, 'I shall remember the look in Margot's eyes all my life.'

Five hundred and fifty-nine people, including every child under fifteen, were sent from the searchlight-strafed platform to the enveloping blackness of the gas chamber. Judith de Winter was able to speak to her father as they left the train: 'Despite all the confusion, I saw that my father was apprehensive and very dispirited, so I told him, "Come on, we have to fight this. Don't lose hope." But he already had. We were parted and minutes later he was amongst those selected for the gas chamber. I didn't see it, but found out much later, actually only a couple of years ago. He was fifty-five years old.'

Otto Frank was the same age as Manuel de Winter, but he escaped the selection. His bearing and determined spirit saved him, so people who knew him assert. Together with Fritz Pfeffer, Hermann and Peter van Pels, he was among two hundred and fifty-eight men who were permitted to live. His wife and daughters, and Gusti van Pels, disappeared into Birkenau with two hundred and twelve women who were also spared.

Otto and his fellow inmates were marched in rows to the main camp, Auschwitz I. It was a two-mile walk over unfamiliar terrain in darkness. Upon reaching Auschwitz, the men were herded into the quarantine barracks where they would spend the first six weeks of their camp life. They were stripped, shaved of all their hair, and despatched to the cold showers. Afterwards they were ordered into a square and given the striped prison uniform and wooden clogs. They were then tattooed with numbers ranging from B-9108 to B-9365. Otto was branded prisoner B-9174.

After the quarantine period, the men entered the regular camp and were assigned to their huts. Otto and his friends were allocated to Block II. The barracks were filthy, glacial, and filled with wooden bunks in narrow tiers of three. Several people had to sleep in the same bunk on mattresses made of straw but turned to pulp by bodily fluids. Since there was no sanitation except out of doors, the floors swam underfoot. As the Westerbork Häftlinge (new arrivals) tried to find places on the bunks, one of the senior men in the block approached Otto and his companions. They recognized him as Max Stoppelman, the son of Miep and Jan Gies's landlady in the Rivierenbuurt. Through Jan Gies, Stoppelman and his wife Stella had found refuge with a Dutch family but after only six months they were betrayed. Peter van Pels told Stoppelman that his mother was still alive; Miep had recently visited her in her hiding place outside Amsterdam. From then on, Stoppelman protected Peter and told them all how the camp functioned, although the rules fluctuated from day to day.

At 4.30 a.m. the following morning, the men of Block II were shouted out of their bunks for roll-call. Prisoners stood, often for hours, as each of them were counted. They were then assigned to work details. Otto, Hermann van Pels and Fritz Pfeffer were given one of the heaviest duties: digging ditches. Somehow, Peter was able to gain a better position, as Otto recalled: 'Peter was lucky to get a job at the post office in the camp which was established for the SS soldiers and the non-Jewish prisoners who got mail and parcels.' He received more rations than the others, but would hide whatever he could in his clothing to share amongst them later. Otto and his 'comrades', as he now referred to all the other prisoners with whom he was familiar, were given coarse, stale bread and a soup that bordered on inedible. Their diet resulted in 'scurvy and skin diseases, strange afflictions like noma, a gangrenous ulceration that creates gaping holes through the cheek, and phemphicus, whereby large areas of the skin become detached and the patient dies within days'. The rigidity of the routine and the overriding fear of execution was evident in their appearance: 'Facial transformations were so rapid among the prisoners that if a few days elapsed without their meeting, it was hard for them to recognize each other.' In addition to their mistreatment by Kapos or 'God Guards' who supervised their work, punishments were doled out as a matter of course. These were medieval in their cruelty: public floggings by chains, whips or clubs, fingernail extraction, and imprisonment in cells so small it was impossible to stand, lie or sit. Block 10 received prisoners who were chosen for medical experiments. Most of the records from the department were destroyed before the liberation, but one report shows ninety castrations in a single day. The rare prisoners who survived such tortures were sent to the gas chambers.

'The average life expectancy of a Jew who was not gassed on arrival was between six and seven weeks in Auschwitz.' The mortality rate amongst Dutch Jews (60,000 of whom were transported to Auschwitz) was high even by the camp's standards. Perhaps because they had been able to live their lives without interference from anti-Semites for so long, and because their existence in the Netherlands had been less harsh than the Jews of Eastern Europe, the Dutch Jews found adapting to camp life even harder than many of their co-religionists. Prisoners had to learn to take the most basic necessities – food, drink and sleep – where they could. They had to steal food or barter it ('organizing' in camp slang), and to be alert to everything around them. It also helped if they had faith of some kind, whether religious or emotional – for instance, a belief that there was someone who needed them to survive.

It was a tremendous benefit to speak German, since that was the language of the camps, twisted crudely by the SS and the Kapos:

The orders were bellowed in German, and if they were not carried out at once they were repeated in conjunction with a beating, and perhaps an explanation of the beating, because the shouting and the beating were parts of the same speech. Those who did not understand that speech were always the last, always too late, and too easily cheated and deceived. 'Language was the first cause of drowning in the camps.'

German, according to Primo Levi, was life. And prisoners like Otto Frank, who could understand not only the regular German but the 'old German of Prussian barracks' had a distinct advantage over many of their comrades. When asked personally how anyone was able to survive Auschwitz, Otto answered, 'You needed luck, optimism and moral strength, but even this did not help if one was starving from malnutrition or caught a disease.'

Hermann van Pels's luck ran out after a month in the camp. He injured his thumb while digging a trench, and appealed to his Kapo to be transferred to indoor work the next day. The Kapo agreed. The following day there was a selection amongst those men, and Hermann van Pels was condemned to the gas chamber. Otto never forgot watching him being led away: 'Peter van Pels and I saw a group of selected men. Among those men was Peter's father. The men were marched away. Two hours later, a lorry came by loaded with their clothing.'

Otto and his comrades tried to retain their belief that they would survive. Sal de Liema, who was in the same barracks, recalled, 'I saw [Otto] when we came out of the wagon. And then we walked to Auschwitz. To the stone barracks of Auschwitz I . . . We tried to like each other, to help each other mentally. We couldn't do anything for food or clothes. Mentally.' Yearning for his children, Otto asked de Liema to call him Papa, although he knew that his real father was hidden in the Netherlands. At first, de Liema refused, but Otto explained, 'I'm the type of man who needs this, I need somebody to be a Papa for.' The younger man finally agreed. He remembers Otto's soft-spoken strategy for staying alive: 'He said, "We should try and get away from these people because if you talk all the time about food and stuff, your brain is going to go, we should try to survive mentally" . . . The biggest problem was to save your brain. Don't think about every day. We talked about Beethoven and Schubert and opera. We would even sing, but we would not talk about food.' Otto's intelligent approach was vital to survival. At the Eichmann trial, the courtroom heard how, 'by way of conditioned reflexes, talk about food increased the production of acids in the stomach, and hence the appetite. It was essential to refrain from talk of food. When someone lost his self-control and started to talk about the food he would eat at home, that was the first sign of Muselmannization . . .'

To prevent themselves from joining those wretched prisoners who were labelled 'Muselmen' because they had lost all hope, Otto and his comrades would discuss art, music and literature. This sort of aesthetic experience was prevalent in the camps as a means of survival, giving the inmates a feeling of moral victory over their captors. The knowledge that the SS also took pleasure in arts and music made the prisoners react with revulsion and incomprehension. One performer in the men's orchestra at Auschwitz spoke of his bewilderment: 'Could people who love music to this extent, people who can cry when they hear it, be capable, at the same time, of committing so many atrocities on the rest of humanity?'

★

Autumn brought mist and rains to the vast open expanse of Auschwitz. As the Allies progressed through devastated Europe, Himmler ordered the gassings at Auschwitz to cease. A group of 1,700 Jews from Theresienstadt were the last to enter the gas chambers on 28 October 1944.

The following day there was a selection in the men's barracks for all those qualified as physicians to be transferred to Sachsenhausen camp in Germany. Fritz Pfeffer applied to leave, having obviously decided that his chances of survival were better there. Otto recalled that he and Pfeffer had grown closer during their time in Auschwitz: 'As long as we were together he discussed more frankly personal matters with me than he had done during the time of our hiding.' Pfeffer was one of sixty doctors who boarded the train that day and disappeared into the unknown again.

In November, Otto was sent to work indoors and was given the task of peeling potatoes. Joseph Spronz, whom Otto would later befriend, had the same duty for a while and outlines in his memoir of the camp exactly what the work entailed:

The first thing we had to do was to carry eighty cases full of potatoes to fill the kitchen preparation basin. The potatoes were of a kind destined for feeding animals; only the biggest ones were peeled, and the remainder thrown into the machine unpeeled. All these tasks were exceedingly tiring. Four weeks passed in this manner, but instead of becoming weaker, which we had expected from the heavy job, we had grown stronger, thanks to the turnips and other vegetables which we were eating from morning to evening together with some left-over bread. Of course, we only did so when unobserved by the SS. We felt we were living like princes. Also, our vitamin requirements were satisfied to a great extent.

The biggest drawbacks were the heavy beatings dealt out to inmates seen taking a break from carrying the cases, and the discovery of filching from the stock:

Those peeling the potatoes were searched three times a day, for fear they could take something . . . Those caught having something on them got a horrible beating and were put into the Commando 'Vollgas' where they had sewage jobs to do. All the same, many of us took the risk of smuggling food from the kitchen . . . The Kapos very often forced us to smuggle in food for them; in return, we were not beaten up on such occasions. Another popular method of 'organizing' was to barter with the potato-peelers to exchange potatoes for bread. If they took the risk of being hit, and smuggled out ten potatoes, they could get the equivalent of the daily ration of bread from other inhabitants of the camp.

One Kapo took a powerful dislike to Otto and beat him regularly. Otto's health began to fail, lessening his work rate which resulted in further attacks on him by the Kapo.

Otto also had a fight with another inmate. During an interview conducted with Otto's second wife in the 1980s, it emerged that when Otto returned after the war, he asked Miep to accompany him to a shoe shop on the Leidsestraat, whose owner he had known in Auschwitz. Otto said to Miep, 'I want to visit this man because I had a fight with him in the camp. I punched him in the face.' Miep was taken aback by this revelation; it was not the sort of thing she could imagine the Otto Frank she knew doing. Although worried about the possible repercussions a confrontation might bring, she went with Otto to see the man. When Otto entered the shop, the man recognized him instantly, and walked toward him. There was a brief moment of hesitation and then he and Otto embraced. When Miep asked about the incident later, Otto told her, 'In the camps, tempers could run high at times because of small, unimportant things.' Evidently, the man had done something Otto did not like, but after the war it was forgotten.*

Sometime in November 1944, Otto reached the limits of his endurance. Severely depressed, starving, and racked with diarrhoea, he was unable to lift himself from his bed. He remembered,

On a Sunday morning I could not get up, being exhausted from hard work and little food and having been beaten the day before by the Kapo . . . That had really affected me also in terms of my morale. I said, 'I can't get up,' and then my comrades, all Dutchmen of course, because I was the only German, but I was totally accepted by all the others, said to me, 'That's impossible – you must get up because otherwise you are lost.'

Someone sent for a doctor, who happened to be a Jewish man from Amsterdam. Otto recalled, 'This Dutch doctor came to my barracks. He said, "Get up and come tomorrow morning to the sick barracks and I'll speak to the German doctor and you will be saved." And this is what happened and through that I was saved.' Dr S. M. Kropveld, the doctor who admitted Otto to the hospital, remembered visiting Otto in the barracks and finding him

incredibly filthy and covered with lice. He said, 'Doctor, please help me,' and I went to a Jewish Czech colleague [not a German doctor, as Otto recalled], Fischer,

* Dienke Honduis, the interviewer, told this story to Fritzi, after having heard it from Miep. Fritzi knew nothing about it.

to ask him for advice. Fischer was a neurologist, an extraordinary man, and he was willing to admit Frank for psychological observation . . . Thus Frank was hospitalized and tucked away in a corner, where he still was when the Russians liberated him.

In the hospital (which Otto described as 'a so-called hospital. It was not treatment. It was really that you weren't hit and you had not to work and you had not to be outside'), Otto met Joseph Spronz, with whom he would enjoy a life-long friendship. Spronz had arrived in Auschwitz in June 1944, from his native city of Budapest. He had been sent to the hospital following an accident in the kitchens of the camp during which his hands had been badly burned. In the hospital he became close to a Hungarian doctor who kept him on to act as his assistant. While there, he formed a group who would recite poetry and liked to discuss cultural matters. This was how he and Otto met, as Spronz's second wife Franzi recalls:

My husband had a strong soul, and true, and he formed a circle in the hospital of people who, despite their illnesses or whatever had brought them there, were interested in music, literature and art. They each took turns to sing or speak about their love. One evening my husband was whistling Bach's St Matthew's Passion and Otto Frank appeared, walking slowly towards him, also whistling the tune. When it was over, Otto said, 'I know that you are Hungarian and I am not, but please, may I join you and your friends?' They invited him to sing or to talk and he stood up and recited Heinrich Heine's poem about losing his religion. And then their friendship began.

In his memoir of Auschwitz, Spronz outlines the schedule Otto encountered in the hospital, and makes clear that conditions, although improved, were very far removed from standard medical proceedings: 'The first thing done to those who were sent there was to rob them of their footwear, the very last one of the things brought from home. Furthermore the captives' garments, and all the small belongings secured with the utmost difficulties, were taken away . . . In the hospital we were allowed to retain only our night-shirts.' The actual design of the hospital was similar to the regular barracks: 'Their equipment did not differ from the rest: tri-level beds, outworn straw mattresses full of fleas. The floor was mostly made of planks, in some places of concrete. Washing contrivances were only on the ground floor as were the toilets.' The food was also no better:

In the hospital people got less food than the men who worked elsewhere; this was meant to be a deterrent; otherwise too many people would have schemed to get there . . . We had more leisure to feel how hungry we were, not to speak of our low morale, which was greater in the hospital; also we simply had more time to look into our innermost soul, and to become aware of how precarious the fate was of our dear ones . . . and how little hope our own present situation held out for us.

Fortunately for Otto, his admission to the hospital coincided with the dismantling of the gas chambers. Those who were already in the hospital wanted to stay there: 'We did our best to hold on in the hospital, as this had various advantages. The weather had turned cold, and the approaching winter foreshadowed great suffering.' As snow fell on Auschwitz that December, thousands of inmates died. In a letter written a few months later, Otto recounts a sorrowful memory of Christmas in Auschwitz: 'The last music I heard was at Christmas in the camp, when two comrades played violin and cello very nicely at the hospital.' He added, 'I know that they are dead now.'

In the early days of 1945, the dull boom of Russian artillery and the crackling of automatic rifles could be heard not far from Oświęcim. In mid January it was joined by the rumble of fleeing Wehrmacht vehicles on the roads. Aware of the Red Army approaching, the SS began to destroy parts of the colossal death factory that was Auschwitz. Gas chambers were blown up, crematoria dismantled and the mechanisms sent to the camps of Mauthausen and Gross-Rosen. Many of the barracks, electrified fences and guard towers at Birkenau were torn down. Clothes, spectacles, suitcases, jewellery and other personal effects brought into Auschwitz were despatched to Berlin. Documents and registers were set on fire in both Auschwitz I and Birkenau. Corpses from hastily dug mass graves were exhumed and burned in open pits. Despite, or perhaps because of, the threat to the end of their power the Germans persisted with the torture and murder of prisoners.

On 12 January the Russians made headway, training the forces at their disposal – over 1.5 million men, more than 3,000 tanks and 10,000 aircraft – on the inadequate German defences at Baranow. Somehow, the inmates in the hospital received the news, as Spronz recalled: 'When the German lines were pierced at Baranow, we grasped at once that this was to bring on the evacuation of the camp. Excitement was enormous.' On 16 January Russian planes attacked the Auschwitz area, destroying the kitchen and food depot in Birkenau. On 17 January units of the Red Army approached outlying areas of Kraków from the north and the north-west, surprising the German positions. The Germans had finalized their plans for the departure and had already decided what to do with the Auschwitz prisoners:

In the first days of January 1945, hard pressed by the Red Army, the Germans hastily evacuated the Silesian mining region. But whereas elsewhere, in analogous conditions, they had not hesitated to destroy the Lagers and their inhabitants by fire or arms, they acted differently in the district of Auschwitz: superior orders had been received (given personally, it would seem, by Hitler) to recover at all costs every man fit for work.

All prisoners in the regular barracks were to be evacuated on foot, while those in the hospital, like Otto, would be abandoned. As the fog obscured the roads around the camp, and snow continued to fall heavily, Auschwitz itself lay silent, 'finally exposed to imminent assault'.

The young man walked quickly through the snow in Auschwitz I Main Camp, keeping his head down. He had made the journey from his own barracks to the camp hospital almost every evening for two months, when the small group of friends with whom he had lived since his arrival in Auschwitz had become separated from each other. Peter van Pels, only nineteen, was the youngest amongst them. Otto later recalled: 'Peter acted like a son to help me. Every day he brought me extra food . . . He never could stay long. We never discussed serious matters and he never spoke about Anne. I had not the impression that he matured much.' Peter intended the night of 18 January 1945 to be his last visit to the hospital. He was leaving Auschwitz, and he hoped to persuade Otto to do the same.

Otto had heard at noon that day that the camp was to be evacuated. His friend Spronz recalled:

At midnight the SS roused physicians and nurses, and me as well. We were deeply disturbed by the order given us – to burn by hand the sick-cards of all personnel and patients then in the hospital. This might have meant the extermination of everybody who was unable to walk. It was very painful for both physicians and nurses to abandon the sick, yet we had to do it to prove our fitness.

Spronz then found Otto, and told him to stay in the hospital if he possibly could. Otto decided to take his advice, hiding in the toilets when he thought danger came too close. He later recalled the evening's events: 'It was twenty below zero. Peter came to me and said, "We leave." He was well fed and had a good position. He was young. He told me, "I am working with them. I'll make it." I said, "Peter, hide yourself. You can hide yourself here in the hospital upstairs or somewhere . . ."' Peter was too afraid of the conse-quences of discovery and felt that participation in the march was the lesser of two evils. He and Otto argued back and forth, and, finally, Peter left the hospital, alone. Otto shed tears for him: 'Peter was a very good boy, really a good-hearted boy. But he wasn't very intelligent.' He was convinced that Peter would not survive the march and knew that he would now be unable to realize his own hope of helping Peter to develop his potential in the future.* Outside the snow continued to fall.

Shortly after midnight, the first column of prisoners began marching away from Auschwitz. In Birkenau,

it was about ten degrees below zero when the SS began routing the ragged prisoners out on to the snow-covered fields and bullying them into the customary ranks of five. Even then, there were long delays, roll-calls, shouts and confusion. Several thousand prisoners in the camp hospital argued about whether to join the evacuation, and those who wanted to flee fought over the few pairs of wooden clogs that the authorities had left them in order to use for going to the latrines . . .

Groups left at intervals throughout the night and the following day. The women and children from Birkenau left first, then the men from the camp. Sometimes there would be only a hundred prisoners in a column, but there were also groups of over 2,000 people who set off on foot westwards towards the cities of Silesia. Upon reaching the railway stations, prisoners were pushed into open goods-wagons and sent on a journey lasting often more than a week, without food or water. The vast majority perished. The survivors 'threw the bodies of the frozen dead on to the railway track, and licked snow off the ledges of the wagons to ease their thirst and hunger. There were instances of cannibalism, when starving captives were driven to consume parts of their comrades who died.' The ones who were forced to cover the distance entirely on foot were beaten, shot and starved, and were offered little assistance from the ordinary German civilians who saw them.

At 1.00 a.m. on 19 January the last transportation of 2,500 prisoners waited by the Death Gate of Birkenau. Documents and clothing were still burning inside the camp. The lights on the main switchboard nearby the entrance gate were flicked out and darkness descended upon the camp. The group then marched down to Auschwitz I to await further orders. When they left, the whole area seemed deserted. Six thousand prisoners too sick to join the evacuation columns, among them Otto Frank, remained behind. Through the woods, fields and villages of Upper Silesia 58,000 former

* Peter was sent to Mauthausen; see Chapter Five for details.

inmates marched in appalling weather, often freezing to death, while far below, 'the grim and partly gutted ruins of Auschwitz lay abandoned in the snow'.

A few hours after the last evacuation column left the camp, Allied aircraft launched a substantial attack on the IG Farben factories in Dwory, very close to Auschwitz I. The heads of IG Farben – employers of slave labourers from the camps, and manufacturers of Zyklon B, the chemical used to kill thousands in the gas chambers – set fire to their archives. For Otto Frank and the 1,200 inmates of Auschwitz I, the Allied raid, though helpful to their morale, was a disaster in immediate, practical terms: it cut the water and electricity supplies to Oświeçim and, consequently, all the camps. It was like being trapped in a sunken ship: there was no light, food or drinking water, just starvation and thirst, and outside a perpetual black fog. The prison compound was buffeted by waves of rain and wind, while the sky above shook with bombs from the Soviet forces.

Otto recalled: 'After the Germans left, we were alone. People from the hospital, and quite a number. And then we found so much food, cellars of food belonging to the SS, but there was no water because everything was frozen and broken. There were lakes in the neighbourhood, though. So we went to break the ice and we made water [melted the ice] from the lakes.' Spronz recalled how they managed: 'Every patient who was able to move was busy carrying water to the kitchen. We drank only boiled water, but black coffee was freely available thanks to the stocks we'd found.' Inmates from Birkenau, where the SS had set fire to the 'Kanada' warehouses and shot two hundred women at random, also managed to salvage supplies from the main camp. Aside from this welcome find, the fog and the rain continued their chill, despondent grip and the rumour spread that the Russians were still only in the Zakopane mountains, far away from the haunted ramp of Birkenau.

It began to sleet heavily on 25 January. At two o'clock in the afternoon an unexpected detachment of the SD strode into Auschwitz I. Five days earlier, SS Sturmbannführer Franz Xavier Kraus, Head of the Auschwitz Liaison and Transition Offices, had received an order from SS Obergruppenführer Schmauser to liquidate every last prisoner in the camps of Birkenau and Auschwitz. Dozens of armed SS entered the hospital barracks, screaming at the patients and dragging them from their beds. Otto and his comrades were forced to their feet and marched down the camp street towards the main gate. Prisoners emerged from the decaying barracks, stumbling and falling as the SS punched and kicked them through a path of frozen snow. The SD yelled orders at the SS, who moved swiftly among the tottering, keeling prisoners, pushing them into line. German Reich prisoners formed the first rows, followed by the Aryans, then other Jews, and finally those inmates unable to stand were dropped into rows on the ground. Otto stood in the middle, knowing exactly 'why we were there. We knew we were finished.'

Spronz was also amongst the prisoners: 'The SD began to consult one another. We realized that an execution was to come, for leaving the camp in an organized way was out of the question. The Germans were playing with their hand grenades and machine-guns and we felt the bullets penetrating our bodies already. Those were moments of mortal anguish . . .'

The SD lined up before the prisoners in a single row, under the black iron gate bearing the maxim: '*Arbeit Macht Frei.*' The sleet turned to rain as they raised their machine-guns.

An officer stepped forward to give the order to fire.

Suddenly three loud, snapping explosions echoed in the air. The prisoners in the front row looked at each other in a daze; no one had been killed. There were two further explosions, clearly from outside the camp, and then an armoured car appeared from the main road carrying several SS men. One of them jumped out and addressed the officer in charge of the murder squad. The exchange was brief but plainly urgent. As they were talking, a small convoy of cars pulled up beside the main gate. The conversation between the two men ended and the officer motioned to the guards. They threw their guns over their shoulders and ran towards the vehicles.

'Return to barracks!' yelled the officer to the bewildered prisoners before climbing into the car nearest him.★ The guards no longer paid the inmates any attention and, within seconds, every vehicle was gone. The stunned prisoners, including Otto, began to walk back to the barracks, helping the lame along the windswept camp street. They discussed what they should do. Franzi Spronz recounts the story told to her by her husband:

The Germans had fled and were not coming back. They were cowards, every one. The prisoners began to talk amongst themselves and said, 'Well, my God, what do we do now?' During the confusion, Otto found my husband and said to him he was sure that the end must be close, no matter what, and he was determined to

---

★ None of the inmates had heard what the officer had been told: that the Red Army was encircling the area; they had just liberated Libiąž, less than 10 miles north-east of Auschwitz. Otto gave a full account of the terrifying incident in his interview with Arthur Unger and mentioned it in a letter to his mother. However he always dated the incident wrongly; it occurred on 25 January, not 26, as Otto remembered.

survive until the Russians arrived so that he could return home and be with his children again. My husband gave him his address and then they parted.

Liberation came quietly, two days later. There had been dog-fights in the sky at night over the camp and fighting near Oświęcim. The SS returned to Birkenau and dynamited Crematorium V at one o'clock on the morning of 26 January before leaving in armoured cars. In the early hours of 27 January Wehrmacht troops blew up the railway bridge over the human ash-filled Vistula and Sola rivers, and the wooden bridge over the Sola which had been built by prisoners from Auschwitz. At three o'clock in the afternoon as snow was once more beginning to fall, reconnaissance scouts from the First Ukrainian Front, wearing white capes, made their way out of the woods near Auschwitz and saw the barbed wire of the camp. As they advanced upon the gate, a group of German soldiers appeared. A fierce battle ensued, at the end of which the Germans had run off, leaving two Russian soldiers fatally injured. Elsewhere in the vicinity, two hundred and thirty-one Red Army soldiers died while fighting to liberate Auschwitz and its sub-camps. After removing a number of mines from the area, the Russians finally entered the compound of Auschwitz I.

When the soldiers entered the hospital, Otto Frank was too weak to stand up to greet them. His only memory of the event was of the Russians' 'snow-white coats. They were good people. We did not care if they were Communists or not. We were not concerned with politics, we were concerned about our liberation.'

The 60th Army of the 1st Ukrainian Front, under the command of General Pawel Kuroczkin, conducted a search of the camp. Lying about the grounds of Auschwitz I they found forty-eight corpses; at Birkenau there were over six hundred. All had died in the last few days. Of the millions who had passed through the gates, only 6,000 remained alive at the time of liberation. Less than one per cent of those admitted to the camp had survived. In the partially destroyed 'Kanada' warehouses, the Russians found 1,185,345 pieces of women's and men's clothing, 43,255 pairs of shoes, 13,694 carpets, 15,000 lbs of women's hair, and piles of toothbrushes, shaving brushes, artificial limbs and babies' clothing. A Polish officer reported that the survivors 'did not look like human beings; they are mere shadows'. The writer Primo Levi, formerly an inmate of Monowitz, arrived in Auschwitz I and found 'innumerable gloomy, square, grey stone edifices, three floors high, all identical; between them ran paved roads, straight and at right angles, as far as the eye could see. Everything was deserted, silent, flattened by the heavy sky, full of mud and rain and abandonment.'

On 28 January the thaw began, though it rained heavily on 29 January, by which time the entire main camp of Auschwitz I had been transformed into a massive temporary hospital. The sick were bathed by strong Russian nurses who 'laid them on the ground on wooden racks, then briskly soaped and rinsed them from head to foot . . . the Russians split the survivors into national groups . . . they gave out clean shirts and underwear . . . the infectious ward, Block 20, [became] a huge dormitory where a single doctor found himself in charge of eight hundred sick and dying patients.' There were no drugs or medical equipment, and few real doctors, yet the Russians did what they could, distributing rations and clothing from former SS stores, and separating the chronically sick from those more likely to survive. Otto fell into this latter category. He was given his own bunk in another barrack, inside a long room where single rows of beds in three tiers reached up to the low ceiling. The hut thronged with women: they were the mothers, daughters, sisters, cousins and friends who had walked over from Birkenau to search for their relatives and loved ones. Otto found the strength to ask every woman from Birkenau who entered the building about his wife and daughters. One of the teenage girls who spoke to him then was Eva Geiringer, a former neighbour from Merwedeplein. She describes their meeting:

I saw one face that looked vaguely familiar. He was middle-aged with hardly any face left at all, just a skeleton's skull out of which stared pale brown enquiring eyes. 'I know you,' I said in Dutch, almost sure in the back of my mind that I had seen him before. He stood up slowly and painfully, tall and dignified still, and bowed slightly to me.

Eva could not tell him what had happened to his children, and he was unable to give her news of her father and brother. They talked further, nonetheless: 'I sat on his bunk for a while and told him all the news that I could, and he thought it was a good idea that we [Eva and her mother] move into Auschwitz where the Russians had permanent headquarters and were going to look after the prisoners. I promised to come back and see him.'

Gradually the sick survivors began to recuperate and move about the camp. Eva recalls how the soldiers organized 'able-bodied people to help peel the vast mounds of potatoes which were tipped into heavy black cauldrons and made into potato and cabbage soup. It was the mainstay food for everybody, troops included. Large chunks of rough, coarse maize bread were distributed and there was now sufficient food to halt the symptoms of starvation.' Water could still only be had from the blocks of ice that were cut from nearby lakes and melted down. On Friday evenings Otto joined a group of his fellow inmates to celebrate the Sabbath. None of the men were religious but they found comfort in the small congregation.

It began to snow again but the long camp streets were still brisk with activity. More Russian soldiers appeared each day, either by truck or on horseback. On the outskirts of the main camp, Russian lorries blocked the roads. Eva remembers 'burly fur-clad, fur-capped Russians' who were busy repairing engines and cleaning guns. Everywhere in Auschwitz there was 'an air of activity, organization and permanence about the Russian presence . . . Russians had set up their headquarters and field kitchens and the military appeared to be in complete control . . . There seemed to be a small permanent band of soldiers who were coping with the problems of the abandoned concentration camp.'

Immediately after his liberation, Otto Frank began to keep a diary.* It is remarkable that this has remained unknown for so long, and it must be one of the very few diaries – if indeed there are any others – which details an Auschwitz survivor's journey, both spiritual and physical, from liberation until the moment of arrival home. Otto never spoke about its existence, but then he never spoke at length about anything connected with his incarceration in Auschwitz. He was apparently able to obtain the pocket-sized red notebook from the Russian soldiers, who handed out pens and paper to those hoping to be able to make contact with people they knew in the outside world. Although Otto was alive, and his mind was intact, it is evident from the diary that he was not functioning normally in those early days of liberation. Like a camera, he could only record what he saw; his emotions were kept at bay. His friend Joseph Spronz described his own paralysed state as 'a being without soul, nothing but flesh'. Otto's entries between 11 February and 23 February when they left the camp read starkly:

11.II.45: block 18 (kitchen).
14.II.45: Sal de Liema [reunion with his friend].
16.II.45: Russian cinema.
17.II.45: first stroll outside.
19.II.45: Auschwitz.
23.II.45: day of the Red Army.

* I am especially grateful to Yt Stoker for informing me about the diary, which is kept in the archives of the Anne Frank Stichting.

Later, the entries become much more descriptive, but Otto focused his attention for the time being on informing his family that he was alive. He wrote many letters, some of which are still in existence. The first was written on 23 February 1945, and was addressed to his mother and sister in neutral Switzerland:

> Dearest Mother,
>
> I hope that these lines get to you bringing you and all the ones I love the news that I have been saved by the Russians, that I am well, am full of good spirit, and being looked after well in every respect.
>
> Where Edith and the children are, I do not know. We have been apart since 5 September 1944. I merely heard that they had been transported to Germany. One has to be hopeful, to see them back well and healthy.
>
> Please tell my brothers-in-law [Julius and Walter] and my friends in Holland of my liberation. I long to see you all again and hope that this will be possible. If only you are all well. Indeed, when will I be able to receive news from you?
>
> All my love,
> greetings and kisses,
> Your son,
> Otto

He drafted a similar letter to his brother Robert and sister-in-law Lottie in England, telling them he was 'lucky to be saved by the Russians. I am well and in good spirits and well kept . . . Don't worry about me any more. I do about you all, but am confident just the same. How much I have to tell you since we met last.' Shortly after writing these lines, Otto and his comrades were told they were leaving the camp. Eva, Otto's visitor in the barrack, recalls:

During a night of the third week we heard the crack of gunfire near to the camp. Then the boom of artillery. The barrage continued throughout the night . . . When we went down next morning the street was full of agitated inmates and soldiers. We gradually realized that the Russians had suffered a severe onslaught from the Germans and had lost ground. Our mutual enemy was advancing towards us once more. We were terrified. Having been through all that suffering and survived, we knew that if they were ever to return they would take bitter revenge and murder us all in cold blood. Eventually, several Russian officers appeared and calmed us down. They indicated in broken German that they were going to move us back behind the lines to Katowitz which was in a safer zone. We had to be ready within the hour.

It did not take long for Otto to pack his possessions. They fitted into one small, striped cloth bag: a needle and thread, and some pieces of paper. He then walked on to the main camp square, where about one hundred and fifty men and women were standing around, talking nervously. A dozen trucks waited along the street. At a signal from the Russian soldiers everyone began climbing into the back of the vehicles. The seating was uncomfortable, but there was plenty of food and water. When the lorries were full, the engines started up, and they made their way out of the camp, driving slowly through the rain along the straight roads towards the main gate.

Less than one month earlier, Otto Frank had stood under that portal, waiting to be shot. Together with everyone else in the Russian-led evacuation, he watched silently as the black iron lettering faded into the mist.

PART TWO

Publish Without a Doubt
1945–1980

5. Everything is Like a Strange Dream

On 5 March 1945 the large, wide Russian trains carrying the Auschwitz survivors arrived in Katowice, the capital of Upper Silesia. On a scrap of card, the Polish Red Cross confirmed on that date that Otto Frank and two Dutch nationals from Camp Auschwitz would return to their own homes. The former inmates' accommodation in a large public building was unpleasant, although Otto noted in his diary that the local people were 'hospitable' to them. On 12 March he and his comrades were moved to the Ferdinand in the centre of town. It was one of several collection centres for concentration camp and slave labour camp survivors in the region. Although Poland was under Russian law, the atmosphere in the area was uncertain since the Russians were still fighting Hitler's armies in Hungary, Poland and eastern Germany. Everywhere was chaos and uncertainty; few resources could be spared for the survivors of the concentration camps.

The Poles with whom Otto came into contact were sympathetic towards him. In his diary on 13 March he names Zofia Kukulska of Katowice as being particularly kind. She and her husband invited him to eat with them on several occasions; Otto kept in touch with the Kukulskas for the rest of his life. His diary entries for the next few days are hard to decipher. On 15 March he wrote to his mother from the Katowice school that he was 'fit and well. We are here now and we are waiting for a transfer to Holland. I know nothing of Edith and the children. Presumably they have already departed for Germany. Do you think we'll see each other again fit and well? How I do demand everything and anything of you! It's a miracle that I'm still alive – I have had a lot of luck and should be grateful.' Another card written that day is straight to the point: 'We own nothing [any] more. I hope you are well when you read these lines. I will write more soon. Love, Otto.'

Two letters from 18 March give greater detail about his circumstances. The first is addressed to his cousin, Milly Stanfield:

> I hope that this letter may reach you giving you the news that I am living. It really is a wonder . . . We were liberated by the Russians on 27 January and it was lucky that at that time I was staying in the hospital, as this was left by the Germans intact. They tried to make me leave with them, but I managed

to escape and stayed; that was my chance. I do not know how many of my comrades, who had to retreat with them, are still living. I don't believe there are many.

Here we are waiting to be repatriated, but there is still war and we are far from home, Holland still being partly occupied. Of Edith and the children I know nothing . . . We were hiding for more than two years in Amsterdam and our friends cared for us, looking after our food and all our needs in spite of all dangers. Luckily I earned enough money in those years to pay our way, but now I am a beggar, having lost everything except life. Nothing of my household is left, not a photo, not a letter of my children, nothing, nothing, but I don't want to think what will happen later and if I shall be able to work again. There are as many in the same situation.

I long for you all and am so much better now, weighing 60kg [130lbs] again. How shall I find you all and all my old friends? I always was optimistic and I am still trying my best.

Milly received the letter in May 1945. It was her first direct communication from Otto, but she knew he was alive by then because Robert Frank had already informed her. The second letter was addressed to Otto's mother. He was contemplating how much information he should impart:

I still cannot decide whether to tell you more comprehensively of some of my experiences – the main thing is you know I am alive and well.

How the thought always torments me, that I have no idea how Edith and the children are, you no doubt understand. I do however hope to see all well again and I do not want to lose hope . . . We are being looked after satisfactorily and I will always think of the liberation by the Russians with gratitude. If I hadn't been in hospital due to a weak body – I weighed 52kg – I doubtless would no longer be alive. I have had a lot of luck and a lot of friends . . . One could never place a value on what our Amsterdam group of friends – Miep Gies, Kleiman, Kugler, Bep – have done to look after us in the hideout. Kleiman and Kugler were arrested with us by the Gestapo and were also taken to a concentration camp. The thought of this pursues me continually – I only hope that these people are now in the meantime free . . .

I can hardly imagine normal circumstances. I don't want to think about the future yet. Here I am a beggar and even look like one. I am still fresh in my mind and my body has recovered, mainly because we don't have to work here. I hope that I can send you further news and that I will hear from you.

On 19 March Otto was able to take his first decent bath, although a stringent disinfecting of his body followed it because of lice. According to the diary, on the same date he had a conversation in English with a Polish doctor (perhaps about his health) and was given 'two shirts, trousers, food'. The next day he was invited to eat at another Polish lady's house, where the main dish was potatoes. Then, on 22 March, he discovered what had happened to his wife.

In the Ferdinand school, Otto was sitting alone at a long table, lost in his thoughts, when a woman entered the room. He recognized her as Rootje de Winter, whom he had met in Westerbork. She was able to tell him that after arriving in Auschwitz on 5 September she and her daughter Judith had been placed in a barrack with Edith, Margot and Anne. On 27 October there was a selection in the block for the youngest and strongest to be transferred to a munitions factory in Czechoslovakia. Judith was taken; Rootje had not seen her since. Margot and Anne should have gone too, but Anne had scabies and was rejected. She was sent to the scabies block soon afterwards and Margot joined her there voluntarily. Edith, Ronnie Goldstein-van Cleef (whom they had met in Westerbork) and another woman whose daughter was also in the scabies block, smuggled food into them every day. On 30 October there was a mass selection in Birkenau. Those sent to the right would be gassed while those sent to the left would be transferred to another camp, although they did not know which. Anne and Margot were selected for the transport. Rootje and Edith were sent to the right. While they were waiting to be taken to the gas chambers, a woman entered the barracks and told them to run to another block. Together with a group of twenty women, they were able to escape the gas chamber.

Rootje told Otto what happened next. In her memoir of Auschwitz, she recounts:

Edith falls ill, has a high fever. I want her to go to the hospital. But there is a great fear of being gassed because every week Dr Mengele goes to the sick barracks to pick out those women who in his eyes are too emaciated to remain alive. Despite everything I bring Edith there. Her fever is higher than 106 degrees F and she is immediately admitted to the sick barrack.

Rootje also entered the sick barracks, but in another block. A few days later, 'New patients arrive. I recognize Edith. She comes from another sick barrack ward. She is but a mere shadow of herself. A few days later she dies, totally worn out.'

Rootje recalled Otto's reaction to the news of Edith's death: 'Mr Frank did not move when I told him. I looked into his face, but he had turned away. And then he made a movement. I no longer remember exactly what it was, but it seems to me he laid his head on the table.'

In his diary, Otto recorded the news numbly, while tormenting himself over his children: 'Mrs de Winter, Zutphen. Message of death of Edith on 6 January 1945 in the hospital, from weakness without suffering. Children Oct. to Sudentenland, very brave, especially Anne, miss special Anne.'

Otto wrote to his mother on 28 March, but was unable to continue

> because Edith's news from 6 January, which I now have, affects me so badly that I am not quite all with it . . . Edith died in hospital with weakness caused by malnutrition, her body could not hold out any longer. In reality she is another person murdered by the Germans. If she had managed to survive another two weeks, everything would have been different after the liberation by the Russians. I have to ask myself whether we can get to Holland, I do not know. I hope, however, that we can still get there, in spite of the fact that Holland is still not liberated. I do not wish to write any more today.

Otto and his comrades waited anxiously for a week as rumours that they were to be transported to Odessa grew, but failed to materialize. His health was still very poor and he was in pain from severe diarrhoea. At night they were locked into the school, but during the day and evening he ventured out, full of wonder at the spring weather and noting in his diary the catkin buds on the trees. He sold his sweater for 350 zolty and his socks for 100 zolty; he then bought bacon, eggs and beer.

On 31 March the train which would take them to Odessa arrived at last. Before leaving, Otto noted in his diary: 'Transport about to happen. Departure after dinner.' He then wrote briefly to his family in Switzerland in a slightly more positive mood: 'How often I think of you and long to see you all again. It may be possible that people here can travel on, but nobody can say when we will be back in Holland. Indeed it seems that the war is coming rapidly to an end. I am well and am standing up to things reasonably, in spite of the sad news of the death of my wife. I only hope to find my children back at home!'

Otto boarded the train the following day ('thirty-two persons per car on planks, and a heater'), but it was several hours before it began to move, and it made frequent, nonsensical stops, although this gave the survivors the opportunity to climb out and talk with each other, and to exchange information. He and sixteen-year-old Eva Geiringer met again during the journey. She recalls him

standing alone at one of the stops. He looked worn out and sad. Mutti [Eva's mother, Fritzi] was with me then and asked to be introduced to him. She knew he'd just heard from Rootje that his wife had died, and she felt great pity for him. I took her over and they exchanged polite words, but there was little to console him and he had no interest in anything. He seemed to want to keep himself apart and remain alone with his grief.

Otto recorded the journey, and their eventual arrival in Czernowitz, in his diary. His entries become more detailed, presumably as he began to take more interest in his surroundings. The diary reveals exactly how obsessed he and his comrades were with food. After months of starvation, Otto listed every bit of food he ate, unable to believe such luxuries as fresh chicken and beer were available to him at last. He enjoyed the landscape from the train, noting on the evening of 2 April that Tarnow was 'a little hilly, homes poor but neat, mostly wooden, no animals'. The train was slow to advance, delayed further by cargo trains approaching, and hardly moved at all at night. During the daytime, the passengers climbed down to trade with the farmers. Otto recorded swapping his shirt for a loaf of bread and a potato dumpling. On 5 April he wrote: 'Moving much more regularly. Villages/community houses with straw, much destroyed. Farmers with eggs, chicken and bread. We are on our way to Odessa, but have to return to Tarnopol, because our goal is Czernowitz. Villages in better state.' He noted with delight the 'black sheep, storks, some pigs', but was upset that the farmers at the next stop were not willing to trade with them.

On the evening of 6 April they arrived in Czernowitz. The following morning Otto climbed down from the train and stood in the rain for a while before walking three kilometres through the town to the barracks where they would be housed. He met a number of Jews who 'generously gave bread, eggs, money, liqueur, tea. An enormous reception from all sides, the people seemed to be very compassionate'. The barracks, although new, were cold, and the survivors had to sleep on the floor. What mattered to them most was the food, however, and that was good. Otto's health had suffered a relapse and he was barely fit enough to manage the ten minute walk to where he could receive something to eat, and hindered further since 'the streets are full of mud because of the rain. They claim that a few days ago it was the height of summer. My intestines are not okay yet, which depresses my mood. Late bath and disinfecting, afterwards in different building.'

The next day he was still sick and stayed indoors, but the following day he sold some tobacco to buy bilberries which he had been told would help his stomach. He then visited a market where the people continued to be compassionate. 'Invited by lady for tea and cake.' He must have felt physically better by then, for he and two of his comrades decided to get drunk on double vodkas and wine, which he recorded with satisfaction helped him to sleep. The next day he visited the very colourful market again, having refused a steam bath, and stood watching the 'farmers in old traditional clothes, lots of chickens, eggs, geese, apples, fowl being bought alive'. Later he ate a substantial meal of 'noodle soup, meat, fried potatoes, pudding with fruit sauce, and tea (was given 2 eggs). Treated two ladies to milk and pastries . . . Postcard to mother, girls did not accept payment.' The postcard to his mother read simply: 'On our onward journey we have landed here and now are hoping to be able to travel on to Amsterdam. I am well, and we are well looked after in all ways. I send my closest greetings to everyone.'

Otto's luck in meeting generous people continued, as did his enthusiasm for recording the food on offer, and his skill in bartering. On 12 April he wanted to find a synagogue, but could not. Instead he sat in a park for a while in the sun, then walked around an old villa before meeting a family who invited him into their home and cooked the eggs he had bought, as well as giving him 'butter, pastry, a chicken leg and eggs'. They asked him to visit them again, but despite being so far successful in leaving the collection centre when he should not have (by slipping under the fence while the guard's back was turned), he was unable to return on the day he had been invited. The weather had turned cold and windy, so he remained 'locked up' in the building, having signed himself in for the day.

On 17 April he watched the train being readied for travel, but was angry and hurt that his name was not on the list for transportation. He noted in his diary: 'All those born in Germany are not allowed to go along (about seventy). Big commotion about all the trouble to change this regulation. Discussed power of attorney with Konijn and Fonteyn and others.' The following day it snowed, but Otto sneaked into town to sell his blanket, and bought bread and apples. He was spotted, however: 'Was picked up by Russians and brought back to camp. It turns out well for me (rain in the evening and all night).'

On 21 April he noted excitedly: 'The weather has improved – sun! I was placed on the list, all of a sudden I am due to leave this afternoon. Delays: the train does not leave yet. The Russians say that Berlin has been taken. In full wagon, 54, did not sleep.' Berlin had not fallen though, and the train remained in the station until the following afternoon, when some people who had secreted themselves in the wagons were discovered. Otto wrote in his diary: 'Terrible for those people. I was almost among them. In the afternoon the train leaves, slow speed. Wagon without planks, no sleep, too many people.' Diphtheria broke out in one wagon and those who were able to move transferred to Otto's compartment. He had 'a very unpleasant night' due to the overcrowding and his diarrhoea.

Late in the evening of 24 April the train arrived at the Black Sea port of Odessa. The passengers remained in the train overnight, and were taken to their accommodation the following day. It was a five-kilometre walk to the collection centre and one of Otto's shoes split on the way. Around him, the landscape was ruined: 'Everything blown up. Mortar.' Otto and his comrades were bathed and deloused. He managed to buy eggs, meat and red wine and the next day noted that the weather was beautiful and the food good. Some Red Cross packages were distributed and lists drawn up for the imminent sailing. Otto was delighted by the food and items they had been given, sharing with one of his closest friends from Auschwitz 'butter, meat, cheese, jam, soap, egg, salmon, chocolate, tea, milk, oatmeal'. They were then sent to another barracks, which was less comfortable than the last.

On 2 May he wrote: 'Tomorrow morning the boat leaves! Exchanged white bread for cigarettes.' A moment later he was told that the transport had been cancelled: 'Pity. They say that Hitler is dead and Goebbels in the hands of the Russians. In the evening another thirty cigarettes and double chocolate on account of visit by Mrs Churchill.' His references to the Dutch royal family (his diary entry for 30 April included the line 'Birthday of Juliana') and the British prime minister's wife are interesting. He was also correct about Hitler, who had committed suicide in his Berlin bunker on 30 April. Berlin surrendered to the Red Army on 2 May. The official German capitulation followed on 8 May. In the Netherlands, the Germans had surrendered two days before.

On 4 May he wrote that he had acquired another shoe but was bored and unhappy about receiving less food than before. The entries for 7 and 8 May read: 'Ships to Naples, they negotiate with Moscow whether we can come along', and 'Lists for information to Red Cross with names. Entry Americans in Utrecht (bad weather). Impatience increases that we are not getting away yet. Lots of noise and shouting for joy during the night.' On 11 May they were moved to a sanatorium twelve miles away where they slept three people to one straw mattress. Otto walked over to a meadow to take in the amazing view of the Black Sea. He was angry that the French were being given preference to travel, but tried to take his mind off it by sitting on the beach in the sun. He noted there were 'no sea birds, almost no shells so also few fish and crabs'. There was also 'no talk about transportation yet. Everybody is impatient, in spite of daily chocolate and cigarettes.'

On 14 May the Auschwitz survivors were told to move to a house a kilometre away but Otto and some of his comrades returned in disgust to protest against the conditions there. In his diary Otto wrote about a 'sit-down strike. Remained in our room with about thirty men. Others moved.' They stayed in the room that night and the following morning were promised 'a tent if we are not satisfied with the home. Move. Very bad room. Bath and clean underwear. Wonderful weather. Rain at night.' The next day Otto and his comrades were angry again at their treatment: 'The sea is calm, see a ship now and then. The *Nijkerk* is in port, but little hope that we are allowed to go with them. Protest telegram to embassy because of discrimination of the Dutch people as opposed to the French.' On 19 May he wrote: 'They talk of transportation aboard an English warship. Tomorrow or the day after. The rumour is confirmed. Great joy, but also still mistrust.' A day later his fears were swept away: 'The boat has not arrived yet. Exchanged shoes. Cooked oatmeal and cocoa. Lay at the beach in the sun. Sword-lilies and tulips are in bloom. [Later] After the meal all of a sudden the order: pack. With the tram and luggage to the harbour area. After that walk for about three kilometres in the dark. In the harbour large boat about 18,000 tons (English). What a feeling!'

The *Monowai*, a New Zealand ship, had returned from Marseilles with repatriated Russian prisoners of war. The journey from Odessa to Marseilles with the concentration camp survivors would be the second of three trips of its kind. Otto and his male comrades were given hammocks below decks on which to sleep while the women were assigned to cabins. Also on board were French and Italian prisoners of war and a group of voluntary workers. The crew, in their neat uniforms, looked after their passengers well and were keen to see that they received nourishing food. Headwinds delayed their departure until the afternoon of 21 May. In the evening sun, Otto ate a meal on the deck, only to find the mattress he had been able to procure had been stolen. His hammock was comfortable enough, and on the morning of 22 May he woke up with hope for the future, buoyed by the beautiful weather and the extensive breakfast. He spent the afternoon 'in the sun on deck, passed Bosphorus towards half-past five. No war. Streets, minarets, old bastions on the hills, but see also barbed wire. Standing still. Dutch consul on board, worried. Cranes. Little traffic. Ferryboats. Rowboats.

Almost all men.' The view the following day was equally enticing: 'Many minarets and mosques. Asiatic side, mountains, Istanbul enlarged with suburbs. Everything visibly well taken care of. Lake. Eleven o'clock roll-call. Lunch: apricots with vanilla sauce. Sail mostly along south side. About five o'clock Dardanelles. Lice check. Calm sea!' On the evening of the 25 May they passed the volcano of Stromboli, which they could see smoking in the distance. The next day the weather was 'a bit stormy, but the boat is excellent. About three o'clock between Sardinia and Corsica. Strong surf, waves came all the way on deck with sunshine. Letters to mother and Robert.'

Otto's letter to his mother has survived. In it he expresses his longing for his children:

> Tomorrow we will be in Marseilles . . . We don't know yet whether we can return to Holland or if we'll have to spend a while in England. The main thing for me is that we've left Russia and with this have the possibility to be with our loved ones again . . . My entire hope lies with the children. I cling to the conviction that they are alive and that we'll be together again, but I'm not promising myself anything. We have all experienced too much to pin our hopes on that kind of thing. Only the children, *only the children* count. I hope continually to find out how they are . . . Perhaps there are people who have news of the girls . . . I'll have to stay in Holland, because I don't have any identification – apart from a number – and can only expect to be with you later on. The most important thing now is that we know we'll see each other again soon.
>
> All my best greetings and kisses.
>
> Love from your Otto.

On 27 May *Monowai* arrived in Marseilles. Otto noted in his diary:

About five o'clock French coast in view. About half-past seven anchor out. Landing at ten o'clock. Many large ships and large reception by the French with music. Dutch consul takes letters to mother and Robert with him. By car to station. Lots of forms, questions. Wine, sandwiches, Red Cross packages. Telegram to Basel. By car to restaurant. Warm food (cherries). Car-train to Paris eight o'clock. Joy and help everywhere.

Otto's telegram to his sister in Basel read: 'Arrivee bonne sante marseille partons Paris baisers – Otto Frank.' This caused confusion among his relatives when it arrived (it was the first of his many communications to reach them), for his mother assumed he meant that the whole family was together, and filled with joy and relief, she informed everyone that this was the case.

On 29 May the train arrived, amid torrential rain, in Lustin, where Otto was billeted for the night in a Displaced Persons Camp. He was given coffee and bread then gave his details to an official. His registration card has been preserved. Aside from his name and address, the notes read that he was fluent in Dutch, English, French, German, did not claim to be a prisoner of war and had almost six hundred French francs on his person. The following day, Otto boarded the train again after a breakfast of coffee and marmalade. At eleven o'clock, the engine started up. As they travelled through Belgium the weather improved and Otto watched the villages rush by, decorated with flags to welcome the Allied liberators. At night he and his comrades disembarked at 'very badly damaged' Roermond and waited through the night for another train. They travelled a short distance the following day, and then a few kilometres further the next, spending the night at a school in Arnhem where 'everything is destroyed'.

On 3 June 1945 Otto finally arrived in Amsterdam. He ended his diary: 'By car ten o'clock to Utrecht – Rotterdam – Amsterdam. At eight o'clock everything fine. With car to Miep. All healthy, Kugler, Kleiman and Lotte Pfeffer. What a joy to see each other again and how much grief! A load off my mind that all are here!'

Since 1943 the Dutch government-in-exile in London had been making preparations for the repatriation of Dutch citizens, estimating that there would be 600,000 returnees, 70,000 of whom would be Jewish. In a letter to his family in Switzerland, Otto hazarded a guess at how many would return: 'Of the 150,000 Jews in this country, I do not believe that there will be more than 20,000 left.' Otto's estimate of how many survivors there actually were is in line with the failure of most to comprehend the scale of the Holocaust. The actual number of Jews who returned to the Netherlands was 5,500. The Dutch government had decided to implement a policy of blanket treatment for all returnees, whatever their background or situation. There would be no special care for the Jews, who were expected to look for assistance from Jewish organizations in the Netherlands and abroad. Fearing an outbreak of disease and lice when the survivors returned, the government closed off as much of the country from the east as was possible.

Those who were kept in centres and camps for Displaced Persons were often housed in abysmal conditions and treated with abhorrence. General George S. Patton, controller of the DP camps in Bavaria, described the displaced persons in his custody as 'a sub-human species without any of the cultural or social refinements of our time'. The DPs returning to the Netherlands were housed anywhere and everywhere. A yard under a Vroom & Dreesman department store was officially home to a number of survivors for a while, but far worse even than this was the situation in which many DPs found themselves: billeted in former concentration camps alongside members of the NSB and the SS. This was more likely to be the case with German Jewish refugees hoping to return to their former homes in the Netherlands. The predicament arose through the Dutch government's repeal of the anti-Jewish laws on 17 September 1944. German Jews were henceforth classified as stateless people of German origin, and thus categorized as enemy nationals. Only those who could guarantee their solvency and assure the authorities that they had homes to which to return were permitted to re-enter the country normally. Others were arrested and imprisoned. A number of Jews returning from Germany and Poland were interned in Vilt Camp with former members of the SS and NSB, and forced to work, attend roll-calls and received beatings. Female survivors whose hair had not yet grown back were assumed to be collaborators whose heads had been shaved to shame them.

The problem arose not only through the mishandling of the situation by the Dutch government, but also because the non-Jewish Dutch population were waiting anxiously for their own relatives who had been deported to labour and concentration camps during the occupation. The war had brought devastation to the Netherlands and the Dutch had suffered ordeals of their own, including thousands of fatalities during the Hunger Winter in the last months before liberation. So when the Jews began trickling back into the country, they were often met with a wall of silence. Those who spoke about the recent past were regarded with scepticism, while others were simply shunned. Jewish survivors were unable to participate in discussions of how life had been in the Netherlands during the Hunger Winter, the 'common currency of conversation after the liberation'. The Dutch had no wish to listen to accounts of gas chambers, typhoid epidemics, medical experiments and death marches, which diminished their own experiences in comparison. It also reminded many of their own culpability in not having attempted to resist the anti-Jewish measures more.

As newspaper reports and photographs from the liberated camps were released into the public sphere in the summer of 1945, people often chose not to see them. Many felt the important thing was to begin looking ahead, and while there were those who had no wish to be reminded that they could have done more to help the Jews, others felt that they had done quite enough. The Franks' former neighbour on the Merwedeplein, Laureen Nussbaum, explains:

The general view among the Dutch was: we gave you shelter in the 1930s and hid you in the first half of the 1940s, so now go back to where you came from, our job is done. The Dutch wanted us to fade into the background, they weren't interested in us or what the Jewish people had suffered in those years. They thought their own problems were far more important.

On 2 July 1945 the former resistance paper *De Patriot* commented on Jews who had been in hiding and owed their lives to brave Dutch citizens:

The re-emerging Jews can thank God for the help they received in that form, and feel humble. Much better people might have been lost because of it. And that too is something all those who were hidden should consider: they have much to repay . . . There can be no doubt that the Jews, specifically because of German persecution, were able to enjoy great sympathy from the Dutch people. Now it is appropriate for the Jews to restrain from excess . . . They are truly not the only ones who suffered and were badly off.

Jewish people would often return to their previous homes only to find old acquaintances living there, people who claimed not to recognize them and refused to move out. Old friends who had been entrusted with possessions denied they had been given anything to look after in the owner's absence, or swore the items had been taken by the Germans. Otto told his brother in a letter that it was 'extremely difficult' to find somewhere to live, adding, 'If I was going to live alone I would not be entitled to get a flat, and at the moment they don't give any to people not yet naturalized.' Another survivor of Auschwitz told the author, 'When I came home to Holland, there was nothing for me. The Dutch – not the Germans, but the Dutch – had taken everything.' He paused. 'Still, I suppose the main thing is to live.' In these instances, as with so much else, the authorities claimed to be powerless. There were also many examples of bureaucratic insensitivity, such as demands for rent and insurance premiums covering the period of deportation.

Anti-Semitism among the Dutch, little heard of before the war, became more apparent. In a letter to his brother in London, Otto wrote sorrowfully, 'The situation of those not yet naturalized is still pretty difficult here. I am sorry to say that the war and Hitler propaganda have a very bad influence still. There are quite a number of people coming back from concentration camps who are retained at camps [here] or are not allowed to come back at all.' The years of constant propaganda had left their effect on the general public, government agencies and official bodies. One Jewish woman overheard a comment made about her as she walked through Amsterdam, 'Look at that, they're wearing their furs again,' while a survivor registering as a repatriate in Eindhoven was told by a clerk, 'Not another Jew, they must have forgotten to gas you.' Judith de Winter who had known the Frank family in Westerbork and Auschwitz recalls,

I was in a mess, thin as a needle, so when we got home, I was sent to be examined by a doctor. It was a strange moment. He looked at me as if I came from another world. I could sense a sort of fear, because my experiences were so totally alien to anything he had encountered. He was not unpleasant, but I could tell by his manner and the way he touched me that he was frightened of me.

Judith went back to school, but found it impossible to relate to the other students. Eventually she went to live in Israel for a while, but her mother advised her to return home and find a job, experience real life first and then return to Israel if she wanted. Judith did as she was advised: 'I came back to the Netherlands and looked for a job. I applied for one position at a chemists in Amsterdam and they turned me down – because I was Jewish.'

By the mid 1950s, prejudice towards Jews amongst the Dutch seemed to be lessening, and anti-Semitic remarks were more often viewed as offensive. And for all those who did not welcome their Jewish countrymen with open arms or were unwilling to listen to their experiences, there were also many Dutch – like the friends of Otto Frank – who were loyal, supportive and considerate to the level of virtuousness. In an interview given only months before his death, Otto confirmed, 'My greatest support was the five non-Jewish friends who had concealed us in our hiding place. I believe that what our helpers did for us was only possible because we in our firm were what today one calls a team. If I had not had such a good relationship with my employees, nothing would have been possible . . . They were friends unto death.'

Working for the Volksherstel (People's Recovery) organization at Amsterdam's Centraal Station, where he registered survivors of labour and concentration camps, Jan Gies asked all the repatriates arriving in the city whether they knew anything about the Frank family, the van Pelses or Fritz Pfeffer. On 3 June a former concentration camp inmate told him that he had seen Otto on his own journey home. Shortly after Jan had returned home to give Miep the news, Otto himself knocked on the door of their apartment. Miep rushed out to him: 'We looked at each other. There were no words. He was thin, but he'd always been thin ... "Miep," he said quietly. "Miep, Edith is not coming back ... but I have great hope for Anne and Margot."' Unable to say anything other than 'come in', Miep guided him indoors.

Later that evening, after Otto had told them his story, he learned what had happened to his Dutch friends. Kleiman and Kugler had been held for a month at the prison on Amstelveensweg in Amsterdam. On 7 September they were taken to the Weteringschans prison and on 11 September they were sent to Amersfoort transit camp. Their treatment there was brutal, there were frequent roll-calls and heavy labour. Kleiman's health, always fragile, deteriorated until a gastric haemorrhage prevented him from working. On 18 September 1944, through the efforts of the Netherlands Red Cross, Kleiman was released and returned to Amsterdam. Kugler remained in Amersfoort until 26 September when he was transferred to the labour camp at Zwolle. On 30 December he was sent to Wageningen where he worked first as an electrician under German supervision, then as a translator for a German army organization. On 28 March 1945, during a forced march into Germany, Kugler was able to escape when a group of British Spitfires opened fire on them. He hid first with a farmer before making his way home to Hilversum.

While Kugler and Kleiman were imprisoned, Miep had taken charge of the business at Prinsengracht, gaining authorization from the bank to sign cheques and to pay the staff. Bep continued to work there as usual. Daatselaar, the sales representative who was an NSB member, suggested to Miep that they try to bribe the Gestapo into releasing her friends. Miep went twice to the Euterpestraat in the hope that this might work, but to no avail. Van Maaren, the head warehouseman, told Miep that he had been sanctioned by Silberbauer to act as 'administrator', which Miep reluctantly accepted, anticipating that it would ensure the company's survival. When Kleiman began working at the office again, he dismissed van Maaren as soon as he could. On 6 November 1944 Kleiman had registered at the Chamber of Commerce as acting director of Gies & Co.

The following day, Monday 4 June 1945, Otto returned to the Prinsengracht. Asked years later if he had found it almost unendurable he replied: 'Yes it was. It was a weight.' When he opened the door to the annexe, he saw on the floor three brown beans from a sack which Peter had dragged up from the office one evening. The sack had burst as Peter tried to carry them to the upper floor. Otto picked them up and put them in his pocket. In the room he had shared with Edith and Margot, the dark-green paint was peeling from the wainscoting and the wallpaper, stained by damp, bulged out from the walls. The map of Normandy, on which he had marked the beginnings of the Allied advance, was still there, as were the lines against which he had measured his growing daughters. In Anne's room all her pictures of film stars, babies, art works, and the other images which so appealed to her lively imagination, remained glued to the walls. The thick curtains which he and Anne had tacked up at the windows to protect their safety were yellow from never being washed, and the smell of neglect hung throughout the closed-off rooms.

Otto had several meetings with old friends that day. The closest to him among the acquaintances whom he saw were Kugler, Kleiman and Lotte Pfeffer. Lotte still had no news of her husband; Otto could only tell her that Pfeffer had left Auschwitz for another camp. The whereabouts of Anne and Margot, Peter and Gusti van Pels were not known. In the evening, Otto ate with Miep and Jan again, and accepted the offer of a room in their apartment. After years of hearing Miep address him as Mr Frank, he now asked her to call him Otto. She agreed, but only when they were at home. In the office, he would still be Mr Frank. 'And I never made a mistake in that,' Miep recalls. 'No. That is maybe why I can handle so many different situations with different people. That is how I am. I can do one thing, yet at the same time think differently about it. I can join in, but in my heart I may think very differently about things . . . I am a person who can be silent.'

Otto visited one of his sales representatives, Ans Broks, who gave him back some clothes that belonged to him and which she had kept safely during the war. There were also a few items of furniture he was able to retrieve, including the antique pieces that had formed part of Edith's dowry. He presented these to Miep, along with a painting that he owned and she had always admired, and later he gave her some real cocoa sent to him from friends in America. After years of eating poor-tasting ersatz products, Miep was so moved by the significance of the gift that she began to cry as she prepared it. He also visited Hendrik van Hoeve, the greengrocer who had provided them with food during the war. Van Hoeve's family had been shocked by his arrival in Amsterdam, having heard from the Red Cross that he was dead. Otto gave him a large basket of fruit which he had somehow managed to find, and listened to van Hoeve's experiences of incarceration in four concentration camps.

Otto began work at the Prinsengracht again, although there was very little to do except contemplate how he could boost the flagging business. His second wife explained much later, 'He was determined to give those good friends of his who had risked their lives in helping to hide the family the reward of a secure existence again.' For the time being they had to wait until the economy stabilized, and there were occasions when Otto had to tell them that they would not be receiving a salary that week; income from the business was almost non-existent. Otto wrote to his brother-in-law Erich later that summer: 'We try to work but, as there are virtually no basic materials, it is difficult. The costs go through but there's no profit . . .' The actions of Otto's friends during the occupation, and the 17 September 1944 ruling by the Dutch government which reversed the Nazi law removing Jews from business life, meant that Pectacon could be reactivated. Otto and Kleiman were once more directors of the company, and appointed Kugler as their proxy. Gies & Co. continued to trade as before, but there were problems with Opekta. The exchange of letters with the Rovag Company in Switzerland concerning the loan and licensing agreement, as well as the letter Pomosin sent to the BEI about the matter, affected a statutory order made by the Dutch government in exile in 1944 regarding the property of enemy nationals. Otto told Erich, 'As regards the Opekta shares, my lawyer takes the standpoint that the old contract between you and me is still in force and that all contracts made under the German oppressor are no longer viable.' Which was correct, but as a person officially classified 'stateless' yet of German origin, Otto was seen as an enemy national himself, and for the next two years the difficulties remained unresolved.

While Otto was at work on 8 June a postcard arrived which his mother had sent to Kleiman in May requesting 'with fear and much sorrow' any information about her son and his family. It was the first sign Otto had that his mother, sister, brother-in-law and nephews were all well. His friends in Amsterdam had already told him that they had not yet received his letters to them, therefore Otto had no idea whether any of his postcards or letters to Switzerland had reached their destination. He wrote to his mother immediately, condensing all that had happened over the past three years into a few short sentences, unable or unwilling to go into detail. He confessed,

Everything is like a strange dream. In reality, I can't sort myself out yet . . . I don't know where the children are, but I never stop thinking of them . . . Our entire household has been stolen from us. I had kept some things in other places, but not very much. I have neither a hat nor a raincoat, neither a watch nor shoes, apart from those others have lent me, and you can't get anything here, there aren't the supplies. I'm living with Miep Gies. I have enough money at present, I don't need very much anyway. I long to be with you all . . . I'm waiting to hear from you soon, to learn about everybody – particularly those whom we've heard little about for such a long time. I'm afraid I only wrote a short letter to Robert, as I can't go into detail. I'm not yet normal, I mean I can't find my equilibrium. Physically though, I'm fit.

Despite Switzerland's sustained neutrality during the war, the Eliases had also known prejudice and hardship. After being forced out of his job with Opekta, Erich joined another company, Uni-Pectin, which was involved in a similar line of business. Uni-Pectin was based in Zurich, and Erich had to travel there every day by train. The company folded during the war and Erich was out of work. He tried various related schemes but none came to fruition. Panicked by the rumour that a German invasion of Switzerland was imminent, Leni fled with Buddy, her youngest son, to another part of the country. Having always been thought of as an impractical social butterfly, she returned home with a pragmatism few thought she possessed. Searching for some means of earning a living, she hit upon the idea of buying shoes and clothes from refugees and then selling them at a profit. Her business soon expanded to include household goods and furniture, which she sold from a small room in Basel's town centre. Before long she had a shop which eventually became a thriving antiques store.

Robert and Lottie in London were safe, and within a few days Otto had a letter from his older brother. His younger brother Herbert had spent two years of the war in Switzerland, travelling there with the passport of his dead cousin, Jean-Michel. He had returned to Paris only to be imprisoned in the camp at Gurs, but had managed to survive the starvation, dysentery and typhoid fever that claimed the lives of thousands and was once more living in Paris. Erich was also searching for a relative, his brother Paul who had tried to obtain a Swiss visa in 1939. Despite repeated efforts, and a guarantee of support from Erich before he lost his job, as well as the promise of funds for Paul to emigrate to Bolivia, his applications were turned down and he was deported. Erich never discovered what had happened to his brother during his lifetime, but after his father's death in 1984, Buddy received confirmation that Paul Elias had been killed in Auschwitz.

Otto's engagements diary for 10 June 1945 notes, 'Dinner at Kleiman's. Moving house.' When Miep and Jan's landlady, Mrs Stoppelman, returned home after being in hiding, she and her tenants found themselves suddenly incompatible. Perhaps the house felt too small with four people living there, and she was unhappy to have gained an extra tenant. Whatever the reason, the Gieses decided to leave. There was a housing shortage at the time, but Jan's sister, who lived further along the same street at Hunzestraat 120, suggested that the three of them move in with her. The sleeping arrangements were not to her advantage (Jan and Miep took her room while she slept in the sitting room, and Otto had a small room at the back of the apartment), but she appears not to have minded.

Two days after moving into his new home, Otto's thoughts were fixated on his youngest daughter. It was 12 June: Anne's sixteenth birthday. In his engagements diary, he wrote simply but forcefully, scoring his pen deep into the page, 'Anne.'

'For the time I go on living. How hard it is to walk about on earth that is so saturated with Jewish blood.' These agonized sentiments expressed by one survivor were shared by many. Those who survived, especially those who had lost their entire families, often felt a keen combination of self-recrimination and anguish. This was not helped by other Jews, such as those who had remained in hiding until the liberation, and those abroad, who suspected the survivors had collaborated with the enemy in some way, or supplanted their fellow inmates in the camps. The problem was caused largely by the sheer lack of survivors. So few were alive; on Otto's registration card from Auschwitz, the Red Cross worker had written triumphantly: 'Return!' To his cousin Milly, Otto admitted that people were suspicious of him: 'People who meet me here always wonder how it was possible for a man of my age to get through this hell. It just was chance.'

In the poem 'Return to Amsterdam', Eli Dasberg writes of walking along city streets with endless rows of dead close behind: 'There is no square, no street without memories.' Familiar places were changed unutterably by the survivors' conception of them. One returnee perplexed by his arrival in his old home explained, 'For about an hour I was all alone in our apartment. Virtually nothing had changed. I sat in an armchair and tried to comprehend that I was back home . . . I couldn't wrap my mind around it, this situation.' Hilde Goldberg's parents had died in the camps, but she and her brother survived the war in Belgium. She joined the Red Cross and worked in Belsen after the liberation where she met her husband, Max. There was never the slightest doubt in her mind that she would not return to the Netherlands permanently: 'After the war, I did not want to meet people I had known from those days again. I didn't look for any of them. It would have been too painful for me. And I still don't. The Netherlands was a cemetery.'

Rabbi David Soetendorp, who became a close friend of Otto Frank, and whose parents and brother had been in hiding during the war, recalls the agony of the survivors:

There was this horrible period of waiting to see who would return and so few of them did. There was so much anger at that time towards the Dutch, it was never-ending. There was an ocean of suppressed anger and grief. It was very oppressive for a child. There were hardly any Jewish children – they had all been killed – so when other Jewish people saw you, they would stare. I once said, 'I'm tired of being a miracle.' And any non-Jewish visitors to the house were questioned intently for the first ten minutes to determine what they had done during the war. If he could not give satisfactory answers, then that was it, he was a collaborator and he would have to leave.

This simmering resentment was felt by all who survived: 'Everyone who saw himself spared by what seemed like a series of miracles knew that he would be pursued to the end of time by the question, "Why?"' One survivor walking through his old neighbourhood found himself gazing at the houses and thinking, 'How many Jews could they have hidden here?'

Otto joined the legions of Jews throughout Europe who spent hour after hour trying to piece together the last known movements of their families. He scoured the lists of victims and survivors printed regularly in the newspapers, placed his own adverts in the press enquiring for any information about Margot and Anne. He called the Red Cross, and tried to trace others in the hope of finding a trail which would lead to his children's safe return. His family encouraged him to think positively and not to succumb to pessimism. They tried to convey their own grief through letters, the only form of communication available. Otto's brother Robert wrote of the difficulty in doing so:

> How we deplore the loss of Edith, and how we feel with you in your anxiety about your children we cannot describe, just as you have hardly given us a hint of all you have been through during the last few years. May God grant that your children will come back to you soon and in good health. Every other question seems unimportant compared with this one.
>
> You say it's a miracle that you are alive and I believe you and am thankful for it, and that you are in good health and prepared to start a new life. I trust that after all you have been through you are not unduly worried about economic questions. They will be settled in due course and I can promise you our and Stanfield's help. We managed to make a living all through these war years and Lottie is working with me after having been employed as a secretary by different firms . . .
>
> Of course we are longing to see you again and hope that all the restrictions

of travelling, etc., will soon be lifted. Having not seen mother for practically eight years now we also long to see her and all the dear ones in Basel.

Lottie . . . was especially fond of Edith and she suffers most terribly thinking of her death. Do you want some clothing? I believe that one is allowed to send some and I can fully supply you with this. Tell us as much about you as you feel you can tell us at the moment and believe me that our fondest thoughts are with you all the time.

Desperate for some form of contact with his missing children, Otto sought out their friends. On 14 June he visited Anne's schoolfriend from the Jewish Lyceum, Jacqueline van Maarsen. She remembers, 'He was alone; I didn't understand. I didn't understand the sad eyes on his sunken face either until he told us his story . . . By the time Mr Frank arrived on our doorstep he had already heard that his wife Edith had died, but he had heard nothing about Margot and Anne.' Otto was among the first to visit Laureen Nussbaum's family, who had been neighbours before the war, and were still living in the same house. Laureen recalls,

Rudi, the young man whom I later married, hid in our apartment. He came to us in September 1944 and remained with us until the liberation. His parents had been deported and we found out they did not survive. Otto came to us not long after his return to Amsterdam. We hadn't moved and that really did delight him, to see us all there, in the same place.

Otto wanted to talk about his children and hoped to hear news of them, but he was also anxious to be of assistance to those in need. Miep confirms, 'He was constantly involved in reuniting displaced concentration camp victims with their friends and families.' He maintained contact with his former comrades in the camp, visiting those who lived in Amsterdam or its environs whenever he could. Max Stoppelman had returned from Auschwitz, but his wife had been killed. He had to build a life for himself again and had taken a job in the textile industry. Sal de Liema and his wife Rose, who had survived a labour camp, were reunited at the end of June and saw Otto usually two or three times a week. However, many survivors had still not returned in the summer of 1945; some were in DP camps while others were in hospitals and sanatoriums. They were not pleasant possibilities to consider, but Otto felt that this must surely be the fate of Anne and Margot, as he wrote to his family in Switzerland: 'There is never any communication from Russian-occupied territory and that's why I cannot get any information about the children, since they might be in Germany.'

On 19 June Otto's mother wrote of her own distress:

To know that you are alone in your mourning for Edith and still without
news of your beloved children is the most terrible experience I have had to
bear in a life that has often been very hard. What Edith must have suffered
without you and the children, one cannot imagine. We had no news from
Czernowitz or Katowice. All the same, my thoughts during that time were
always with you . . . [Edith] was always such a staunch support to you through
thick and thin and for the children a devoted mother and the best of friends.
I feel the most sorrow for her. I know I could not be of much help, but it
would be such a consolation for me to see you and just be at your side . . . I
take my leave of you today with a heavy heart. I want to tell you over and
over how much we are thinking about you and would love to comfort you
in your unspeakable sorrow. Don't lose your courage and your hope and rest
assured that deep love embraces you.

Alice had contacted the International Red Cross herself in an attempt to
discover what had happened to her granddaughters, and had forwarded a
copy of Otto's letter where he wrote about Edith's death to Julius and
Walter Holländer in America. Otto was expecting to hear from them at any
moment.

On 21 June Otto wrote to Leni and Erich, for the first time admitting
that he was no longer so certain he would be reunited with his children:

Up to now I was convinced I'd see them back, but I'm beginning to doubt
it. Nobody can imagine how things were in Germany who has not suffered
himself! . . . As regards the children, I know that nothing can be done. We
have to wait, that's all. I go to the office daily because that's the only way to
divert myself. I just can't think how I could go on without the children,
having lost Edith already. You don't know how they both developed. It's too
upsetting for me to write about them. Naturally I still hope, and wait, wait,
wait.

On 24 June Otto visited Eva Geiringer, the young woman he had met
immediately after the liberation of Auschwitz. Eva remembers,

I heard a knock at the front door and found Otto Frank standing there. His grey
suit hung loose on his tall, thin frame, but he looked calm and distinguished. 'We
have a visitor,' I said, as I took him in to see Mutti [Eva's mother, Fritzi]. He held
out his hand to be introduced to Mutti. 'But we've met already,' she said, 'on the

way to Czernowitz.' He shook his head. His brown eyes were deep-set and sad. 'I don't remember,' he said. 'I have your address from the list of survivors. I am trying to trace what has happened to Margot and Anne.' He was desolated that he had not yet found them but he sat and spoke to Mutti for a long time, building up her confidence.

Fritzi told him that she was waiting for news about her husband and son and was trying to get their apartment on Merwedeplein back from the tenants who were currently occupying it. She later recalled little of the visit, except that he was 'broken-hearted over the loss of his wife, Edith'.

The official celebration of the liberation was on 28 June, known as Bevrijdingsdag. Otto spent the day quietly in the company of Miep, Jan and Bep. The following day, Edith's brother Julius sent Otto a letter, hoping to persuade him to join them in America:

> My last hope is that you will find the children. Walter and I will do everything for you. In case you want to come to the USA we have money saved for you three. Send me a cable when you have found the children. There are nine food parcels shipped to you care of Max Schuster. Let me know if you need food. We will send it.

Otto's letter to Robert and Lottie in London on 7 July illustrates the difficulty in obtaining accurate information about those who had not yet returned, and was aware that the reception of the survivors was not as sympathetic as it should have been:

> As much as I feel the loss of Edith, the sorrow about my children is still prevailing. I *have* to take the fact of Edith's fate, but I still hope to find my children and that is at the moment all I live for. By chance I heard that a girl returning from Theresienstadt told another girl that she saw Anne and Margot there after the liberation but very ill with typhoid fever. I asked quite a lot of people coming from there but nobody confirmed the news up to now. On the lists their names do not appear, but that does not mean much as the lists are not reliable and very often the names of stateless people are not taken. I do all to find out more about it and I waver between hope and fear. The girl who told the story is not back yet, the girls met at Leipzig, so I can't speak to her myself.

A few days later, Otto received another letter from his brother-in-law Julius: 'I hope you are doing well in Amsterdam. Every day I expect news from you about the children. Even more than the passing away of Edith, the destiny of the two girls is on my mind day and night. But it is of no use to make life more difficult for you than it is . . . Please inform us at once and by using the shortest way when you hear of them. Wishing you all luck.'

On 18 July 1945 Otto finally found out what had happened to his children. Checking the Red Cross lists once more, he saw at last 'Annelies Marie Frank' and 'Margot Betti Frank'. But beside their names were the dreaded symbols of crosses, which could mean only one thing. Upon receiving the name and address of the woman who had made the marks, he travelled to Laren, where he met Lin Brilleslijper, who was renting a small house there with her husband Eberhard Rebling.

Lin, who later spoke often about her experiences, and also recorded them in writing, told Otto that at the beginning of November she and her sister Janny were transported from Auschwitz to Bergen-Belsen in Germany. The camp was situated on heathland, open to the elements. The Germans had planned originally to use it as a holding station for Jews who could be exchanged with German hostages abroad, but nothing ever came of the idea and in late 1944 thousands of sick prisoners being evacuated from other camps were sent to Bergen-Belsen. There were not enough huts to accommodate the newcomers, so vast tents were erected upon the windswept heath. Immediately after their arrival, wrapped in blankets, Lin and Janny walked to the water-pipe on the hill to wash. 'Two scrawny threadbare figures emerged,' Lin wrote in her memoir. 'They looked like little frozen birds. We lay down in the bunkhouse and wept.' The frozen birds were Margot and Anne Frank. They told the Brilleslijper sisters that they had been on the Auschwitz transportation, and that their mother had been selected. The four of them went over to the tents. 'We lay down on some straw and cringed together under our blankets. In the first days it was warm, we slept a lot. It started to rain.' Despite their weakened state, the women were forced to work, pulling apart old shoes in a long barracks. A storm broke out one night, and the tents were ripped from their moorings. Barracks were eventually constructed, but more transportations were arriving each day: 'We were displaced from our bunks. Now we had no roof over our heads. Every day there was roll-call. But at dusk we had to be back in the bunks, or we would have been shot.'

In the early days of 1945 a typhus epidemic raged through the camp. Thousands were dying from that, and the hunger and the thirst. The guards had cut off the water supply deliberately. Bodies lay everywhere. For a time, the Brilleslijpers did not see Margot or Anne, but in March when 'the snow was already melting', they found them in the sick barracks. Both girls had typhus. 'We begged them not to stay there, as people there deteriorated so quickly and couldn't bring themselves to resist . . . Anne simply said, "Here we can both lie on the plank bed; we'll be together and at peace." Margot only whispered; she had a high fever.' The girls then returned to their usual barracks, where Margot's condition quickly worsened. Seeking to rise from her bunk one day, she fell to the floor. The shock killed her.

Janny, whom Otto called upon after visiting Lin, recalled later, 'At a certain moment in the final days, Anne stood in front of me, wrapped in a blanket . . . she told me that she had such a horror of the lice and fleas in her clothes that she had thrown all of her clothes away . . . during dreadful hallucinations.' Without her sister, not knowing that Otto was alive, but realizing her mother was dead, and suffering from a violent strain of typhus, Anne died in the camp in late March 1945. Lin and Janny found the bodies of Anne and Margot and carried them over to one of the mass graves where up to 10,000 corpses were buried in each. Bergen-Belsen was liberated three weeks later.

In the engagements diary which he kept at the time, and in which he always recorded any significant events, Otto could find no words for the worst day of his life. The diary only discloses the fact of his meeting with Lin Brilleslijper, and its gravity:

'18 July 1945: *Lien Rebling* >!'★

Two days after Otto learned of his daughters' agonizing deaths in Bergen-Belsen, on 20 July 1945, he wrote one word in his engagements diary: 'Ahlers'.

Tonny Ahlers had been arrested on 6 June 1945, less than two weeks after his second child, another boy, was born. At the end of the month he was sent to the Scheveningen Prison, some distance from Amsterdam, and he was still there on Friday 20 July when Otto recorded his name in his engagements diary. Did Otto visit him in prison? Presumably so, since Otto later stated that 'after the war, when I came back from Auschwitz, I looked for the man'. 'Ahlers' appears again in Otto's agenda three days later on Monday 23 July. (Alternatively, Ahlers's wife, Martha, may have contacted Otto on her husband's behalf.) Whatever took place on those two dates, the fact is that on 24 July 1945 Otto wrote to the prison authorities that 'in passing' he had heard that Ahlers was 'currently interned' with them and that, 'I have some information about this man and would like to know to

---

★ Otto misspelt Lin's first name, and Rebling was her married name.

which address I should send my information.' Scrawled across the envelope is Ahlers's cell number.

The following month, on 21 August 1945, Otto sent a letter to the BNV describing his first meeting with Ahlers in 1941. He avowed that after two meetings during which he had voluntarily given Ahlers money, 'I never saw him again.' This remark was not the only curiosity in his letter. Otto had forgotten the date of the encounter with Jansen, who tried to betray him to the SS, but he vividly recalled when he met Ahlers. Likewise, Otto could not remember Joseph Jansen's first name, despite the Jansens being 'well known to me', and yet he recalled Ahlers's full name and address from 'one' meeting in 1941. The business arrangement between Otto and Ahlers is one explanation, of course, but the additional, very precise information presumably came from Ahlers himself during these meetings in summer 1945. What is astonishing however is that Ahlers had the original of Otto's letter (a fact that emerged a few years later). Only one person could have given it to him, since the police would never have done so: Otto Frank. Otto ended his letter to the BNV: 'Ahlers, I feel, saved my life, because if [Jansen's] letter had reached the hands of the SS, I would have been arrested and executed . . . I know nothing else about this young man.'

Otto's engagements diary reveals two more dates on which the name 'Ahlers' features; Friday 27 August and Monday 30 August. Whether the references were to meetings with Ahlers himself will probably never be known, but it certainly seems the most logical explanation. Otto would write one more letter about him that year, but in the meantime Ahlers was released from prison and attended a family wedding. The shock of 'seeing this creature again' impelled his brother-in-law to send a blistering letter to the Dutch authorities. The letter outlined how Ahlers had been ostracized by his family before the war for anti-Semitism, his love of National Socialism, and his violent behaviour; it also explained how the family had dreaded his visits during the war:

Perhaps you can imagine that on a day like that we were in a state of extreme tension in order to make sure that the people who were in hiding got away, or that those who happened not to be at home, would not return that day, that no people came calling to ask for distribution documents or false identity cards for people in hiding and that our children would not let slip any word about who was in our home or about the wireless . . . Tonny would tell us about his good relations with the SD in Amsterdam, about his beautiful Jewish home in Zuid and such matters and he did not miss an opportunity to show us his identity card as a member of the SD. We were always immensely relieved when he left again.

In March 1945 Ahlers had visited his sister and brother-in-law and had suddenly begun talking about his work for the resistance: 'He said he had been through the Front to Den Bosch for the resistance movement in order to carry messages. Knowing his imagination, I asked him for several particulars about this to which he could not respond satisfactorily. If he tried to make himself useful after September 1944, then that was certainly calculated . . . If he was released [from Scheveningen] because of his conduct during the last months of the occupation, then there is something not right about this.' Ahlers's brother-in-law ended his letter, 'For us he will always be a traitor, someone who was hand-in-glove with the Germans.'

On 27 November Otto wrote another letter about Ahlers from his office on the Prinsengracht, but it is not clear to whom it is addressed. He reiterated everything from his letter to the BNV, adding enigmatically, 'When I found out later that Mr Ahlers, who had passed himself off as a courier between the NSB and SD, had been locked up in the penitentiary at van Alkemadelaan in The Hague, I felt compelled to write to the Nationale Veiligheid in The Hague, to declare what Mr Ahlers had done for me. When Mr Ahlers returned from prison some months ago, he came to visit me and told me what had happened. From his remarks I understood that he was very active underground. How it all occurred, I cannot judge, I can only express my gratitude for the great service that Mr Ahlers has rendered me.'

The day after writing this letter, Otto and Ahlers apparently had another meeting, for Ahlers's name appears in Otto's engagements diary again. What is striking from Otto's letter is the emphasis he puts on Ahlers's 'good' deed; it almost seems too much. Ahlers may have saved Otto's life in 1941, but he did it in order to gain money and come to a business arrangement with Otto Frank. What is most intriguing is why Otto was so preoccupied with Ahlers at such a traumatic point in his own life. Two days before 'Ahlers' first appears in Otto's diary in July 1945, Otto had learned that his daughters were dead; on the day when he first wrote to the prison authorities in defence of Ahlers, he also wrote to inform his family that same day that Anne and Margot were never coming home. Otto was always scrupulously honest, yet he was clearly evasive about his association with Ahlers in regard to the Dutch authorities, changing his story repeatedly in regard to how often they met, whether money was involved and whether Ahlers had asked for payment or not. Comparing the dates of the post-war meetings with the letters Otto wrote about Ahlers, it is evident that there was a pattern to these events. The meetings in July and August always took place on Mondays and Fridays, although the reason for this is not clear, but what is certain is that the meetings in July, August and November occurred within a few days of Otto writing his letters in support of Ahlers. Why did Otto defend him?

At that point, Otto had no reason to suspect Ahlers of his betrayal; as far as he was concerned, Ahlers had given him the letter from Jansen and they had then reached a business arrangement, with Otto delivering to Ahlers's company. But when Otto returned to the Netherlands in 1945, he did so as 'a stateless person of German origin', an enemy national, and the persecution he had suffered because he was Jewish meant nothing to the Dutch government. As such, he was due to be investigated for his political allegiances during the war. Ahlers could spin an unpleasant tale around Otto's deliveries to the Wehrmacht, the NSB men he employed while dismissing the Jewish secretary who once worked for him, and the business with the Armee Oberkommando in Berlin. Otto's company, which had struggled throughout the 1930s, had made a small, but significant profit during the war. In a declaration to the authorities in which he denied all wrong-doing, Ahlers pronounced himself appalled that 'these firms and their owners' who had traded with him now spoke 'with abhorrence about the dirty collaborators and traitors of their country'. He claimed that his company was 'the only one that can know anything about their aspirations to being important during the war'. Ahlers was unscrupulous, as Otto knew only too well. The letters Otto sent to the authorities on his behalf would ensure that Ahlers kept his silence.

While Otto hoped his business dealings during wartime would not return to haunt him, his hope that his children would come back was gone. In his memoir, Otto wrote, 'I found two sisters who had been with Margot and Anne in Bergen-Belsen, and they told me about the final sufferings and deaths of my children . . . My friends, who had been hopeful with me, now mourned with me . . . It took many months for me to get used to a normal life without my loved ones.'

Three days after hearing about Anne and Margot's deaths, Otto wrote to inform Robert of the news. The letter has been lost, but from Robert's reply it is obvious that Otto asked him to let the rest of the family know, unable to bear the thought of writing such a letter himself again. Otto confided to Herbert later that month, 'I try to think of other things and cannot sit still. No one must know how I grieve inside. Who can understand anyway? My wonderful people here, but only these few.' The first of the myriad condolence letters arrived at the end of July, from Julius Holländer:

'Walter and I can understand how you feel. We loved Margot and Anne as if they were our own children. Our life is empty now. Edith and the girls were all we had.' Of his comrades from Auschwitz, Sal de Liema comforted him: 'You have been much more than a father to me but your own daughters can never be replaced. I think about you a lot and hope that you are keeping busy at the office. Although I should have found it somewhat of a relief to have you here for a short time, it really is best to stay at work. Perhaps there will come a moment when you have a real need to go out for a short time. Papa, our house is always open to you, for as long as you want.'

Otto sent Robert and Lottie another letter on 26 July, but could not bring himself to write more fully about Margot or Anne:

> I'm cared for in every respect. I behave surprisingly calmly. There is so much misery around me that I try to help wherever I can. I feel no bitterness, dear Robert, because I saw so much misery, lived in such wretchedness, and meet all over the same situation. So I cannot say: Why me? Out of the more than 100,000 Jews who were deported, about 2,000 have returned as yet. From the thousands who were forced to flee with the Germans, I met *three* who escaped being shot or frozen to death. I always say again that only those who lived under the oppressor know what it means. I could talk to you for hours about Edith and the girls, but it doesn't help and it's very upsetting for me. So I'll leave it until we meet again.

He wrote a little more about his inner turmoil to Milly on 27 July, beginning his letter with the avowal that he would 'never be able to bear' the truth about his children's deaths. He continued, 'Nobody can really help me, though I have many friends. Useless to say much about it, I know quite well those who mean it and those who just only talk.' Milly later recalled that in another letter, Otto wrote almost positively about the time in hiding: 'You can have no idea how the girls had developed, because you only knew them as attractive children. Living so close together, we watched them grow into mature human beings and realized their true potential. You will hardly believe it, but in spite of the constant strain and tension, the ever-present fear of discovery, we were really happy because we were sharing everything.'

In August, letters for Otto came swiftly and in great number from his family. All were eager to convey their own distress about the death of the children, and to express their concern for him. Robert expressed sentiments which would be repeated often in the future by those who met Otto: 'We admire you greatly for the way you can think and act without a word of bitterness or hatred after all you have been through.' The whole family in

Switzerland sent him a telegram on 6 August: 'Received sad news we all mourn our dearest ones fondest love and thoughts keep strong and healthy kisses mother – Elias Frank.' They began to put all their efforts into persuading him to try to visit Switzerland as soon as he could, but for the time being it was not possible for Otto, as a stateless person, to travel beyond the Dutch border.

On 9 August 1945 the second of two atomic bombs was dropped on Japan by American forces. The Japanese government surrendered on 14 August and the war officially ended.

Otto had worked on the assumption, since his return to Amsterdam, that very few, if any, of his family's personal belongings could be recovered. His assumption was incorrect.

On the day of the arrest at the Prinsengracht, when the police had gone, Miep found herself alone in the upstairs offices, with the warehousemen still busy on the ground floor. Kleiman had given Miep the keys to the building, but in the afternoon, the senior warehouseman, van Maaren, took possession of them. Miep gave little thought to this, simply assuming that the SD had guessed that he had not known about the hidden Jews and had therefore placed him in charge. Around five o'clock, Jan returned, as did Bep. Together with van Maaren, they went up to the annexe. It was in chaos, but amongst the papers, books and numerous other objects scattered across the floor, Miep recognized Anne's diary. Miep picked it up and then pointed out the other ledgers and loose pages Anne had used to continue writing on when her original diary had overflowed. She and Bep gathered up all the pages they could find, along with several items belonging to the people in hiding, and deposited them in Miep's desk drawer. The following week, Miep asked van Maaren to check the annexe for more papers. He obliged, and having found a few more papers, handed them to her. A week or so after the arrest, the annexe was emptied of its furniture by the Puls removal agency.

Miep did not tell Otto that she had managed to salvage the diary, but when Otto told her that his children were dead, she thought of it immediately. She recalls,

I didn't hand [Otto] Anne's writings immediately on his arrival, as I still hoped, even though there was only a slight chance, that Anne would come back . . . When we heard, in July 1945, that Anne, like Margot, had died in Bergen-Belsen, I gave what pieces of Anne's writing I had back to Mr Frank. I gave him everything that I had stored in the desk drawer in my office.

Otto's initial reaction to seeing his daughter's cherished diary again is not known, for he never spoke about it. However, in a letter to his mother a few days later he wrote,

Miep by chance saved a [photograph] album and Anne's diary. But I don't have the strength to read it. There's nothing of Margot's left any more, only her Latin work, because our whole household was looted, and that's why everything we used so often and all Edith's and the children's lovely little possessions are lost. I know there is no sense in thinking about them, yet a human being isn't just a mind, but has a heart too.

The diary remained unread, but not forgotten.

6. This at Least Has Survived

Within the coming months, Otto learned of the fates of Fritz Pfeffer, Gusti and Peter van Pels. Fritz Pfeffer was transferred from Sachsenhausen to Neuengamme, near Hamburg, where the work and treatment affected him swiftly. He died in the sick barracks of Neuengamme on 20 December 1944. His cause of death was recorded as enterocolitis, a disease of the intestine.

Shortly after her arrival in Auschwitz, Gusti van Pels had become separated from her group of friends. On 26 November she was sent from Auschwitz to Bergen-Belsen where she met Anne and Margot again. On 6 February 1945 she was transferred to the aeroplane factory in Raguhn, part of Buchenwald camp. She was transferred again, either by train or on foot, to Theresienstadt, arriving there on 9 April. Her final whereabouts are unknown; the Netherlands Red Cross dossier gives her date of death as between 9 April and 8 May 1945 in Germany or Czechoslovakia.

After bidding Otto farewell in Auschwitz at the end of January 1945, Peter had arrived in Mauthausen where he worked in Melk, the name given to the outdoor commando unit who toiled in the camp's rock quarries and underground arms factories. At the end of April 1945, Melk was disbanded and Peter was sent to the sick barracks where he died on 5 May 1945, the day the camp was liberated.*

Otto avoided depression by keeping himself as occupied as possible. He told his mother, 'I usually succeed in that – only occasionally do I get distressed.' In his memoir, he recalled: 'Again and again, I resumed contact with earlier friends, who had likewise hidden and survived . . . I tried to build a new existence in Amsterdam with the helpers who worked for my spice-importing business. I tried to rebuild the firm. I also attempted to reunite orphaned children with their relatives. I visited patients in various sanatoriums. All of this gave me new goals in life.'

Among two of the orphans he helped were Hanneli and Gabi Goslar. Hanneli's mother died in childbirth in 1942, along with the baby she was carrying. Her father Hans and grandparents had died in the camps at

* See the relevant individual Netherlands Red Cross dossiers in the archives of NIOD.

Westerbork and Bergen-Belsen, where Hanneli and Gabi spent almost a year as 'exchange Jews' who were never exchanged. Hanneli had seen Anne in the camp in February. They met two or three times, Hanneli recalls: 'She told me that her father had been killed – her mother too, she thought. It was a pity she thought her father had died when he had not. The way she idolized him perhaps she would have had the hope to live if she knew he still lived.' Hanneli and Gabi were deported from Belsen in a transportation of 7,000 persons headed for Theresienstadt. Their two-week journey through ravaged territory ended on 23 April 1945 when they were liberated by the Russians. Hanneli was later admitted to a hospital in Maastricht. Her young sister, Gabi, was cared for by a family friend. When he heard what had happened to the Goslar children, Otto visited Hanneli in Maastricht, after travelling fourteen hours in a lorry to reach her (in a letter to his mother, Otto confided, 'For me, Hanneli will always be the connection to Anne'). Hanneli recalls, 'I was so excited when Otto came to see me. The first thing I said was "Anne is alive, she's in Germany!" He already knew the truth. We talked for a long time. Otto had me moved from Maastricht to the Joodse Invalide in Amsterdam, which was much better. The sixth floor was for Jews returning from the camps.' Otto told Hanneli that he had arranged for her to be transferred to a sanatorium in Switzerland, where her uncle lived. It was through this connection that Otto obtained the necessary documents for her and Gabi (then in an orphanage) to leave the Netherlands.

Otto visited Jacqueline van Maarsen again, now that he had news of Margot and Anne: 'He cried and cried. He came to see me often, and I was at a loss as to how to console him. The only thing I could do was talk to him about his children, and that was really the only thing he wanted . . . Mr Frank also visited Jetteke often . . . It was Jetteke whom Mr Frank wanted to talk to about Margot. Both of his daughters had been equally dear to him.' Jetteke Frijda had gone into hiding with her younger brother during the war and both of them had survived. Her father was killed in Auschwitz and her elder brother, Leo, was shot by the Germans for his activities in the resistance.* Her mother had escaped to Switzerland. Jetteke remembers, 'I worked in a library in The Hague. Somehow Otto found out that I was there and he came to see me. He told me about his family and what had happened to them. He also told me about my father, because they had been together in Auschwitz.'

Otto wrote about daily practicalities to Julius and Walter, beginning:

---

* There are now two streets named for Leo Frijda in Amsterdam.

Everything seems unimportant, senseless. But life goes on and I try not to think too much and to be angry. We all have to bear our fate. Here all the money I had was taken but it may be that I get a part of it back. I don't need money now, I receive what I need in the firm. I am not working officially and the laws for people not yet naturalized are a handicap in some ways.

Business continued to be dismal. Otto explained some of the problems to friends: 'I have to build up and work. In poor Holland it is so difficult, especially if you're stateless. Everything is export, not import and only the most vital of commodities, certainly not pectin. I wish I could work with Uni-Pectin in Switzerland.' In another letter, he chastised himself to be grateful that he at least had something upon which to build: 'Luckily I have a base here to start again . . . if the money will be restored the Germans took from me, I needn't complain . . . There is nothing one can buy anyway. Holland is looted to a great extent . . . I try to get permission to go to Switzerland for business and to see mother, but it will certainly take a few months to get the papers.' The outstanding amount from the Pectacon liquidation was transferred from the Nederlandse Bank to the Liquidatie van Verwaltung Sarphatistraat (Liquidation of the Sarphatistraat Administration or LVVS), in 1947. The LVVS dealt with the repayment of Jewish funds deposited with Lippmann, Rosenthal and Co. The credit balance determined by the LVVS was duly paid back to Otto, the rightful owner.

He sent an affectionate letter to his cousin Milly, and was able to find the courage to write about his children but could still not bring himself to read Anne's diary:

As the girls grew older they were real friends, especially when we were forced to be together for more than two years in two little rooms. I had time to tell them everything about the family and Anne made a genealogical tree of the family and she wanted to know all about every member. I always impressed on the girls to stick together even if characters were different, and they did. Margot was very good in English, she read *Hamlet* and *Julius Caesar* in the original language, Anne of course only started but worked daily. She read little stories. So great was her interest that she pinned photos of the royal family to the wall – they are there still. Of course I know that I shall never get over it and I miss the children far more than Edith. It was the hope and the future, and that counts more than the present life. I informed the children about everything as I thought that we might not return, but I trusted they would. By chance the friends here could save some photos and the daybook of Anne. I had it in my hands but I couldn't read it yet. Perhaps I shall have the force to do so later.

Obviously Miep and Jan had told Otto about Jan's resistance work and the fact that they sheltered a Jewish man in their own home, for he told Milly that they were

really darlings. They did quite a lot of illegal work besides doing all for us . . . Much will have to be changed as far as social law is concerned. As far as I can see there is no progress in humanity yet. This needs to develop, the cruelties of the war have still too much effect on the people. Besides there are impediments all over. I only need to think how the 'staatenlos' [stateless] are treated. It is a shame for humanity, but I do hope that all that will be regulated soon in a decent manner.

Otto's letters to the family in Switzerland began to contain more and more information about his murdered wife and children, and the people they used to know. His letter of 1 September reads:

On Monday evening, I went to Hilversum, to the Hof's house. I took nearly all our silver cutlery there and it's still there, safe. Mrs Hof was always very kind and Edith never forgot her. She helped Edith in 1933 when Edith didn't know how things worked here, the schools and so on . . . I will do all I can to come soon. I'm a bit afraid of that, though. I'm really on the verge of tears and find it so easy to cry. But I have to tell you that I'm healthy. I'm now more than 150 pounds. I try not to think too much and I'm sleeping very well. Of course, the thoughts of Edith and the children never leave me, but I'm trying to look more on the positive side of things than the negative . . . Sometimes I can't believe that I'm fifty-six years old. But for me, life does not have meaning any more.

On 6 September Otto wrote to his mother about an incident that had provoked him into losing his fragile composure. A letter had arrived from a girl in America, who together with her sister, had exchanged 'pen-pal' letters with Anne and Margot before the war and now hoped to do so again. Otto acknowledged how deeply he had been affected: 'Some days ago, a long letter from America arrived for Margot and Anne from a girl with whom they had had no actual contact. This girl wanted to start their correspondence again. I wrote to her in floods of tears. Things like that upset me very much. But it doesn't matter . . .'

Otto spent Yom Kippur with Hanneli Goslar. 'I will not go to the synagogue,' he wrote to his mother. 'The Liberal service doesn't exist or I *would* have gone, but the orthodox one means nothing to me. I know Edith was not so narrow-minded in her thoughts. She never expected or wanted me to fast, and she understood that I went to synagogue only because of her. I would have gone with her or the children, but to go alone makes no sense and would only be hypocrisy.' The Liberal Jewish community in Amsterdam was no more; so many of them had been slaughtered. The historian J. Presser contemplated the post-war Jewish society in the Netherlands, asking,

Can we really call it that? The writer himself prefers to speak of a group. A group pieced together after the Liberation, from a host of fragments; a few thousand men and women married to gentiles and spared for that reason, a few thousand who emerged from hiding, the survivors of Westerbork, the very small number who returned from Theresienstadt and the other camps.

Despite the abatement of Jewish religious life, former members of the Liberal Jewish Community began to consider whether it was feasible to attempt to rebuild their community. They approached Otto to join their board. He recalled, 'After the war a few of the Jews who were there before the war said we have to start a Liberal community again. Mr Frank, will you join us? So I did right away, and I worked with them too.' His involvement arose more from a sense of community than for his own needs, but when the synagogue opened for services, he attended regularly on Friday evenings. From that time, Otto took to always carrying with him a notebook in which he had copied some lines from a Jewish prayer book and a prayer by Saint Francis of Assisi. He remained ambivalent about his faith, however: 'I see how much help religion can give, but it's not for me.'

On Saturday evenings Miep and Jan invited Lotte Pfeffer and a small group of friends to play Canasta with them. Otto would not play, but talked to whoever was present. One Saturday Lotte told him about a letter she had received from Werner Peter Pfeffer, Fritz's son who was living in England. The content of the letter is unknown but it had evidently upset her. Otto offered to write to Peter (as the young man preferred to be known) on her behalf. His letter is full of kind advice and an offer of help, should Peter ever need it. They obviously had not yet heard that Fritz Pfeffer was dead, for Otto writes,

We still wait for your father, we may still hope . . . I try to place myself in your position. You were about twelve years old when you were separated from your father. You cannot know how he lived in the meantime, what happened in all those years. I on my part know nothing about your mother, your father never spoke about her and he introduced Charlotte [Lotte] as Mrs

Pfeffer to all his acquaintances. Nobody knew that he was not really married to her and it was not his fault that it was not done, but the laws that prevented it being done. For Charlotte this situation is a very difficult one. She did everything possible for your father, she was the greatest support for him, and I know and admire her. I would do anything to help her, she is worth it. And I feel it my duty to tell you that, to inform you. It is impossible for me to judge your feelings towards her, but I know it to be in the sense of [loyalty to] your father that you respect her for what she is and that you have all the confidence in her and keep in closest connection.

Unfortunately, the letter did not reconcile Peter and Lotte, and their relationship never improved. Further difficulties arose when Lotte had her common-law marriage to Fritz Pfeffer officially recognized. A friend of Peter's recalls,

I'm not sure what happened between them, but he told me that he and Lotte were not on good terms. He said something about reparations payments – she had married his father posthumously and I think those payments went to her when he thought they should go to him. He regretted the animosity between them, but felt it was too late to change anything.

In November 1946 Peter emigrated to America and established a successful office furniture and supplies company under his new name Peter Pepper. It was many years before he and Otto were in contact again.

On 24 September Otto wrote to someone else with whom he had had no communication during the long years of war, Nathan Straus: 'Dear Charlie, you told me once that I am the only one who calls you by this name, but I feel more the old relations between us if I still call you by that name . . .' He outlined the events of the last two years before concluding, 'I have to bear my fate. I suppose you have heard and read enough about the horrors of the Polish concentration camps. It surprises all imagination. Luckily I lived there only for a few months, but even then every hour one is under the caprice of these tormentors is too much.' Straus replied the following month, having cabled Otto $500, which he hoped would be 'of some assistance to you in what, despite your unwillingness to speak of it, must be difficult financial circumstances. Don't trouble to acknowledge it. You just forget about it.' He was now president of the radio station WMCA in New York and wrote from his office to offer his condolences, admitting, 'Words are quite useless in such a situation as this. In fact, the huge scale of the tragedy which has befallen innocent people is almost beyond the human mind to encompass.' Otto acknowledged his friend's generous gesture as soon as he had discovered the money had been transferred into his account: 'I know you don't like me to speak about it but nevertheless I thank you with all my heart.'

A few days later Otto wrote to his mother about another breach of his fragile self-defences: 'I have just been in the synagogue for a children's festival. Anne and Margot always went to this event together, even when they were in Aachen. On the outside, I was smiling, but inside I was crying bitterly.' For other parents too, whose children had been killed in the Holocaust, the spectre of the lost child or children would be ever present, and many found themselves questioning why they had been chosen to suffer. The psychiatrist Eli Cohen confessed: 'It remains painful to examine a child that was born in the same year as my little boy, and I no longer even try to repress my thoughts. It's pointless anyway. But over and over I ask myself, "Why was this child able to stay alive, when my son was murdered?" ' Otto sent a supportive letter to Leni, urging her to be strong: 'human beings can withstand so much when they really must'. He mentioned then not only his plans to visit them in Switzerland, but also revealed that he had finally begun to read Anne's diary and was captivated by it.

Otto tried to find the words to express to his family in Switzerland his astonishment and fascination with his daughter's diary, but could not:

> What I'm reading in her book is so indescribably exciting, and I read on and on. I cannot explain it to you! I've not finished reading it yet, and I want to read it right through before I make some excerpts or translations for you. She writes about her growing up with incredible self-criticism. Even if it hadn't been written by her, it would have interested me. What a great pity that this life had to go . . . We are all changed, only the core of our being remains.

Otto's method of coping with grief before reading Anne's diary had been to keep himself busy with work or surrounded with company. Now he was obsessed with the book and his discovery of Anne's unexpected gift for writing:

I can't put Anne's diary down. It's just so astonishing. Somebody has begun copying out the 'fairytales book' that she wrote because I don't want to let it out of my hands for a moment, and it is being translated into German for you. I *never* allow the diary out of my sight because there is so much in it that no one else should read. But I will make excerpts from this.

At the start of November 1945, Otto asked his friend Anneliese Schütz whether she would be willing to help him translate some passages of the diary from Dutch into German for his mother in Switzerland. Otto described her to his mother as 'a lady of about fifty. She hardly sees anyone and she's very lonely. She was a journalist and was always very interested in the children. Margot had literature lessons at her house.' Laureen Nussbaum, who was also part of the study group, recalls, 'Anneliese Schütz was a journalist from Berlin. She wore heavy glasses, had that Berlin snappiness, and was rather masculine as professional women sometimes were then.' During the war Schütz had worked for the Joodse Raad but had been deported first to Westerbork and then to Theresienstadt. In the summer of 1945 she returned and moved in with friends, one of whom remembered,

One evening, I think it was in November 1945, Anneliese Schütz came home with the handwritten diary of Anne Frank. She had got it from Otto Frank. I seem to recall a 'poetry album' and a large format, school exercise book. I got this from Anneliese Schütz and spent one night reading it and looking at it. The original diary was thus here in my house for at least one night.* That same winter of 1945/1946 – I can't give a more precise date than that – Anneliese Schütz began, at the request of Otto Frank, to do a German translation. She did this from a typed Dutch copy. I believe that Otto Frank had typed this himself. Together Anneliese Schütz and I tried to use the language of a young girl as far as possible.

Miep, who had so far resisted all Otto's pleadings that she must read the diary, recalls that after their evening meal, Otto would work on the translations from Dutch into German: 'Sometimes he'd come walking out of his room holding Anne's little diary and shaking his head. He'd say to me, "Miep, you should hear this description that Anne wrote here! Who'd have imagined how vivid her gift of observation was all the while?" . . . I could not bring myself to listen.' In his memoir, Otto related how overwhelmed he was by his youngest daughter's talent:

I began to read slowly, only a few pages each day, more would have been impossible, as I was overwhelmed by painful memories. For me, it was a revelation. Here was revealed a completely different Anne to the child that I had lost. I had no idea of the depth of her thoughts and feelings . . . I had never imagined how intensely Anne had occupied her mind with the problem and meaning of Jewish suffering

---

* This conflicts with Otto's letter, quoted above, in which he states he never lets the diary out of his sight.

over the centuries, and the power she had gained through her belief in God . . .
How could I have known how important the chestnut tree was to her when she
had never seemed interested in nature . . . She had kept all these feelings to herself
. . . Occasionally she would read humorous episodes and stories out to us . . . but
she never read out anything which was about herself. And so we never knew to
what extent she went on to develop her character, and she was more self-critical
than any of us . . . Through Anne's accurate description of every event and every
person, all the details of our co-habitation became clear to me again.

Otto's family were amazed by the excerpts sent to them, as he had expected.
Otto was hoping to travel to Switzerland in time for his mother's birthday
in December, when she would be eighty years old, and wrote:

> You would not be able to imagine how busy I am at the moment, and quite
> often I haven't a clue where the time goes. The main thing for me was to
> establish, in my own way, an equilibrium and I hope now that the healing
> process will happen gradually . . . All my wishes are with you. If only I could
> be there now! Everything seems to be so endlessly slow. I have also been to
> the solicitors in order to finally get my naturalization, however they told me
> that it depends on a relaxation of policy and that they are getting prepared. It
> has become twice as hard for us in the meantime . . . I am counting on my
> trip and am not giving up. So hopefully we will see each other soon.

In the autumn of 1945, after witnessing the reactions to the diary by his
family and a number of friends, Otto began to consider whether he should
attempt to have it published. In addition to the excerpts sent to his mother,
he had typed out another copy of the diary. This was based not on Anne's
original diary alone, but on that and the revised version she had written
herself. After hearing a broadcast by the Dutch Minister for Education, Art
and Science on 28 March 1944, in which Gerrit Bolkestein announced a
repository after the war for diaries, letters and documents depicting 'what
we as a nation have had to endure and overcome during these years', Anne
had begun to rewrite her diary with a view to publication. She was never
able to complete the rewritten version; the entries end in March 1944, while
the original diary continues to within three days of their arrest. Otto used
both of these versions in compiling his typescript, and added four chapters
from her book of *Tales*, which also detailed aspects of their life in hiding.
There were deliberate omissions to the typescript: passages he judged
uninteresting or too intimate and some unpleasant remarks Anne had made.
He typed everything out on paper and then cut and pasted the sections

together. On 16 November he wrote to his cousin Milly that he was not through copying the diary yet:

It does not grieve me what she writes and I know quite well that there are several things she did not see right and she would have changed her ideas. In fact she was in very good terms with her mother at the camp later, but it is a disagreeable feeling to publish things against her mother – and I have to do it. There are passages I can scrape [sic], f.i., what she thought about my marrying Edith, our marriage, her views on politics as the relationship between England and the Netherlands and others. It keeps my brains busy every day . . .

Otto visited his friend Kurt Baschwitz, himself a writer and then living on Rooseveltlaan, to ask his opinion. Baschwitz's daughter, Isa, remembers Otto arriving at her father's apartment with a small case containing the diary and various loose sheets: 'Otto felt that Anne's diary should be published, that it was important for children, especially German children. He came from a business background and my father was one of his few intellectual friends, and one who also wrote books. Otto wanted to ask me, in particular, whether this would catch on with young people.' Isa was uncertain, feeling that the passages where Anne had written harshly about her mother and Anne's references to sexual matters, should not be published. Her father agreed, as did Otto, although he did not know how this could be achieved. Isa goes on, 'My father felt that the diary ought to be published as authentically as possible, and that any justified omissions should be indicated by means of dots or the like. He did not have much faith in the message for German youth. These two matters are the source of the falling out between Otto Frank and my father.'

Otto also showed it to his friends Werner and Jetty Cahn, whom he had known since 1933; before her marriage to Werner, a German-Jewish refugee, Jetty lived in the boarding house on Stadionkade where Otto rented a room. Werner Cahn recalled,

One day Otto Frank came in with a number of handwritten loose sheets, from which he read aloud. These were the diary entries of his daughter Anne. He came back on various occasions to read from them. It made a great impression on us. I told Otto Frank I wanted to try to find a publisher. I also advised him not to let the original out of his sight, and initially to have it typed up.

Excited, Otto wrote to his mother:

Friday I was with Jetty Cahn at her house, and I started to read out some of Anne's diary, to get Werner's opinion about it. He's been with the publisher Querido for ages, where Jetty was too. Next Friday is the big decision, but already I have the impression: publish without a doubt – quite a big item! You can't imagine what this means. The diary would come out in German and English, telling everything that went on in our lives when we were in hiding – all the fears, disputes, food, politics, the Jewish question, the weather, moods, problems of growing-up, birthdays and reminiscences – in short, everything. Frau Schütz, whose house I was at yesterday, wants to translate a story called *Blurry The Explorer*. The story of a hero.

Cahn approached Querido's Alice von Eugen-van Nahuys but she 'haughtily rejected it. The German publisher Gottfried Bermann-Fischer (S. Fischer Verlag), which at that time was in Amsterdam, did the same.' Kurt Baschwitz gave the manuscript to the publisher Blitz. And they too turned it down. Disappointed, but not discouraged, Otto asked his friend Ab Cauvern, a dramatist employed by VARA, the Workers Broadcasting Channel, to check the typescript for 'grammatical errors and to remove Germanisms, that is, to correct expressions my daughter had borrowed from the German language and which were therefore bad Dutch'. Cauvern remembers, 'My wife and I knew the Frank family before the war. Margot and Anne stayed with us in Laren. My wife was Otto Frank's secretary . . . I read through the typescript and only corrected the typing errors (in the margin). Finally, I added the afterword . . . I did not have anything to do with the further preparation for publication.'

Cauvern's epilogue was simple: 'Anne's diary ended here. On 4 August, the Green Police made a raid on the "Secret Annexe". In March 1945, two months before the liberation of our country, Anne died in the concentration camp at Bergen-Belsen.' Isa Cauvern then typed the manuscript anew. In a letter to his mother dated 12 December 1945, Otto mentioned taking the diary to the Cauverns 'for corrections and copying out. I have got so far with it now, and I would like to have it finished so that I can show it to publishers . . . I can hardly get away from it all – and do not want to either.' He showed the new typescript to those people 'who I believed would be interested in these notes, from which much that concerns our fate emerges'. Jacqueline van Maarsen's reaction to Otto's declaration that he hoped to find a publisher for the diary was incredulous: 'I thought, how crazy, who would want to read a book written by such a young child? And I didn't like the idea because I knew my name was going to be in it, but luckily for me, Anne had changed my name to Jopie, and though I didn't like that either, I was much happier not to have my real name published.' Eva and Fritzi Geiringer also saw the diary. Eva recalls, 'He showed it to us, and then he read a few pages from it, and he burst into tears. He couldn't carry on. He was very emotional about it and quite shocked by the fact of its survival, and also by what he read. I found reading it very strange myself.' By this time the Geiringers had learned that Eva's father Erich had died on one of the death marches and her brother Heinz had died three days before the end of the war in Mauthausen.

The majority of Otto's family and friends encouraged him to proceed. Hilde Goldberg recalls,

On my first leave from Belsen where I had been working as a nurse, I came back to Amsterdam and as I was walking down Waalstraat, I saw Otto. We just could not stop crying. I think he already knew what had happened to his daughters then, yes, he must have done, from the Brilleslijper sisters, but I was able to tell him a bit more about what Belsen was like. He told me about the diary and I said he should publish it. Why not? It was all he had.

Kurt Baschwitz may not have agreed with all the sections which Otto decided to retain, but he had no doubt of the diary's power: 'It is the most moving document of that time that I know of, and a literary masterpiece as well . . . I think it ought to appear in print.

On 1 December 1945 Otto attended the funeral of his close friend Johan Voskuijl, Bep's father. Four days later, Otto accompanied Hanneli and Gabi Goslar, together with two other children, to Schipol Airport. Hanneli recalls,

Otto helped us to get to Switzerland – not money-wise but with papers. He sorted that out, I couldn't. On 5 December he took me, my sister and two of my friends to Schipol to see us off to Switzerland. Before we left he gave us necklaces made of a chain and a Dutch coin with the date inscribed upon it. That was such a good, kind thing to do. I was in a sanatorium for three months in Switzerland. Then I went to a Swiss school. When I lived in Basel for a while, I would sometimes visit Otto's family there and I felt so strange and guilty the first time I had to go to see his old mother. I had survived and her own grandchildren had died. In 1947 I emigrated to Palestine. Gabi was not allowed to go with me then; she came in 1949. Otto and I stayed in close touch.

Hilde Goldberg, who had married a doctor she met in Belsen, also emigrated permanently, settling first in Switzerland, then in Palestine, and finally in

America, where she and her husband Max, brought up their three daughters. Five thousand Jews left the Netherlands after the Holocaust; it had become for them 'the place where they did not know anybody any longer, and where they were confronted with so many sad memories'. Most went to the US, but after 1948 many also emigrated to Israel.

Otto wrote to his mother on 15 December that he would not be there for her birthday five days later, but still hoped to visit them as quickly as possible:

> I always have so much to do, that I never get round to complaining . . . And, indeed, if for a moment one looks back, one should only think of the nice things there were and not mourn the past . . . As sad as much of it was, in the end we were together for a long time, and even though the children were killed for some unknowable reason, their spirits remain eternally childlike.

On 17 December 1945 Tonny Ahlers was again arrested by the POD. On Christmas Eve, he wrote to his captors frantically, having compiled a fictitious list of good deeds he had done during the war. He claimed to have saved many lives but could only recall one name: Otto Frank. He wrote down how he had 'delivered' Otto from 'the hands of the SD' and that 'this man (Mr Frank) was 100 per cent for me!' He told them that Otto had obtained his address 'so that he could thank me in the highest possible terms. And this man was then unknown to me!' On 6 January Ahlers's wife wrote to the authorities, begging them to free her husband since she had two tiny children and no income. Ahlers remained in jail, accused of being an 'informant for the SD, for betraying people to the SD, and a director of the Wehrmacht Einkauf Buro PTM'. Witness after witness confirmed that Ahlers had worked for the SD, including his mother who told the police, 'During the war he has done all kinds of terrible things.' It emerged that when the police had first tried to arrest Ahlers after the war, he had sent them to another man named Ahlers who lived nearby. The man's hysterical wife visited Ahlers's father, hoping to convince him to intercede. He merely laughed and said she 'could not touch' his son, who had 'good papers and was protected by rich Jews'. Ahlers's former boss, Kurt Döring, was interviewed in relation to the case, but since he was due to stand trial for war crimes he was unwilling to incriminate himself and would only say, 'My impression is that Ahlers is a big talker, very ignorant and capable of anything.' Listed among the other members of the SD and Zentralstelle staff due to be questioned about Ahlers was Maarten Kuiper. The interview never occurred.

Despite Ahlers's protests to the authorities and his requests to the police to interview the 'Jewish Director of Opekta', Otto Frank wanted no more to do with him, having at last been confronted with the evil of which Ahlers was capable: '[Ahlers] was in prison as a political criminal. I went to the commission . . . They showed me the documents on him, and I saw that I was the only person he had saved. He had betrayed a great many others.' If Otto had suspicions that Ahlers was involved in his own betrayal, he kept them to himself for the time being; in 1946, the investigation into his own political background would begin.

Towards the end of 1945 Otto finally received all the documentation he needed to travel to Switzerland. Kleiman was to have accompanied him but he once again fell ill with a haemorrhage. Otto took the train alone from Amsterdam to Basel, where he arrived to celebrate the New Year, 1946. In the expansive, welcoming house on Herbstgasse, Otto was surrounded by faces he had not seen since before the war: his mother, Leni, Erich, Stephan, Buddy, and Erich's mother who also lived with them, Oma Ida.

Otto returned to Amsterdam in late January, writing to his family immediately afterwards, 'The trip went well. I was the only passenger and Bep met me at the station. I was bombarded with questions. Everything I brought back with me was so gratefully received. There's too much to discuss. I haven't even checked my post yet . . . It is strange, all these same people and yet so different . . . It was wonderful to be with you again.' They had spoken little of the events of the past year, and Buddy sent Otto a letter explaining why: 'We didn't have enough time to talk during your stay in Basel, to say what is in our hearts . . . You can't imagine how much I wanted to hear about your life . . . But to be honest, I was frightened of re-opening old wounds.' Otto reassured him; he had understood and found it difficult to speak himself of all that had happened without breaking down. He hated to dwell on the tragedy of the past: 'There is no point in wasting away in mourning, no point in brooding. We have to go on living, go on building. We don't want to forget, but we mustn't let our memories lead us into negativity.'

Following his return from Switzerland, Otto gave the revised typescript of the diary to Werner Cahn, who was keen to get a second opinion on its potential: 'I knew the Romeins via the journal *De Nieuwe Stem*. I took the typescript to Annie Romein-Verschoor, whose opinion I valued highly. Jan Romein saw the typescript lying there that evening. He read it through in one sitting and immediately wrote his piece in *Het Parool*, which was printed the next day.' Jan Romein was a very well-respected Dutch historian.

On 3 April 1946 his article appeared on the front page of *Het Parool* under the title, *A Child's Voice*. It began:

By chance a diary written during the war years has come into my possession. The Netherlands State Institute for War Documentation already holds some two hundred similar diaries, but I should be very much surprised if there were another as lucid, as intelligent, and at the same time as natural. This one made me forget the present and its many calls to duty for a whole evening, as I read it from beginning to end . . .

Later that day, publishers began to call Romein, who referred them to Cahn. He remembers, 'Fred Batten, who was at that time with the publisher Contact, also rang and his enthusiasm led to my giving him the typescript on approval.'

Everyone at Contact agreed the diary should be published, but there were difficulties. Otto recalled the managing director, G. P. de Neve, 'telling me that religious advisers had objected to the printing of certain passages (e.g. about menstruation). It is evident I myself do not object to these passages as they are included in the German version and other translations.' De Neve also demurred over Anne's angry outbursts against her mother and the entry where she describes her curiosity about a friend's breasts. The manuscript was thus amended and its style brought in line with house rules. Some changes were also made in the choice of words and some lines rephrased. Twenty-five full passages were omitted. Otto agreed to the alterations: 'The text was edited at the request of the publishing house. Some unimportant changes were made. These were entries which might cause offence to the readers.'

In June five excerpts from Anne's diary were published in *De Nieuwe Stem*, the left-wing newspaper for which Werner Cahn worked. Otto had found a list of pseudonyms among Anne's papers for all those in hiding, and decided to use them in place of real names. Nonetheless, some people found it inconceivable that he would publish it. Rabbi Hammelburg, with whom Otto was on the board of the Liberal Jewish congregation, told him he thought it was wrong to publish the diary: 'Otto Frank was what I call a good man, but also sentimental and weak. He told me for the first time about his daughter Anne's diary when the manuscript was already with the publisher, Contact . . . I didn't read *Het Achterhuis* until it was in the shops. Nor did he ever speak to me about the whole commercial hullabaloo which went on, and I have never appreciated the Anne Frank House. The same goes for all thinking Jews in the Netherlands.' Annie Romein-Verschoor also had misgivings, despite her own involvement (she wrote the introduction to the first Dutch edition):

The overwhelming success of the book exceeded all my expectations and even now I cannot really explain it . . . Success breeds success and the desire for money. This is not an imputation against Otto Frank, who, when he came to tell me that the diary should be published, with tears in his eyes, assured me that he did not wish to profit from the suffering of his child, and I assumed that he meant it and has held to that . . . Otto Frank was certainly opposed to the success and the subsequent myths and speculative defilement which inevitably came with it, but he could not stop it.

Otto was convinced that he was doing the right thing: 'Anne would have so much loved to see something published . . . My friends' opinion was that I had no right to view this as a private legacy as it is a meaningful document about humanity . . . Anne would have been so proud.'

On 15 May 1946 Bep Voskuijl married Cornelius van Wijk and gave in her resignation at the Prinsengracht. Otto, Miep, Jan, Kleiman and Kugler all attended the wedding. The first of Bep's children was born the following year; Bep named her daughter Anna. A young man was hired to take Bep's place at the office. Erich Elias was in Holland in summer 1946, to discuss business matters with Otto.

In July Otto attended the first post-war conference of the World Union for Progressive Judaism in London as a delegate. This provided him with the opportunity to see Robert, Lottie and Milly again. Milly recalls,

Knowing how happy Anne would have been that her diary became an international bestseller brought Otto his first glimmer of consolation, but when he came to England in July 1946, this healing process had hardly begun. We met at the London hotel where my mother and I usually stayed. He got there first, and we found him resting with his eyes closed. I thought I had never seen such a sad face. When he saw us, he brightened up, and we talked for hours. He told us in full the story of his escape . . . he also spoke of the terrible journey from Holland to Auschwitz in 1944 and the agony of parting when the men and women were separated . . . He described the scenes in the camp, when the prisoners were lined up to be chosen as victims for the gas chambers: his neighbours were picked repeatedly, but somehow he was left unnoticed.

Otto's friend Isa Cauvern, who had typed the diary manuscript as a favour to him, committed suicide in late 1946, leaving her husband alone in the

large apartment he only shared with his daughter Ruth when she was home
from boarding school. Ab Cauvern invited Miep and Jan, who were still
living with Jan's sister, to move in with him. Miep recalls, 'Jan and I discussed
the situation with Otto. Otto said that if it was all right he'd like to move
along with us to this apartment . . . "I prefer staying with you, Miep," he
explained. "That way I can talk to you about my family if I want." In fact,
Mr Frank rarely talked about them, but I understood what he meant.'

The investigation into Otto's background as an enemy national was
conducted throughout 1946. This was done by the Nederlands Beheers
Instituut (NBI) – the body charged with 'the administration of enemy
property in the Netherlands, of the property of the members of the NSB,
and of the property of deported Dutch citizens who had not returned'. Otto
'insisted' that the NBI act quickly to clear his case so that he could travel
abroad on business. In order to satisfy them that he was and had been
'politically trustworthy', Otto had to ask his friends and employees, as well
as several people who had been with him in the concentration camp, to
attest to his good character. Jan Gies, Dunselman, Kleiman and Otto's friend
from the Foreign Police, detective Gerard Oeverhaus, all wrote on his
behalf. Oeverhaus asserted that he had known Otto since 1933 and judged
him 'One hundred per cent a friend of Holland, the Dutch people. He was
and is anti-German and anti-National Socialist.' Otto also drafted his own
declaration.

Although the NBI were thorough, they apparently did not discover
Otto's sales to Berlin and business with the Wehrmacht (van Keulen is
mentioned several times but no connection is made with the Wehrmacht).
On 7 February 1947 the NBI found Otto free of all charges of being an
enemy subject and declared him 'no longer an enemy national in the sense
of the Order concerning enemy property'.

The diary was originally to have been published in March 1947 according
to a letter Otto wrote to Gertrud Naumann early that year. He was staying
in Basel for two weeks, having arrived on 6 January, and reminded her,

Today it is two years ago that Edith perished in the camp. You can't allow yourself
to give in to your feelings otherwise it would be unbearable. Margot remained the
quiet, delicate one. Anne was like quicksilver, but inwardly just as good. Her diary
will be published here in March and I'm negotiating with Switzerland and the
United States for a German and an English edition . . . Apart from you and Mrs
Schneider, there are few people in Germany who I care about . . . In life one must
search for the bright spots, so I must be glad to have my mother and to have the

opportunity to see her and my brothers and sister again. But there's no substitute for a wife and children. As I'll soon be fifty-eight years old I can't expect much from life any more.

Otto comments on the expected date of publication in another letter to a friend that month and on the issue of his feelings towards his former homeland,

> The diary will come out in book form in March. I take it that later an English and German translation will come out so you can read it then. It's a unique document, not written to be published, but written from the heart, for herself alone. It's astonishing how a young girl between thirteen and fifteen could write. How everything affected her. This at least has survived. In spite of all my experiences, I am not given to hatred. I don't generalize because I know how many injustices occurred, though people do generalize. I still have a lot of friends in Germany. Their behaviour was correct and they also suffered . . . I understand your longing for your homeland but there's nothing that would drag me back to Germany.

Otto's sentiments were in line with many Jewish survivors of the camps: 'For most European Jews, post-war Germany was a land stained with blood in which self-respecting Jews should not live. Even some of the Jews in Germany themselves felt that they were merely a "liquidation community" living in "a stopping place between the camps and the grave".'

Just as Bep had resigned from the Prinsengracht offices in the summer before, in May 1947, Miep gave in her notice. She remembers,

> At the office real products were again for sale. The business had never ceased to function at any time. Since his return Mr Frank had again become the slightly nervous, soft-spoken man he'd been before the hiding time. The change that had taken place when he'd gone into hiding, the calm authoritative personality he'd assumed, had vanished. But Mr Frank's interest in the business seemed to be waning . . .

Difficulties with Opekta remained. The loan given to Otto by Erich Elias in 1933 was due to be repaid to the Nederlands Beheers Instituut (NBI) under the terms of the order concerning enemy property. The governing body were not satisfied that the loan had been 'a friendly arrangement' of a personal kind and they now ruled that the loan must be transferred from Otto to Pomosin-Frankfurt. Otto was granted permission by the NBI to repay it in small instalments because of his claims against the LVVS and because profits at Opekta since the end of the war had been so poor. The matter was finally resolved, in 1950, by a decision of the Minister of Internal Affairs. Under the terms of an agreement between the Netherlands and Switzerland relating to settlement of conflicting claims to German property, Opekta-Switzerland was removed from the list of enemy nationals. The money repaid by Otto was transferred to the Nederlandse Bank on behalf of the Swiss concern.

In 1947, however, Otto was still trying to find a way to supplement his low income as he explained to his old comrade from Auschwitz, Joseph Spronz:

Everything is better here now. We're not hungry but business is very difficult. I'm trying to develop some import–export business, but just about everything I attempt runs aground on currency regulations and other problems in various countries. I can't get artificial silk – the big firms won't let anyone in. I don't have much experience in textiles and work more in foodstuffs and chemicals . . . I have talked with a friend about importing braces and other such clothing accessories. He said he would try to find interested parties but he needs prices, samples, photos of the goods . . . Another friend of mine would like raw products of different kinds . . .

Otto also felt able to write about his emotions to Spronz, who had lost many of his family, including his first wife, in the Holocaust: 'I'm happy to hear that you got married again and wish you and your new wife all the best. I can understand how you're looking forward to your baby . . . on the outside I know I seem okay but my life is in fact over. Without children, there is no point in life.'

Anne's eighteenth birthday would have been on 12 June of that year. And, despite feeling that his life was over, 25 June 1947 was an important day. Otto noted in his engagements diary: '*BOOK*'. The diary was issued in an edition of 1,500 copies, with a foreword by Annie Romein-Verschoor. Otto published it under the title Anne herself had chosen: *Het Achterhuis: Dagboekbrieven van 14 Juni 1942 – 1 Augustus 1944*.*

Asked years later about his editing of the diary – that is the changes to the text Otto made before handing the manuscript to the publisher – Otto replied, 'Of course she didn't want certain things to be published.

---

* *The Back House: Diary letters from 14 June 1942–1 August 1944.*

I have evidence of it . . . Anne's diary is for me a testament. I must work from her perspective. So I decided to do it through imagining how Anne would have done it. Probably she would have completed it as I did for a publisher. She would have shown it to us anyway. She would have discussed it.'

Since the early 1980s, when it became apparent that it was *The Diaries of Anne Frank* rather than *The Diary of Anne Frank* which formed the basis for the world's greatest bestseller, controversy has raged not only over whether Otto had the right to tamper with his daughter's literary masterpiece, but also over the extent of his editing. When an interviewer asked him how much had been omitted, he answered, 'Nearly nothing has been withheld. A few letters were withheld which deal with personal affairs . . . of people still living. But these don't affect the diary in the least. Practically everything is published.'

Anne herself never intended to publish her complete diaries, but instead a book based upon them. After hearing Bolkestein's broadcast, she wrote, 'Just imagine how interesting it would be if I were to publish a novel of the Secret Annexe. The title alone would be enough to make people think it was a detective story.' A month later she declared, 'My greatest wish is to become a journalist someday and later on a famous writer . . . In any case, I want to publish a book entitled "Het Achterhuis" after the war. Whether I shall succeed or not, I cannot say, but my diary will be a great help.' By May, she was ready to begin. Out of necessity, the new version was compiled on sheets of coloured carbon paper which had been given to her from the office supplies. Here and there she changed the odd word, removed a reference, added a sentence, deleted whole passages and added scenes from memory, as well combining entries to make the writing flow. Among those loose pages which Otto removed, perhaps intending that they should never be published, were two sheets on which she had written an introduction to the diary:

Writing in a diary is a very new and strange experience for me. I've never done it before, and if I had a close friend I could pour my heart out to, I would never have thought of purchasing a thick, stiff-backed notebook and jotting down all kinds of nonsense that no one will be interested in later on.

But now that I've bought the notebook, I'm going to keep at it and make sure it doesn't get tossed into a forgotten corner a month from now or fall into anyone else's hands. Daddy, Mummy and Margot may be very kind and I can tell them quite a lot, but my diary and my girlfriend-only secrets are none of their business.

To help me imagine that I have a girlfriend, a real friend who shares my interests

1. Robert, Otto, Herbert and Leni Frank, around 1895. *Photo courtesy Buddy Elias, private collection.*

2. Otto Frank in 1900.

3. Otto (*centre*) with friends in Frankfurt. The caption on the back reads: 'So you won't forget the dancing lessons of winter 1906/07!' *Photo courtesy Buddy Elias, private collection.*

4. Otto and his mother, Alice, on holiday in Granada.
Photo courtesy Buddy Elias, private collection.

5. Otto around the time of his
sojourn in New York.

6. Otto and his siblings shortly before the outbreak of the Great War. *Photo courtesy Buddy Elias, private collection.*

7. Otto Frank as a German soldier. *Photo courtesy Buddy Elias, private collection.*

8. Otto being given a haircut whilst serving on the Somme, 1916. *Photo courtesy Buddy Elias, private collection.*

9. Edith Holländer, around the time of her engagement to Otto Frank.
Photo courtesy Buddy Elias, private collection.

10. Otto and Edith's wedding day (and Otto's 36th birthday), 12 May 1925.
Photo copyright AFF/AFS/Archive Photos.

11. Otto and his children, Margot and Anne, 1930. Anne captioned this: 'Papa with his two sprogs.'
Photo copyright AFF/AFS/ Archive Photos.

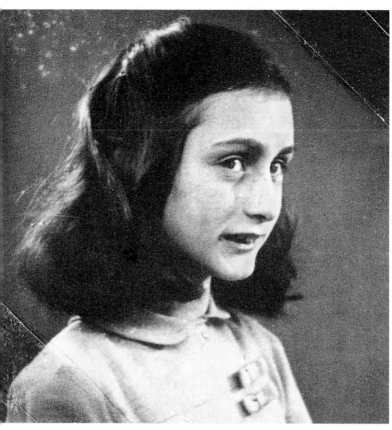

12. Previously unpublished photo of Anne Frank. It was taken shortly before the family went into hiding, and Anne pasted it on to the last page of her first diary. *Photo copyright AFF/AFS/ Archive Photos.*

13. The secret annexe during the war years.
Photo copyright AFF/AFS/ Archive Photos.

14. Three of the helpers (*front*): Victor Kugler, Bep Voskuijl and Miep Gies. (*Back right*): Pine, and the smiling girl (*left*) is Esther, who was forced to leave Otto's employ when the anti-Jewish laws came into effect. May 1941.
Photo copyright AFF/AFS/Archive Photos.

15. Tonny Ahlers's identity card from the Fokker factory in Amsterdam, 1941.
Photo copyright Rijksinstituut, Den Haag.

16. Tonny Ahlers at the funeral of WA man Hendrik Koot. From *De Telegraaf* newspaper, 18 February 1941. Ahlers is in the white raincoat.
Photo copyright De Telegraaf.

17. Karl Josef Silberbauer. He led the raid on the secret annexe on 4 August 1944.

18. Euterpestraat 99 (now Gerrit van der Veenstraat) the headquarters of the Sicherheitsdienst (German Security Service and Security Police).
Photo copyright NIOD.

20. Charlotte Pfeffer, before the war.
Photo copyright AFF/AFS/ Archive Photos.

19. Otto Frank, sole survivor of the eight in hiding, reunited with his brothers and sister in Switzerland after the war.
Photo courtesy Buddy Elias, private collection.

21. Wedding day of Otto and Fritzi, 10 November 1953, in Amsterdam.
Photo copyright AFF/AFS/ Archive Photos.

22. Otto in his private office at 263 Prinsengracht in 1953. His concentration camp number is visible on his inner arm.
Photo copyright Maria Austria Instituut, Amsterdam.

23. Otto and his brother Herbert accompany a group of young Japanese readers of Anne's diary around Basel Town Hall.
Photo courtesy Buddy Elias, private collection.

24. Otto in 1967. His great passion was travel.

25. Otto the grandfather. Otto and Fritzi with Zvi Schloss (*right*) and Zvi and Eva's three daughters, Jacky, Caroline and Sylvia, whom he loved dearly.
Photo courtesy Eva Schloss, private collection.

26. Otto a year before his death, with the Orde van Oranje-Nassau medal on his coat. He received the honour on what would have been Anne's fiftieth birthday, 12 June 1979.
Photo courtesy Buddy Elias, private collection.

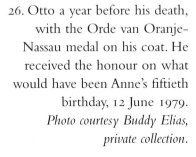

and understands my concerns, I won't just write in my diary, but I'll address my letters to this friend-of my-own-imagination, Kitty.

So here we go!

Otto chose not to use this introduction.

Curiously, although Anne wrote two versions of her diary, both are incomplete. The original diaries are missing the entries for the year 1943 (this book has been lost, although Anne must have had it when she was working on her revised version), and the second draft finishes four months before they were arrested. This presented Otto with the problem of having 'two incomplete versions to work with. With unprecedented skill Otto Frank shaped these two into a single version of which, of course, the second version formed the basis. Necessity therefore brought a third version into existence.' For the period from June 1942 until December 1943, Otto had both diaries from which to work, and usually he stuck to the revised version. For the year 1943, he had only the revised version. For the period from December 1943 until March 1944, he again had both at his disposal.

It has always been thought that Otto removed the sexually explicit passages and those where Anne wrote most harshly about her mother, but in fact it was more often Anne herself who eliminated these details from her revised diary entries; her original entry for 6 January 1944, for instance, begins with a long passage about her feelings towards her mother, then proceeds to a discussion about sexuality before ending with her decision to become friends with Peter. In her revised diary, Anne completely cuts the paragraphs dealing with her mother and sexuality and omits much from the section concerning Peter. For his version, Otto turned the long original entry into two (dividing them unnecessarily into '5 January 1944' and '6 January 1944'), and kept almost all of the original version intact.* Otto realized that part of the power of the document lay in entries such as these and, despite having no background in writing or publishing, his editing of the diary, particularly for that time, was ingenious.

In a private letter, Otto clarified his position: 'Anne made an extract of [revised an entry in] her diaries in which she deleted and changed a great deal of material . . . But I thought that much of the deleted material was interesting and characteristic . . . so I made a new copy in which I re-inserted passages from her diaries.' Otto's prologue to the first edition in 1947 read,

---

* Laureen Nussbaum's article *Anne's Diary Incomplete* in *Anne Frank Magazine 2000* discusses this entry in particular; she was the first to point out that Otto actually reinstated much of the material Anne herself deleted.

'With the exception of a few sections, which are meaningless to the reader, the original text has been printed.' The former would have made a more accurate introduction to his daughter's legacy.

Most reviews of *Het Achterhuis* hailed it as an outstanding book. *De Groene Amsterdammer* praised 'the intelligence, the honesty, the insight with which she observed herself and her surroundings, and the talent with which she was able to depict what she saw was astonishing . . . [Anne is] the symbol of those who shared her fate, those murdered by the Germans.' On the other hand there were others such as the critic in Amsterdam's *De Vlam*, who were dismissive: 'By no means a war document as such . . . but purely and simply the diary of an adolescent girl.'

Otto sent scores of copies of the diary out to family and friends, and to the writers, politicians and heads of state mentioned in the book (the Dutch prime minister, Gerbrandy, made the terrible mistake of addressing his letter of acknowledgement to 'Miss Frank'). Now that the diary had been published, Otto wanted it to enjoy wide success. In a letter to Anne's former boyfriend Hello Silberberg (in which Otto explains that the other name changes in the diary had been made by him), he urged, 'You can be content with the description of those days, without knowing it your person will be fixed for the next decades as you were in those years of youth . . . It is in Anne's spirit that the book should be read as widely as possible, because it should work for people and for humanity. Speak about it, recommend it to others.' Silberberg replied a month later, in July 1947: 'I have never found it as hard to write a letter in my life as I do now. I am convinced that it doesn't serve any purpose to describe my emotions to you . . . I am convinced I will never know another person who can fix these thoughts for the future in such a clear, touching and at the same time *accusing* way.'

In 1947 Otto signed a contract with Ernest Kuhn, a New York attorney, who agreed to represent him in negotiations with American and Canadian publishers. Included in the contract were drama, radio, film and television rights. Twentieth Century Fox expressed an interest in the book, but this came to nothing. In October Otto received a letter from Paul Zsolnay of Heinemann & Zsolnay Ltd in London whose reader in Vienna had given the diary,

> an excellent report . . . Consequently, I shall be very pleased to publish this book in Austria if you will give the German translation rights to my Viennese firm. The translation is quite satisfactory and small improvements can be put in, if necessary, by my Viennese reader . . . Mrs Frank told me that you were

also interested in having an English version of the book published in London. I shall therefore submit the original Dutch book to William Heinemann Ltd and will recommend it very strongly.

Mrs Frank was presumably Leni, who sent the German manuscript to publishers Amerbach-Verlag, Basel, without success. Ultimately, Heinemann did not publish the diary.

In the Netherlands the diary was in its second edition by the end of the year, as Otto told his cousin Dora: 'Anne's book is a big success here . . . There have been readings from the book four times already. I hope I can succeed in seeing that English and German editions are also published . . . I get reports from Germany often. As a whole they are not going to change, but single cases deserve help. Thus mother sends to people regularly who deserve it.' Milly visited Otto in Amsterdam that winter and he seemed brighter than when she had last seen him in London. She recalled,

The country was certainly at its worst, deep snow everywhere, trams few and far between. But the people were so sturdy and uncomplaining that I found it energizing. Otto showed me all over the annexe and introduced me to the wonderful group who, for over two years, had risked their lives daily to help them . . . The rooms were as Anne described them. Her collection of photos still hung on the walls.

In 1948 an investigation was launched into the betrayal at 263 Prinsengracht. Kleiman had taken the first measures to bring the traitor to justice in February 1945 by visiting the Politieke Opsporings Dienst (Political Criminal Investigations Department or POD) with a letter detailing the arrest, warehouseman Wilhelm van Maaren's unpleasant interest in the secret annexe, Lena van Bladeren-Hartog's dangerous gossip to Anna Genot, and other noteworthy incidents. On 11 December 1945 Otto had written to his mother that he hoped the investigation could begin:

I was at the Security Police. We did all we could to try to get out of them who had betrayed us . . . yesterday we all went to the police station to study photographs, to see if we could recognize anyone who had arrested us and then perhaps learn more from these people about those who betrayed us. The photos were astounding – we could identify two of the men. They're still in prison and we're going to confront them . . . If only this might work, but quite often the people themselves don't know who the actual traitors were, and simply did what their whiter-than-white superiors told them.

The two men identified from the photographs were Willem Grootendorst and Gezinus Gringhuis. Grootendorst, born in Utrecht in 1889, had worked in the Amsterdam police since 1912, first as an agent, then as a detective, and later for the Zentralstelle. He could not remember the arrest at 263 Prinsengracht, but recalled a raid at 825 Prinsengracht on 8 April 1944, the date of the worst break-in at the annexe, when the fugitives were almost discovered. He admitted having assisted SS Oberscharführer Silberbauer during arrests of Jews and had worked with Gringhuis on several occasions. After the war he was tried and imprisoned for 'delivering Jews to the SD'.

Gringhuis, who was later sentenced to death but never executed, was born in Onstwedde in 1895. Employed by the Amsterdam police, in 1940 he joined the NSB, then the Rechtsfront and the WA. In 1942 he was transferred to the Zentralstelle, working alongside Ahlers's friend Peters. He was arrested by the Dutch authorities in May 1945. In his declaration about the secret annexe betrayal, Gringhuis told the police, 'I cannot remember anything about an arrest on 4 August 1944 in a house at 263 Prinsengracht in which ten people, among them eight Jews, were taken into custody.' Somewhat peculiarly, Gringhuis did say, however, that he had spoken to Otto Frank, who had received an anonymous letter in which a member of the Joodse Raad was named as their betrayer. Otto did not know the man, but Gringhuis did and felt there was no reason to suspect the man's integrity. Interestingly though, the letter contained the sentence, 'Your hiding place in Amsterdam was mentioned at the Zentralstelle.' One person who had connections with both institutions was Tonny Ahlers: he occasionally acted as a supervisor at the Expositur department of the Joodse Raad on Jan van Eyckstraat, and he was a familiar face at the Zentralstelle, where his closest friend was a staff member. If Ahlers was the writer of the accusatory letter, it would not be the last time he would name another man as the Franks' betrayer. Gringhuis also told the Dutch detectives that, regarding the betrayal at 263 Prinsengracht, 'I have heard the name Silberbauer. I think that he was also employed at the Zentralstelle. I have never been friends with the SD man Kuiper . . . or have I been with him at an arrest?'

Kuiper was not brought forward at either of the two visits made by Otto and his loyal friends to identify their captors. In 1947, a year before the investigation into the betrayal at 263 Prinsengracht began, Kleiman made a statement to the POD about Kuiper and the fact that he was not questioned in relation to the arrest. In a letter to Otto dated 1958, Kugler refers to Kuiper as 'a Dutch Nazi with a thick head . . . about whose deeds a lot has been published in the newspapers' and wished that Kuiper had at least been mentioned publicly in connection with their case. He then recalled the confrontation with Gringhuis and Grootendorst, during which 'the civil servant said that unfortunately the third person [Kuiper] could not be presented' because he had been sentenced to death. As Kugler said, the Dutch newspapers were filled with reports about the Kuiper trial in 1947. The *Elseviers Weekblad* described Kuiper, the 'Criminal of the Euterpestraat', as 'a tall man with a sharp nose in a small face, a short upper lip and a thin mouth . . . His eyes have the burning look of a lunatic. Hard throat muscles run under his jaws, the chin is aggressive.' It was impossible to name all those whom Kuiper had betrayed; he admitted himself that the figures ran into the high hundreds. Reporters wrote at length about some of the murders for which he was known to be responsible, including the shooting of Hannie Schaft, one of the Netherlands most well-known resistance fighters. On another occasion he had killed a young man and his parents, running out into the street to shoot the young man who had desperately tried to escape; for this, the press noted, 'the bloodhound received fifteen guilders'. The Judge declared Kuiper's history to be 'one immense indictment of manhunt, murder and manslaughter'. On 6 December 1947 Kuiper was sentenced to death, whereupon he screamed to the courtroom: 'I have not committed any betrayal, I have not arrested anybody, I have never denounced Jews! I acted under orders of my superiors! I regret my actions . . . !' His appeal against the death penalty was dismissed. On 30 August 1948 Maarten Kuiper 'the SD detective who arrested numerous Jews, people in hiding and others', the man whom Tonny Ahlers had idolized, was executed.*

The official investigation into the betrayal at 263 Prinsengracht began in January 1948. Otto had visited the Politieke Recherche Afdeling (Political Investigation Branch or PRA) in June the previous year to give them a copy of Kleiman's 1945 letter and, according to his engagements diary, on 20 and 21 August 1947 Otto spoke to van Maaren (who had been edged out of the business) himself. Presumably he asked him whether he had played any part in the betrayal. No record of their conversation has been found. On 12 January 1948 Kleiman was interviewed by the PRA. He told them that Silberbauer and his men had 'seemed to know precisely what they were doing, for they went straight to the hiding place and arrested all eight persons present there'. Kugler and Miep were interviewed two days later but had

---

* Almost all Dutch war criminals and collaborators received light sentences; few were actually sentenced to death or to long years in jail (and those who were frequently had their sentence considerably shortened). Only thirty-six were executed, 'among them not only German Nazis and Dutch collaborators, but also the Jewish woman Ans van Dijk, found guilty of betraying more than 100 Jews'.

little of any interest to say to the detectives, unlike van Maaren, who gave the PRA a written declaration in early February in which he wrote that upon seeing the entrance to the secret annexe for the first time, he had been 'dumbfounded by its technical ingenuity . . . the SD would never have been able to find out anything about this secret door without inside information'. He also stated, 'I was told that on arrival the SD went straight upstairs to the bookcase and opened the door.'

On 10 March Petrus and Anna Genot were interviewed and confirmed that Lena van Bladeren-Hartog had said that she had heard there were Jews hiding at 263 Prinsengracht. Petrus Genot told detectives that he had guessed as much as early as 1942, having cleaned out the annexe prior to its clandestine habitation and having noticed the large amounts of food delivered to the offices. On 18 and 20 March Lena van Bladeren-Hartog and Lammert Hartog were questioned by detectives. Lena was clearly evasive in her replies, but understandably so even if she were not guilty of making the phone call to the Gestapo; she would not want suspicion brought upon herself. Lammert Hartog told the police he had seen the great quantities of food deposited in the building, but had only connected them with fugitives concealed on the premises when van Maaren confided in him 'about fourteen days before the Jews were taken away that there were Jews hidden in the building'. Hartog had not liked van Maaren but, nonetheless, he considered it improbable that he would betray anyone. Hartog had one further comment to add: 'I was struck by the fact that the detectives who raided the place were not just on the lookout for hidden Jews but were, you might say, completely in the picture.' Van Maaren was questioned on 31 March and admitted that he had had suspicions that 'something peculiar was going on in the building' for some time, having also noticed the food deliveries. He was adamant that he was not the betrayer.

While the investigation was in progress, a second, almost concurrent inquiry into Otto's attempted betrayal by Joseph Jansen in 1941 began. His name had come up during the investigation into the secret annexe betrayal, but he was not pursued in connection with it; having spent the large majority of the war years in The Hague, he was therefore unlikely to have been aware of Otto's movements in Amsterdam.* During the Jansen inquiry,

---

*Jansen did not appear to know about Otto's deliveries to the Wehrmacht or to the Armee Oberkommando in Berlin. Otto never asked for him to be investigated in relation to the betrayal at 263 Prinsengracht, but he did contact the Political Criminal Investigation Service about the letter of 1941:

'*Concerning Mr Jansen:* Together with this I send you a copy of my letter concerning Ahlers that I sent to Scheveningen. I do not know if this man whom I call Jansen in my letter

Miep had a new statement to add to those she had made about him in 1946: 'Later on I found out from Mr Frank that the NSB man who had given said letter to Mr Frank was Anton Ahlers who resided at Hoofdweg in Amsterdam at the time.' When the police arrived to question Ahlers in his prison cell about the matter, they were given unexpected news: he had escaped. It was not the first time he had done so; during his imprisonment he had been transferred from one penitentiary to another, and had managed to slip away on several occasions, always returning to his wife. During one bout of illicit freedom, he was captured while committing a theft. He remained at large during the Jansen inquiry and by the time he was caught and imprisoned once more, the police had apparently forgotten to interview him; he never was questioned by them.

The investigation into the Franks' betrayal was closed on 22 May 1948.

---

is caught already because this is the man who is actually doing the dirty work. I have forgotten his forename initials and I do not know where he lives but there is a woman who lives on the Amstelveensweg and has a flower stall at Amstelveensweg 72 who can tell you all about him. She separated from her husband and she is of Jewish origin and has nothing to do with all this stuff. But you can certainly get information from her. I hope that Mr Jansen is already behind bars or will be caught through this letter.'

During the war, Jansen betrayed his own son to the Germans; he wrote to Seyss-Inquart to inform him that his son had said all Germans should be shot. In September 1941 the Jansens' two sons were arrested in the night. Jansen dismissed this to his terrified wife with the words, 'Well, there are bound to be victims.' Jetje did all she could to have her sons set free – even appealing to Ahlers's neighbour Friedrich Christian Viebahn, who knew her husband – but to no avail. One son was shot in Neuengamme, the other was liberated at Ebensee. On 31 March 1945 Joseph Jansen was arrested. Otto and his employees all gave evidence against him. Jansen's wife, Jetje, recalled, 'About the letter to the NSB, which my husband is said to have written concerning Mr Frank, I cannot tell you anything because I was notified of this fact by Mr Frank after the war. It is indeed correct, that my husband carried addresses of Jewish people in his wallet during the war. I do not know what he intended to do with them, but out of concern for their safety, I had my children warn the persons concerned, so they could take their measures.' She did say that when Otto told her about the letter, 'I thought that the ground had disappeared from under my feet.' Questioned about his attempted betrayal of Otto, Jansen denied having ever written the letter, 'It could not have been my handwriting. I believe that, if I were to stand and look Mr Frank full in the face, and would tell him that I was not the writer of the letter, he would certainly believe me. I am not an anti-Semite and I have always respected Mr Frank and considered him to be a man of high standing. I do not know the solution to this . . .' Jansen was sentenced to four years and six months in jail. His doctor filed a report on him shortly before he was freed, confirming that 'Now when we go over all this with the accused, everything that he is charged with, it must be said that the accused fully acknowledges it. He knows he has been wrong and he positively feels that denouncing Mr Frank is a very damaging fact to his name.' On 21 March 1949 Joseph Jansen was released. He died a few years later.

In the process of that inquiry, Johannes Kleiman, Wilhelm van Maaren and Lammert Hartog had all given statements to the effect that the Gestapo and NSB were acting upon inside information, yet the detectives failed to ask how any of them had reached their conclusions. Van Maaren, the main suspect but against whom nothing could be proved, was granted a conditional discharge. He was cleared of all charges in an appeal on 13 August 1949.

Tonny Ahlers was released from prison on 3 October 1949 and stripped of his Dutch nationality as a mark of disgrace.

Due to the Dutch East Indies' independence from the Netherlands in 1949, Gies & Co., which depended upon the spices imported from the former colony, experienced a fall in profits. Otto hoped to import pectin from America, and his cousin Dora provided a connection to a company in Kansas named Speas Co. The head of the company assured Otto that his associate, Mr de Wijk of Renkum, in the Netherlands, would call upon Otto to discuss the matter with him. Otto replied with sharpness and anger; he had already worked with de Wijk in 1935 when he and his partner, W. Vermeer, manufactured 'pen-jel' which Otto bought from them. Otto wrote to Speas Co., 'I know that Mr de Wijk was your agent before the war, but I did not know that he is still acting for you as no activity from his side could be stated in the market. I do not wonder that this "gentleman" is *not* sending the booklet as his conduct during the war was of such a kind that he would not dare visit my firm.' There was no further communication between them.

In July 1949 Otto travelled to London and Paris to meet with publishers who had expressed an interest in the diary. He signed a contract with Calmann-Lévy, who would publish the diary in France the following year. The translators worked from *Het Achterhuis* rather than from the diary itself. Upon his return to Amsterdam, Otto sent a copy of the German translation to a Mr Koretz of Fox Film, Paris on 5 August. Presumably this came to nothing, but in January 1950 Francis (Frank) Price, the head of Doubleday's office in Paris, was given an advance copy of *Le Journal* by the author Manès Sperber, an adviser to Calmann-Lévy. Price's first impression was that 'the volume [was] of little importance' and he instructed his assistant Judith Bailey to reject it. Bailey read it, and asked Price to reconsider.

In the Netherlands, the diary was into its sixth edition by July 1950, but 'the time lapse between the fifth printing in February 1949 and the sixth printing in July 1950 gave the publisher the impression that interest in the Second World War was declining, and the book was not reprinted between 1950 and 1955'. Otto divided his time between his business, diary-related matters, and his friends. The year before Gertrud Naumann had married Karl Trenz, and in 1950 Hanneli Goslar married Walter Pick, an Israeli army major. Otto kept in regular contact with them both. On 13 July 1950, after a pregnancy that came as a surprise to everyone, at the age of forty-one, Miep gave birth to a boy, Paul. She and Jan were ecstatic, and Otto was delighted for them. Ab Cauvern, whose apartment it had been originally, had moved out the year before, but Miep, Jan and Otto stayed on. Otto continued to live with them after the baby's birth, but he was more and more often away, promoting the diary.

Le Journal was a critical and commercial success upon publication. In August 1950 the American writer Meyer Levin was given a copy of it by his French wife, Tereska Torres. Levin was a forty-four-year-old novelist and freelance writer. During the war he was employed as a battle correspondent in France. His experience of the liberated camps was first-hand; he helped trace relatives and friends of the survivors. In his book, *In Search,* he said: 'I realized I would never be able to write the story of the Jews of Europe . . . Some day a teller would arise from amongst themselves.' When reading the diary, he realized he had found that 'teller' and, remembering the dead in Belsen, wrote, 'I must have gazed down on the body of this young girl . . . The voice reached me from the pit.' He vowed to avenge her. 'Isn't there something we must do to pay for being alive?'

Levin contacted the French publisher to enquire if English and American rights had already been placed. If not, he would like the opportunity to act as agent. Calmann-Lévy passed the letter on to Otto, who replied to Levin on 19 September, explaining that, 'My Paris agent Maison D. Clairouin are busy at present to place the English and American rights of Anne's diary, so that I cannot give you an option at present.' Although this was true, Otto had already written to Nathan Straus, who had spoken to Random House on his behalf, to say that he did not wish to pay agents' fees unless a firm offer was made. On 21 September Levin wrote to Otto again, enclosing a copy of *In Search,* with another idea: 'My interest in the diary is not commercial so much as one of sympathy and I would be glad of the opportunity to translate it.' He also asked permission to speak to his connections in the film and theatre world, feeling that the diary could be adapted into 'a very touching play or film'.

Otto replied to Levin on 25 September, doubtful that the diary would make the transition to stage or screen well, but 'in case you should have some ideas on the direction of the film, you are absolutely free'. He had faith that the diary would be taken by a British and American publisher eventually: 'I know it is difficult to find the right editors in England and

USA but I am sure that it will come someday.' He then told him, 'In Germany the book will be published before Xmas in Heidelberg by the firm: Lambert Schneider.'

The publication of his daughter's book in Germany was of great importance to Otto: 'I thought they should read it. But in Germany in 1950, I had difficulty. It was a time when Germans didn't want to read about it. And Schneider of Heidelberg wrote to me. He said, "I have read the book and feel it has to be published, but I don't think it will be a financial success."' Part of the problem lay with Anneliese Schütz's translation. Otto had translated excerpts from the diary from Dutch into German himself in 1945 for his mother, with help from Schütz, but this was not suitable for publication. Schütz then made a more copious translation for submission to publishers based on the Dutch typescript Otto had given to Contact and retaining some of those passages the Dutch book had omitted. Schütz did not include certain references which were only comprehensible to the Dutch reader and Otto later admitted, 'She was too old for the job, many of her expressions were pedantic and not in a youthful enough style. In addition she . . . misunderstood many Dutch expressions.'

The Diaries of Anne Frank: The Critical Edition lists a number of examples, among them her confusion over the Dutch word 'rataplan', which she translated from Anne's Dutch sentence, 'the whole bag of tricks', into 'the whole rats' nest', and 'my telling replies' became 'my bewinged replies', apparently because Schütz had looked up the Dutch word 'gewiekt' which followed the correct word 'gewiekst' in the dictionary. She also made peculiar additions of her own:

The sentence: 'He actually got Miep to bring him a banned book,' was expanded in the German translation to 'He got Miep – who of course had not the slightest suspicion – to bring him a banned book', and the statement 'she forgot all about the soup so the peas were burned to a cinder and utterly refused to leave the pan' is amplified in the German with: 'What a pity I can't tell Kepler about that . . . Theory of heredity!' Nowhere in the Anne Frank manuscripts is there any reference to the theory of heredity; in addition we have here the confusion of the astronomer Kepler with the geneticist Mendel, who based his laws of heredity on experiments with peas.

Otto still felt that her translation 'could by and large be called faithful and in the spirit of the original'. His friend Werner Cahn was less certain, for him the translation, 'although correct, did not always reflect the style of the young Anne Frank. That is, in any case, a particularly difficult thing to do.

But this may well be the reason why well-intentioned German literary circles occasionally expressed doubts about the authenticity of the diary.'

There were also some changes 'of a more political nature'. These were made on account of Schütz's attitude that 'a book intended after all for sale in Germany cannot abuse the Germans'. Thus the following differences to the text occurred. Anne's description of conditions in Westerbork and the line, 'We assume that most of them are being murdered', from her entry of 9 October 1942, were cut. The self-imposed rule in the annexe that 'only exceptionally could one listen to German stations, for instance to hear classical music and the like', was cut. Similarly, the house rule 'Only the language of civilized people may be spoken, thus no German' became 'all civilized languages . . . but softly!' (Otto professed the change had been made by the German publisher, but it is clear from the typescript that the change was made earlier.) The sentence, 'He ended up looking like a giant and he was the worst fascist there was' was changed to 'watching him grow into an invincible giant'. Anne's line concerning 'heroism in the war or when confronting the Germans' was altered to 'heroism in the war and in the struggle against oppression'. And her declaration that, 'There is no greater hostility than exists between Germans and Jews' was transmuted into 'There is no greater hostility than between *these* Germans and Jews!'

Otto said that the last change was made at his suggestion, and his explanation of why reveals sentiments akin to Schütz's own:

There is one sentence which I changed a word of purposely. Anne writes about the Germans, what terrible people the Germans were. And I made it *these* Germans. Because there were other Germans too. And I'm sure I thought of it discussing it with Anne. It is a matter of character, a matter of responsibility which I feel. We had friends in Germany. Anne had a very good friend in Germany . . . and I had a secretary – we knew these could never have been Nazis. The secretary was caught out when she tried to smuggle a Jewish cousin of ours to Luxembourg . . .

Asked whether he thought Anne would have changed it later, Otto replied firmly, 'Yes.' Perhaps he would have been less keen on approving such differences to his daughter's text if he had known the results of a poll conducted in Germany. In 1947 three-quarters of all Germans considered the Jews to 'belong to a different race than ourselves'. In October 1948 41 per cent of Germans still approved of the Nazi seizure of power. In 1952 37 per cent of the population felt it was better for Germany not to have any Jews and, in the same year, 88 per cent said they had no personal responsibility for the mass exterminations. Removing the German references not only offered its readers absolution, it also pandered to the widely held view that Jews could never be German. For over forty years the German text of the diary retained its delicate editing. The publication of the complete diaries in 1986 rectified this bias, but, by then, it had ceased to be an issue because few people were aware of the reinstatement of the original meaning.

The first German edition of 4,500 copies sold moderately well, though booksellers were reluctant to push it. In a letter dated 14 December 1952, Otto wrote, 'In Germany they sold very little, as the newspapers do not collaborate . . . I hope to be able to stimulate the sale and shall work out a scene as I agreed with Lambert Schneider.' In 1955, a paperback edition of the diary was issued in Germany. It was a runaway bestseller, but by then the diary had already achieved worldwide fame.

On 29 September 1950 Otto wrote to Meyer Levin about the reactions of the British and American publishers who had rejected the diary, and in response to Levin's repeated requests to approach people in the movie industry, Otto told him, 'You just go on and I shall not interfere. It even would be possible to film the original place and I would try my best to overwin [overcome] my inner feelings.' In England Gollancz, Heinemann, Allen & Unwin, Macmillan and Secker & Warburg had all turned the diary down and in the US the publishers Scribners, Viking, Vanguard, Simon & Schuster, Appleton Century, Schocken, Knopf, Harper and Harcourt had done likewise. Random House mentioned the possibility of making an offer if a British publishing company would also agree to publication.

In late September the Jewish publishing house, Vallentine Mitchell & Co., contacted Otto's Parisian agent Clairouin to ask about British rights. When he was in London, Levin visited them: 'I have just talked with a representative of a rather new British publishing house, the firm of Vallentine Mitchell. They are eager to have Anne's diary . . . I hope you will feel that it would be a good idea to have them do it.' When Otto replied on 30 October he told him, 'Secker & Warburg wrote to me and asked for an option while considering the matter. So I postponed Vallentine Mitchell a little while until I get a definite answer from Martin Secker.' It was Levin who had alerted the other company, as he confessed to Otto, but added, 'They have had long enough on it. The Jewish Chronicle group is really eager to publish it . . . it would be my suggestion, if I may offer it, to let Vallentine Mitchell have it and to ask him to get in touch with Random House about the arrangements and have it done here also.'

Levin had already begun to call upon his contacts in New York theatre and film, and sent out scores of letters to agents, producers and directors, none of whom were willing to commit themselves. On 11 November Janet Flanner's 'Letter From Paris' in *The New Yorker* referred to the diary as 'one of the most widely and seriously read books in France'. Despite her condescension (she called Anne 'a precocious, talented little Frankfurt Jewess'), it was a valuable piece of promotion, as was Levin's essay about the diary in *Congress Weekly* on 13 November 1950. Under the title, 'The Restrictive Market', he attacked the American market for not publishing more books about Jews and cited the diary as an example of how the European market was not so narrow-minded.

Dutch refugee writer Dola de Jong had seen both pieces. She recalls,

I was what is commonly called 'a scout' for the American publishers . . . I found out about the diary and ordered a copy of the book. But, believe it or not, I couldn't interest the American publishers. I was well connected in those days, but all the publishers I approached rejected the book. One of the big houses who rejected the diary was Doubleday (they later bought the rights from Frank!). But, in the end, I found a junior editor at Little Brown in Boston who had the right instincts and feelings. His name was Ned Bradford.

On 18 November Otto told Levin that he had offered the diary to Vallentine Mitchell in London after Secker & Warburg had rejected it: 'Now I have to wait for their answer and if we agree on conditions I will ask them to take up negotiations with Random House.' The problem now was who would do the English translation. Otto wrote,

I *have* an English translation [by Rosie Pool], but my friends in London told me that this translation was not good, and advised me not to give it to [the] publishers. So I kept it, but it certainly is a good base for another translation. The French one seems to be alright, but it is made by *two* persons, one understanding perfectly Dutch, but not being French, and the other one *not knowing* Dutch but a real young French woman, knowing the language of a young girl! This is essential. Therefore I even do not know, if a translation made for Britain is just as good for USA. An American girl probably uses other expressions.

Otto wrote about Rosie Pool's translation to Vallentine Mitchell on 21 November concluding, 'My New York friend [Straus] wrote me that it was insufficient.' Straus later admitted that the translation was 'almost incomprehensible' and that he felt 'Otto's enthusiasm for the manuscript might be inspired by affection for his lost little daughter rather than based upon any real merit inherent in a child's diary . . . I believed – as most people did –

that the American public was tired of hearing of Nazi atrocities and would not pay to see them depicted again on the stage.' Otto paid Pool for her work, but did not have the heart to tell her that he could not use it. Levin had offered to do the translation, an idea Otto disliked but thought could still prove useful: 'I do not want to accept this, but perhaps he could make the necessary corrections.'

On 22 November 1950 Ned Bradford of Little Brown sent a cable to Otto: 'This is definite offer to publish Anne Frank diary in US. Excellent chance simultaneous British publication . . . Prefer Dola de Jong to translate, much enthusiasm for book here. Little Brown & Co.' Otto also received a reply from Vallentine Mitchell: 'You will doubtless be pleased to know that, in principle, your offer has been accepted by our directors. What we should like to do is to acquire from you the English language rights and to come to an arrangement with an American publisher – Random House has been suggested – whereby the latter buys from us the rights to reproduce the book in USA. This procedure has the merit of simplifying the business of sharing the costs of getting your daughter's journal into English.' Otto told Levin, 'I wrote Vallentine Mitchell explaining the whole situation and asking them to get in contact with Random House first. I told them about the affair Little Brown and did send them the translation of Mrs Pool to judge themselves, if this translation is worth-while as a base to be overworked. Vallentine Mitchell asked for the Hebrew rights too.' Otto travelled to London the following day to discuss matters with Vallentine Mitchell.

His companion on the journey was Fritzi Geiringer, who was going to visit her parents and sister in England. He and Fritzi often attended the Friday night services at the Liberal Jewish synagogue together. She recalled,

As time went on I became his confidante and, in turn, I took my problems to him . . . having gone through the same experiences, Otto and I found that we had a lot in common and he also took an interest in [Fritzi's daughter] Eva. When he was chosen, as Holland's representative, to attend the conference of the World Union of Progressive Judaism in London, he took Eva along to represent Dutch Jewish Youth. I often invited him to go to lectures and concerts with me.

The meetings with Vallentine Mitchell went well enough for Otto to accept their offer upon his return to Amsterdam. He told Levin he had also accepted Little Brown's offer:

Now I want the two firms to get in contact about translation. This is a difficult question, as London would not accept an American version and USA wanted Mrs de Jong to translate. I warned Little Brown to have it translated by someone who was not in school in USA as the charm of the book could be spoiled. Of course Vallentine Mitchell want to sell sheets to USA to make everything cheaper. These questions the two firms must figure out themselves.

He also told Levin – who had advised him – that he did not want to surrender dramatic rights to the publishers.

On 10 December Otto confided his worries about the translation to Levin: '[Mrs de Jong] was not satisfied, that I did not want her to translate, as I know that she is not American and was afraid that she would not find the right style. But it seems that I am mistaken and that Little Brown want her to translate . . . I had a pretty sharp correspondence with her, but I hope that she understood the situation now and that everything will be settled.' Otto later said that he had agreed to de Jong's 'request that she was to be the translator, but never wrote her to start or urged her to go on with this work. On 12 February 1951 she mentions in a letter that she had started to translate. But at this date I had not even received contracts.' De Jong remembers events in a very different light, but it is evident that she took the decision to begin the translation without a contract and of her own free will:

Because of the urgency of the cause and because both Ned and I were convinced of the importance and the eventual success of the diary I threw caution to the wind and reluctantly proposed to do the translation on spec. Ned hated to see me make that commitment, but, on the other hand, we trusted Otto Frank . . . It was a difficult job because Anne Frank was what in those days was called a teenager and this category had its typical mode of expressing itself. A famous proponent was Cissy van Marxveldt [Anne's favourite author]. Her books were enormously popular with female teenagers and she established the 'teenage language', the way of expressing itself . . . what I'm trying to emphasize here is that my translation followed Anne Frank in her way of expressing herself. The [other] translation didn't.

Besides the problems with the translation, disputes emerged over other issues of production and promotion with Little Brown, including their tussle with Vallentine Mitchell over Canadian rights. Otto said they had asked only for US rights, and, since Canada was a Commonwealth nation, those rights belonged to Vallentine Mitchell, as was usual at the time. Otto signed a contract with Vallentine Mitchell on 15 January. His payment was £50 and

10 per cent of initial sales. He still had not signed a contract with Little Brown.

On 8 March 1951 Mr Jaap of Vallentine Mitchell announced to Otto that Barbara Mooyart-Doubleday had been chosen as their translator. Mooyart-Doubleday was a British woman in her twenties living in Amersfoort with her Dutch husband and two children. Barry Sullivan, a friend of hers who worked for Vallentine Mitchell, suggested her as the translator. He contacted her in November 1950 to tell her about the diary, which was 'rather a special case. The translator should, I think, be an English woman, with an idiomatic knowledge of Dutch, she should understand the mind of a gay, true and rather sophisticated teenager; she should be able to convey the flavour of the original and not be afraid of a non-literary translation or of using English schoolgirl expressions.'

Mooyart-Doubleday bought a copy of the book and set to work:

I was deeply moved by the diary. I read it in one breath – took it to bed with me and read it through. I did my small bit of translation, and then it must have been a matter of weeks before the publisher came back to me and said they wanted me to do it. They had asked a man working at the Embassy in The Hague to have a go too, but his approach was all wrong, and it's unthinkable really, Anne's diary translated by a man!

The translation took approximately four months to finish:

I sat at the dining-room table and wrote it all out in longhand. I had a couple of dictionaries for if I was in any doubt. I would do one page in the afternoon while my little boys slept or played in their play pen, and then I'd get them into bed at 7 o'clock and then I'd work from 7 until 9. My husband told me I had to stop then, otherwise I wouldn't sleep, but I had a notebook beside the bed because, occasionally, I would think of things in the night and write them down. Each new day I would read the three pages I had translated the day before, because sometimes after a night's sleep I would think, 'I don't like the way I've said that, that could be improved.' So I would go through the three pages again each time. I was to have been paid sixty pounds, but when I was halfway through, Vallentine Mitchell wrote to say, 'We are in negotiations and we may be able to sell your translation to Doubleday. If that is the case we will raise your fee to £100.' And fairly soon they told me they were selling it but they told me not to panic with finishing the translation because there were all sorts of questions yet to be settled. Later the proofs came and Otto sat with me out on the balcony of my home and we read it through.

She remembers her first meeting with Otto vividly:

Having finished the main work of the translation, I had a day alone. I left my boys at home and travelled to Amsterdam by train. I remember walking from the station and seeing the Westerkerk in the distance, knowing Otto was in the office on the Prinsengracht. Then ringing the bell there . . . It was very strange and I was very impressed by the whole experience. I was charmed by Otto. He was tremendously courteous, old-worldly in that sense. He showed me around the '*Achterhuis*' and it was very different then to how it is now. There seemed to be unexpected trap doors and things everywhere. Creaking wooden stairs and torn paper on the walls. When he was showing me around he was not especially emotional for the simple reason that he had something to do, but then we walked over to Hotel Krasnapolsky and, during lunch, talking one to one, tears came into his eyes several times. He was a very sad man and, at that time, it was all still very close. I was later once very emotional and remember bursting into tears before him. That was when he took me to meet Fritzi. We were having lunch, and, I don't remember quite what he said, but I know he turned to Fritzi and said something along the lines of, 'You can see now how bound Mrs Mooyart is to Anne and the diary.'

Doubleday had come back into the picture through Frank Price, who after his second reading of the diary had grown more enthusiastic about it. On 14 March 1951 he wrote to Otto, offering terms similar to Little Brown. Otto replied that he already had an American contract in place, but had refused to sign it because of difficulties over dramatic rights, concerns which were 'more a matter of sentiment on my side than a financial one. I do not want a film to be made based on terror, bombardment and Nazis spoiling the ideal base of the diary and therefore want to keep these rights under control.' He warned Price that he was so keen to see Anne portrayed correctly, his decision 'depends on it to a great extent' and he would discuss contract possibilities with Doubleday only when 'I know your standpoint about the film question'.

After receiving Price's assurance on the matter of dramatic rights, Otto wrote to Little Brown on 27 March to inform them that he would not be signing a contract with them. Whoever made a note of Otto's decision did not tell Dola de Jong:

One morning, I found the announcement in the *New York Times* that Otto Frank had sold the rights to *The Diary of a Young Girl* by Anne Frank to Doubleday. I was nearly finished with my translation. Of course, Ned Bradford and I talked on the phone. There wasn't a darn thing he could do. After all, this business was his secret.

We hadn't informed his superiors of our decision. We would have gotten hell for getting caught up in such an unprofessional affair. As for me, I was so incensed with Papa Frank that I simply dropped the matter.

On 30 March 1951 Otto met Frank Price in Paris. Later he had lunch with Levin and his wife at their home. Otto recalled, 'The greater part of our conversation was personal. Levin mentioned his activities in the Jewish field, he wanted to know more of my experiences.' When he returned to Amsterdam, Otto found that he had upset his French agent Clairouin by negotiating with Doubleday on his own. The agency demanded their fee, since they had provided the initial contact with Price. Otto refused to pay at first but then conceded to pay a third of what he owed. Obviously, Otto had not told Price either that Levin had been trying to provoke a response from film and theatre people for the diary, because on 9 April 1951 Price wrote to him to ask if he had been correct in understanding from their discussion in Paris, that Otto wanted Doubleday to 'handle any approach . . . from a film or radio concern, should there be interest in the dramatization in one form or another'.

After seeking advice from his friend Fritz Landshoff, who had connections with Querido, Otto signed a contract with Doubleday on 27 April 1951. Frank Price and his colleagues Barbara Zimmerman (the book's editor), Jason Epstein and Karen Rye 'playfully' formed the 'Informal Society of Advocates of Anne Frank', filled with enthusiasm for the book. Nonetheless 'the prevailing assessment at the firm was that the sales potential was small' and the marketing team were ordered to 'play down the grim aspects of the story' and stress instead the 'beauty, humour and insight of this document of sensitive adolescence'.

With an American contract in hand, Otto began to feel more confident that a play or even a film was viable, and asked both Levin and Price what they thought about approaching Italian film producers to see if their response was any more positive. Levin told him that a film was far more likely to be produced in England or America, and to allow him to continue searching on his behalf. Otto concurred, writing to Levin on 17 May, 'I have enough confidence in you and your wife to leave the film question to your judgement, knowing that you will not start any binding agreements and keep things in hand.' Neither Levin nor Doubleday knew about the other at this point, but Otto may have felt there was no need to inform both parties yet, since there was no firm interest from a film company or producer.

In July 1951 Otto travelled to London again in order to deliver to Vallentine Mitchell those passages from the original Dutch typescript which had been omitted from the book when it was published in the Netherlands. They included Anne's letters of 3 August 1943 and 15 April 1944 where Anne discusses menstruation and her curiosity about a friend's breasts. Barbara Mooyart-Doubleday can no longer recall whether the impetus to include them came from Otto or from the British publisher, but on 17 August, after receiving her additional translations, Mooyart-Doubleday's editor wrote, 'Today the last batch went on to America. Everyone feels, who has read it, that it's going to be a wonderful book. Some passages go on moving me so deeply though I've read them four or five times now.' Regarding the new sections, 'nearly all of it will go in'. It had taken some time for them to decide upon a title. Suggestions were 'The Hidden Annexe', 'The Secret Annexe', 'Behind the Hidden Door', 'Families in Hiding' and the very 1950s 'Beauty Out of the Night' and 'Blossom in the Night'. They finally agreed upon 'Anne Frank: The Diary of a Young Girl'.

On 2 October Price informed Otto that publication would be delayed to take advantage of a serialization of the diary in *Commentary* magazine. Two weeks later Barbara Zimmerman, the diary's editor at Doubleday, wrote to tell Otto that (on his suggestion) they had begun negotiations with Eleanor Roosevelt to write an introduction. Her letter was warm and enthusiastic, much appreciated by Otto who wrote to Zimmerman on 2 November that he had 'the feeling that the matter of Anne's book is not only a commercial question for you but also a personal one'. Their friendship rapidly developed through their letters. Zimmerman was at twenty-four years old the same age Anne would have been. On 2 January 1952 Otto wrote to her regarding Meyer Levin, who had contacted Doubleday for a copy of the manuscript. He told Barbara Zimmerman she could send it: 'He is an able man and the only one who had the right sentiment in regard to the book.'

Publication had been postponed until June to coincide with Anne's birthday. On 11 February Zimmerman sent Otto a copy of the introduction signed by Eleanor Roosevelt, adding, 'We are enormously pleased, a fine tribute to the book.' Otto was happy with the introduction but told Zimmerman that he was worried the book was sinking under commercialism and reminded her, 'For me it is still the human spirit that counts.' She did not respond to Otto's gentle chastising, but sent Otto proofs of the book, along with further ideas for promotion of the diary, which she thought 'might well become a minor classic'. In his reply, Otto tried again to emphasize Anne's ideals, as he saw them expressed in the diary. He was very pleased by the introduction, which he felt was 'a splendid piece, not too long and very impressive. I felt that she understood Anne and she picked out her ideals in many of the letters Anne was writing.' He wrote to Eleanor

Roosevelt himself, expressing his gratitude 'from all my heart for the interest you are taking in [Anne] and for the help you are giving by your writing in spreading her ideals . . . Reading your introduction gives me comfort and the conviction that Anne's wish is fulfilled: to live still after her death and to have done something for mankind.' According to two recent books about the Meyer Levin affair, the introduction was actually written by Zimmerman and signed by Eleanor Roosevelt.* When the author questioned Zimmerman about it, she laughed: 'What can I say? Mrs Roosevelt was a very busy woman!' Otto never learned that Zimmerman was the real writer of the introduction.

Gearing up for the publication in Britain, Vallentine Mitchell contacted child psychologist Dr Emmanuel Miller, rather than a historian, for his reflections on the diary to use as publicity material: 'Although it was written by a young girl it is unlikely it will be read by adolescents. We believe it will be of interest to parents and for all those interested in the inner problems of growing children. The book is exceptionally honest and intelligent and seems to reveal authentically all the pains and joys of adolescence.'

Levin replied to Otto's letter of 6 March with the news that he had been assigned to review the American edition for the influential *New York Times Book Review*. He told Otto that he was confident the diary would find someone to transfer it to the stage and screen and hoped Otto would send any enquiries he received about it on to him, since he felt he could write the adaptation. A week later, he said that he wanted to know who Otto would prefer to act as his agent for the adaptation: 'I will try to do the things an agent would normally do, but without obligating you in any way . . . I say this again to make sure there is no embarrassment between us or between myself and Doubleday.' He offered to step aside if necessary, since his real desire was to work on an adaptation. Otto answered that he preferred Levin to act as his agent rather than Doubleday, of whom he was not entirely confident. He preferred, 'to leave things in your hands, and to pay agents' taxes to you. Why should another earn it when we know best what is in the line of Anne's book and that the ideas prevail?' Levin then contacted Darryl Zanuck at Fox to let him know he was hoping to adapt the diary, and told him that the film, if Fox produced it, should be shot in Amsterdam.

At Levin's request, on 31 March Otto signed a document authorizing

---

* Lawrence Graver, *An Obsession with Anne Frank: Meyer Levin and the Diary* (California: University of California Press, 1995) and Ralph Melnick, *The Stolen Legacy of Anne Frank: Meyer Levin, Lillian Hellman and the Staging of the Diary* (Connecticut: Yale University Press, 1997).

Levin to 'negotiate for motion picture, television, radio and dramatic adaptation for a period of one year from this date, with the stipulation that I, as sole owner of these rights, shall require to approve any such agreements, and any adaptations of the material in this book, before public presentation'. Otto did not give Levin authorization to adapt the diary in the document, though Levin later claimed he had. Levin persevered in pressing for interest in the diary from theatre and film producers; Hermann Shumlin read the proofs of the diary and told Levin he liked it, but wanted to read his adaptation before taking out an option on it. On 23 April Zimmerman met Levin for lunch, knowing he had a keen interest in the diary. She wrote to Otto that she found Levin 'very charming and he has many fine ideas about the book'.

Vallentine Mitchell's choice of novelist Storm Jameson to write the introduction to their edition did not please Otto as much as Doubleday's choice had, though she at least wrote the piece herself. Otto felt that, despite 'being a first class writer', Jameson was 'not popular enough'. He had hoped for a bigger name. In April the first reviews of the diary prior to publication began to appear in Britain. One of the earliest was by Mary Stocks in the *Manchester Guardian*:

There is something about this particular war book which strikes very hard on the imagination . . . It may be that this particular mixture of danger and domesticity has a peculiar poignancy; or perhaps the intensity of the close-up presented to us makes it seem so. If one reads the book in a single sitting, one emerges with the sensation of having actually lived for a while in the 'secret annexe', shut up with its inhabitants. But there is more to it than that. This book comes to us in translation fairly late in the day. We have begun to forget Belsen and the persecutions and pogroms that led up to it. Later persecutions of different origin and claiming different victims have obscured those evil memories.

The *Newcastle Journal*'s review on 13 May was appreciative and expressed similar sentiments: 'The chill of Belsen pervades these trivialities. "She'll grow out of it," one thinks. And then one stops, and remembers that she was never given the chance.' Another reviewer prophesised that 'From this one girl's diary a gleam of redemption may arise.'

In May 1952 *The Diary of a Young Girl* was published by Vallentine Mitchell in an edition of 5,000 copies. As had been anticipated by the publisher, the response was cool; Florence Greenberg's Jewish cookery book far outsold the diary in its first few months. Vallentine Mitchell, although only a small Jewish publisher, was then partly funded by Captain Ian

Maxwell, who became better known as Robert Maxwell. He employed quite a large sales team but by September 1952 his representatives were reporting that 'the book was not selling very well in the provinces'. In two weeks, they had sold only three copies. The problem lay partly in the fact that Britain, unlike Germany, had no suppressed memory to confront, and the Holocaust was not part of the general consciousness. In a private letter to Barbara Mooyart-Doubleday, Vallentine Mitchell's Barry Sullivan explained that it was necessary for Storm Jameson's introduction to 'dwell a little on the concentration camp angle' because 'in England, Belsen is a hazy, almost "historical" fact and the word is often used in jokes'.

In America the diary's serialization began in a May issue of *Commentary*, after Levin had negotiated first serial rights. Otto worried that Doubleday might want him to travel to America to promote the book. He wrote to Zimmerman, 'It would be terrible for me to have to speak to someone interviewing me. I have to get out of a situation of that kind. I could not stand it.' On 12 June, Anne's birthday and four days before publication, Zimmerman informed Otto that 'of the great many exciting things that have been happening this week' Levin's review in the *New York Times* was one of the best: 'This is one of the most important things to happen to any book, especially since the *Times* is the most influential paper in the country. The review itself is a beautiful one . . . I feel sure the sales will be extremely good. *Anne Frank* will receive a wonderful reception in America!' With hindsight, Zimmerman admits that, despite all the trouble that followed with Levin, 'I have to give him credit for that review. It was damn good, very dramatic and really hit hard. It struck a chord with people and made them race out to read the diary. There really hadn't been anything like the diary before, you know. It was devastating and it was immediate. It was in the voice of a child which made it both more unbearable and yet more accessible.'

Levin's 'authoritative, dazzling, compelling' review appeared on the first page of the *New York Times Book Review* as 'The Child Behind the Secret Door'. It begins:

Anne Frank's diary is too tenderly intimate a book to be frozen with the label 'classic', and yet no lesser designation serves . . . This is no lugubrious ghetto tale, no compilation of horrors . . . Anne Frank's diary simply bubbles with amusement, love, discovery. It has its share of disgust, its moments of hatred, but it is so wondrously alive, so near, that one feels overwhelmingly the universalities of human nature. These people might be living next door; their within-the-family emotions, their tensions and satisfactions are those of human character and growth, anywhere

. . . Surely she will be widely loved, for this wise and wonderful young girl brings back a poignant delight in the infinite human spirit.

Levin's review in the Jewish *Congress Weekly* was very different in tone. There he described the diary as 'without doubt the most important human document to have come out of the great catastrophe . . . The Holocaust at long last comes home, and our defences are shattered. We weep.'

On 16 June 1952 *Anne Frank: The Diary of a Young Girl* was published in America. Contrary to initial expectations and promoted by Levin's impassioned, triumphant review, the first print run of 5,000 copies were snatched from the shelves so quickly that by the afternoon every single copy had been sold. A second edition of 15,000 was rushed through, a huge advertising campaign organized, promotional items placed in all the major newspapers across the country and syndication rights snapped up. By late afternoon, theatrical agents, producers and television executives had converged upon Doubleday's New York office demanding to know who they should contact for dramatic rights.

In Amsterdam, Otto received the news about his daughter's shoot to literary stardom in a state of shock.

7. The Question of a Jewish or Non-Jewish Writer

America was not the only country where the diary had exceeded all expectations. In 1952, after Doubleday placed the book with a Japanese publisher, it received huge acclaim there. The marketing strategy in Japan had been to sell the diary as a 'protest against the great misfortunes brought by war', and to the Japanese public, Anne Frank, despite being European, was 'an acceptable and accessible cultural figure of the war – a young victim, but one who inspired hope for the future rather than a sense of guilt for the past. Her sex further emphasized the stress on innocence.' Anne Frank became a national heroine and the mid 1950s became known as the Anne Frank Years in Japan. Oddly enough, because the diary was one of the first books to mention menstruation openly in Japan, 'Anne Frank' also became a euphemism for having one's period. Since the 1950s, five million Japanese editions of the diary have been sold.

Late on the day of publication in America, Otto received a cable from Doubleday, jointly signed by Zimmerman and Levin, in which they said they (Doubleday and Levin) wanted to act together as his agents for dramatic rights. Levin then sent a separate letter to Otto telling him that, at Doubleday's request, he had resigned as his co-agent for dramatic rights and now wished only to write the adaptation. He asked Otto to authorize him to do so, promising, 'Of course, should the situation arise where a production by a famous playwright is possible only if I step aside, I would step aside.'

The following day, in an internal memo, Zimmerman wrote to Frank Price that Levin's actions concerning dramatic rights 'seemed to be screwing the whole deal up . . . it would be best if we handled the rights and worked closely with Levin'. Theatre producer Cheryl Crawford had already called Doubleday to enquire about the rights. Not knowing that Levin planned to write the adaptation, she suggested Lillian Hellman and Clifford Odets for the task. On the same day Zimmerman told Otto that it would be in his interests for Doubleday to work closely with Levin, thereby ensuring that the diary adaptation would be handled 'suitably and with taste'. Otto cabled Doubleday on 18 June: 'Consent to give you authority to handle film and play rights with usual agent fee, providing conditions of any sale of such rights be approved by Meyer Levin and myself, as desire Levin as writer or collaborator in any treatment to guarantee idea of book.' However, he was not satisfied with the recent turn of events and told Zimmerman, 'Mr Levin did a lot for the book and is entirely filled with it. I know that he understands Anne perfectly and therefore I have all confidence in him. On the other hand I imagine that no one who buys the rights wants to have a prescription what he has to do. How do we get over this point?'

On 23 June Zimmerman told Otto that his daughter's diary was 'one of the biggest books that has been published in America in a long time'. She had not intended to talk about dramatic rights, but felt compelled to mention the wonderful offers they had received 'from some of the most important playwrights in America today!' Levin wrote to Otto after a meeting with Joseph Marks, a Doubleday vice-president, to inform him that he (Levin) had received seven serious offers of production, but was worried about another playwright whose name had been mentioned by Marks and whom Marks seemed to favour.

On 25 June Marks and producer Cheryl Crawford met. She offered to give Levin the opportunity to write a script within two months, after having discussed his ideas with him first. If she was not completely happy with it, but felt it had promise, then she wanted to call in another writer to work with him. Levin agreed to her terms. The next day Otto wrote to assure Levin that he would 'not decide anything or give any authorization without first having been in touch with you and Doubleday . . . Let us hope the results will be gotten and of course I want you to have a share, both financially and as a writer.' Levin now began to write an adaptation. A third edition of 25,000 copies of the diary had reached the bookstores. Zimmerman asked Otto if he would be willing to travel to America 'to talk to these producers and playwrights with us'.

Levin's wife Tereska sent Otto an angry letter on 28 June, following a phone call from Otto which had evidently upset her husband in some way. She railed against Doubleday, who were in her husband's debt for the review which sparked so much interest in the diary and were now trying 'to get rid of Meyer. It's been an incredible and (in a detached way) fascinating thing to watch – the big company against the writer who was not *their* writer!' She knew that Doubleday aimed to find 'a big American name for the big public'. Tereska told Otto he had to name a producer and make the agreement with Levin firm, ending her letter, '*Do you want Meyer to try to write that play for her?* Your decision at this point is indispensable.'

Otto's next letter to Levin did little to allay his fears; he wrote that Levin should work with another playwright on the adaptation. He admitted that his change of position was due to the 'long talks' between himself and Doubleday's Frank Price during the latter's recent visit to Amsterdam. He told Levin: 'I have faith in you but I also have in Doubleday after all they did, knowing Mr Price and reading the beautiful letters of Miss Zimmerman . . .' Referring to Levin's earlier statement that only a Jewish writer could suitably adapt the diary, Otto declared,

> As to the Jewish side you are right that I do not feel the same way as you do. I always said that Anne's book is not a war book. War is the background. It is not a Jewish book either, though Jewish sphere, sentiment and surrounding is in the background. I never wanted a Jew writing an introduction for it. It is (at least here) read and understood more by gentiles than in Jewish circles. I do not know, how that will be in USA, it is the case in Europe. So do not make a Jewish play out of it!

Upon sending the letter, Otto a felt pricking of regret and sent Levin another missive, worried that his first letter was 'more harsher than I meant it'.

At the beginning of July, Cheryl Crawford was told by Doubleday that the project was on hold until Otto's visit to New York. Levin was increasingly mistrustful of everyone around him, particularly Joseph Marks, and told Otto that he suspected Marks was trying to oust him from the play. He also repeated his belief that only a Jewish author could successfully write the adaptation since 'a non-Jew would be handicapped with this material', but that he himself would not write 'a Jewish play . . . The emphasis was on the lack of opportunities open to Jewish writers to deal with their own material, not on any undue emphasis they might give to the Jewish quality of the material.'

On 7 July Doubleday cabled Otto to inform him that they would no longer act as his agent in dramatic rights. This was slightly a bluff in that they hoped to shock Otto into dropping Levin once and for all. In fact, Otto then wrote to Levin, asking him to act as his agent once more, 'I never lost confidence in your person!!!! I won't do anything without your advice . . . I am a terribly nervous man near to a breakdown and *must* be careful not to hasten matters.' Producer Crawford then wrote to Otto, telling him that if Levin could not write a worthy script within two months then she would call in Elia Kazan, the director, to work with him on it. If it still was not up to scratch, then she would employ another playwright and pay Levin for his work.

On 21 July 1952 Otto was in Basel, making arrangements to move there permanently. Despite being granted Dutch citizenship, he found Amsterdam too filled with memories for him to be able to progress with his life. Earlier he had confided to Zimmerman: 'I am attached to Amsterdam, to my friends there and to my work. The most important part of my life I spent in this town, all the past is in some way connected with the city and her inhabitants. Anyhow, I have the intention to move to Basel. I cannot explain to you all the details . . .' In another letter to Zimmerman he discloses another reason for leaving Amsterdam; he told her that more and more often he was approached by people who had read Anne's diary and wanted to visit the hiding place: 'I never refuse to speak to people interested in Anne, only I do not like Press interviews. Often people come here to see the annexe, every individual person I can see and talk to, is welcome. (To you: it is always exciting for me, but I feel it a duty, even if it is a strain on my nerves.)' Otto also wanted to be with his family in Switzerland, and in 1952 he arrived at the house on Herbstgasse, where he had his own room on the top floor. Curiously, his quarters were physically similar to those of the secret annexe. Behind a plain door, a short flight of twisting steps led up to a corridor. To the right was the large attic of the house, and immediately in front, behind another door, was a large square room, whose low ceiling made it humid in the summer months. A long window overlooked the garden at the back, and the rear balconies of the surrounding houses. Otto took Anne's diaries with him to Basel, but kept them in a bank safe. He later told an interviewer that he could never break his ties with Amsterdam: 'I live in Basel today because I can no longer live in Amsterdam. I often go there, but I can't stand it for more than three days. Then I go to the Prinsengracht where we hid for two years . . . Sometimes I look at our hiding place; it has not been changed . . . I look around and then I leave. I cannot bear the sight any longer.' Despite the past always surrounding him, Otto's life was about to enter a new phase. Not only was he emigrating to Switzerland; at the age of sixty-three he was to marry again.

Laureen Nussbaum, who remained friends with Otto after moving with her husband to Bern in 1956 and then to the US a year later, recalls,

Before he married Fritzi, Otto had other relationships, of course he did. He returned to Amsterdam in 1945 and did not marry for almost ten years. Although it took him a long time to recover from his experiences, he was a very handsome man with a lovely personality. A lot of women were widowed during the war. He really did his best for a lot of people. Women liked him and why not! I know that Mrs van Collem had her eye on him when Anneliese Schütz lived with her during working on the German translation, and Lotte Pfeffer, too, hoped something would happen.

Lotte and Otto had been friends for many years. When he returned from the camps, Lotte began to rely on him for advice, especially when she had made up her mind to have her relationship with Pfeffer legally recognized. It was Otto's groundwork which led to Lotte's posthumous marriage to Fritz Pfeffer in April 1953. Lotte had always been admired for her beauty, which had not faded after the war. Every week, she, Otto, Jan and Miep would play bridge together, and a romantic relationship between Otto and Lotte gradually developed. At some point, he asked her to accompany him to Switzerland, to meet his family there. Lotte was thrilled, and bought herself a new outfit for the journey. When they returned, it was obvious that things had not gone according to plan, for Lotte was upset about something and her relationship with Otto suffered as a result. He was already close to Fritzi Geiringer by then, and it may well have been that Lotte had expected more from the holiday than Otto had intended. Hilde Goldberg, who was a close friend of both Lotte and Otto, recalls,

We were all sure that Otto would marry Lotte. But sometimes things just don't work out. I could understand him moving to Switzerland when he did. He was living with Miep and Jan and they had a little boy, but, mostly, I think it was the situation with Lotte that brought matters to a head. It was a bad time for him as far as Lotte was concerned – he really needed to put some space between them. She was madly in love with him, but he wanted Fritzi.

Fritzi (Elfriede Markovitz) was born into an assimilated, middle-class Jewish family in Vienna in 1905. At the age of eighteen she married twenty-one year old Erich Geiringer, an Austrian businessman. Erich was very attractive, and unfaithful in the early days of their marriage, which Fritzi was able to forgive if not forget. Nonetheless, their marriage remained strong, and in 1926 their son Heinz Felix was born, followed in 1929 by a daughter, Eva. In May 1938, Erich emigrated to the Netherlands to go into partnership with the owner of a failing shoe factory which he subsequently turned into a success. When war broke out between England and Germany, Fritzi and the children joined Erich in Amsterdam, at Merwedeplein 46. Their life there was happy at first, but after the invasion, and their failed attempt to join Fritzi's family in England, things became increasingly difficult. Erich lost his job in the shoe factory but began another lucrative business producing snakeskin handbags.

On 6 July 1942 Heinz received the same call-up notice as Margot Frank. Erich and Fritzi had already made preparations to go into hiding, and the following day, like the Franks, they too disappeared from public life. Erich and Heinz hid in the Dutch countryside, while Fritzi and Eva found refuge with a teacher in Amsterdam-Zuid. On 11 May 1944 Fritzi and Eva were betrayed by a nurse who worked for both the resistance and the Germans. When they arrived at the Gestapo headquarters on the Euterpestraat they found Erich and Heinz had also been arrested. Like the Franks three months later, they were sent to Westerbork and Auschwitz. Fritzi and Eva remained together for much of their time in the camp. Upon their arrival, Fritzi's quick thinking saved her daughter from the gas chambers. She made Eva put on a coat and hat, which made her look much older than her fifteen years. On one occasion Fritzi herself was selected, and when, by chance, Eva saw her father in the camp, she told him that her mother was dead. Fritzi had actually been saved by a cousin, who intervened on her behalf, but Eva never saw her father again to explain that she had been wrong, and believes that this mistaken knowledge contributed to his death. After Fritzi and Eva's liberation and journey home, they eventually moved back into their old apartment, where Otto became a frequent visitor. Fritzi remembered, 'I didn't know how I could carry on. Erich had always organized everything for the family and now, without him, I felt lost.' Otto also supported her when their betrayer was found and tried. Eva recalls, 'My mother attended the trial but came home very upset. They had let our betrayer go. And for one reason: a famous Dutch opera singer claimed she had been saved by the same woman. And so she was acquitted. My mother wanted to kill her.'

Eva was aware that Otto wanted to marry her mother before Fritzi herself knew: 'Otto came to visit me in England when I was thinking of getting married. I didn't see how I could marry, because I didn't want to leave my mother on her own but Otto said, "Now, look. Don't worry about this, because after you are married and settled, your mother and I are going to marry."' In 1952 Eva married Zvi Schloss, an economics student from Israel then working for a London stockbroking firm in Amsterdam. Otto was a witness at the wedding. Eva and Zvi set up home in England and had three daughters. Eva worked as a freelance photographer until 1972 and then started an antiques business in north-west London.

With Fritzi, Otto discovered the romance his marriage to Edith lacked. They addressed each other by pet names; Fritzi was 'Putzeli' or 'Sugarli', and Otto was 'Burscheli'. His letters to her from America in 1952 reveal his deep affection for her (and are very different from his anniversary letter to Edith): 'I'm looking forward to seeing you as much as you are with me. In my head you're always with me. I don't think you will have anything to complain about in the future. I haven't experienced real femininity until now. I want to send the letter quickly. Do the zoentjes (kisses) do the trick? They're included.' Otto's reference to 'real femininity' presumably means that he felt he had found the right woman at last. Otto's nephew, Buddy, remembers, 'Fritzi was terrific for Otto. They were a real partnership in every sense. She helped him so much with the diary – writing endless letters, inviting people to meet them, attending functions and so on. She was always at his side and he relied upon her. I liked her – she had a tremendous sense of humour and would roar with laughter at any joke.' Father John Neiman, who became close friends of the couple after writing to Otto about the diary, recalls, 'Fritzi had great dignity and was as kind as her husband. They were both very easy to get along with, not aloof at all, just the opposite. It was clear to see that they were so right for each other. As husband and wife, they complemented each other perfectly.'

On 21 July 1952 Otto wrote to Cheryl Crawford, expressing his doubts about Levin:

> I like Meyer Levin, I trust him and know that he has the right feeling for the book, but how can I know if he is the right dramatist? I would be more than glad if he was and I hope he will realize his plans as he himself is confident and convinced. He is a fine novelist and judged right from the beginning with sensitiveness the value of the Diary for dramatization. Your proposal is a fair one and I rely upon you.

He then wrote to Levin that he had accepted Crawford as producer; Levin could make the knowledge public if he wished, provided that the news was not brought to the attention of the Dutch authorities; Otto wanted to avoid the tax liability which he would incur since he was emigrating to Switzerland.

In August Otto received a letter from the distinguished theatre producer Kermit Bloomgarden enquiring about dramatic rights to Anne's 'fine sensitive diary which you have considerately and generously given to all of us'. Bloomgarden's greatest successes had been productions of plays by Lillian Hellman and Arthur Miller. Otto informed him that he had 'cabled to Miss Crawford my consent in principle. Of course I have not yet signed any contract but a given word is sacrosanct and only if *serious* differences would arise in making the contract' would he renounce the agreement. Otto told Levin about the exchange with Bloomgarden, wondering whether it might have been 'better to give the rights to him' rather than Crawford. Levin told him that he doubted it; in the era of McCarthy's House of Un-American

Activities Committee, Bloomgarden's left-wing politics and friendships could do damage to the play, or so Levin thought.

Levin had written a radio script based on the diary to be broadcast on CBS the night before Rosh Hashanah, the Jewish New Year. He sent his first draft to Otto, who liked it but told him not to be afraid to experiment with the material more: 'Don't think that I would like to have everything as it *was*. Take the liberty of the writer and make it as good as possible to make an impression on the public . . .' Levin's radio play proved a success, with *Billboard* praising it for retaining 'all of the sensitivity and moving qualities of the original'. Levin was on a high; he had spoken to Crawford about the stage adaptation and she admitted she 'liked his approach and the way he planned to break it into scenes'. He sent her a copy of his first complete draft and waited to hear from her.

On 24 September 1952 Otto boarded the *Queen Elizabeth* at Southampton for New York, ready to discuss matters pertaining to the diary and the play. He was accompanied by his cousin Milly, who was delighted to see him again and to have the opportunity to spend a few days with him on the ship. On 29 September the boat docked in New York. Otto wrote of his arrival: 'My brothers-in-law and Miss Zimmerman were waiting for me. A huge cadillac took me to the hotel . . . Mr Marks from Doubleday had left whiskey and flowers at the hotel and he came at six o'clock to greet me. They have opened a bank account for me at the hotel. I only need to give a signature or ask for more money (which I don't do). The thing I wanted most was to talk to my brothers-in-law.'

Otto's reunion with Edith's brothers Julius and Walter was emotional, though tempered by the presence of Zimmerman. Otto described Julius, who had suffered from depression all his life, as 'a wreck about the past, very depressed and nervous and I felt deeply sorry for him. The younger one is much better'. He arranged to meet with them privately at a later date. His first impression of Zimmerman was that she was 'a sweet thing, Anne's age . . . She is so pleasant . . .' Zimmerman herself recalls,

Otto turned up with this really beautiful zippered leather notebook which was for a much older person, and I was rather surprised but very touched by the fact that he thought to bring me something. He was a beautiful, tragic man. I didn't know what to expect when I met him, but he was very spiritual. His two brothers-in-law were there, waiting for him. They were adorable. Refugees. Sad. A lot of people wanted to meet Otto. I tried to protect him from that a bit, but there were a *lot* of people, especially Jewish groups, who wanted to talk to him or listen to him. We became extremely fond of each other during his stay.

Zimmerman told Otto she had not arranged any interviews for him, although Otto soon discovered he had barely a minute to himself during his time at the Madison Hotel.

On the afternoon of 30 September Otto met Levin, who handed him the script. The following day Otto wrote to Fritzi that since his arrival,

> I've had no peace and no quiet, and I'm quite excited although I try to be calm. But in the first days so much is lined up and therefore I can't sit down properly to write to you and answer your questions . . . Yesterday in the morning I was at Doubleday. They had just had a meeting of travelling salesmen and Marks wanted me to say a few words. I did this but was very nervous . . . In the afternoon I was with Levin, who brought me the first script. He said that Miss Crawford agreed in principle and that only a few changes would be necessary. I will hear this for myself this afternoon as we have an appointment at three o'clock . . . This morning I started to read the script. I can read it only in long intervals because it excites me terribly and I have to cry all the time. The book is in many shop windows.

At 3 p.m., Otto, Levin and Crawford met in Crawford's office. She liked the script and a discussion about directors followed. Otto dined with Levin and his wife that evening. They were joined by William Zinneman, a film executive who had read Levin's theatre script and was full of praise.

On 3 October Crawford sent a letter to Otto at the Madison Hotel and told him that she had read Levin's script again and now felt it 'did not have enough theatrical potential for Levin to continue working on it, nor did she think there would be any use engaging a collaborator'. Levin was 'stunned' by her pronouncement.

After a drawn-out argument, Crawford agreed to allow Levin to rewrite his script. On 3 October Otto wrote to Fritzi, telling her nothing of the upset between Crawford and Levin. He did say that he had read Levin's first draft and his instinct told him that, 'Psychologically it's excellent, but I can't judge how it will be on a stage, that's a matter for Miss Crawford. On Monday we'll have another meeting.' He turned down all interviews and requests for appearances: 'Lots of people want me to give speeches, but I refuse them all. I've refused, for instance, the Zionists, B'nai B'rith, etc. My arrival here was broadcast on the radio.' On 6 October Otto told Fritzi:

> It continues with Levin – I saw the lawyer this morning and am going to him again this afternoon to try to reach an agreement. This morning Morton

Wishengrad, who wrote the text for a TV special to be aired on the sixteenth, read his text to me. I have the feeling that it's better than Meyer's text, which we read together. It made a certain impression on me. All this is more than exciting for me as you can imagine. The text made me think of how a film could be if it is well written, so I can relax and be optimistic. It *will* come.

Joseph Marks had suggested to Otto that he find himself a good lawyer to handle the negotiations for the play adaptation. Nathan Straus, whom Otto met frequently while in New York, recommended John Wharton of the firm Paul, Weiss, Rifkind, Wharton and Garrison. Crawford had informed Otto that she wanted a second opinion on Levin's script and proposed Kermit Bloomgarden. Levin could do little but agree. Otto confided to Fritzi: 'I have the feeling that problems will arise if Crawford doesn't agree with Levin's work, but I don't want to speculate.' It was several days before Otto learned Bloomgarden's damning opinion of Levin's script. In the meantime, Levin asked Otto to accompany him to his synagogue and then invited him home for the Sabbath dinner. Otto told Milly about his evening with the Levins. She thought it was a calculated move: 'When Otto visited him in New York, Levin took him to his synagogue, hoping that Otto would share in his discovery of Judaism.' But by then, Otto had already decided that Levin was not the right person to write the adaptation, having heard the views of Bloomgarden and Crawford: 'From this moment on, my confidence in Levin's script was vanishing.'

On 20 October, after ten static days, Otto wrote to Fritzi:

I'm getting impatient. This afternoon I have a meeting with Miss Crawford as I already wrote. Saturday I was with Levin, but had the impression that he's not happy that he has to make more changes to the script. I told him that Bloomgarden and Miss Crawford didn't think his script was dramatic enough and these two were recommended to me as the best. He didn't want to go into that. He still has hope, which I find uncomfortable because this particular knot needs undoing.

Two days later, Otto was introduced to Myer Mermin, a lawyer with much experience of theatrical business matters, through Paul, Weiss, Rifkind, Wharton and Garrison (the company also represented Bloomgarden and Lillian Hellman). Mermin and Otto quickly became friends, and it was he, rather than John Wharton, who handled most of the future negotiations. Otto wrote to Fritzi that evening:

Last night I had a long talk with Marks who was always suspicious about Levin. Levin doesn't want to give in as his heart is set on writing the script for the dramatization. It's understandable, but I have to rely on the experts. I cannot use my own judgement because it's too important a matter. Crawford also apparently thinks things will be difficult with Levin because she knows his talent as a writer but not as a dramatist. Therefore, she asked her lawyer to speak to him and Marks thinks I should ask mine to do the same. This seems right, I have to get things moving and will try to get my lawyer, Wharton, together with Crawford, to sort things out finally with Levin. Then we can begin discussions about the dramatization with another writer.

Otto wrote again on 24 October, outlining some of the problems facing him:

I had a meeting with my lawyer who sees great difficulties ahead in that another author would naturally turn in a script which has similarities to Levin's, and he said that a well-known man wouldn't contemplate beginning a dramatization until Levin is satisfied . . . In the afternoon Levin himself came by and declared that although he has no money he wouldn't think of taking a salary for a play that isn't up to standard. His reputation as a writer would be tarnished. I think he should have the opportunity to find other producers if Crawford and Bloomgarden don't like his script . . . The real problem is that Crawford didn't arrange a real contract with him and now it's too late. I'm staying impartial in all this . . . I'm not doing anything without a lawyer . . . Sometimes I wonder whether I shouldn't just drop the whole 'show business' because there are so many difficulties. I said this yesterday to Levin and explained to him that it's not right for the ideals of Anne to do something that might end up in a court case, and that it's better to do nothing than for that to happen. I think it made an impression on him.

Levin contacted Crawford to inform her that he had received firm offers from producers who were interested in his play. He told her to step aside and release Otto 'from his present sense of obligation' to her. Discovering what Levin had done, Otto turned to Mermin for advice. Mermin wrote to Levin on 29 October recommending that he, rather than Crawford, should withdraw, adding, 'Mr Frank, being the kind of person he is, will prefer to withdraw the book entirely from dramatization rather than prolong a painful controversy'. Crawford still wanted to produce and Levin still wanted to adapt, and with no formal contract between them, the situation had reached stalemate.

★

On the afternoon of 11 November Otto had a meeting with Zimmerman and Crawford who now had an entirely new proposal for him: playwright and novelist Carson McCullers should write the play. Otto agreed, presumably feeling that he could trust Zimmerman and Crawford above Levin (unknown to Otto, Frank Price had already spoken to McCullers about the play adaptation; her response had been cautious but positive). On 15 November Otto returned to Europe.

On 21 November 1952 Levin signed 'under protest' an agreement allowing him one month in which to find a producer from a list compiled by himself and approved by Crawford and Mermin. After that date, he could not perpetrate his own adaptation 'in any manner whatever' and Otto would have the right 'free of any claims by you, to engage any other dramatist or dramatists to dramatize the Book and any producer or producers to produce such dramatization'. On 21 December, having been unable to secure a written agreement to produce his script from any of those on the approved list, Levin renounced all his rights to the play. The following day he sent Otto a furious letter claiming he had never stood a chance with Doubleday and Mermin against him; they had rejected perfectly good producers proposed by him. He did not include Otto in his attack: 'My anger is not against you. It is against people who use deception and manipulation . . . We all feel that you were absolutely straight and generous with us, and that there were simply professional things in the background which you could not understand.'

Otto must have experienced relief as well as misgivings now that Levin was obliged to surrender his rights, but his thoughts were more on personal matters, as he informed Zimmerman from Basel: 'Today I expect Fritzi. We shall stay here together up to the end of the month and go to the mountains in January . . . Mother was eighty-seven on 20 December. She was in good condition and joined us for dinner. She rose and made a wonderful speech! My brother came from London, so we were together (her four children). This is an exception we are grateful for.' Otto's pleasure did not last long. On 25 December Levin sent him a second letter, now directing his anger at him, after having read in the newspaper that Carson McCullers would probably write the stage-play of the diary. He seethed:

> I am disgusted and enraged at the thought that a non-Jew has been selected to write this play . . . You may say it does not matter and all the rest of it, but, after the way my work was treated, to bring in a Gentile writer over dozens of excellent Jewish writers that are here, to have it produced by a Gentile when important Jewish producers who were eager to do it were ruled off the

list, is scandalous beyond measure. I will not stand for this. I will write about it wherever I can. It is adding insult to injury. I will tell the whole story . . .

On 7 January 1953, having learned of Levin's tirade, Zimmerman wrote to Otto about

the question of whether a Jew or a non-Jew should write the play. Naturally a Jew will feel in certain ways more strongly about the book, but in other ways this might be a disadvantage. I don't believe that a non-Jew will not feel as strongly in other ways about Anne's book, and at the same time they will not have the danger (which a Jew might have) of limiting the play to simply Jewish experience. The wonderful thing about Anne's book is that it is really universal, that it is a book, an experience, for everyone. And I think that just a little objectivity would, on the part of the writer, ensure this very broad appeal.

In a conciliatory letter to Levin, Otto tried to impress upon him that 'the greater part of the readers are non-Jews. I am sure that it is necessary to have sensitiveness for the Jewish sphere but on the whole it must not prevail'. A Jewish director 'can do much to preserve the Jewish sphere', but 'even I cannot interfere about the writer'.

Levin continued to harass all those concerned, however, and, after discovering that Crawford had decided to consult her lawyer, Zimmerman wrote angrily to Otto that Levin 'has done everything in his power to ruin everything . . . Meyer must stop this needless destruction. He is behaving more rashly than one could ever imagine . . . He is impossible to deal with on any terms, officially, legally, morally, personally . . . a complete neurotic who was destroying himself and Anne's play.' In answer to Otto's question about whether the director should be Jewish, she replied that most of them were, and asked Otto to simply trust her, 'since I have no literary reputation to gain or lose, simply your very valuable to me friendship and my very deep affection for you'.

Zimmerman today is unrepentant about her views at that time:

Otto was so vulnerable, especially then. He was moved by anyone who loved the diary. Levin acted that up a bit, although I know he cared about it really. I did read Levin's play at the start. And I was very young and naive then, but I could see for myself that it just would not work. The *Anne Frank* play Levin later published was not the one he was touting at the time. He had years in which to perfect it, and he was the sort of person who would do that, over and over. The original was no good at all. He completely misread the family, turning them into very observant Jews when actually they were upper-middle class and highly assimilated. It was not so much a play as a series of religious celebrations. It didn't happen! And Levin's play wasn't going to happen either, it was hopeless.

Zimmerman was not the only person Otto consulted regarding the issue of a Jewish playwright; he also asked Nathan Straus his view. Straus replied in terms very similar to Zimmerman, confirming, 'As far as the world is concerned, it would seem to me a distinct advantage if the play were written by a non-Jew. In the first place it would emphasize the universality of the theme. In the second place, there is, to my mind, little doubt but that the play would be much more readily accepted on its merits if it were written by a non-Jew.' There were few people whose opinion Otto respected more than his old friend from Heidelburg University. His comments had satisfied Otto that his own feelings – that it did not matter whether the writer was Jewish or not – were legitimate.

Having heard that Levin was threatening to sue Crawford (against the wishes and advice of his wife, Tereska), Otto wrote to him in exasperation: 'I told you that it is against the ideas and ideals of Anne to have disputes and quarrels, disagreements and suing . . . I start to see you as a different person . . . I would be very much pleased if you would stop with every kind of trouble-making as this is unjust and below your standing. Get awake, use your good and common sense.' Typically, Otto regretted sending the letter and sent a second which was not so forthright, although he told Levin, 'Every agreement verbally or in written form is sacred to me, even if the result turns out to my disadvantage. You are a bad loser.' Nevertheless Otto was deeply unhappy about the state of affairs, and suspected that Levin had not been fairly treated by anyone. During his stay in New York, he wrote to Fritzi that 'actually it is Doubleday who always warn me off [Levin] and in a certain way agitate me, which I try to resist'. Nonetheless, Levin's actions since his play had been rejected upset him and he told his friend Rabbi Bernard Heller that, 'I never in my life got so disappointed by the character of any man as Meyer Levin's.'

Eventually, both producer Cheryl Crawford and writer Carson McCullers withdrew from the play, and Kermit Bloomgarden stepped in to produce. From their correspondence, it is clear that both Zimmerman and Mermin were pleased to have Bloomgarden on the diary team. Otto felt that Crawford had behaved badly, so much so that he could almost justify Levin's behaviour. John Van Drieten and George Tabori were among the names proposed as playwrights for the diary adaptation. Levin tried to insinuate himself upon them yet again and brought on board a young producer named Teresa Hayden. Otto was encouraged by Hayden's letter to him but Zimmerman warned him off immediately, condemning Hayden as 'generally unstable, inexperienced and difficult . . . *not* a particularly bright person . . . associated with a string of failures'. She saw Levin beginning 'the same old pressure and nastiness again' and his 'pathological hatred for successful people' had made him 'the least trusted man in America next to McCarthy probably . . . We *have* to trust [Bloomgarden's] judgement and put the fate of the play in his hands.' Levin bombarded Otto with aggressive letters after the failure of his most recent attempt to inveigle himself into Otto's affections, and professed that his play meant to him what Anne meant to Otto. Mermin sent Levin a sharp letter, doubting that he could persuade Levin to desist with his battle, 'but who knows? I am neither a psychiatrist nor a magician – and again we have to wait to see what will happen.'

In March, whilst staying with Fritzi and Eva in London, Otto heard that his mother was seriously ill and flew out to Basel to be with her. He told Zimmerman on 16 March: 'I stayed a week and as she felt better, I returned to London . . . We hope for the best.' Three days later he wrote again: 'Mother was better, but today my brother called up and told me that mother died last night after having had a stroke. So I am returning to Basel again . . .' Alice Frank's funeral was the last time Otto, Herbert, Leni and Robert would all be together. Two months later, on 23 May 1953, Robert Frank died in London.

Otto's method of dealing with grief had always been to keep himself occupied, and following the deaths of his mother and brother, he immersed himself in business connected to the diary. He was troubled by the lack of success of the British edition. Whereas in America the book had sold spectacularly well – Zimmerman wrote to Otto on 28 April that there was no possibility of the diary going out of print since 'even ten years from now (as well as beyond that time), everyone is convinced it will continue to be in demand and as important as it is now' – in Britain, once the current stock had been sold, no further print run had been ordered. Otto's letter to Vallentine Mitchell's Barry Sullivan protesting against their decision shows how forceful and determined he could be when roused: 'You seem to be satisfied with the sale but I am not, and I am convinced that many more books could have been sold . . . I was influenced even from friends from Paris and New York to prefer your firm and to take a Jewish publisher. I honestly and frankly must say that I feel let down by you.' Sullivan tried to placate Otto, explaining the diary's sales as due to 'a definite turning away from books which deal with the deep and poignant aspects of World War II'.

Otto was not to be pacified: 'Had I known that you wanted the book so badly mainly on account of its commercial outlook, I never would have entrusted it to your firm ... I am not the only one who regards it as a disgrace that this book is not available on the English market.' David Kessler, the managing director of Vallentine Mitchell, became involved in the dispute on 17 June, reminding Otto 'that when the book came to our attention it had been rejected by more than one English publisher, as well as, I understand, by several American publishers ... 5,000 copies have been sold and, in the circumstances, I do not regard that as a bad figure.' In an internal memo, Kessler noted, 'it was a rather strange feature of this book that although the reviews were excellent the demand was not particularly strong and, in fact, we sold far fewer copies than were sold in other countries'. Pan Books issued the diary in late summer 1954 as a cheap paperback and at last it began to achieve the kind of sales which Otto had been convinced were feasible. The first two Pan editions of the diary ran to 75,000 copies and by the end of the decade it was one of their bestselling titles.

On 19 March 1953 Otto told Zimmerman that the owner of 263 Prinsengracht intended to sell the building (he retired from Opekta that year and Kleiman replaced him as the company director). The asking price had been increased from fl.20,000 to fl.30,000, but Otto wanted it: 'I shall do everything to get the house but of course my means are limited.' The idea to buy the house and set up some sort of educational organization relevant to its wartime history and Anne's diary had come from Joseph Marks of Doubleday. On 1 October 1952 Otto wrote to Fritzi: 'Marks has this plan whereby all publishers of Anne's book should club together to buy the house at 263 and install a library for young people. That's the way they think here.' Otto liked the plan but could not see how it could be accomplished. On 19 April 1953, after receiving Otto's letter about the selling of the house, Zimmerman wrote to him that she had discussed it with Frank Price and they wondered whether 'perhaps [the Dutch government] or some organization might have the sense of how very worthwhile this would be'. At the meeting of the shareholders of Opekta on 27 April they agreed to buy the property which was 'of special interest' to Otto, and that 'a foundation appointed by him' would be established there. Unfortunately, the building was quite literally falling apart and the renovation costs would be enormous. Having been informed of the strategy, Zimmerman wrote to Otto on 20 May confirming that 'after the house is saved from destruction, we can try to realize the plan of Mr Marks for an Anne Frank Foundation'.

By the summer, however, there was a further troubling development.

On 14 August Otto told Zimmerman, 'Yesterday I had a letter from Mr Kleiman urging me to come to Amsterdam immediately.' Berghaus, the firm who had purchased the neighbouring house, Number 265, intended to demolish and rebuild it. The structure of Number 263 was so weak that it would probably collapse in the process (and the new roof which had been fitted was already leaking). The only solution was to plough more money into the renovation. Otto wrote despondently,

Mr Kleiman wrote that he is in favour of selling the house rather than investing another fl.10,000 – though he knows how I feel about the secret annexe. In case a show or film would have given an outlook of further income I would not have hesitated to pay amounts needed to preserve the house. But in my present situation living outside of Holland, not earning a salary, I cannot afford it. I have to look at this matter in a realistic manner even if it hurts me to a great extent to be unable to realize the idea originated by Mr Marks to have an Anne Frank Foundation in the house and to preserve the secret annexe for future generations . . . I feel it is my duty to let Mr Marks know the state of this matter. His original idea worked in my mind all this time and became a sort of ideal, trying to make from the secret annexe not only a dead monument but to make it a youth centre for people from different countries. I intend to stay in Amsterdam a few days only to get a clear picture of the situation. Maybe a show or film will come one day – too late to help me with this project.

On 9 September Otto told Zimmerman the latest news:

In the matter of the house I feel that I should not take the risk of rebuilding if I can avoid it. The experts told me it might just as well get to cost double the amount they originally taxed. So I have to be reasonable. A decision will be taken definitely by the middle of December if the house next to us will be torn down with the consequences for our lease, and if they want to buy our house too or not . . .

His next report was even more dismal: the entire row of houses from 265 to the corner of the street would be torn down. Berghaus offered a good price for 263 Prinsengracht, and it was accepted. Opekta were permitted to conduct business from the building for one more year. After that, a different address would have to be found: Berghaus had included the building in their plans for demolition. The secret annexe would be razed to the earth.

★

On 10 November 1953 Otto Frank married Fritzi Geiringer at Amsterdam's City Hall. The only guests were Miep and Jan Gies, and Kleiman and his wife. Fritzi's daughter, Eva, was unaware that they were getting married then, and only found out when they called her. After the ceremony, there was a dinner at the Hotel de l'Europe before the newly weds departed to spend the night at a small hotel in Arnhem. The following day they travelled to Basel, where Fritzi was to share Otto's room in the house on Herbstgasse. Erich, Leni and Stephan continued to live there (Buddy was working abroad as a skating star and actor), and Herbert joined them permanently in 1955. Otto was once more in the family atmosphere he had craved, and liked being seated at the long table in the front dining room, discussing matters pertaining to the diary and news about friends with his wife, brother, sister, brother-in-law and nephew. They used his parents' silverware for meals, and were surrounded by the oil paintings and stalwart, rich furniture from the Frankfurt home of his youth. He enjoyed the little displays of familiarity: Leni's scolding of Herbie, who would sit growling in his throat and rapping his fingers on the table when nothing was being said, Erich's quiet, sensible advice and his wife's ringing laughter at some joke Buddy had passed on in his letters to Stephan. Leni conducted her antiques business in a resolute manner that surprised Otto. She was successful enough that Erich never had to work again, and each day he would take his newspaper into Leni's shop where he sat drinking tea and chatting with the customers, to Leni's amused irritation.

On 11 December Otto's lawyer Myer Mermin wrote advising him to approve the suggestion of Frances and Albert Hackett as dramatists of the diary. Otto's request to Lillian Hellman for her to write the play had been refused, but she suggested her friends the Hacketts as ideal. Their forte was light comedy, which they had employed to successful effect in their award-winning screenplays *Father of the Bride* and *It's a Wonderful Life*. Their efforts in writing for the theatre had been ineffectual, and they had also been investigated, though not subpoenaed, by the House Un-American Activities Committee. The Hacketts were eager, though unsure that they were 'the people for the job' of adapting the diary with its 'tense drama, the possibility of great intimacy in the scenes . . . And moments of lovely comedy which heighten the desperate, tragic situation of the people.' Bloomgarden re-assured them that he did not want to 'wring tears out of people' and felt that 'the only way this play will go will be if it's funny . . . get them laughing, and that's the way it's possible for them to sit through the show'. Mermin's only reservation to Otto about the Hacketts was the difficulty of their agent,

Leah Salisbury, who was 'studying the contract now and has already indicated to Bloomgarden that some of the provisos are not satisfactory to her'.

On 19 December the *New York Times* announced that the Hacketts would be adapting the diary for the stage. Levin contacted them immediately, reiterating every detail of past events. Otto had also seen the article, and confided to Frank Price that he was nervous about the choice: 'I confess that I am a little afraid, as most Europeans are, of a "Hollywood" writer for such a serious and delicate subject.' He was happier when he had received their first letter, in which they declared themselves 'very honoured and very humble in approaching the task. It is a very beautiful, and very moving book . . . We pray that we may be able to capture its quality . . . the spirit and indomitable courage of your daughter.'

As Mermin had forewarned, Salisbury negotiated a contract that was slanted in her clients' favour as writers rather than Otto's as the father of the murdered girl. By the time it was finalized, Levin had placed an advert on the theatre page of the *New York Post*, accusing Bloomgarden of killing his play. He asked the public to contact Otto and demand a test reading. Quite a large number did, but Otto ignored the letters on his lawyer's advice, feeling his former friend had 'the mind of a psychopath'. Bloomgarden paid no attention to Levin either. Price, who had taken over the business of the diary since Zimmerman had left Doubleday after her marriage, censured Otto for his 'gentleness of spirit' that 'allowed this matter to go on to the point where it has reached this impasse'.

The Hacketts were busy with the script, paying particular attention to a scene which would depict the Hanukkah service in hiding. They consulted a rabbi and 'got Jewish prayer books, hymn books', but were treated coldly in the Jewish bookstore they visited and enquired nervously of Bloomgarden: 'Will [Levin] be able to marshal all the Jewish people against us?' Otto's response was kinder; he recalled 'every detail' he could from their observance of Hanukkah in the annexe. After gathering their information, the Hacketts later said their aim with the Hanukkah scene had been to see 'what liberties we could take without offending anyone'. For background about Dutch wartime history, they consulted Tony van Renterghem, a former resistance fighter. He recalls: 'The Hacketts knew absolutely nothing about Holland or the war. I had to brief them extensively.'

Otto was perturbed by the lack of contact between himself and Bloomgarden; he had not yet received any correspondence from him which, he told Frances Hackett, 'I resent a little' not because it was 'a business matter to me, though business is connected with it, but everything relating to the book is real life . . . Anne's diary is a link between those who work on it . . . and myself and it creates a certain personal feeling.' She and her husband were too busy with the script to intervene. They had finished their second version, but Frances wrote in her own diary that they were 'so afraid of making people unsympathetic that we have not made them human. Started over again.' Otto sent them a copy of Anne's composition 'Give', which he hoped would be useful in helping them understand 'the rather childish idealism . . . so typical of Anne'. Frances responded that it was 'naïve, I suppose. But somehow I cannot believe that such gifts of love and the understanding that she pleads for might not well be what is most needed in these chaotic and terrible times'. At the end of May the Hacketts sent copies of the rewritten script to Bloomgarden, Hellman, Salisbury and Otto. They were nervous; the main change from the previous script was in the voiceover technique which was originally spoken by Elli (Bep), but had been altered to Otto, because they felt he was the one 'responsible for Anne's development'. They were worried not only about Bloomgarden's reaction, but also Otto's: 'He may be shocked at the amount of comedy we have in it . . . but I think it is true to the character of Anne . . . and consequently in the spirit of the book.'

Otto sent Mermin his opinion on the script on 2 June. He hated it, and confessed his surprise at his own 'negative' reaction: 'Whereas with the Levin play, I felt that the psychological development and the characters were good, but that I could not judge the dramatic value, my first impression of the Hackett version is to be excellent routine work, but giving the spirit of the book . . . I cannot say that the script is against the spirit of Anne but it is not working up to the high spirit of Anne and in its present form would never convey the message which the book contains. You can imagine that I feel very miserable about the situation. What I wrote to you I shall never be able to write to the Hacketts, who are such fine and sensitive people.'

Otto waited three days before sending the Hacketts his views, beginning his letter, 'I have a lot to object.' Listed as causes for his dislike was the 'rather humouristical touch' in the first act, the relationship between Anne and Edith, as well as that between Anne and Peter, which was 'too compressed' and their depiction of Margot as 'snappish'. What was needed, he told them, was a clear illustration of Anne's 'optimistical view' of life. He continued, 'Having read thousands of reviews and hundreds of personal letters about Anne's book from different countries in the world, I know what creates the impression of it on people and their impressions ought to be conveyed by the play to the public. Young people identify themselves very frequently with Anne in their struggle during puberty and the problems of the relations mother-daughter are existing all over the world. These and the love affair with Peter attract young people, whereas parents, teachers, and psychologists learn about the inner feelings of the young generation.' He felt that their play 'failed to do justice to the circumstances', and his confidence was so low he was uncertain whether 'the points I raised could be corrected'.

The Hacketts were depressed by Otto's response. Sensing their dejection, Bloomgarden gave them something concrete on which to build: three pages of necessary amendments to their script, including the change of the Hanukkah scene from serious to celebratory. He suggested that they write a scene in which Pfeffer ('Dussel' in the script) stole bread, and wanted the relationship between Anne and Peter to be given much greater attention. In conference with the Hacketts, Bloomgarden suggested writing the play as a depiction of Anne coming to terms with the normal problems of adolescence under extraordinary circumstances. Anne's own description of the diary as a chronicle of 'how we lived, what we ate and what we talked about as Jews in hiding' was dismissed. The Hacketts and Bloomgarden were in agreement that the worst thing they could do was to show 'a collection of disagreeable people on stage and too much of the depressing atmosphere of nightmare and horror . . . we should [not] worry too much about reactions to showing oppressed Jews in an unfavourable light'. Throughout the sweltering summer of 1954, the Hacketts worked on their script in the apartment they had rented in New York. In September, after having been told by Bloomgarden that he would only consider producing the play if there was 'more spiritual lift for Anne', the Hacketts met Lillian Hellman in Martha's Vineyard to ask for her advice on the script. They returned to New York with fresh enthusiasm: 'Went to see Lilly. She was amazing. Brilliant advice on construction.'

On 6 September, waiting anxiously to hear from the Hacketts, Otto informed George Kamm of Pan books about the diary's worldwide sales: 80,000 hardbacks in the USA with 200,000 sales of Pocket Books; 135,000 in Japan; 30,000 in the Netherlands, 35,000 in Sweden; 4,600 in Britain and 4,500 in Germany, although Fischer's cheap paperback would be issued the following March in an edition of 50,000. In his letter, Otto notes that there had been some changes of words and phrases even in the text of the Pocket Book edition. Later Otto wrote to suggest some ideas for a window display promotion and included a pamphlet he had paid to have designed and reproduced 1,000 times to distribute in bookstores.

On 25 October Otto told Mermin that he had received a copy of the revised script and was 'really satisfied'. Otto was in hospital at the time, after having suffered a nervous breakdown. His fragile state of health had finally given in to the strain. In his letter to Mermin though, Otto insisted that he now felt 'quite well' and went on to admire the Hacketts' approach to the material 'from an entirely different direction. I must confess that I am now very confident concerning the success of the play . . .'

On 29 October Garson Kanin was appointed as director and it was at his suggestion, more than anyone else's, that the script lost some of its most vital elements. In an article he wrote for *Newsweek* in 1979, Kanin looked back on his involvement in the play with excessive sentimentality, calling Anne a 'bright and wondrous kid . . . Her father was the man who said, a moment before their inescapable discovery, "For two years we have lived in fear; now we can live in hope."' Queried on French television about whether he had actually uttered those words, Otto shook his head and laughed. In his article, Kanin recalled for his readers Anne's 'bright, sweet, smiling little Jewish face – an admixture of humour and tragedy' and compared her to 'the Mona Lisa (which she strangely resembles)' and 'many classic figures in the world's lore' including 'Juliet, Peter Pan, Albert Einstein (was he *ever* a small boy?), Gertrude Stein, Grandma Moses, John F. Kennedy, Shirley Temple'. His appointment as director came at the instigation of Lillian Hellman, and he reflected on a project that 'turned out to be not so much a theatre job as a rare religious experience'.

Under Kanin's guidance, Dussel's reports about the ordeals suffered by the Jews and the non-Jewish Dutch disappeared to be replaced by the single sentence: 'No one in Holland has enough to eat.' Otto's speech about the horrors of the camps was removed and the arrival of the Nazis at the annexe became dramatic; jackboots on the stairs, thundering at the door and German voices screaming to open up. Specific references to the Holocaust were excised. The lines uttered by the stage Anne (adapted from Anne's own words): 'We're not the only Jews that have had to suffer. Right down through the ages there have been Jews and they've had to suffer' were altered. Kanin noted,

People have suffered because of being English, French, German, Italian, Ethiopian, Mohammedan, Negro, and so on. I don't know how this can be indicated, but it seems to me of the utmost importance. The fact that in this play the symbols of persecution and oppression are Jews is incidental, and Anne, in stating the argument so, reduces her magnificent stature . . . In other words, at this moment, the play has an opportunity to spread its theme into the infinite.

The lines were changed to 'We're not the only people that have had to suffer. Right down through the ages there have been people that have had to suffer. Sometimes one race, sometimes another.' In an effort to secure 'better audience identification with the subject and the characters' almost all references to Jews and Jewish suffering were erased.

Otto supported the Hacketts in their striving to make the play more universal: 'It was my point of view to try to bring Anne's message to as many people as possible even if there are some who think it is a sacrilege and does not bring the greatest part of the public to understand.' However, the fact remained that scenes invented by the Hacketts, such as the one in which Hermann van Pels steals bread (an incident which never occurred) were deeply misleading. They disregarded historical fact, suggesting to members of the audience who had not read the diary that Anne must have written about such events herself. Originally, the Hacketts had depicted Dussel (Pfeffer) as the thief, but Otto himself advised them to change this to van Pels (because of his own friendship with Lotte Pfeffer). He then became fearful of a potential law suit from Hermann van Pels's brother, who was living in New York. Nothing came of it, but his friends in Amsterdam would later question how he could have allowed this scene (and several others) to be included in the first place.

On 6 December, following three weeks of intensive work on the script in London, the Hacketts and Garson Kanin arrived in Amsterdam. In her diary, Frances recorded how they found 'presents from Mr Frank waiting in the hotel room. This is St Nicholas Day. Garson, Albert Hackett and I met Mr Frank for first time.' The following day, they visited the annexe, which Frances wrote was 'very harrowing. Stood in Anne's room, stretched out my arms, touched walls on either side. This is the room she had to share with the crotchety dentist. Saw Garson looking at one of the photographs Anne had pasted on her wall. It was Ginger Rogers in a picture he had directed – *Tom, Dick and Harry.*' They also walked around the Rivierenbuurt, taking in Anne's Montessori school, their former apartment and the 'ice-cream parlour where Jews were allowed', before meeting people: Miep, Jan, Bep, Kugler and Kleiman. Otto introduced them to his friend, historian Louis de Jong, who offered to read their script to check 'for mistakes in documentation'. On 10 December Kanin arranged for a photograph to record every physical aspect of the annexe, 'doorknobs, stairs, sink, stove, windows', while Frances and her husband 'got recordings of Dutch children's games, street organ, got books on Amsterdam'. Kanin organized 'a tape recording of Westertoren carillon, the tram car that runs to end of line a block away, canal sounds, street sounds, bicycle bells'. Throughout the day there were 'questions, questions, questions, to Mr Frank'. The following day was their last: 'Had luncheon with Mr Frank. Final evening in Amsterdam. Back in London, really spent. I thought I could not cry more than I had. But I have had a week of tears. (We heard later that Mr Frank was ill for a week.)'

Kanin's impressions of the visit were documented in an article he wrote for the *New York Times*, ending with a histrionic flourish:

In all my meetings with [Otto] he was unhurried, casual, old-worldish. He talked about the hideout and the arrest without an ounce of emotion. "This is a cold fish," I told the Hacketts. Anyway, after I left for Paris, I had to telephone Mr Frank. I didn't get him to the phone for days. Finally I learned why. The moment we'd left Amsterdam he collapsed. He had been crushed, but he had not shown it. He had been as he had been in the days when the Gestapo was outside the door – a modern miniature Moses.

The day after the Hacketts' departure to America and Kanin's to Paris, Otto informed Mermin about his more restrained perceptions of the play's team:

I spent an entire week here with the Hacketts and Mr Kanin and I must say that it was a wonderful experience to be with them and to discuss all the details of the play. Knowing me you will understand that it was very exciting too. They all are very sensitive people and I am convinced that we could not have a better director than Mr Kanin . . . They are all working with the greatest devotion and I have every possible confidence in their work. Now more than ever I am convinced that it was my duty to try to get the best script possible.

Knowing that Kanin was keen to rewrite parts of the play, Otto told Bloomgarden that he was satisfied that now that the 'very sensitive' writers had 'undergone the influence of the hiding place . . . the spirit of the script will not be changed'.

On 30 December 1954 Otto was given news he had been dreading all year: Levin had begun litigation against him and Crawford. His charge was the breach of agreements made between 1950 and 1952 permitting him to write or collaborate on the stage play of the diary. He wanted the November 1952 agreement overturned on grounds of fraudulence, and the opportunity to be given the chance to write or collaborate on a script based on the diary. He claimed $76,500 in damages from Crawford for persuading Otto to break the terms of the contract of March 1952. For much of 1955, lawyers on both sides explored possible resolutions of this particular disagreement, as well as other conflicts, between the parties. Levin placed various articles in the press requesting to have his play performed.

★

Otto would have been deeply hurt to know that two pages of suggestions for script improvements which he had carefully compiled were dismissed by Kanin as unimportant. On 10 January 1955 Kanin had told the Hacketts, 'I think all is handleable, don't you? I just glanced at them.' The Hacketts' agent, Leah Salisbury, wrote to her clients that she was worried about Otto's promise to Levin that he could have his play performed in Israel, though nowhere else. She had told Mermin she wanted 'various changes in the foreign contract', since Otto had 'too much control . . . and that all steps within our legal rights should be taken to prevent such a thing from happening'.

On 22 March Joseph Schildkraut, who would portray Otto in the play, wrote to his real-life counterpart. He had read the diary, and felt Anne, 'that wonderful *girl-woman*', was 'a *heroine* and is *immortal* – as immortal as the Macabeans were – or Joan of Arc – or any other heroine or martyr of history'. Schildkraut, born in Vienna in 1896, had been a child actor. In the 1920s he usually played a handsome rogue, but by the 1930s he was working as a much respected character actor. He told an interviewer that *The Diary of Anne Frank* was 'not primarily a Jewish play . . . In this adaptation, the sectarian nature of the story is not emphasized. These people could be any refugees, not just Jews.' He told his producer that 'each time I think or talk of "our play" – (don't laugh, Kermit, please) – I get an almost sacred feeling inside me'. During the auditions for Anne, he favoured a young actress named Natalie Norwich, and described her as 'Overwhelming! – Unique!' a '*dark-haired, dark-eyed, Jewish (not Yiddish!!)* Julie Harris. This is our girl!!!!!! . . . this *revelation* for "Anne"!!!' Eventually, the role of Anne went to Susan Strasberg, the talented young daughter of stage impresario Lee Strasberg.

The casting of Edith Frank caused a few rumblings of discontent and outrage in the press. The actress who portrayed her, Gusti Huber, was reported to have a 'former Nazi affiliation and special friendship with Josef Goebbels'. The accusation came from another actress, Lotte Stavisky, who would not work with Huber on account of her involvement in Nazi propaganda films. The Hacketts consulted Otto, who said he had asked his wife, Fritzi, who was also from Vienna like Huber, whether she knew anything about her. Fritzi did not, but was anxious to know more. A look at Huber's biography reveals nothing about the work she undertook in the war, but a journalist who had been interned in Dachau sent Bloomgarden a 1935 Vienna newspaper article in which Huber stated her resolve not to 'associate with non-Aryan artists [who] would endanger her stature in Nazi Germany'. In 1946 she arrived in America, after having married a US Army officer. The journalist queried how someone with Huber's tenacious 'anti-Semitic leanings prior to the incorporation of her homeland into the Greater German empire' could work with 'performers such as Joseph Schildkraut and Susan Strasberg, with director Garson Kanin. Yet today she has the nerve to utter the word "Shalom" from the stage.' Huber remained cast in the role of Edith Frank, and went on to portray her in the film.

On 31 August Otto wrote to the Hacketts: 'I pray that the spirit of Anne's book will be transferred to the public', but admitted 'the whole idea of having all represented on the stage is depressing me always' although he could 'bear it for the *Good*'. He wrote again later, to remind them that the men must have their heads covered for the prayers during the Hanukkah ceremony, as they had in hiding. Rehearsals had begun, but were not going well; both Bloomgarden and Kanin felt it was 'too serious'. A preview of the play was held on 15 September at the Walnut Theatre in Philadelphia. Frances was pleased that the play 'went well in spite of terrible heat . . . Notices good in two papers. Radio review "First act fine, second weak."' They added another scene to the second act which seemed to balance the whole play.

There were more changes to the script as opening night came closer. The Maoz Tzur, sung during the Hanukkah ritual, was transposed by 'O, Hanukkah', a popular song among American Jews. A passage lifted from the diary where Anne talks about her deep unhappiness at the enforced isolation was replaced by a line about the 'miracle' of menstruation. More references to Jewish suffering disappeared from the script, including Peter's angry vituperation about their imprisonment, 'Because we're Jews! Because we're Jews!' In an interview given three days before the premiere, Kanin declared, 'I have never looked upon it as a sad play. I certainly have no wish to inflict depression on an audience; I don't consider that a legitimate theatrical end. Anne Frank's death doesn't seem to me a wasteful death, because she left us a legacy that has meaning and value . . .' He viewed the play as an 'honest telling of a breathlessly exciting story . . . a chronicle of the dignity and nobility of common people'. Bloomgarden informed all those involved in working behind the scenes that the play was 'a theatrical experience . . . so real it might be your own,' while Frances Hackett described Anne Frank as 'a young girl like other young girls who wriggled, giggled and chattered . . . a sprite . . . a captivating, bright spirit . . . She might have been your neighbour's teenage daughter – or your own.'

The rehearsals were coming to an end. Susan Strasberg recalled her despair at Schildkraut's frequent tantrums in the role of Otto Frank:

Pepi [Schildkraut] was unhappy at having to mute his flamboyant style and . . . it was traumatic for him to shave his head in order to look like Mr Frank . . . He complained that I was stealing scenes or upstaging him, that my parents were helping me to do this . . . He was even unhappy because it was called *The Diary of Anne Frank*. Before we left town, the producers spoke about replacing me: I was too inexperienced and Pepi was unhappy with me. He was creating problems, and every other day he threatened to quit, accompanied by torrents of tears, which I later learned he could turn on or off at will. Fortunately, all this was forgotten in the rush of opening-night madness . . .

On 5 October 1955 *The Diary of Anne Frank* premiered at New York's Cort Theatre. Among the many fur-stole clad, couture-dressed stars emerging from their limousines was Marilyn Monroe, a close friend of Susan Strasberg. Backstage, tacked to the bulletin board with small pins, was a letter from Otto Frank:

> You will all realize that for me this play is a part of my life, and the idea that my wife and children, as well as I, will be presented on the stage is a painful one to me. Therefore it is impossible for me to come and see it. My thoughts are with every one of you all the time, and I hope the play will be a success and that the message which it contains will, through you, reach as many people as possible and awaken in them a sense of responsibility to humanity.

While the real Otto Frank slept thousands of miles away in Switzerland, the lights in the New York theatre dimmed and his alter ego climbed the creaking stairs to a dark and dusty attic.

When 'Otto' closed the diary and bowed his head, and the curtain fell on that first performance, everyone in the theatre that night was aware they had just witnessed a resounding success. Even those few who disliked the play knew it was a hit. The reviews were ecstatic. Echoed by his contemporaries, the critic from the *New York World Telegram* proclaimed, 'The genius of this play is that there is nothing grim or sensational about it . . . it relates the flowering of a youngster who was pure in heart . . . in the end they must go to the concentration camps. And Anne goes, smiling.' The *Herald Tribune* said the play was

as bright and shining as a banner. *The Diary of Anne Frank* is not in any important sense a Jewish play . . . it is a story of the gallant human spirit . . . Anne Frank is a little Orphan Annie brought into vibrant life . . . without the gallantry of the human spirit, this apartment could be a hell a few storeys above the earth . . . but this place is not a hell above ground; it is a testing place in which men and women and children earn the blessed right to be alive.

Frances Hackett wrote in her diary the following day: 'Every notice good! Walking on air! It was worth the tears, the months we worked, the miles we travelled. We only wish that Anne could have known.'

Algene Ballif, writing in *Commentary* in November 1955, demurred: 'Seldom do we glimpse the Anne Frank of the real diary.' For her, Anne had undergone a 'Broadway metamorphosis into [an] American adolescent.' The overall effect was of 'superficiality and inarticulateness that renders the script so poor, does pitiful injustice to the diary and proves too much even for those of the actors who try to make up for it'. Ballif prompted theatregoers to return 'to her real diary for the kind of memorial she requires'. The first Dutch press review, in *Vrij Nederland*, reproached Broadway's distortion of 'things which are sacred'. In America the play was simply 'a thing of amusement' and Anne herself 'ridiculous ... The entire performance is sacrilege, sacrilege to all those who were tortured.' The idea of 'well-fed people entering the theatre ... laughing' was loathsome. The writer condemned everything about the play, including the fact of its existence, feeling that the only place where Anne should be remembered was 'on a field over which the sun sets or in the synagogue on J. D. Meijersplein'. *Het Parool* denounced the play as 'kitsch, which I hope we shall not see here'.

The dissenters were few, however, and the play made Anne Frank a household name. Susan Strasberg was a star overnight, and featured on the cover of every newspaper and magazine in the country. Levin was frantic, telling anyone who would listen that his play had been 'killed by the same arbitrary disregard that brought an end to Anne and six million others. There is, among the survivors, a compulsion to visit on others something of the evil that was visited on them.' He tried to marshal writers against the play, but with little impact. The play was breaking all records: it ran for 717 performances in the 1,000-seater Cort Theatre and then toured twenty major North American cities. In New York alone approximately one million people sat through a performance of *The Diary*.

In November the Hacketts visited Otto in Basel, staying at the Three Kings Hotel. A mutual friend of theirs, Calvin Fox, wrote to Otto about a film based on the diary, for which the Hacketts hoped to write the screenplay:

The Hacketts ... also mentioned that there had been a number of negotiations for picture situation, but that nothing had been concluded. They would prefer to produce independently a picture that would retain all of the integrity and truth you insist upon. I have the feeling that they feel as insecure about a Hollywood production as you do . . . they share with you all of your intense emotional involvement . . . at least as intense as they can be under the circumstances.

It seems unlikely that the Hacketts were 'insecure' about a Hollywood film given their background, but Fox obviously wanted Otto to believe that the Hacketts were the right people for the adaptation. The Hacketts' agent, Leah Salisbury, was also keen to convince him, and wrote to him on 1 December offering to represent him, having 'loved you and suffered with you' and having taken 'all of you Franks to my heart'. She hoped 'of course that the final deal will assure us the Hacketts as the screen writers and Kanin as the director'.

Otto replied to Salisbury on 13 December, thanking her for her 'warm personal interest in everything concerning Anne's diary'. Although he realized that 'the play means more to you than business' and was 'tremendously . . . impressed' by her letter he rejected her offer. Frances Hackett, having heard about the exchange, sent Salisbury a letter in which she explained why she felt Otto had declined to be represented by her: 'He is a very frugal man . . . and I think he will think twice before paying 10 per cent [Salisbury's fee].' In her dealings with him she had found him 'a curious mixture of great emotion and business' who 'gives his money away while taking care to secure its source', and was intrigued by how he was 'unable to speak of the diary without crying' and yet was quite willing to have scenes invented and changes made to Anne's words. Otto's aim, of course, was that the 'message' of the diary should reach as many people as possible, and when those whom he trusted advised him that the best way of doing that was to change this and alter that, he believed them. The Hacketts, Kanin and Bloomgarden had long ago learned that they could manipulate him by appealing to him as Anne's father, assuring him that they, too, wanted what was best 'for the diary', 'for the play' and now 'for the film'.

Otto would have been deeply wounded had he seen the cruel letters passing between the Hacketts and their agent, who were perplexed by his resistance to committing the diary to film. On 9 January, after an unpleasant remark in one of Salisbury's letters about Otto's emotional state (and hearing that Otto intended to travel to America), Albert Hackett wrote to Salisbury that 'I thought I was the only one who dreaded his visit. He lives in the past and, once he gets talking about the diary, the play or Anne, he has very soon reduced Frances to tears.' They were fearful that Otto would allow changes they did not have any right to protest in the European production of the play. On 12 January, following a meeting with Bloomgarden and Kanin, Salisbury said she was worried about letting Otto have 'too much control. Kermit and Garson agreed with me completely – said it was dangerous and must not be allowed to happen.' By 26 January, Salisbury was able to inform the Hacketts that she had revised her wording on the contract in such a way that it would be 'impossible for [Otto] to insist upon change in the American text, or the sequence of scenes' or 'to impose his ideas regarding deletions or additions because the play is "too glamorous" for Europe'.

Meanwhile, Levin continued with his efforts; in February he sent Otto a list of over a hundred rabbis who had signed in favour of allowing his play to be performed. That same month he brought a second lawsuit against Bloomgarden and Otto charging 'fraud, breach of contract and wrongful appropriation of ideas, Levin as plaintiff asked damages of $150,000 against Otto, and $100,000 against Bloomgarden'. His actions meant that Otto's royalties from the play (30 per cent, payable directly to him) could not be released. In reply to Otto's furious letter to her husband, Tereska wrote to Otto in a rage herself, calling him 'a very obstinate man . . . you *must* believe that you are *always* right'. Otto refrained from answering on the advice of Mermin and his assisting lawyer Edward Costikyan, who were keeping a careful eye on proceedings.

Otto decided against travelling to America, feeling it would be 'a tremendous strain not mainly in connection with the lawsuit, but my visit would be known all over, and I could not escape many people wanting to meet the real Otto Frank after they had seen the play and this would be very emotional'. He was also concerned about costs: 'As Mr Mermin knows I am not a fortunate man and though I am convinced we will win the cause, I feel it my duty to tell you about my financial position . . . The business in Amsterdam does not bring me more than about $1,000 income a year [the agreement between Otto and Kleiman] and the capital I have in Switzerland originates for the greater part from what I received from Doubleday for the book. All the other countries did not pay much. I am living here in a very modest way, using two rooms in my sister's house. I do so because I did not want to use the money from the play for personal purposes.'

The play continued to win accolades; having already been the recipient of the New York Drama Critics Circle Award for the season's best American production, on 7 May 1956 it won the Pulitzer Prize for drama. An article in the *New York Sunday News* noted that it was not 'a Jewish play' but 'a drama about human beings. They happen to be Jewish because those were the people who had to hide from the Germans in all of Europe, but their race and religion are incidental details.' By mid 1956 the play was grossing more than $30,000 a week. It was a long-standing tradition that the Pulitzer prize-winning play was performed at the Paris drama festival, but in 1956, tradition was broken: *The Diary of Anne Frank* was not performed. The US State Department, nervous of upsetting Franco–German relations, had decided that the play must not be staged.

On 24 May Otto divulged his qualms about the play being adapted for the screen by the Hacketts. He was nervous that their film 'would not contain the mission of the book'. His letter also reveals that he felt guilty about the portrayals of Pfeffer and van Pels on the stage, and this had caused problems for him amongst those closest to him, for he was unhappy in the knowledge 'that some of the characters would be represented in a wrong light. How could I face the reproaches of my conscience, of my family, of Miep, Kleiman and the others, who never understood that I gave away the rights to get money without any promise from the producer to respect the quality of the material'. His 'personal feelings and . . . conscience would not be at rest when, in a film in which my family and my friends are represented, characters or situations would be falsified'. Otto would have been horrified to know that Mermin passed this, and all his letters on the subject, to Salisbury. Mermin, Salisbury and the Hacketts worked together to convince Otto that 'he would never be able to sell the play for pictures if he insist[ed] on approval of the script'.

Otto had incurred the wrath of the Hacketts and Kanin by pleading for the Maoz Tzur to be reinstated for the Hanukkah scene in the European performances of the play. He told Salisbury: 'It would make a very strange impression among all Jews and those who knew a little about Judaism if the usual Hanukkah song would not be used. It even should be sung in Hebrew.' Salisbury told the Hacketts to inform Otto that 'O Hanukkah' would remain in the script: 'What you say will influence Mr Frank – if anyone can influence him on this point.' On 2 July Kanin told the Hacketts he had hoped 'that this subject was closed for ever. The ending of the first act will be flat as a latke unless the song which is sung there is a gay one.' A Hebrew song would be 'a great mistake . . . it would simply alienate the audience'. He urged them not to 'be afraid to speak firmly to Frank' and to persuade him that it would be 'damn foolish to horse around' with the play.

The following day both Kanin and the Hacketts wrote to Otto about the Hanukkah scene. The Hacketts explained that they felt singing in Hebrew would 'set the characters in the play apart from the people watching them . . . for the majority of our audience is not Jewish. And the thing that we have striven for, toiled for, fought for throughout the whole play is to make the audience understand and identify themselves . . . to make them feel "that, but for the grace of God, might have been I".' Salisbury was so exasperated by Otto's repeated attempts to ensure he had final approval of the way characters were portrayed in the film that she was considering drafting a contract whereby only the basics would be written into the agreement, i.e. 'The family must be Jewish, in Holland at the time of World War II, and all except Mr Frank must die in concentration camps.'

On 12 July, after receiving a letter from Levin's wife, Otto contacted Mermin: 'I have the feeling from Tereska's letter that Meyer is in a very bad state of mind. Of course I do not know if her letter was written with his consent. Just imagine that Levin really would break down and commit suicide. We do not want to have to reproach ourselves that we did not try everything. Might be that he really is now willing to agree to a favourable settlement.' A few days later, Tereska wrote to him again: 'Otto, this case against you has ruined my marriage with Meyer . . . it has come to the point where I don't even know if Meyer still loves me. He is like frozen now, so bitter, and he can't think about anything else, he says he lost all his faith in people . . . if a solution is not found quickly, and some way to end all this, it will probably end our marriage.' Unhappy about Tereska's evident misery, Otto proposed to Mermin a new idea on 26 July: 'Let [Levin] have amateur rights *in Israel* only, in case his play would be accepted in one of the big theatres there. This would not hurt, as he would make his play more Jewish anyway.' The matter remained in the hands of the lawyers.

In August 1956 the European premiere of the play was held in Sweden. It was well received. Otto gave an interview to coincide with the opening in which he insisted, 'This is not a play for me, or even for Jews or Germans – it is a play for all the world.' But it was the reception to the play in Germany, where *The Diary of Anne Frank* had its opening night in October in the cities of Aachen, Dusseldorf, West Berlin, Karlsruhe, Hamburg, Constanz and Dresden simultaneously, which caught the headlines of news-papers across the world. In the country of his daughter's birth and her murder, Otto watched from the sidelines in amazement as the play 'released a wave of emotion that finally broke through the silence with which the Germans had treated the Nazi period'. One reviewer later recalled:

No one was prepared for what actually happened on the evening of 1 October 1956, when seven theatres, ranging from West Berlin's swank Schlosspark to the drab Soviet Zone drama house of Dresden, premiered the German version of *The Diary of Anne Frank* . . . In Berlin, after the final curtain, the audience sat in stunned silence. There was no applause. Only the welling sound of deep sobs broke the absolute stillness. Then, still not speaking and seeming not to look at each other, the Berliners filed out of the theatre.

The day after the premiere, every German newspaper carried the story of the play and how audiences had reacted to it. One review described the play as having 'the effect of a present day requiem: the audience seemed to be engaged in an act of contrition'. Theatre playbills included photos, Otto's memories of the period in hiding, accounts of Anne's final days in Belsen and articles with titles like 'Are We Guilty?' but most of the youth of Germany identified themselves with Anne and her 'adolescent problems' and did not even consider the political context in which the diary had been written. Over the next few months the play was performed 1,984 times in 58 other German cities and was seen by more than a million people. Anne was hailed as a national heroine. Schools, streets and refugee villages were given her name and her old friends in Germany were bemused to see a plaque attached to the wall of the Franks' house on Ganghoferstrasse. A pilgrimage organized by the Hamburg Society for Christian and Jewish Co-operation marshalled more than 2,000 teenagers to walk to Bergen-Belsen in 1957 to remember her death. 'We feel,' cried Erich Luth, one of the teenage speakers, 'that Anne Frank died for all of us, for freedom and human dignity.'

An article titled 'The Diary That Shook A Nation' reflected upon the response to the book:

At Dusseldorf, Ernst Deutsch, who played the role of Anne's father, Otto, was inundated by emotional fan letters. 'I was a good Nazi,' one read, 'I never knew what it meant until the other night' . . . Another surprise occurred in Mainz, Germany. The local theatre was thrown open after the second performance of the diary for a public discussion of the play. Unexpectedly, hundreds of teenagers jammed the house . . .

It soon became apparent that German teenagers were searching for something their parents wouldn't give them. 'The growing adulation of Anne Frank by young people,' worried a Berlin periodical,

gives cause for some concern. More and more often, parents find themselves confronted with disturbing questions about wartime events, especially the persecution of religious minorities. Children no longer ask, 'What happened?' but 'How could it have happened?' Their emotional intensity tends to create a sense of isolation between our own generation and our youth.

In October Otto wrote to novelist Carson McCullers, with whom he had remained friends after her decision not to write the play, 'My brother went to Karlsruhe to see the play and he told me that after the interval as well as at the end the public did not dare to move and only after a certain time it started to applaud . . . It gives me satisfaction that Anne's voice is heard now in Germany too . . .' A reporter from the *Hadassah Newsletter* was present at the occasion and recounted:

When the final curtain fell, the packed house remained silent. Respect and awe united a deeply moved audience. Minutes later, I went backstage, accompanied by Herbert Frank, Anne's uncle. When the play's producer introduced the brother of Anne Frank's father to Maria Magdalena Thising, who had so convincingly recreated the martyred girl on stage, the young actress burst into tears. Refusing to accept Mr Frank's compliments for her fine performance, she sobbed, 'I won't take your hand – I am a German.'

The author Alvin Rosenfeld reflects: 'Out of both sorrow and shame, Germans have named streets, schools and youth centres after Anne Frank, but to this day most probably do not comprehend why, a generation ago, a significant number of their countrymen deemed it necessary to hunt down a fifteen-year-old Jewish girl and send her off to suffer and die.' Hannah Arendt condemns the admiration for Anne Frank in Germany especially as a form of 'cheap sentimentality at the expense of great catastrophe'. In an essay on Anne Frank's place in post-war culture, author Alex Sagan argues that a more realistic play would never have succeeded on the level of *The Diary* (the works of Primo Levi and Elie Wiesel were largely ignored at the time):

A play or film that treated the Holocaust could only reach a large German public if it were somehow adaptable to the prevailing cultural mood. The Hacketts' play was uniquely suited to this task. Even as the play forced Germans to think about the Holocaust, it did so in ways that accommodated German discomfort with the subject. To begin with, depiction of German criminality was held to an absolute minimum. Even at the moment when those in hiding are arrested, no Nazis or Germans appear on stage. Nor did the play highlight Anne Frank's own eloquent remarks about German anti-Semitism and Nazi brutality. The play's director in Munich sought to remedy this by emphasizing that the story's unseen aggressors were Germans. His method was to play recordings of German beer hall songs at certain moments, perhaps to indicate that singing Germans prowled the streets of wartime Amsterdam. The Hacketts' agents put a stop to this 'enhancement' . . .

But, if Germans felt accused, the psychological discomfort of this situation was relieved by Anne's famous words, which could be deeply reassuring. Germans need not think the worst of themselves, for 'people are really good at heart' . . . The Hacketts' formulation seemed to grant forgiveness for German crimes by affirming the inner goodness of all . . . German audience members could breathe easier, for the most part families of Holocaust victims seemed to recognize their 'inner goodness'. If the Germans 'accused themselves', Anne Frank seemed to forgive them.

In the five years following the publication of the paperback edition of the diary by Fischer Bücherei in 1955, the book was reprinted eighteen times and sold in excess of 700,000 copies. On its cover were the words: *'I still believe in the good of people'* and that one, penultimate line from the play, which was lifted from its darker context in the diary, is believed by many to be the last line of the diary; it is quoted as such by the editors of the *Oxford Companion to American Theatre* (1992) and *Cambridge Guide to American Theatre* (1993). Otto himself ended an article he wrote about Germany with those lines, insisting, 'I must keep talking to [the youth of Germany] for, like Anne, "in spite of everything I still believe that people are really good at heart."' His second wife's daughter, Eva, has often thought about that:

I always say that Anne might not have held that view had she come through the camps. But recently I thought about Otto, and the person he was. He was such a gentle person, so lacking in hate. When I was in despair and filled with anger about all that had happened, he told me repeatedly, 'You must not hate.' I'm sure Anne learned that expression, or the idea behind it, from Otto. He would have tried to lift her out of her despair by saying to her, 'Don't give up, there is still so much good in people.' He was a very spiritual man.

Otto always refused to be drawn into the debate about Germany's search for absolution through his daughter's diary. He did not believe in collective guilt and condemned Germany only once publicly in a 1959 speech before the American Anne Frank Foundation (a sister to the Amsterdam-based Stichting), when he told the audience: 'In 1952 the book was published [in the place] where Anne was born and where she was brought back later by her German murderers to find an early death.' Despite this, he never relinquished his pride in his German roots. When there was a motion by the board of the Anne Frank Stichting to ban Germans from visiting the house, Otto stopped the idea. He recalled, 'They were all against Germany. And I said that you have to allow Germans. You don't refuse the Jews of Germany. You don't refuse your own people.' Zvi Schloss remembers Otto was 'very military in some sense – tidy, punctual, exact. You could see that he had been in the German army. You see, he never had to overcome his hatred, like most German Jewish survivors do. He never hated Germany. He loved his country to the end.' Eva agrees:

He was very proud of having been in the German army and always remained so. He said often, 'I'm a German from a very good family.' My mother, Fritzi, was quite the opposite. She had been born in Austria but she hated Austrians and never wanted to go back to Austria. I found Otto's attitude difficult, very difficult. It caused problems between us for a while. But let me put it this way: Germany was to him like a wayward child to a parent. You love your child, but dislike their actions. Otto always loved Germany. He would never abandon Germany, but he was appalled by it just the same. And that hurt him until his death.

Asked in 1959 about how he felt towards Germany, Otto replied,

I realize that at present there are many former Nazis in important positions. Also, anti-Semitism is not diminishing . . . due to the fact that people who are over forty have been in one way or another connected with the Nazi movement and indoctrinated with its ideas. There is great danger from parents and teachers of this sort. On the other hand, there are many young people who understand the crimes which have been committed and want to remedy them. So you see, we are not allowed to generalize and I, for my part, am always ready to help those, no matter where they are, who want to work in the direction of good. Of course one cannot forget the atrocities nor forgive the guilty ones.

Otto told the same interviewer: 'I have lived through two world wars and witnessed the power of a criminal dictator system and its consequences. The great dangers are mass movements, slogans, materialism and egotism. I believe in the freedom of the human spirit.'

A year later, he wrote an article for *Coronet* magazine under the title, 'Has Germany Forgotten Anne Frank?' Although he ultimately expressed the view that it was more important to look to the future, rather than the past, he admitted that he would never trust his former homeland:

The older generation of Germans cannot yet face up to past history and communicate its lessons to the future. I believe that unless it does, unless the questions of German youth are answered fully and frankly, the fragile growth of democracy in Germany may come to an end . . . I am intensely interested in Germany, its future and its youth. My concern is that never again should Germany experience the madness of racial prejudice and that Anne's life should not have been empty and without meaning . . . Of all the letters inspired by a reading of *The Diary*, I have been most diligent in answering the ones from German youth. For their education – in democratic ideals and ways of life – is of paramount importance to me . . . I was born and raised in Germany but I do not have any greater insight into the future of Germany than do other Europeans or Americans. I look about me and I am often baffled by what I see . . . Germany is a busy, busy land. But when it comes to the education of its youth towards democratic values, the clocks of Germany are running all too slowly . . . Europeans remain concerned about Germany. They are repelled by the past and worried about the future. They know that they cannot very well live without Germans and never have learned quite how to live with them. In that respect I am a typical European, for those are my reactions too.

In October 1956 Otto cabled the Hacketts to inform them that he had decided to approve them as the writers for the diary screenplay. Frances Hackett was not pleased though by Otto's expressed belief that they would allow him consulting rights, and she told Salisbury he was 'bedevilling' them. On 27 November, in the presence of Queen Juliana, the play premiered in Amsterdam. Otto attended the opening ceremony with several of his friends and all the 'helpers' apart from Kugler, who was by then living in Ontario, Canada with his second wife, Loes van Langen, whom he had married in June 1955 (Kugler's first wife died in 1952). Miep later reported to Otto how she and Jan had reacted to the play itself:

Jan, who usually can stand quite a lot, wasn't able to say a single word to me during the play and the break. When it was over I saw his face was wet, and in the street he told me he was very glad he'd seen it. And I myself, too, Otto. In spite of the fact that it was devastating. I thought the beginning was scary and I had the feeling I wouldn't be able to cope, but when all the players are on stage it is all right. And at the end there is this immeasurable anger, you'd want to drag the 'Moffen' around the room if you'd seen them, it doesn't matter that they are not real.

In January 1957 Otto was informed by his lawyers that a Hebrew production of the Hacketts' play had opened in Israel. Otto was shocked himself, having refused to allow the play to be performed there until the matter with Levin was resolved. Mermin requested to the management that they cease performing the play, but was ignored. Otto had no wish to provoke either the Habimah theatre company or Levin, who had begun a new round of campaigning for his play to be produced. Galvanized into responding to Levin's claim that he had rejected his play because it was 'too Jewish', Otto said categorically that this and other allegations made by Levin were untrue. As regards Levin's example of the suppression of the Jewish material in the diary (Margot's wish to emigrate to Palestine), Otto stated, 'Margot saying "I want to go to Palestine" was not of the level of significance Levin wants to give it. She would not have done so and it was only a one-off remark, which was not to be taken too seriously.' He made one concession which must have pleased Levin, however: he admitted that there were passages from the diary concerning Jews and Judaism which he would have been pleased to have seen included in a dramatic adaptation.

In early 1956 Otto received the miraculous news that the annexe was no longer under threat of demolition. The Dutch press had been alerted to the situation the previous year and had devoted several articles to it, including a major piece in *Het Vrije Volk*: 'Anne Frank's Secret Annexe Awaits The Wrecker's Ball', which urged, 'The Secret Annexe . . . has become a monument to a time of oppression and man-hunts, terror and darkness. The Netherlands will be subject to a national scandal if this house is pulled down . . . There is every reason, especially considering the enormous interest from both inside and outside the country, to correct this situation as quickly as possible.' The local historical society *Amstelodamum* asked: 'How could people better honour the memory of Anne Frank than by saving this house, which is forever connected to Amsterdam's darkest years of occupation in terms of both literature and history?'

After relinquishing 263 Prinsengracht to Berghaus, in 1955 Otto and Kugler retired from Pectacon and from Gies & Co. (together with Jan Gies), and the business was sold. During a visit to Amsterdam that spring, Otto had written to Kanin: 'The office moved from Prinsengracht to new quarters which, as you can imagine, was for me personally a very difficult and enervating matter. In fact, it still is.' The new offices were in a modern building in Amsterdam-West.

In April 1955 the seventh edition of the diary was published in Holland to coincide with the tenth anniversary of the liberation. By then, Otto and Fritzi were spending the greater part of their day replying to the letters Otto received from ardent readers of the diary. Some were simply addressed, 'Anne Frank's father, Amsterdam,' but the Dutch postal system knew where to forward his mail. Increasing numbers of people visited the annexe and asked to see inside. Kleiman had been given a key by the Berghaus company and took people around himself. On the day of the premiere of *The Diary of Anne Frank* in Amsterdam, he was there with several actors from the play. He recalled, 'When we were in the van Pels's room, we heard a loud banging downstairs. It sounded menacing and made them understand even more the fears which ruled the lives of the people in hiding.' In November 1956 Otto spoke to the Mayor of Amsterdam about the public interest in the building, hoping to raise the funds to prevent its destruction. Otto told him he wanted to buy the house himself but felt he should not, since his aim was to establish a foundation there one day. Kleiman spoke to the press about their objectives, adding, 'We get a lot of money from abroad. But it shouldn't be like that, with the Dutch not giving anything themselves. We need fl.350,000 by 1 July to save the houses next door from demolition.'

Finally, in January 1957, the Amsterdam City Council offered Berghaus an alternative location in which to situate their offices. The following month, during the commemoration of the February strike, Kleiman met several men who told him they were interested in forming a society to preserve the house. Otto recalled, 'They formed a committee and when I came to Amsterdam in May, I learned of their intention to incorporate an Anne Frank Stichting.' Otto would be represented on the Board of Trustees by Kleiman. Other board members included Truus Wijsmuller-Meijer, a former resistance worker; Floris Bakels, concentration camp survivor and publisher; Jacob van Hasselt, the notary; Hermann Heldring, the director of KLM; and Ton Koot, the secretary of the Bond Heemschut (Landmark Preservation). The organization stated its goal as: 'the restoration and, if necessary, renovation of 263 Prinsengracht and especially the preservation of the attached annexe, as well as the propagation of the ideals, left as a legacy to the world, in the diary of Anne Frank'.

In autumn 1957 Berghaus presented 263 Prinsengracht to the Anne Frank Stichting. There was still the matter of 265 and the houses at the corner of the Westermarkt. Berghaus wanted fl.350,000 for the entire row. The Stichting managed to raise fl.250,000 and the outstanding amount was donated by the bankers Pierson & Co. The buildings would be replaced by student housing and a youth centre, where courses and conferences could be held. With the houses saved, Otto could begin finalizing his plans for a museum dedicated to his daughter's memory, and continued his 'mission to spread her ideals as much as possible' in earnest.

8. I Have No Scars Left

On 8 April 1957 Lotte Pfeffer sent a wrathful letter to the Hacketts. She remonstrated with them about the Hanukkah scene, in which her husband was portrayed as ignorant about the ceremony when, in reality, 'his religion meant everything to him' and he spoke Hebrew fluently. She objected to the characterization of him as a ridiculous, bumbling loner, informing them that he was 'neither an inveterate bachelor nor a man without relations', but was survived by a wife, brothers and a son, and warned, 'I do not wish my husband to be shown in the film as a psychopath. I think it enough that this had been done already in the play.' Lotte closed her letter with a request to see the completed screenplay.

The Hacketts' response was cool; they replied that 'a play cannot mirror reality' and that 'in order to inform the non-Jewish audience about the Hanukkah service and its significance, they needed one character (Dr Dussel) unfamiliar with it so that another character could explain it to him – and hence to the audience'. They told her that they were not permitted to send her a copy of the script, and that the final decision about the way in which the protagonists were represented did not lie with them. Salisbury, their agent, had already advised her clients to be 'evasive' with Lotte: 'don't admit anything and don't encourage her'. Suspecting that Otto retained the right of approval over the screenplay, Lotte contacted him – and threatened him with a lawsuit for libelling her husband.

Otto wrote to Frances Hackett on 22 April expressing his doubts about the film: 'In my innermost I cannot feel happy about it as long as I do not know how matters will develop further', and telling her about his problems with Lotte: 'She is demanding from a film historical truth. This she cannot ask, nor does the public expect it . . . I can only pray that everything will turn out the way that you and I hope.' Frances replied that as far as Lotte was concerned, their lawyer was 'always cutting down on any sympathy for her claims or any admission of our sympathy to her'.

On 11 May Otto apprised Frances of the latest development; he had spoken to Lotte and asked her 'not [to] be so childish as to believe that [you] had not taken every information from the legal point' and had told her that they knew exactly what the law permitted them to write. Amongst the documents found after Otto's death was a curious handwritten declaration drawn up in 1956:

Agreement:

Mr Otto Frank, Basel, Herbstgasse and Mrs Charlotte Pfeffer, Amsterdam, IJselstraat 18, agree:

1. Mr Frank renounces for himself and his heirs repayment of all the sums of money he has given so far to Mrs Pfeffer.

2. Mrs Charlotte Pfeffer renounces all former claims to *The Diary of Anne Frank* and the play and the film which have been made from it.

Enclosed with the declaration was a letter from Lotte, dated 5 September 1956: 'I include the agreement, which I thought I would be able to give you personally, but so far have not been able to do. There were no bad intentions, as was assumed . . . I heard the news that my son has died. Up till now I still quietly hoped that he would be in Estonia with farmers and I believed I would hear from him one day. Another illusion lost.'

Presumably that was the last stage in the conflict between Lotte and Otto, who had also received a letter from an old friend of Pfeffer in Germany, admonishing him,

I had the pleasure of working for [Fritz Pfeffer] in his house for more than a year, taking care of him and his son. I know that he was a truly religious man . . . I assure you that I will do my utmost to tell everyone who I speak to about the play how Fritz really was. Do you actually believe that an idiot could ever become a doctor or a dentist? I don't. Have you ever thought about why Fritz became a complainer during the hiding period? Until the betrayal, you and the van Pels family were all together and could share your burden. Fritz was a stranger among you. Certainly you must have known how much he worried about his wife. He was all alone . . . Friends and acquaintances of myself and Fritz are enraged about the way in which the character of Fritz was portrayed . . . I am sorry to write such harsh words to you, but my sense of justice does not allow for somebody to be made a laughing stock, especially when that person is dead and can no longer defend himself.

It was the end of Otto and Lotte's friendship; she wanted nothing more to do with him, or with Miep and Jan, with whom she had always had a close relationship. Lotte became increasingly isolated, and ventured out less and less. She died in Amsterdam in her apartment on Deurloostraat on 13 June

1985. Her neighbour below called a junk dealer to remove her belongings months later. Entering the apartment, the dealer found

a complete mess. Nothing was packed. I could tell from the décor that the occupant had a certain taste that did not quite look Dutch. For instance, there was a Gispen lamp from the thirties . . . There were still a couple of unwrapped packets of lumps of sugar and many old shoes in boxes. There were also boxes full of buttons and tiny bars of soap . . . There was also a hat box. And we found photo albums . . .

Her effects were deposited at the Waterlooplein market in the old Jewish Quarter of the city. Shortly thereafter, when shopping at the market, an employee of the Anne Frank Stichting, Joke Kniesmeyer, noticed a pile of books and bent down to examine them. She read the name *Ch. Kaletta* in one of the books, and then discovered a folder of yellow newspaper cuttings about *The Diary of Anne Frank*. With a shock, she realized what lay before her. Although it was too late for Lotte to know it, she had left behind enough books, letters and photos documenting the warmth and humanity of Fritz Pfeffer to reverse much of the damage done to her husband by the Hacketts' ruthless dramatization.

Otto himself previously tried to correct the picture when the play was later performed by amateur groups and schools. In 1970 he sent a request to one American school: 'As to Mr Dussel, one should realize that he was a single man between two families and therefore felt lonely. There is sometimes the tendency to play this role humouristically but it should be played rather in a tragic way.'

On 2 April 1957 Eleanor Roosevelt wrote to Otto, having reacted sympathetically to a letter she had received from Levin. She advised Otto to avoid a court case 'which would bring out so many disagreeable things, such as why you moved to Switzerland, [and] would be harmful to the feeling people have for you and for the play and particularly the diary from which the play was written'. Levin had told her that Otto had moved to Switzerland to avoid high Dutch taxes and he asked her to persuade him to settle out of court.

Otto was dismayed by Eleanor Roosevelt's pleas on Levin's behalf. Although he had indeed managed to avoid Dutch taxes for the year he moved to Switzerland, that had not been his reason for emigrating. His purpose had been to be with his remaining family and to escape the memories Amsterdam held for him – factors which Levin had known but dismissed.

In his 'very distressed' reply to Mrs Roosevelt, Otto explained, 'I had the full agreement of all Dutch authorities for my moving and still now have my business in Amsterdam but, besides, this matter has nothing to do at all with the merits of the case . . . I am not led by financial interest. It always has been and still is my intention to give all the net profits of the play and the film to institutions in Holland and Israel in memory of Anne.' The court case was necessary to 'free me for ever from [Levin's] unjustified attacks'. He hoped that Eleanor Roosevelt would now 'form your own opinion . . . on Mr Levin's behaviour'.

Otto contacted Frank Price to tell him that Levin had 'hurt my reputation . . . I am very much disturbed that Mrs Roosevelt seems to be doubtful about my character . . .' and appealed to Price to write to her, 'telling her a little about me and the bad character of Levin'. He also pressed Nathan Straus into defending him from Mrs Roosevelt's 'rather hostile' letter. Straus sprang into action and 'set to work to draft as effective a letter as possible . . . for Mrs Roosevelt's enlightenment'. On 19 April Straus wrote to her, concluding his letter, 'It is scarcely necessary to have me add the statement that Otto is an unusually fine, sensitive human being,' or that 'a bitter and disgruntled man has seen fit to attempt to besmirch a fine and dedicated life, oblivious alike to the mandates of justice and to the potential injury to the message carried by the play . . . Otto would seem to have suffered enough without being forced, in his old age, to endure character assassination, slander – and, worst of all, loss of respect of fine people.' Mrs Roosevelt quickly changed her mind once she had received Straus's letter and apologized to Otto: 'I have read the material you sent and I think you are probably right in your stand.' She wished him good luck with the court case.

On 20 May 1957 Otto signed a contract with 20th Century Fox for the film version of *The Diary of Anne Frank*. In June he was in Amsterdam to meet George Stevens, who would direct the film. As a young American soldier Stevens had witnessed the liberation of Dachau. Otto told a friend, 'We had a very favourable impression of his personality and all our discussions took place in a spirit of friendship and understanding. As the Hacketts are writing the script we have the confidence that something good will be created.' Otto remained in the Netherlands until July, when Nathan Straus flew over from New York. Straus was presenting $10,000 to a student housing foundation in Delft as an expression of his 'respect and gratitude' for Dutch aid and hospitality to 'the victims of Nazi terror'. Straus said in his address: 'The kindness shown by the people of the Netherlands to the victims of the Nazi terror has touched me personally because of a personal circumstance.

Otto Frank, the father of Anne Frank, is one of the oldest friends I have in the world, our friendship dating back to the time when he and I were both students at Heidelberg University.' The money was spent on restoring a canal house (Nathan Straus Huis) a few hundred yards from the Delft Technical High School.

Throughout the summer of 1957 articles appeared about the forthcoming film, questioning whether the Jewish element so lacking in the play would be reinstated on the screen. Although the question of which song should be sung at the Hanukkah celebration scene had been settled, conflict arose over whether the prayers should be said in English or Hebrew. The Hacketts were very firmly in favour of the former, explaining on 8 August to the rabbi they had consulted, that if they were said in Hebrew,

this identification of the audience with the people in hiding would be shattered . . . they would be alienated . . . What we all of us hoped and prayed for, and what we are devoutly thankful to have achieved, is an identification of the audience with the people in hiding. They see them, not as some strange people, but persons like themselves, thrown into this horrible situation. With them they suffer the deprivations, the terrors, the moments of tenderness, of exaltation and courage beyond belief.

Towards the end of the month, a quarrel arose between the Hacketts and the French translators of the play. The Hacketts felt too many changes had been made to their script, and on 23 August they sent an explosive letter to Marguerite Scialtiel, the translators' agent:

It is curious that you have put us on the defensive about this play. We have had to explain everything, the reasons why we have done everything. This is not an unproved piece of work . . . But the unhappy part of this whole experience is that throughout your letters to us, and throughout all of M. Neveux's [one of the two French translators] work, we see a very real contempt for our play. Why did you want to do it? Why did M. Neveux ever touch it? We cannot understand.

In notes dated 21 August 1957 the Hacketts fumed: 'The whole purpose and meaning of the play have been destroyed. The characters have been made so disagreeable, so unpleasant, so vulgar, that the audience would welcome the Gestapo's coming for them.' They insisted, 'This is not a play like other plays . . . Practically every line of the play is taken directly from Anne's diary.'

Marguerite Scialtiel replied on 26 August, assuring the Hacketts that their requests would be met, but unable to resist several tart remarks of her own: 'I attribute the comparative failure of the play in England to the fact that there the family, except for the adorable father and the girl, were *not* attractive.' She went on,

As to Dussel . . . when we [she and Marguerite Jamois, the other translator] were in Amsterdam Otto Frank was having great trouble with Mrs Dussel and we understood he *wanted* to make up for having portrayed him as so disagreeable . . . If you had lived with the Germans as we did for these terrible years . . . what is bitterly hurtful is your assertion that the play puts the *JEWS* back 2000 years. How do you justify this?

Otto was horrified when he heard about the row. He had already cautioned Marguerite Scialtiel to allow few changes to the Hacketts' text – 'It might be fatal for the play if the public get the impression that it contains horrors and tortures,' – but he wondered whether it might be a good idea for the Hacketts to consult again 'a Jewish personality'. Salisbury, the Hacketts' agent, told Scialtiel she felt the characters were portrayed so darkly in the revised script that 'audiences would end by hating the family, and the Jews . . . that the final effect is a kind of anti-Semitism'. Salisbury told another acquaintance that the Hackett script had 'merged in popularity with the book'. Letters flew back and forth between Scialtiel and the Hacketts that autumn. The Hacketts threatened to call in their lawyer, but eventually the French production proved triumphant, winning a prize for best 'mise en scène' of the year from the Ligue de la Fraternité, a society fighting anti-Semitism and racism. The translators asked for the money from the award to be donated to children orphaned by the Holocaust.

A report about the proposed 'Anne Frank House' appeared on 15 September 1957 in the *New York Times Magazine*:

Mr Frank sat alone in a nearby coffee-house the other day while reporters were shown through the Prinsengracht building by the executives of the newly organized Anne Frank Foundation . . . The founders themselves offer to an unusual degree both professional and spiritual qualifications for the aims of the foundation. Many political parties and religious faiths are represented. Their outlook is simultaneously limited and broadened, however, by one fact: unlike the Franks, not one of the founders is a Jew. The founders themselves do not stress that fact, nor try to explain it. Nevertheless, a suggested explanation is this: the Prinsengracht story was a Dutch tragedy that happened to take place in Amsterdam. The victims were Jews, as Jews were the victims of Nazism everywhere. But in the Netherlands, the pain was felt by people of all conscience, regardless of faith.

The restoration of 263 Prinsengracht began. There were several major changes to the front building, although Otto had told Kleiman that, 'as far as the front house is concerned, if it is in any way possible I would give it preference for restoration because I would like the front house also to be preserved as Anne described in her diary'. Exhibitions about Anne Frank, National Socialism and the war in the Netherlands would be held in the old offices. The annexe remained empty, on Otto's orders:

After the Anne Frank House was restored, they asked me if the rooms should be furnished again. But I answered, 'No!' During the war everything was taken away and I want to leave it like that. But after the house was opened to the public, people said they felt that the rooms were very spacious. I answered that they were getting a wrong impression and said, 'You mustn't forget the unbearable tension that was constantly present.'

On 13 December 1957 the Levin trial opened at the Supreme Court of the State of New York before Justice Samuel Coleman. Levin promised that the money he was seeking from those he accused ($600,000 from Otto and Bloomgarden, and $450,000 from Crawford), after deduction of his expenses, would go to Jewish charities. On 30 December the Judge dismissed Levin's charges of fraud and breach of contract, but, on 8 January 1958, the jury found in Levin's favour, having been asked to consider whether the Hacketts had plagiarized his play in any way. Otto and Fritzi, who had travelled to New York for the trial, sent a telegram to Switzerland about 'this greatest injustice'. Bloomgarden had suffered a heart attack during the proceedings. Samuel Silverman, the lawyer who represented Otto and Bloomgarden in court, said he would consider leaving the bar. Justice Coleman told him hundreds of rabbis agreed with the verdict, whereupon Silverman 'shouted back that he did not think much of American rabbis'. Zimmerman recalls,

I couldn't attend the trial every day because I had a small child, but I went a few times and it was so awful. It was a great strain on Otto's English. He really couldn't understand the language the lawyers were throwing at each other. Levin's lawyer was a divorce lawyer anyway. He would fire something out and poor Otto would stand there, blink and smile, and the jury just did not get it. They saw him as a slinky foreigner.

In an appeal, Otto's lawyers succeeded in having the verdict overturned and a new trial was convened. Talks amongst the lawyers dragged on for over a year.

The film of Anne Frank's diary began shooting in the spring of 1958 with a budget of $3,000,000. Stevens filmed the exterior scenes in Amsterdam, but had the annexe recreated to scale on a Hollywood studio lot. Otto flew to America for two weeks to 'provide much technical information – what the family took with them into hiding, what they wore, what they ate – and also talked at length to the cast'. Kleiman was also an adviser on the project, and told a journalist, 'The film people are very precise, I had to send all sorts to America. Pencils, milk bottles, rucksacks, stamps. Mr Stevens, the director, asked for photographs and exact descriptions of the spice mills. Everything in the film had to be right.' Bread was purchased from a Dutch baker residing in California, and Kleiman sent over samples of the spice jars for use in certain scenes. Louis de Jong, director of RIOD (now NIOD), was also consulted for the authenticity of the film and later wrote to Stevens: 'Of course, I as a historian have discovered here and there some slight touches and details which did not correspond with reality, but these will not hinder the general public and I realize that sometimes certain dramatic effects are necessary in a work of art, even if they did not occur in reality.' A visiting journalist described the set: 'Around the fringes of Stage 14 are large bulletin boards set up in such a way that the actors cannot miss them as they walk to and from the set. Stevens has covered them with pictures. Predominating is an enormous blow up of the familiar photograph of Anne, thoughtful-eyed and hesitantly smiling. Other pictures, made during the war in Amsterdam, show fenced-in ghettos, Jews being chased and beaten in the streets.'

The casting of Anne Frank caused great speculation in the press since Susan Strasberg had decided not to participate in the film (Joseph Schildkraut and Gusti Huber were repeating their performance as Otto and Edith Frank for the screen; curiously, Hendrik van Hoeve, who had provided the people in hiding with groceries, played himself in the film). Otto wanted Audrey Hepburn for the part of Anne.* Hepburn, born in Brussels in 1929, had lived through the war herself in the Netherlands. She recalled how, as a young girl, she had seen the cattle trucks leaving Arnhem station 'filled with Jews . . . families with little children, with babies, herded into meat wagons . . . all those faces peering out. On the platform, soldiers herding more Jewish families with their poor little bundles and small children . . . It was very hard to understand . . . all the nightmares I've ever had are mingled

---

* Audrey Hepburn later became a patron of the Anne Frank Educational Trust UK.

with that.' In 1947 she read *Het Achterhuis*: 'When the liberation finally came, too late for Anne Frank, I took up my ballet lessons and went to live in Amsterdam with my mother in a house we shared with a lady writer, who one day handed me a book in galley form and said, "I think you'd like to read this." It was in Dutch, 1947, Anne Frank's diary. It destroyed me. There were floods of tears. I became hysterical.'

Hepburn was one of the first visitors to the building on the Prinsengracht. When Stevens sent her the book asking her to audition for the role of Anne, she read it again, 'and had to go to bed for the day'. Otto then travelled to Bürgenstock to meet Hepburn and her husband, Mel Ferrer. Hepburn recalled,

He came to lunch and stayed to dinner. We had the most wonderful day . . . He came with his new wife, who had lost her husband and children in the Holocaust. They both had the numbers on their arms. He was a beautiful-looking man, very fine, a sort of transparent face, very sensitive. Incapable of talking about Anne without extreme feeling. I had to ask him nothing because he had a need to talk about it. He struck me as somebody who'd been purged by fire. There was something so spiritual about his face. He'd been there and back.

Hepburn kept a photograph of them all taken that day in her copy of the *Diary of a Young Girl*.

On 2 August 1957 Mel Ferrer wrote to Otto and Fritzi from Lucerne:

Dear Mr and Mrs Frank, I am sending you these pictures as a little memento of our meeting that rainy afternoon . . . There is still no news about Audrey's doing the picture, but we expect to hear soon whether or not the Hacketts have completed the script, and then the final decision can be made. We have thought so often of the strange instinct which prompted you to send us your friendly message that afternoon and we are very grateful indeed. It was a wonderful moment to meet and talk with you, and I hope that it will not be too long before we can do so again.

Hepburn also wrote warmly to Leni, having become friends with her through Otto. In the end, Hepburn told Otto she could not take the part: 'I didn't want to exploit her life and her death to my advantage – to get another salary, to be perhaps praised in a movie . . . I could not have suffered through that again without destroying myself . . . I just couldn't deal with it.' She was also honest enough to realize that, at the age of almost thirty, she was too old for the role.

Natalie Wood was then asked to play Anne, but she did not want the role. After a nationwide search for an actress to play Anne (over 10,000 girls auditioned), nineteen-year-old Millie Perkins, a model from New Jersey, landed the part after being approached by a Fox scout in a restaurant. She was modelling for *Paris Match* when she was called for a second screen test. Two months later Stevens visited her in New York and told her she was his Anne Frank. Stevens defended his choice to a cynical press, insisting that he did not want someone who necessarily resembled Anne before she was deported: 'What I want is a general resemblance and a person that is wistful, loveable, fun-filled and precocious all at the same time. Millie is most like Anne Frank in temperament.' Schildkraut said that of all the Anne Frank actresses he had worked with, 'Millie Perkins is the nearest thing to the real Anne Frank.'

Stevens announced that his film would be

devoid of Nazi horrors. It will tell the valiant, often humorous story of a wonderful family hiding out in a time of great stress; the story of a teenage girl's magnificent triumph over fear. Anne Frank was the kind of girl responsible for the survival of the human race . . . Anne didn't know anything about the camps . . . Her diary isn't the book of a young girl looking death in the face. It's the story of someone facing life.

Stevens filmed the end scene depicting Anne in Auschwitz, but it was badly received by the test audience and he replaced it with a shot of the Amsterdam clouds and Anne's ghostly voice proclaiming, 'In spite of everything, I still believe people are really good at heart.'

The film ran to three hours, though European cinemas showed a slightly shorter version. It was neither a critical nor a commercial success. One theatre manager explained the poor audience numbers in New York as being due to people 'growing tired of the past Holocaust. That includes Jews and Gentiles alike.' A British report in the *Daily Mail* thundered:

The Diary of Anne Frank is an outstanding instance of a subject being diminished by filming . . . The girl who wrote the diary must have had something more than the perky charm of a New World Junior Miss . . . the characterization and idiom of the picture are fatal to its effort to recreate an authentic atmosphere. These were European Jews in a European situation. But, as presented here, especially by Shelley Winters and Ed Wynn, they become stock figures from any tragi-comedy of Jewish life in Brooklyn. The only exception is Joseph Schildkraut's admirably managed portrait of Anne Frank's father.

Nonetheless, the film received eight Oscar nominations and was awarded three, one of which went to Shelley Winters for her portrayal of Mrs van Daan (Gusti van Pels).

Otto had slowly begun to understand the dangers inherent in trying to universalize the Holocaust and what had happened to his family. He requested a clarification in future theatre programmes as to the authenticity of the diary, and asked whether it would be possible to provide some sort of list of chronological facts before the film started. He had been shocked by an incident involving a Dutch Jewish acquaintance who had sat next to an American Jewish woman during a performance of the play in New York. When the Dutch woman said that she had known Anne before the war, 'the American expressed amazement that the characters and events in the play were real'. Otto wrote to the Hacketts: 'There are a great number of the younger generation who just do not understand what it is all about and that it is a true story. I spoke to youngsters who told me their classmates laughed right at the beginning when the truck came and there were people on it in "pyjamas". It seems that some sort of explanation should be given at the beginning – before the film starts.'

Barbara Zimmerman defends the play and the film:

Neither were as dreadful as people say now. No one wanted to have a sad, hopeless ending. There had to be something uplifting in the end. Okay, so the Hacketts weren't Shakespeare, but it really was not a bad effort. They used Anne's language and kept it honourable. The ending of the film might be kitsch, but you would have to be an idiot not to know that something appalling happened to the family afterwards. The Hacketts were very modest people, they loved Otto and wanted to do the job well. They were emotional about it. Levin was a manipulator. He was very sentimental and his play was pure propaganda. The Hacketts let the story tell itself. The refrain about people being really good at heart was unfortunate, and it did disguise the real horror somewhat but I feel loyal to the Hacketts. They helped sell a lot more books.

That same year the East German film *Ein Tagebuch für Anne Frank* was released. Completely different in tone from the Hacketts' efforts, here Anne's story served as a background to the unmasking of former Nazis who were living peaceful lives in Germany. One of those named was the former commandant of Westerbork, Gemmeker. His full address was displayed on-screen under a current photograph. The film maintained that little had changed in Germany since Hitler's rise to power: 'The "democratic" system in West Germany is the old system under a new mask, and the new mask is rather transparent . . . The disguises change, but the danger remains.' It was made as 'a memorial to Anne Frank, as a memorial to the millions who were murdered; but also [as] a warning to the living . . .' In the accompanying press booklet, Joachim Hellwig wrote: 'In West Germany the diary of Anne Frank is misused as a symbol of the spirit of tolerance. In this matter there can be no tolerance.' The film received more favourable reviews than the Hollywood spectacular, but was given only a limited release. Otto hated it, dismissing it as 'mere communist propaganda. Anne's name in connection with it, is used in spite of my strong protest . . . Of course I am not opposed to an anti-Nazi film, but I objected to use Anne for political propaganda.'

Het Achterhuis had not been reprinted in the Netherlands since 1950, but between 1955 and 1957 fifteen editions appeared. By 1958 it was published in Holland, Britain, Germany, France, USA, Norway, Denmark, Sweden, Japan, Israel, Italy, Hungary, Finland and Spain. In Moscow the play was not performed but a translation was available. By early January 1958 the play had grossed more than $2.6 million. Otto was keen to use his royalties for the Anne Frank Stichting.

In a letter to Otto, dated 18 June 1958, Kleiman expressed his unhappiness about the manner in which the Stichting was being promoted in the Dutch press. He also disliked Otto's idea of a collection in the streets to try to restore the house: 'I do not appreciate this. When there is a disaster, one can say that we must help at any price, and that all means to collect money are permissible, but that is not the case here.' He worked hard on the business side of the Stichting (in addition to his own work), and continued to guide people through the annexe but warned it was becoming dangerous to do so. He concluded,

> I do not like to write this to you, but I feel that the atmosphere in the Stichting is not very good, especially as far as cooperation is concerned. I am very glad that I cannot attend . . . and that really expresses my sentiment. And another thing: you pass so many messages on to me. Aren't there any that you can pass on to the secretariat directly? I keep having to introduce news that you receive from the USA, either directly or indirectly, while it would have much more impact coming from you. It is not that I mind the work, but in this way my position is not very clear. You understand what I'm trying to say.

Kleiman died on 30 January 1959. Otto flew to Amsterdam for the funeral, which took place in the Zorgvlied Cemetery. He gave a speech at the ceremony which included a quote from Edith that Anne had recorded in her diary: 'When Mr Kleiman comes in, the sun begins to shine.'

With his loyal friend gone, Otto began to pay more attention to the everyday business of the Stichting. He was eager to raise more funds for the educational foundation he aimed to establish in Anne's name, as well as for the museum itself. Anneke Steenmeijer, who worked at the Stichting in the early days, recalls,

Otto was very moved by people's response to the diary. When he wanted to begin something, not to keep the house just as a museum, but to make it active, he went to his friend Rabbi Jacob Soetendorp and asked him if he had any ideas. He told him to go to Henri van Praag – he would know what to do. Van Praag suggested the Youth Centre and, every month, Otto came to Amsterdam to speak to him about the educational courses they would give there. Later he came often to those seminars. For him, the educational side was the most important. He absolutely did not want it to be only a museum.

In January, informing Otto about a $5,000 cheque donated to the Stichting by Bloomgarden, Mermin told him that he (Mermin) had begun 'in the last few days, to write directly to a number of wealthy people, some of whom received the form letter in December, and intend to continue to write a number of such individual letters . . .' Otto sent Mermin an extensive list of people whom he thought able and glad to contribute, including Edith's brothers, Nathan Straus, and many other close friends. Mermin himself sent out scores of letters to wealthy Americans who might be interested in making donations to the Stichting. Otto also expected the money from all benefit performances of the film in America to be given to the Stichting by 20th Century Fox, but the studio had already decided that in order to stress 'the universality of the picture' the funds raised would be divided between various charities. Spyros Skouras, president of Fox, told journalists that neither the Stichting nor any other Jewish organization would receive money from them because it was 'not a Jewish picture. This is a picture for the whole world.' Frances Hackett comforted Otto that although he would be 'very disappointed', other showings 'in Holland and abroad' would benefit the Stichting.

On 20 March 1959 Otto and Fritzi arrived in New York on the liner *United States* for a ten-day stay, whose main aim was to organize the American Anne Frank Foundation. On 24 March they were guests at a dinner in New York's Little Theater where the film of the diary was shown. The American Anne Frank Foundation (whose First Vice-President was

Myer Mermin and whose treasurer was Joseph Marks), based at 12 East 94th Street, had organized a special American committee to sponsor the evening. Among the committee members were Senator John Kennedy, Kermit Bloomgarden, Joseph Marks, Meyer Mermin and Nathan Straus. Eleanor Roosevelt was honorary chairman. Otto talked about the Amsterdam Stichting, hoping to raise funds for it, and presented plans of the 'International Anne Frank Foundation' while Shelley Winters 'detail[ed] the activities of the campaign in the US'. The audience were told that if 263 Prinsengracht could be restored through monies raised then 'the City of Amsterdam and the Government of the Netherlands would reimburse the Trustees part of the costs, to be used for "operating expenses".' Otto himself had donated $30,000 to the project and the City of Frankfurt gave $5,000 in commemoration of Anne's birth in the city. Otto pledged to increase that figure when he received his royalties from the play and the film: 'It is Mr Frank's intention that from the net proceeds which will be available to him from the play and the motion picture he will devote approximately half to the Amsterdam Youth Centre and related foundations (and approximately half to a memorial to be established in Israel).' The aim in America was to raise $300,000, including $10,000 for 'miscellaneous' use, i.e. additional, unforeseen costs incurred during the restoration of the house (which was closed to the public due to its instability) and establishment of a youth centre. Many of those invited contributed sums, large and small. Interestingly, the list of donors names Gusti Huber under 'cannot contribute'.

Otto and Fritzi left their modest hotel for a time to stay with Hilde Goldberg and her husband Max in Rhode Island. Their daughter Ruth recalls,

Otto used to make surprise appearances in Rhode Island or in New York, whisking me off from school for an intimate chat. He always brought books, good books that were carefully chosen and much appreciated. He was always loving and amusing. And most of all, he always, *always* took me seriously . . . Otto filled my life, from the very first book of nursery rhymes he gave me, to my adult sense of the totality of the diary; its answer to violence, despite the reality of Anne's own death . . . for me, and I'm sure for others who loved him, his fearful vulnerability was always apparent and astounding. He was strong and brave because he made himself a living testament to his dead family.

Two months after his visit to America, Otto travelled to Wuppertal in Germany to view the construction of an 'Anne Frank Village' for twenty refugee families, which was intended to provide 'a home, work, friendship and to sink their roots in the good earth'. The words were sealed into the foundation stone containing earth from Belsen which was laid by Otto, who was accompanied by Belgian Dominican priest Father Dominique Pire, with whom he had struck up a close friendship. Pire, a Nobel Peace Prize winner and founder of the 'Aid to Displaced Persons' movement had directed the building of six such villages through his organization, which was also known as 'Europe of the Hearts'. He contacted Otto about his intention to build a village in Anne's name; in answer to Otto's letter and donation, he wrote fervently, 'Thank you for your gift which will be converted into bricks for the Anne Frank Village. For months now, Anne's picture has been hanging on the wall of my little office. In her I see all who have suffered and are suffering. Her courage has been a source of inspiration to me.' At Wuppertal, he declared, 'Let those adults who hear me agree amongst themselves so that little girls will no longer be murdered; build a world of brotherhood based no longer on fear, but on trustful collaboration.' Pire died suddenly in 1969. Otto saw the occasion in the Ruhr city as 'another step along the road that Anne's diary has sent me travelling in the years since the war'.

Not all the events connected to Otto's daughter's diary in 1959 were pleasant. In October 1957 fifty teenagers had disrupted the opening of the play in Linz and the show 'ended in a full-blown Nazi riot'. The following year, a poster for the play in Wuppertal, where the refugee village was located, was defaced with 'Death to the Jewish swine. Too few Jews went up in smoke. Anne Frank was a Jewish swine too.' In that same year, anti-Semitic demonstrations interrupted a performance of the play and Lothar Stielau, an English teacher in Lübeck, and former NSDAP and SA member, alleged that the diary was a fake.★ Fischer Bücherei, publishers of the German language version of the diary, brought the matter to Otto's attention. Stielau stated that he believed Anne Frank kept a diary, but doubted how much relevance it had to the published diary. Supporting his claims was Heinrich Buddeberg, who wrote to the press naming Meyer Levin as the diary's author. The Ministry of Culture ordered Stielau's temporary suspension from his job and

---

★ I have condensed the various legal battles Otto fought to prove the diary's authenticity, since the court cases with revisionist historians contain a great deal of repetitive material that is unlikely to interest the general reader. This is not to imply that the issue was of little importance to Otto Frank; on the contrary, it affected him profoundly. Readers wishing to learn more are directed to Chapter Seven, *Attacks on the Authenticity of the Diary*, in David Barnouw and Gerrold van der Stroom, *The Diaries of Anne Frank: The Critical Edition* (London: Viking, 1989).

in April 1959 the case came to court with Otto and two publishing houses bringing criminal charges against Stielau and Buddeberg.

Seven days into the trial, Stielau asserted that when he made his allegations it was the play rather than the diary to which he referred, although articles in the press had led him to question the diary's authenticity. In interviews given in July, Otto specified the differences between the original diary and the published version, and declared himself willing to allow experts to investigate the actual diary. On 13 October 1959 the three women elected to examine the diary arrived in Basel. In March 1960 they reported themselves satisfied that the writing in the diary was identical with specimen examples of Anne's writing elsewhere. The report found the published diary 'true to its sources in substance and ideas'. Stielau's lawyers demanded a second opinion, which they received, only to tear it apart because it did not provide the information for which they had hoped. The matter limped on until 17 October 1961, when Stielau and Buddeberg's lawyers came to an out-of-court settlement with Otto's lawyers and the lawyers representing the publishers. Stielau's lawyers declared that their client had 'no grounds for claiming the diary was a forgery'. The evidence presented had 'persuaded him to the contrary'.

The affair had exhausted Otto and hurt him deeply. What is more, he was an increasingly popular target for neo-Nazi hate mail. One such letter found after his death came from a British anti-Semite calling himself Peter Dawson (not his real name), a notorious spreader of vitriolic literature:

> Otto Frank, this is to tell you that your stinking diary is a fake and a phoney and that you have done more harm to the recovery of the post-war world than the Jewish-Bolshevists of Moscow and Tel Aviv, in whose pay you are. How dare you say that you are going to sue people because they do not believe all the tripe and piffle that you put out with the assistance of Vallentine, Mitchell, Kermit Bloomgarden and Twentieth Century Pox [sic] Films. Just you wait you criminal you. Your day will come. I would strongly advise you to go to Israel and keep your big lying mouth shut. See you in court, Abe.

The slander against the diary never abated during Otto's lifetime, although he did all he could to fight the accusations by neo-Nazis that it was a forgery. One of the most aggressive revisionists was Robert Faurisson, whom Otto also fought in the courtroom, as he did all those who dared to decry his daughter's legacy. Faurisson contacted Kugler, Miep, Bep and Otto himself to conduct his spurious interviews aimed at discovering 'where the truth was'. Faurisson, a literature lecturer at the University of Lyons, denied that the gas chambers had ever existed. Otto allowed the diary to be investigated to prove its authenticity again in early 1980. When Otto won his cases, any damages awarded were donated to the Anne Frank Stichting. Father Neiman recalls, 'Stories about the diary being a fake cut him deeply. He found defending it very painful and personally wounding. He thought it was terrible that someone could make such accusations and though it cost him a lot personally and financially to fight those people, he did it and he did so on behalf of all the victims of Nazism.' Shortly before Otto's death, the Supreme Court in West Germany ruled that Holocaust denial was an offence. In 1994 the Bundestag passed a law whereby anyone repudiating that the Holocaust took place could be punished by up to five years' imprisonment.

In January 1960 Otto signed the papers to settle the Levin case and hoped that this matter at least was ended.* However, a few days later Levin sent him a vituperative letter: 'While the legal phase of our encounter is over, the moral phase is not done. Your behaviour will remain forever as a ghastly example of evil returned for good, and of a father's betrayal of his daughter's words.' Otto was unable to escape Levin; in March he visited Israel for the first time, only to learn that Levin had published a letter in the *Jerusalem Post* claiming that Otto had told a journalist that he had rejected Levin's play purely because it was not 'universal' enough. At a press conference held in the Ramat Hadassah Youth Aliya Centre, Otto denied Levin's latest attack and told his young listeners that he had never tried to undermine 'the importance of Anne's Jewishness', though her significance 'transcended her specific interest to the Jewish people'.

Levin's son, the poet Gabriel Levin, wrote of his father's involvement with the diary:

I have no doubt that my father was in a sense 'right' in attacking the Hacketts' play for all the obvious reasons. However, I believe – and I say this with pain – that my father was obstinately, even cruelly wrong in insisting that he had a claim over the play/diaries that somehow superseded Otto Frank's legal and moral rights, as the sole survivor, to his daughter's literary remains. I may not agree with the way Frank

---

* Otto paid Levin $15,000 and was in turn able to collect his royalties from the play, which had been tied up during all the legal tussles. Levin relinquished any rights to the diary, but retained the right to discuss the diary as a literary issue, as long as it didn't touch on the question of whether or not his play should have been produced.

controlled the image of Anne (not only in terms of her Jewishness, but also in terms of her sexuality and her relation to her mother), but I do feel strongly that it is not for us to judge the survivors of the camps, and if this is how he decided Anne should be presented to the general public, so be it; after his death a more rounded picture would – and has – come out. I don't believe that Meyer ever lost his mind. But he did lose, I believe, whenever the issue of Otto Frank and the diaries came up, his moral bearings.

Despite his father's 'battles with the windmills of Anne Frank', Gabriel maintains that Meyer Levin

cared deeply for his family, and he was, strangely enough – for a man with such a temper – rather shy, introverted and 'soft' in his approach to people. He was also driven by a deep sense of justice (again, a paradox, when one considers the fierce insensitivity of his letter to Otto Frank) and was undoubtedly a writer of rare integrity – a writer of the Old School, who lived, passionately, by the word.

Otto enjoyed his stay in Israel, despite Levin's attempts to cause him harm, and the press were generally kinder to him than to Levin. One admiring journalist reported, 'I was with Otto Frank when he dined with the children at the Youth Aliya village of Nitsanim. Although seventy-one years old, Mr Frank had swum in Eilat at 7 o'clock that morning: thirteen hours later he had energy and time not only to address the children but also to give an interview to two astute journalists.' Otto himself informed Mermin that he and Fritzi had swum 'in the Dead Sea as well as in the Red Sea, crossed the desert during a heatwave and a sandstorm'. He also saw his old comrade from Auschwitz, Joseph Spronz, his wife Franzi and son Gershon. Franzi remembers:

The political regime in Hungary had kept us apart from Otto for many years, but when we emigrated to Israel, Otto was able to trace us through his friend Gideon Hausner, the Israeli Chief Prosecutor who led the trial against Eichmann. When Otto met my husband again in Israel after all that time apart, he got very emotional – he had a terrible nosebleed because of the excitement. Otto wanted to pay my son's university fees but there was no need, we could do that ourselves. Fritzi and I became great friends. During the festival of Purim there were parades everywhere and we all watched them from a friend's house overlooking the town.

Otto and Fritzi also visited Hanneli Goslar, who was married by then and had children of her own.

Otto always wrote for my birthday and later he visited often. When he and Fritzi came the first time, my children were still small and I was going to bring them to the hotel, but Otto said, 'No, we're coming to you, children have to be seen in their own environment to get to know them best.' Otto had been on a trip to the Massada mountain. He told the story in a very amusing way: they went up in a cable car and it got broken, so they had to do the whole journey on foot. Then when they got back to their hotel, where they were staying on the eighth floor, the elevator wasn't working, so they had to take the stairs. Everything went wrong. Otto was laughing so much as he told me about it and he ended, 'Oh, I never slept so good as I did this night!' He never complained about anything because he always said he had lived through the concentration camps so what was there to worry about now?

Hanneli was also touched on subsequent visits by the fact that Otto kept photos of Fritzi's grandchildren, Caroline, Jacky and Sylvia, in his wallet; he clearly regarded himself as their grandfather and spoke of them with pleasure and deep affection.

At the end of April, Otto and Fritzi flew to Amsterdam for the official opening of 263 Prinsengracht as a museum. On the morning of the event, 3 May 1960, the Anne Frank Stichting held a meeting at the Tropenmuseum under Otto's chairmanship. Afterwards Otto, together with Miep, Jan, Bep, Mrs Kleiman and Mayor van Hall (who had worked hard on the project) travelled the short distance to 263 Prinsengracht and spent some time together inside the annexe before the doors opened to the public. At the opening ceremony, Otto could not hold back his tears, and cut short his speech, imploring the crowd, 'Forgive me for not speaking for longer, but the thought of what happened here is too much for me.' The public were then permitted entrance to the 'Anne Frank House'. The architect Rappange had restored the house (and its neighbour, 265), converting the former warehouse and the spice grinding room on the ground floor into a lecture hall, while the offices on the second floor and the storerooms on the third had been modified to allow for exhibitions and displays. A student would conduct tours of the house, which Otto told journalists was intended as 'neither a museum nor a place of pilgrimage. It is an earnest warning from the past and a mission of hope for the future.'

On the same date, funded by private contributions, the German Federal Republic, and Otto himself, the Anne Frank Stichting Youth Centre was launched with Otto as its chairman. The old canal houses on the corner of the Prinsengracht and the Westermarkt had been demolished and that day the mayor laid the first foundation post on the land where student housing would be built and completed by 1962. During the summer, when the students were absent, the dormitories would house young people who had signed up for the conferences held there. Suggested topics for discussion were the relationship between Judaism and Christianity, discrimination, prejudice and war. Otto was a regular visitor; his aim was that the world's youth would form a common bond and strive together for peace in his daughter's name, fulfilling his interpretation of her words, 'I want to work for the world and mankind.'

On 10 May 1961 Otto wrote to Mermin, 'In October . . . we hope to move into a flat or house of our own after having lived eight years with the family. The main reason is that the younger son [Buddy] of my sister who is with "Holiday on Ice" quits his job and wants to come home for good.' Otto and Fritzi felt that the time was right to move into their own home, after years of always living with other people. They bought a beautiful detached house in the Basel suburb of Birsfelden. There was a spacious basement, above which the Franks lived, and then another floor which they rented out. Surrounding the house was a large garden, which Otto tended himself, growing the 'Souvenir d'Anne Frank' rose around the balcony at the rear. Inside the house, Otto designated one room as the office in which he and Fritzi would reply to the vast correspondence generated by Anne's diary. Above the desk where Fritzi typed while her husband dictated his letters (and to which Fritzi also contributed) was a Star of David created by a nun who had read the diary, and Marc Chagall's lithograph of Anne from a luxury French edition of the book. Later these were joined by a photograph of the statue of Anne in Utrecht and a colourful chain of cranes made by Japanese readers.

Otto had many regular correspondents who were determined to keep writing to him despite his protestations that he did not have the time. A number of the most persistent writers became close friends of both Otto and Fritzi. Among these was Sumi, a Japanese girl who had been placed in a convent by her mother after her father's death; she wrote to Otto after reading the diary and asked to become his 'letter daughter'. A Greek girl named Vassa wrote to Otto in her native language (which Otto had translated by the Greek Consulate in Basel) telling him that her father had been in the resistance during the war and had been killed in front of her. She was deeply depressed, but her frequent letters from Otto helped her to recover. Their correspondence continued at a faster pace once she had learned French in order to communicate with him better. Otto and Fritzi later visited Vassa in Athens. A young American girl, Cara Wilson, started an exchange of letters with Otto in 1960 that continued with Fritzi after his death, and published extracts from them in her book *Love, Otto: The Legacy of Anne Frank* (Andrews & McMeel, 1995).

Another regular writer was John Neiman, now Father Neiman, who began writing to Otto in 1974. He recalls,

I first read the diary in fifth grade. It impressed me hugely. I re-read it every year and bought books on Holland and the Holocaust because I was so drawn to Anne and her experiences. I found Anne's beliefs so moving. In college I decided to write to Otto Frank and tell him how much the book meant to me personally. In June 1976, after many letters between us, I went to Switzerland at his invitation. I stayed near to his and Fritzi's home, at the Hotel Alpha. It was just a dream come true. What impressed me most was Otto's humanity, which he had retained after the most terrible experiences. And to be honest, he changed my life. In 1979 I was thinking about the priesthood but still had my doubts. I spoke to Otto about it at his stepdaughter Eva's home and he said, 'Look, your love for Anne is a wonderful thing, but use it, turn your love into doing good for others.' And suddenly everything became clear to me.

Every year, Otto and Fritzi spent Eva's birthday (11 May) and Otto's birthday (12 May) with Eva and her family, either in London, or on holiday. Zvi, Eva's husband, recalls,

Otto was a very good man. He was interested in me, in Israel where I came from. One thing struck me the minute I met him: he was very, very German. He had a very strong sense of orderliness and cleanliness. Eva is very untidy and he hated it – he used to tell her off a lot. When he came here once, he got dressed in an overall, a grey work-coat and went out. We found him cleaning the garage! And we used to lie in bed late and Otto would come in early with Fritzi and beat on the bed with a walking stick: 'Get up, come on, out of there!' He was very military. You could see that he had been in the German army.

Bee Klug, who met Otto and Fritzi in the early 1960s in London through Zvi Schloss, who worked with her husband, recalls inviting them all to dinner one evening:

The discussion around the table stuck in my mind. My family came from Poland originally and more than seventy relatives died in the Holocaust. Otto described himself as German, a seventh generation German Jew and said, 'If the Holocaust could happen in a country as civilized as Germany, then it can happen anywhere.

But we can prevent it through education. Seeing something like this in Anne's name is a compensation for me, but there is a lot still to do.'

Klug, who in 1991 became one of the founder members of the Anne Frank Educational Trust in the UK, insists, 'Otto was out for justice. So was Fritzi. They dedicated their lives to that end.'

Among the frequent visitors to the Franks' house in Birsfelden was Judith de Winter, who first met Otto and his family in Westerbork, and her husband Henk Solomon. She remembers, 'Otto was always very clear about what he wanted to achieve. He was determined that everyone should know about the Holocaust. He used the money that came from Anne's diary solely for that purpose.' Judith's husband agrees: 'Otto was too careful with money. He would never take a taxi when he could walk. It makes me furious when people say, "Otto Frank lived off his dead daughter." Nothing could have been further from the truth. He wanted money, but only to use for the good of others.'

In 1971 Otto was questioned about his royalties by reporters attending the presentation of a gold statuette of the god Pan to mark the sale of a million paperback copies of the diary in English. His reply was immediate and direct: 'I take the money. I don't give it all to the foundation. There are peace funds and fourteen scholarships in Israel and single scholarships in places like Nigeria. And the tax takes about half.' Otto and Fritzi's one extravagance was travel; they liked to see new people and learn about other cultures. Anne, who wrote in her diary that her father enjoyed reading 'dry as dust' descriptions of people and places, would not have been surprised to see the stack of basic travel books he kept in his bookcase in Basel. Otto's stepdaughter, Eva, recalls that after Otto and her mother moved into the house in Birsfelden, they were visited by a young couple who

wanted to know about the writer Gustav Janouch, who lived in Prague. He had translated Anne's diary into Czech and also written a book about Kafka. The couple told Otto that they intended to visit the writer and Otto said, 'I am sure Gustav will ask you to smuggle his Kafka manuscript to the West. This will be very dangerous. Don't do it. No book, even a very important one, is worth a human life.'

On 24 January 1963 Otto and Fritzi Frank established the Anne Frank-Fonds in Basel. To Otto's distress, the Anne Frank Stichting in Amsterdam was not running as smoothly as he had hoped. In early 1961 he had written to Mermin, 'We have just come back from Amsterdam where, as you probably know, the international youth centre has been opened . . . As a whole this manifestation was a success, though not everything had been organized as I would have wished.' On 9 February 1962 he was more explicit in his disquiet about the Stichting to Mermin:

I am still in a very strong disagreement with the Board, so that I even refuse to take part at Board meetings. One of the main reasons is the contract which has been made between the Anne Frank Stichting and the Foundation for Student House in which the interests of our Foundation are, in my opinion, neglected, favouring the other one . . . The relation between myself and the Board is working very badly on my nerves being so much against everything Anne stands for. If I would not see always again the influence of Anne on youth, as well as from the Amsterdam group and by letters from abroad, I would get discouraged and would think of retiring from the Board.

In a letter to his friends Max and Jean Grossman, dated November 1962, Otto confided that some of the difficulties had been resolved:

I always was very dissatisfied with the Board, but now, after a year of struggle I succeeded with my demands to have three to four new members, among them a new chairman and secretary. We are looking out for the right people now. I finally asked the Mayor of Amsterdam to help in solving the difficulties. He proposed a mediator and with his help I managed to get my conditions accepted.

Otto's faith in his vision of the Stichting had been shaken, however, and he now decided that, upon his death, the copyright of Anne's diaries and other writings would be inherited by the Fonds in Basel. He invited a group of close friends, as well as his nephews Buddy and Stephan, to join the board; unlike the Stichting in Amsterdam, his intention with the Fonds was that it would always remain a small organization whose main aim would be to 'promote charitable work and to play a social and cultural role in the spirit of Anne Frank'. In order to do this, they would receive all royalties from sales of the diary and from the various dramatic adaptations based upon the book. Unlike the Stichting, the Fonds would have a much closer personal link to the diary; among its members, Otto hoped, there would always be family.

A few months after the creation of the Anne Frank-Fonds, the discovery of the Gestapo officer, Silberbauer, who had arrested the Franks in their hiding place, caused a furore in the world's press. Tonny Ahlers, who had slunk back into obscurity following his release from prison, moved swiftly into action, contacting the Vienna authorities involved in the investigation into Silberbauer's wartime past. And from that moment on, Otto Frank publicly avowed that he no longer wanted his betrayer found.

Nazi hunter Simon Wiesenthal had been looking for Silberbauer since 1958, when a group of teenagers handing out neo-Nazi leaflets told Wiesenthal that they would be more willing to believe in the authenticity of Anne Frank's diary if he could find the man who arrested her. Wiesenthal was obstructed in his quest by Otto, who had asked those who knew Silberbauer's real name to refer to him as 'Silberthaler'. This name was employed in Ernst Schnabel's *The Footsteps of Anne Frank*. In the same book, Otto said of Silberbauer, 'Perhaps he would have spared us if he had been by himself.' Otto refused to be of any assistance to Wiesenthal in his search, something Wiesenthal could not understand. Cor Suijk, who knew both men, recalls, 'Wiesenthal knew Otto was deliberately not helping, trying to prevent him from finding Silberbauer. He said, "If it was up to Otto Frank, we would never have found him."' But Otto saw it like this: when Silberbauer discovered that Otto had been an officer in the Great War, he showed respect, giving the family far more time than was usual to pack, and made the NSBers put away their guns. Otto understood him, thinking back to his own discipline as a German soldier, and actually protected the man who arrested his family. Wiesenthal remained angry that Otto had such respect for this man and had caused his team so much unnecessary work. Otto himself was shocked and far from happy when he heard that Wiesenthal had found Silberbauer. He never wanted that to happen.

After years of searching, Wiesenthal tracked down his man in 1963. Karl Josef Silberbauer, born to a police officer and his wife in 1911, and a member of the Gestapo since 1938, had been jailed briefly after his return to Vienna in April 1945. In 1954 he was reinstated into the Vienna police, where he was still working when the inquiry into his past was launched. On 4 October 1963 Silberbauer was suspended from duties. The story broke in the world's press on 11 November 1963. Silberbauer spoke to one journalist at home in Vienna and also granted an interview for *De Telegraaf*, the newspaper for which Ahlers worked.

Following Silberbauer's discovery the investigation into the betrayal was re-opened. A number of new witnesses were heard, while some of those who had given testimonies before, such as the Hartogs, had died in the intervening years. Otto, Miep, Bep and Kugler could give the detectives no new leads to follow. The Dutch police involved in the case again concentrated on trying to prove van Maaren guilty. Otto told a journalist, 'When we were arrested, Silberbauer was there. I saw him. But van Maaren was not there, and I have no evidence about him.' Miep seemed certain that van Maaren was not the betrayer, while Kugler remained convinced that he was their most likely suspect and wrote as much in a private letter to Otto. Extraordinarily, on 4 December 1963, Silberbauer's mother-in-law also wrote to Otto:

> Before anything else, I would like to apologize for bothering you with my writing, Mr Frank, but it is the worries about my family that force me to do this. I am the mother-in-law of Silberbauer, it hurts my heart to have to watch how my daughter is suffering from this. They point after her, the house is often besieged by reporters and photographers. Silberbauer does not even dare to go and feed the birds in the garden, because there are also people in the back . . . he is not a bad human being. He loves children, animals and flowers, and such people cannot do the vicious things he is charged with.
>
> What would you have done, Mr Frank, if one of your soldiers had disobeyed one of your orders? That is what he had to do as well.
>
> His stepdaughter wrote me a letter from the US full of fear, because she has six children and this might hurt them. Thank you, Mr Frank, for the good things you said about Silberbauer . . . I would like to ask you, Mr Frank, if I could lay claim to your goodness, for you to write to Mr Wiesenthal in order to leave the family finally in peace.

Otto kept her letter, but no response to it has been found.

Tonny Ahlers, meanwhile, had evidently continued his practice of watching from a safe distance before deciding to act. The 1950s had seen Anne Frank's diary grow in acclaim and Otto Frank was upheld as an example of Jewish resistance and integrity in the face of evil. Ahlers was livid. It did not matter to him that Otto had defended him when he had been unable to find anyone else able to say a single good thing about him; he hated 'the Jew Frank' as he referred to him in private letters. By the early 1960s, Ahlers was struggling to earn a living as an occasional reporter for *De Telegraaf*, and ran a business, Photopress International ('information service, publicity photos, infra-red and flash photography, the latest news in pictures and sound, day and night'), from an apartment in Amsterdam-Osdorp where he lived with his wife and children.

On 27 December 1963 Ahlers wrote to the authorities in Vienna, explaining that he had '*exonerating* material about Mr Silberbauer'. He referred erroneously to Otto's conduct during the war, adding, 'during the war years

Otto Frank cooperated with National Socialists, and should absolutely not be held to serve as an example of what his co-religionists endured through Nazi Germany. I can substantiate this with more proof.' He told them that Jansen's son was the betrayer almost certainly knowing that the young man was dead (as was Jansen senior). At the same time he defamed Anne's diary, by writing of 'the positive worth of the diary tales of Anne Frank. Just as fairy tales have a positive worth.' He felt that Silberbauer was 'the victim' and 'the extent to which Otto Frank has betrayed his own cause I leave to the judgement of others'. He offered to act as a witness against Otto, but asked them to refrain from passing on the information to NIOD, evidently not wanting his name to be on file for any future researchers. He ended, 'Otto Frank has very good reasons to keep silent.'

On 15 January 1964 Ahlers wrote to Silberbauer at his home address. He began his onslaught with the view that while the betrayal investigation was covered in the press, 'Otto Frank boldly kept silent. I know exactly why. But nevertheless this man is referred to as having "integrity" and is seen as "representative". The question is: of what?' Ahlers claimed to have many interesting documents about Otto's conduct during the war in his possession. He ended his letter: 'It all boils down to the fact that Otto Frank himself, through the so-called diary of his daughter Anne, has acquired an exceptional social status to which he himself has fervently contributed . . . It would cost me little trouble to prove that Otto Frank/Opekta delivered to the Wehrmacht in 1941 and was a profiteer and a betrayer of his own kind.' Several months later, Ahlers telephoned a journalist from *Revue*, whose publication had recently outed van Maaren as the betrayer. Ahlers sent the journalist a copy of Otto's letter to the authorities on his behalf – which he could only have received from Otto – cunningly omitting the first few lines which referred to his own prison sentence. Ahlers wrote in his own letter:

> . . . in April 1941 I went to Frank and told him someone wanted to betray him to the SS and he, also by his own declaration, waited until July 1942 to go into hiding. What he did in the meantime is known to me. And his little game with Gies. Frank's oldest daughter was called up for transport to Germany in the summer of 1942, thus making clear that the NSB-Wehrmacht relationship/deliveries were not a safeguard against being deported.

He concluded his letter: 'This all happened in 1941/1942, a period in which Jews were involved in a life or death struggle and I realize that the behaviour of people in that situation must be judged with clemency. I don't judge Otto Frank's actions during the war years. But I think it's crazy that Otto Frank is upheld as an example of integrity amongst Jews after the war.' Referring to why the betrayer had never been found (while implying again it was Jansen's son and that Jansen had been making the deliveries to the Wehrmacht on Otto's behalf), Ahlers wrote that Otto's guilt about his wartime business transactions prevented him from pursuing his betrayer: 'Because of the understandable fear, he said nothing. Even when he knew someone else could be blamed. It will be difficult to get to the bottom of it all . . .' Ahlers sent a copy of his letter to van Maaren's son.

Why did Ahlers write those letters when he knew that his own past could cause him problems if the police chose to confront him? Clearly, he was keen to 'exonerate' van Maaren and Silberbauer, while damaging Otto's reputation as much as he could without mentioning his own wartime activities. But the Dutch authorities did not question Ahlers, seeing him as a peripheral figure, someone who was 'not to be trusted with the truth' and therefore not worthy of investigation with regard to the betrayal. They thought him a fool, without realizing that, like all fools, Ahlers was dangerous. And they did not know, of course, about the discrepancies in Otto's own letters, his deliveries to Ahlers's company, Ahlers's relationship with Maarten Kuiper who had arrested the family and was a paid informant, other letters written by Otto and Ahlers, the extent of Ahlers's crimes during the war, or Otto's meetings with Ahlers in 1945. Even if Otto himself now suspected Ahlers of his betrayal, he could prove nothing: the people to whom Ahlers may have passed on his deadly information were both dead – Kuiper had been executed and Dettman had committed suicide.

In 1964 both Silberbauer and the wartime head of the Amsterdam Bureau of the Commander of the Security Police and Security Service, Willi Lages, were questioned about the arrest. Both declared that they were sure the telephone call was not anonymous, but came from a known betrayer. During his interrogation (mistakenly thinking that Silberbauer had taken the call), Lages told the Dutch detectives, 'You ask me whether, given a tip off, we would have gone straight there and arrested the Jews. It's not logical. In my opinion a tip would first be investigated into whether it was worthy, unless this tip came from somebody who was known by our organization. In the case of the story of Silberbauer's receiving the telephone tip, to go there on the same day, then I conclude from that the tip giver was known and that in the past his information was always based on truth. If that was the case then when Silberbauer received the tip, he must have known the tip giver.' Silberbauer explained to the investigators that it was Dettman, and not he, who had taken the call. He then insisted, 'The call had to be from someone well known to Dettman.'

In his summary, the Dutch detective heading the investigation into the betrayal wrote: 'Silberbauer also informed us that he was convinced the tip concerning the Franks was made immediately before the arrest. Possibly there is a chance to discover which police officers received a bonus at that time, by making an investigation in the aforementioned "Bundesarchiv".' Nobody attempted to do so. Had they done, they would probably have at least discovered that Maarten Kuiper was a paid informant of Jews in hiding and was present at the arrest.

The Dutch police in charge of the investigation did ask Otto about the accusations concerning the Wehrmacht made by Ahlers, although the climate for such questions was somewhat different from twenty years before. Otto answered that many Dutch companies had made deliveries to the Wehrmacht during the war. He was not asked about 'Berlin'. The detectives compiled a short report on Ahlers, but made several mistakes in it. They ended their declaration with an air of vague puzzlement: 'It is not clear how Ahlers was familiar with the hiding place.'

On 4 November 1964 the investigation into the betrayal at 263 Prinsengracht was officially closed. Otto had given police a statement in which he declared that Silberbauer had not mistreated the prisoners in his care, and that he had only been acting under orders. Yet although Otto was magnanimous toward Silberbauer to the extent that he kept his identity a secret (which he said was to protect other families sharing the name, although there were also people named Silberthaler) and defended him to the prosecution, his attitude towards other war criminals was far more hostile. Possibly this act of direct forgiveness was Otto's way of coming to terms with that terrible day in August 1944 and what happened after it.

Silberbauer was acquitted of concealing his past and returned to the Vienna police force. Otto's statements about his conduct were identified as being crucial to the outcome of his case.

In 1966 Meyer Levin re-entered Otto's life when his *Anne Frank* play was performed by an Israeli theatre company. His book *The Fanatic*, based upon his experiences with Otto, the Hacketts and Broadway, had been published in 1964. Leah Salisbury sent reviews of the book to Otto with a memo: 'Dear Otto, will this man ever become sane? Best regards, Leah.' Otto's lawyers tried to insist upon the closure of the play in Israel, but it ran for another fifty performances. Levin was still pursuing the right to have his play performed, and even wrote to Walter Pick, Hanneli Goslar's husband, to ask them to intervene with Otto. Pick told him that was an impossibility; while feeling that Levin's play was more significant to Jews and Israel, Hanneli would never do anything to upset Otto. Levin was furious, but powerless to change Pick's mind.

Some form of compensation would come for Levin in 1970, when he was awarded the World Federation of Bergen-Belsen Associations' Remembrance Award 'for his memorable dramatization of *The Diary of Anne Frank*'. Days before his death on 9 July 1981, Levin had busied himself with a new campaign to have the Pulitzer Prize for the Hacketts' *Diary of Anne Frank* repealed. The obituaries in the press focused on his thirty-year struggle to have his play recognized and produced. However, Dola de Jong, whose Dutch to English translation of the diary was abandoned when the contract with Little Brown fell through, recalls that, despite having been willing to testify, at Levin's request, in court against Otto, upon reading the play she had been unimpressed: 'I must confess that, though he stayed closer to the truth and intention than the Hacketts' version, his play was very boring and wouldn't have made it on Broadway.'

Levin's play has received limited outings on the American stage since 1983. His widow, Tereska, wrote a memoir about being in the eye of the hurricane of Levin's Anne Frank fixation, remembering that during one argument, Levin had screamed, 'If you really love me, you will take a gun and shoot Otto Frank.' His friend Harry Golden commented that suing Otto Frank was the worst public relations blunder of the twentieth century; it was like suing the father of Joan of Arc. Nonetheless, Levin had been instrumental in bringing the diary to the attention of the American public and he clearly had a more logical vision of how the Holocaust would be represented in the future than the Hacketts, for he wrote: 'The Final Solution was not a common fate. A new word, genocide, had to be found for this mechanized mass murder that included the hunting down for destruction even of infants confided to non-Jews. Generalizing away the particular Jewish doom falsifies the Holocaust and opens the way for today's campaign of denials. It weakens the warning against genocidal methods that could indeed be directed at other peoples, or again at the Jews.'

The Hacketts and their agent continued to jealously guard over all proposals for dramatizing the diary. Otto received many requests, particularly from schools, who wanted to write their own short piece based upon the diary, but under the terms of his contract with the Hacketts, he was compelled always to concur with their position. For instance, in 1974, Irene Lewis of the Hartford Stage Company, Kinsey St, Connecticut asked Otto's permission to stage a play entitled *Annelies Marie Frank: Witness*, a forty-five minute script, documentary style with excerpts from the diary. Otto had no objections but Leah Salisbury did. She wrote to Irene on 4 December 1974, warning that although Otto was happy about it,

> We must call to your immediate attention that the book *Anne Frank's Diary* and the stage play, *The Diary of Anne Frank*, are legally merged, and disposition of stage rights are controlled by the playwrights Frances Goodrich & Albert Hackett. It is inevitable that a forty-five minute compilation would involve material used in the play in one or another location. Furthermore, a forty-five minute stage presentation with four professional actors in a touring theatre production of schools and community organizations would be in conflict with contractual commitments to companies leasing amateur rights to say nothing of the fees to dramatists and Mr Frank. We therefore cannot approve or consent to your presenting such a stage documentary, and must request that you do not proceed with any such plan.

A very puzzled Lewis wrote again to Otto, enquiring, 'I understand that the playwrights control the rights to the play, but how can they control the rights to Anne's actual diary? They are two very separate and different works. Don't *you* control the rights to the diary? . . . I think Anne's words unedited and standing alone, are better than the play could ever be. Let's face it – she was a better writer than the authors of the play!'

Otto replied on 11 January 1975, 'I am sorry to say that there is a merger clause between the play and the book in my contract with the Hacketts. At the time when this contract was concluded I was quite inexperienced in matters regarding theatre production and left everything to my lawyers. I did not realize what the passage really meant. Though I do not quite agree with the interpretation of Mrs Salisbury, I cannot risk a law-suit on account of this matter . . . I regret very much that I cannot help you bring your work to the stage.' Unknown to Lewis, Otto contacted his lawyers, feeling that schools and educational institutions should definitely be allowed to propagate 'Anne's message' in the way in which they wished:

Again there is something I have to ask you in connection with the merger clause in the contract between the Hacketts and myself . . . I am doing this because on thinking the whole matter over, I cannot agree with Mrs Salisbury's standpoint . . . some quotations of the diary are used. I think Mrs Salisbury should have answered that this play does not interfere with the rights of the Hacketts. In refusing consent, she is applying the merger clause in an unjustified way. I kindly ask you to look into the matter and give me your opinion. If you agree with my view, steps should be taken. I think we should not let Mrs Salisbury interfere when citations of Anne's diary are used in cases like that.

Otto's efforts were not rewarded; Salisbury stood firm.

On another occasion, Otto agreed with the Hacketts that another play had to be stopped from production; this was a musical based on the diary by the son of Kermit Bloomgarden. After refusing permission to the deceased producer's son, Frances Hackett wrote to Otto in outrage that Bloomgarden Jnr had 'really said that we (Albert and I) were obstructionists, keeping the story of Anne and the diary from the world. That the world had a right to Anne's story . . . The play *is* the diary, most of it word for word.' During the last year of Otto's life, the Hacketts wrote to him in concern about a cantata by Enid Futterman in which, they informed Otto, 'every spoken word' was a 'quotation from the book of the diary, not the play', and admonished that further performances 'might be harmful to the already established production'. Albert Hackett favoured an outright ban while Frances, unable to 'think of stopping anything that gives Anne's message' was more cautious, especially since the 'shouting song about being glad to be a Jew' had been removed. Fritzi wrote to the Hacketts on Otto's behalf, since he was too ill with cancer by then, admitting that she likewise disapproved of the cantata, and in particular the Yiddish lullabies, 'as none of the Frank family knew a word of Yiddish and singing it would falsify Otto's personality'. In the end, Frances decided they could permit performances as long as the Yiddish 'so completely alien to Mr Frank' was not used. She wrote triumphantly of the play then being broadcast on television, 'just as it has been played all these years!'

In the 1960s Otto lost three people to whom he was close: Nathan Straus, and Julius and Walter Holländer. Straus, his dearest friend, died on 13 September 1961 at the age of seventy-two of natural causes in a Sunrise Highway Motel in Massapequa. Newspapers reported on his long and illustrious career, but Otto knew that Straus himself had been an unpretentious man. Upon his election as Mayor of New York in 1953, Otto wrote to Barbara Zimmerman that he had not known about his designation: 'He did not inform me, he is too modest for that.' In addition to holding chairmanship of WMCA, and serving in 1952 as national vice chairman of the United Jewish Appeal, Straus wrote books about housing and campaigned on behalf of numerous charities. His funeral was held on 15 September 1961 in New York.

Julius Holländer died horrifically on 4 October 1967 when a lift in the New York hotel where he and his brother were living plummeted to the ground from the tenth floor. In January 1968 Otto wrote to his wife's cousin Irene, 'Walter's desperate loneliness is a source of great pain to me. The two brothers turned their backs on everybody and everything and became recluses. Now Walter is more alone than ever.' Walter died later that year, on 19 September, apparently from diabetes. Both brothers had 'saved up enough money for a comfortable retirement which they did not live long enough to enjoy'.

In 1967 Otto was co-plaintiff in a war crimes trial. On 13 January 1966 the chief of the Gestapo in the Netherlands, Wilhelm Harster, was arrested. He had been a major general in the SS elite guard and was responsible for transporting Jews to concentration camps. Himmler affectionately referred to him as 'a real Jew-killer'. Harster was arrested in 1945 in the Netherlands and sentenced to twelve years in prison. After serving six years he returned to Germany where he became an official in the Bavarian State Government until his retirement on health grounds in 1963. Two of Harster's former aides were also arrested: Wilhelm Zöpf and Gertrude Slottke. Zöpf was an adviser to the Nazi security police on Jewish matters and had become a lawyer in Munich after the war. Slottke, who kept records of Jewish families like the Franks who tried to escape Nazi persecution by hiding, had become a saleswoman in Stuttgart. The enormous press interest focused throughout the trial on the connection with Anne Frank. Otto was quoted as saying: 'Anne is always being brought to the fore for the sake of sensation when former Nazi security officials are arrested.' He said he had never heard of Harster but conceded that 'the Jewish man in the street has no idea which Nazi officials were responsible for what happened to specific Nazi victims'.

Harster's new trial began on 23 January 1967 in Munich. Robert Kempner, former US prosecutor at the Nuremberg trials, represented Otto (who was concerned only with the case of Zöpf) at the trial together with the family of Edith Stein.★ There were numerous references to Anne during the trial. Asked if he recognized Anne from a photo, Zöpf replied, 'I know her diary,' and said he was aware that she had been deported under his orders, which as a human being he found very sad. On one occasion when the diary was mentioned, journalists reported Slottke crying ('crocodile') tears as she said, 'I admire that girl. She had to go through a lot.' It was one

---

★ A German Jewish refugee who converted to Catholicism and became a nun; along with other Roman Catholic clergy of Jewish origin she was deported to Auschwitz in 1942 and murdered.

of the shortest war crimes trials ever held, with only two witnesses being called. Harster was sentenced to fifteen years in prison for complicity in more than eighty thousand murders; Zöpf received nine years for complicity in over fifty thousand murders and Slottke faced five years for complicity in forty-two thousand murders. Otto was disgusted at the leniency of their sentences, but told Cara Wilson that 'those accused cannot be regarded as normal human beings, they worked like computers without heart or feelings'.

In an interview he gave in 1965, Otto was asked his opinion about the trials of the Auschwitz criminals conducted in Germany. He answered, 'I think they are necessary. At the Nuremberg trials just after the war, the German people thought it was the Allies taking revenge; you could hear that being said in Germany. Now it is the German courts that discover all these beastly acts. They are just as necessary as the Eichmann trial.' He was questioned about Eichmann's execution and said calmly, 'Killing is not the worst. I think he merited killing, but whether he should have been is another matter. I am not an adherent of killing.'

On 12 May 1969 Otto celebrated his eightieth birthday with a holiday for all his family in the Swiss mountains. After dinner and a few glasses of wine, Buddy recalls how Otto 'got Fritzi up to dance. Instead of adopting the customary dance pose, Otto reeled off a spicy jig. All the young kids were clapping . . . he wasn't showing off, he just jazzed it up a bit. That was Otto. Simple, uncomplicated, with a great sense of humour and dignity.' Otto was always generous with his family. In 1973 Buddy and his wife Gerti booked a much longed for first trip to Israel. Otto visited them at the Herbstgasse a few days before they departed, and took Gerti to one side, into the sitting room and then closed the door. He put 2,000 francs in her hand and told her to enjoy her holiday. In March 1974 Otto lent money to his cousin Milly (who had emigrated to America in 1967) so that she and a friend were able to go to Israel. She insisted on repaying him, but he asked her to leave it to the Fonds in her will instead.

In that same year, a disagreement arose between Otto and Victor Kugler. On 23 April Otto received a letter from Massada Press in Israel informing him that they were planning to publish a book about Kugler's reminiscences of Anne and her life in hiding. In their regular correspondence Kugler had said nothing to him about the book, and Otto was 'astonished and annoyed'. He took offence at the title, *The Man Who Hid Anne Frank*: 'I do not agree with it. *The Man Who Hid Anne Frank* does not exist. There was a group of brave Dutch people to which Mr Kugler belonged, but without the help of

Mr Kleiman, Miep, Henk (Jan) and Elly (Bep), it would never have been possible.' He had spoken to Miep, Jan and Bep and they, too, were dismayed by the news, hoping 'it will not be translated into Dutch . . . They want to keep in the background and they think that what they did was their human duty . . . They do not want to be praised or drawn into publicity.'

A letter from Bep Voskuijl shows just how unwilling she was to be in the public eye:

I would prefer to stay away from it all, by nature I am already nervous and I cannot take any more stress. Also, the pleasant things, like the invitations here and there, give me nervous breakdowns before and after. You know that lack of language plays a major part here. I know you all mean very well and I appreciate it very much and don't want to upset anybody in our Opekta circle . . . I am dead set against publicity . . . I will do everything in my power to keep the symbol of an idealized Anne high, something which to me is connected at the same time to everything that's happened which I was myself a witness to. This immense loss will never leave my heart.

The author of the Kugler book, Eda Shapiro, wrote to Otto twice, imploring him to give his approval to the project. Otto refused and Massada Press cancelled her contract after receiving a letter from him. Otto also wrote to Shapiro, adding that he, Miep and Bep were 'disappointed about the behaviour of Mr Kugler in this matter'. A few months later, Otto responded to a letter sent to him by Robert Rothman, a solicitor who had taken up Kugler's cause and told Otto that Kugler needed expensive surgery on his eyes. Otto was still smarting over Kugler's actions, but promised to help if necessary: 'I know that his health is not very good and that he had to undergo an eye operation, as his wife wrote me all the details. As to his financial circumstances, I know that the Kuglers are living modestly, but I suppose that they are not really in need . . . I shall write to him before the end of the year anyway and if necessary I would of course help him.' In 1977 Kugler received a $10,000 prize from the Canadian Anti-Defamation League, which paid for his eye operation. His wife, Loes, told Otto in a very friendly letter that year that the surgery had been successful. They remained in contact, and Otto never referred again to the matter.

Ever since the founding of the Anne Frank Stichting, Otto and Fritzi had travelled once a month to Amsterdam. In 1964 the Anne Frank Stichting and the Youth Centre were united under the leadership of Otto's friend and teacher, Henri van Praag. In September 1965 Otto wrote to Mermin about changes to the Stichting, 'I was still very dissatisfied with the organization of the Stichting and I kept on asking the board to look out for better people. They understood this very well, but it was difficult to find the right persons. But now I think we have found them. They will start work probably 1 November. Being an optimist I hope again for the best.'

One of the 'right persons' to whom Otto referred was Cor Suijk, who remembers that when he arrived at the Stichting, 'there were two people on the payroll; all others were volunteers. When I left twenty years later, there was a paid staff of over one hundred. I also introduced an admission fee, which Otto actually opposed.' He describes their relationship as 'agreeable irritation' and elaborates:

Otto was a keen observer and a good listener. This attitude of offering people the opportunity to express themselves first provided him with the advantage of making people wonder how well they were doing with regard to their argument. Particularly if they got heated, his calm became a dominating factor . . . He would seldom overlook mistakes the Anne Frank Stichting staff and I, as their director, had made. His dissatisfaction regarding our lack of adequate care concerning the archives, correspondence, the museum artefacts, the upkeep of the place and particularly to preserve the authentic appearance of the house, made the staff fear his regular visits. Not many of these workers were eager to meet him. They usually flew apart, scattering themselves all over the place. His ability to notice shoddy work and sloppy thinking in our publications was distinctly feared. He could be very unrelent-ing, speaking insistently, but would never shout. His prestige and moral authority resulted from him being absolutely right as to his criticism.

Although the internal staffing problems at the Stichting subsided, monetary difficulties came to the fore in the late 1960s. The house received 180,000 visitors in 1970 (100,000 of whom were American), which necessitated an expensive structural rebuilding throughout. In 1971 several articles appeared in the international press detailing the critical financial predicament at the Stichting. One newspaper reported,

Recently re-opened after four months of renovation made possible mainly by the proceeds of a nationwide collection, the house is having difficulty staying open. For the last five years, its organizers have had an annual deficit despite donations from the Amsterdam city council and private groups . . . the Stichting once more is trying for a government grant despite the fact its first application was rejected. 'If we do not get government support, we will have to close the house,' Stichting director Isaac van Houte said.

The admission fee saved the house from closure. The Youth Centre, which had been Otto's dream, was disbanded in 1970.

On 30 July 1977 one of Otto's earliest ardent correspondents, Cara Wilson, arrived in Basel for a short visit. At some point during Wilson's stay, Otto showed her his photo album, and she recalls, 'There was one picture of some beautiful blond-haired moppets playing together in a backyard . . . "You see these children, Cara?" Otto ran his finger across each face. "These were my playmates when I was a boy. And they all became – except that one right there – they all became Nazis." ' Some of Otto and Fritzi's friends and family stopped by in the evening after her arrival:

The group of people who gathered into the Franks' cosy front room were all in their late sixties, seventies and early eighties, but I had never met a group of senior citizens like them before. They were dynamic, teasing, vivacious, very much filled with life and self-esteem. They spoke in rapid German, hands gesticulating, stopping only to briefly translate for me. The gist of their conversation, between talk of vacations and theatre and mutual friends, was their fury over the new generation of Germans.

In October 1978 Otto was delighted to be told by Father John Neiman that he had met Peter Pepper, Pfeffer's son, by chance. Father Neiman recalls,

Peter and I became friends. When someone first mentioned him to me, I thought it was Peter van Pels because, after all, there was, or there seemed to be, a chance that he had survived. Then I spoke to him on the phone and he explained that he was Pfeffer's son. I told him that I was in touch with Otto and he said he would like to meet him again. He went to Switzerland often on business. You know, he had no idea that his father had died in Neuengamme – I told him. Through me, I feel very happy to say, Peter and Otto again became friends.

In December 1978 Pepper travelled to Switzerland. Otto wrote to Neiman, 'He came to see us the day before yesterday and we found him a very sympathetic man. My conversation with him was very cordial and we felt a certain closeness to each other by the link through his father. I could tell him some details about him which his son did not know. It is thanks to you that this reunion could take place.' At the end of 1978 Otto began to suffer regularly from high blood pressure and, on 15 December, he made out his will. His cousin Milly was able to visit him again in March: 'I spent the Sunday at Birsfelden. We had a lovely, relaxing day. He must have known how his illness was gaining on him, but he never complained.'

Otto celebrated his ninetieth birthday in London. His nephew Buddy was also in town, starring in *The Canterbury Tales* at the Shaftesbury Theatre. He and Otto had been invited to a gala concert at the Theatre Royal in Drury Lane to open the 'Anne Frank 50th Anniversary Tribute', for which there would be events around the world. At the press launch Otto was presented with a birthday cake. Newspapers reported, '[Larry] Adler played a jaunty "Happy Birthday" – and Otto Frank blew out all his candles in one go'. Upon his return to Basel, Otto's health deteriorated further; he confided to a friend, 'I am suffering frequently from dizziness and circulation-trouble and am feeling rather weak.' Ignoring the advice of his doctor, on 12 June Otto and Fritzi travelled to Amsterdam to attend the commemoration of Anne's birthday, in the Westerkerk. Otto received the 'Orde van Oranje-Nassau' with obvious pride and then accompanied Queen Beatrix to the annexe. He recalled, 'she was most interested and asked many questions. Of course it was very emotional. She is a great woman and very natural and modest. When she left she said "Shalom" to me!' It was Otto's last visit to Amsterdam. On 9 July he wrote to Father Neiman that he and Fritzi were embarking upon 'a *very* much needed holiday of three weeks in the Swiss mountains tomorrow . . . We hope to gain new strength during our holiday so that we shall be able to go on with our work though on a much smaller scale. I am feeling my age more and more.'

Over the years, Otto received thousands of tributes to his daughter; in September 1961, President Kennedy asked his Secretary of Labor to lay a wreath at the house during his visit to Amsterdam. Otto's willingness to accommodate everyone who showed an interest in his daughter's diary brought him both admiration and criticism; Israeli newspapers reacted with satisfaction when Golda Meir visited the house in 1964, but were outraged by the reports of Otto presenting the Pope with a special edition of Anne's stories in a private meeting in the Vatican. But Otto seemed never to listen to his detractors. He set up competitions for schoolchildren, offering prizes funded by himself, and invited groups of people into his own home to discuss the diary and the lessons he believed could be learned from it.

Interviewed by the son of Nathan Straus in the late 1970s (who described him as 'a guarded individual'), Otto said of his duty towards his daughter's legacy, 'It's a strange role. In the normal family relationship, it is the child of the famous parent who has the honour and the burden of continuing the task. In my case the role is reversed.' He wrote:

When I returned from concentration camp alone, I saw that a tragedy of inexpressible extent had hit the Jews, my people, and I was spared as one of them to testify, *one* of those who had lost his dear ones. It was not in my nature to sit down and mourn. I had good people around me and Anne's diary helped me a great deal to gain again a positive outlook on life. I hoped by publishing it to help many people in the same way and this turned out to be the case. When later the Anne Frank Stichting was established I wanted it to work in the spirit of Anne's ideals for peace and understanding among peoples.

In another interview, he stated firmly, 'We cannot change what happened any more. The only thing we can do is to learn from the past and to realize what discrimination and persecution of innocent people means. I believe that it's everyone's responsibility to fight prejudice.' He believed the best way to do this was through 'communication', by which he meant responding to all those who wrote to him. This exhausted him. For thirty years, every morning was spent answering letters, and often several hours in the afternoon as well.

Otto made a special effort in replying to schoolchildren, although they often asked about the one subject he found it hardest to speak about: his time in Auschwitz. He told one class, on the anniversary of the camp's liberation, that 'though I have been beaten, I have no scars left'. He tried to impress upon them the importance of remembrance: 'No one, especially we Jews, can ever forget the terrible crimes committed by the Nazis, and the younger generation, that looks upon everything as ancient history, must realize that anti-Semitism and the current form of anti-Zionism are still virulent.' The most common question was what Anne would have become had she been permitted to live. Otto usually refused to speculate, but on one occasion he admitted, 'I feel that she would have grown into a truly fine writer.' He was enormously proud of his daughter's gift, explaining, 'Everyone with ambition is hoping for greatness – or at least success, which is not the same. Even if someone produces something great, it is frequently not recognized directly. But a real work of greatness survives generations.' Only rarely was he asked about Margot or Edith, and he did not speak of them often himself. Anneke Steenmeijer recalls, 'He hardly talked about his wife and daughter Margot but you knew when he did that he cherished them in his heart.' His son-in-law Zvi Schloss agrees: 'He talked a lot about Anne, but he did speak about Margot too, though he spoke of her in relation to Anne. It was the same with Edith – she and Margot he spoke of as part of the family, but never as individuals.' Eva explains, 'That's how he felt. Anne occupied his every minute. He admitted that Anne was his favourite, there's nothing wrong with that – all parents have their favourite, though they don't like to admit it.' Father Neiman, who had grown close to both Otto and Fritzi during the long correspondence they exchanged, remembers,

> He never spoke about Edith, but that was probably out of respect for Fritzi, which is understandable. The only person who ever said something about Edith was Fritzi. I remember it clearly. It was after Otto had died and I was in Switzerland again to see her. We were at the Basel Zoo and chatting about Otto. Suddenly Fritzi said, in her thick Austrian accent, 'Otto loved Edith very much, but he loved me so much more.' That made me laugh – it was so typical of Fritzi.

Otto was seldom asked about himself, but three years before his death, Otto met Arthur Unger, a New York journalist who flew to Basel to interview him. Talking about his life at that time, Otto told Unger that though he never attended synagogue in Basel, he did so when he was in Amsterdam, 'just to show I am still here and I am still interested in the Liberal Movement . . . I am not in the Jewish community here. I still am in the Jewish community in Amsterdam.' Questioned about whether the income from the diary was large enough for him to live comfortably, Otto replied that it was, but that most of the royalties were split between the Stichting in Amsterdam and the Fonds in Basel; he also received a pension for his service in the German army in the Great War and 'I sold my business too'. Unger asked him to pinpoint the lessons to be learned from the diary. Otto answered immediately: 'Withhold easy judgement, never generalize and don't expect thanks for what you do for people. That doesn't work. You must have the satisfaction in yourself for having done something.'

At the end of February 1980, Fritzi contacted Father Neiman:

> This is Mrs Frank writing to you to answer your long and detailed letter . . . I have to tell you that Mr Frank's health is very bad. He is so weak that he has to remain on the couch the whole day, not being able to regain his strength. He is suffering from an obstinate form of pleurisy and we have to go to hospital once a week where much water is taken out of his lung and some medicament put in it. Up to now we have not seen much change to the better, but we do not give up hope . . . I read the letters to him if he is not too exhausted.

Otto had already confessed in a letter written in November that he was 'not in a very good state of health. Though I am not really ill I am feeling miserable most of the time'. For the first time in twenty years he and Fritzi had not spent Christmas in London or in the mountains. Eva and her family visited them instead.

Otto's health worsened. Fritzi wrote to the Hacketts that on his birthday in May, although many people arrived in Birsfelden to congratulate him, 'He stayed on his couch and only wanted to see one person at a time.' Father Neiman had visited them a few days before and found Otto

very ill then. He was in bed and I sat with Fritzi for some time. Then Otto woke up and called out that he knew I was there and that he was well enough to see me after all. But he was terribly weak then. Fritzi made some sandwiches and they had one of their typical silly arguments about them. He complained, 'They're too thick!' and she kept saying, 'No, they are thin!' It went on and on. It was the last time I saw him.

Otto's closest friends, aware that he was seriously ill, travelled to see him. Miep and Jan, Judith and Henk Salomon, and Gertrud Naumann and her family all visited. Gertrud recalls that when she entered the room, Otto reached out to her tearfully, saying, 'Gertrud, I've so longed for you.' Suffering from lung cancer, Otto was growing weaker every day.

On 19 August 1980 Otto's old comrade from Auschwitz, Joseph Spronz, visited with his wife Franzi. She recalls,

In February, when Otto was diagnosed with lung cancer, the doctors told Fritzi he had only six months to live. We were in the US and Fritzi did not tell us, and she didn't tell Otto either. Otto would insist, 'Look, it's not that I am sick, it's just that I am tired!' His worried sister Leni told Fritzi that Otto needed specialist care, but Fritzi refused, wanting to care for him herself. And she did a wonderful job. We knew it would be a shock to see Otto, whom we always knew as an incredibly strong and powerful man looking so ill. When we arrived, Otto was in bed, but he heard us and got up, holding out his arms. He looked into my husband's eyes and they embraced. Otto murmured against my husband's shoulder, 'My dear friend, Joseph.' He was so weak. The hospital staff arrived to collect him a few minutes later. We followed them, and my husband was allowed in to Otto's room. I don't know what passed between them, but they spoke of Auschwitz. Joseph was gone a long time. When he came out, he told Fritzi that we would call again tomorrow. I telephoned the hospital in the morning, quite early, and was told, 'We're sorry, but Mr Frank died last night.'

★

Anne's friend Jacqueline van Maarsen heard the announcement of Otto's death on the radio in Amsterdam, though having visited him the month before, she was not surprised by it. She was amongst those who travelled on an aeroplane chartered by the Anne Frank Stichting to Basel for the funeral on 22 August. Fritzi's daughter Eva and son-in-law Zvi flew over from London with their three daughters, who were devastated to lose the man whom they regarded as their beloved grandfather. Otto had requested that his body be cremated (which Jewish law does not permit) and his ashes interred at the Friedhof Birsfelden, a non-denominational cemetery a few minutes away from his home. After the funeral at two o'clock that afternoon, at which poems and prayers of various religions were read out, the mourners walked to the house Otto and Fritzi had shared for almost twenty years. Fritzi played a cassette recorded by Otto some time before on which he talked about his life, and his soft, clear voice filled the room.

In the days following her husband's death, Fritzi received hundreds of condolence cards: one of the Anne Frank Havens in Israel called him 'one of the true humanitarians of the spirit of the nineteenth century'; the Judaic Heritage Society in New York and the World Congress of Faiths (Inter-Faith Fellowship), of which Otto had been Vice-President, telegrammed similar sentiments; Victor and Lucy Kugler sent 'sincere sympathy'; Barbara Mooyart-Doubleday, translator of the diary from Dutch into English, wrote that she would always remember Otto for his 'great mental and moral force, for his courage in the face of difficulties and sorrow, for his kindness of heart and for his never failing desire to turn ill will into good'; the Hacketts cabled Fritzi to say 'our hearts are with you in your great loss'; and Barbara Epstein (formerly Zimmerman) was 'full of memories and sadness beyond words'.★ There were to be no gifts for his family, only donations to charities Otto favoured, such as the Israel Cancer Association. Fritzi replied to all the accolades with a small card on which was printed, 'I would like to thank you sincerely for the friendship and heartfelt sympathy shown to me at the occasion of the passing away of my beloved, unforgettable husband, Otto Frank.' The only sour note was sounded by the obituary in *Jewish Week* which condemned Otto's support for those who had 'eliminated Anne's poetic tribute to Judaism . . . replacing it . . . with a universalistic observation . . . denigrating the importance of Jewish experience'.

On the evenings of 5 October and 8 October respectively, memorial tributes were held for Otto in Basel and New York. The latter was organized by the American Anne Frank Center and featured extracts from the diary,

★ All correspondence in the archives of the Anne Frank Stichting, Amsterdam.

the play, speeches and musical interludes. One of Otto's many young correspondents spoke about visiting him in Basel: 'He took me to what he called an authentic English pub. He was eighty-two then, and there wasn't a person in there over thirty, but he was in his element, surrounded by young people from all over the world who crowded around our table, asking questions. He switched effortlessly from language to language.' On their way home, they missed their tram and Otto decided to walk to the next stop. His companion wanted to wait for another tram but Otto told her, 'I never retrace my steps. I always look ahead. I live with the past every day, but never in it. My place is in the present.' Another speaker said simply: 'Otto Frank was the creator of Anne Frank's spirit. When she died, he lived for her.'

At the remembrance evening in Basel, Fritzi spoke about her years with Otto as 'amongst the happiest of my whole life'. She recalled how 'only people' mattered to Otto and how his greatest affection was for the young. 'He had an innate sense of what it meant to be family and I was very lucky that he viewed my daughter as a blood relative and, in her, he had a child again.' She remembered how, in 1946, Otto had travelled to Frankfurt to find two German friends, 'who he knew were not Nazis. He wanted to show them that, in his eyes, there was no such thing as collective guilt. Although he believed that Hitler's crimes against the Jews should never be forgotten, he also felt that there was no way forward with hatred.'

Otto's close friend Rabbi Soetendorp then read, from a portfolio of writings Otto had collected, a poem:

Let us commemorate those whom we loved,
  those who were taken from us and have gone to permanent rest.
May everything good that they have done,
  every truth and goodness that they spoke be recognized to the full and may it
    direct our life accordingly.
Because through that the living award the dead the greatest honour and they
    are spiritually united with them.
May those who mourn find comfort, and be uplifted by the strength and trust
    in this worldly spiritual power and the indestructibility of life.

Franzi Spronz remembers later during that evening: 'A violinist had been hired to play the music Otto loved. My husband was emotional – after all, he and Otto first met through their love of classical music. When the violinist began to play, my husband remembered that meeting and he wept. It was the music Otto had whistled to him in the hospital in Auschwitz.'

Epilogue: A Driven Man

Fritzi Frank outlived Otto by eighteen years. After his funeral she returned to London with her daughter, 'totally exhausted, morally and bodily'. To Barbara Epstein she confided that Otto had lost the will to live during the final months of his life, and that to witness his despair and weakness was 'agony to me'. She confessed to another friend: 'Though I know that he wanted to die after his long and fulfilled life with the many sad but also happy events, I miss him terribly.'

Otto's marriage to Fritzi had given him another life. He once wrote to a young woman who could only conceive of him as he must have been immediately after the war, 'All you know about me has happened twenty-six years ago and, though this period was an important part of my life leaving unforgettable marks on my soul, I had to go on, living a new life . . . think of me not only as Anne's father as you know me from the book and play, but also as a man enjoying a new family life and loving his grandchildren.' Fritzi supported Otto in his mission to spread the diary's 'ideals'. She recognized its overwhelming importance to her husband, and was only half-joking when she told journalist Arthur Unger, 'That's the purpose of his life really. All else is an ornament. I am an ornament.' Asked by Unger whether sharing a similar experience through the war was an element in the success of their marriage, Otto said, 'Oh yes. It makes a big difference. To get married, if my wife had not been in the concentration camps, it would be impossible. The same experience, she lost her husband, she lost her son, and if she speaks about it, I understand it. And if I speak about it, she understands.'

Otto's cousin Milly, who had known him longer than anyone apart from his immediate family, wrote to Fritzi in August 1992, 'I am so happy Otto had those lovely years with you and your family, after the storms in the earlier part of his life. You were just perfect for him.' After Otto's death, Fritzi wanted to stay in touch with all those who had written regularly before. It helped stave off the loneliness. She continued Otto's work, and took a keen interest in everything connected to Anne and the diary. Fritzi was a founder member of the Anne Frank-Fonds and remained actively involved with them until she became ill in 1993. She also tried to remain abreast of activities at the Anne Frank Stichting in Amsterdam and was dismayed to hear that they had paid for one of the employees to fly to New

York to collect Milly Stanfield's papers to add to their archives, and wrote to Milly of her 'astonishment . . . I wonder that they could spend their money making the trip'. She also wrote to the Hacketts about efforts to stage Levin's play, fuming to them in July 1983, 'You can see that even after his death Meyer Levin is making trouble.'

Although Fritzi's health had always been robust since the war, she suffered a near-fatal tram accident not far from her home in Basel and never fully recovered from it. Following the accident, a Polish woman named Katja Olszewska was employed as a companion for Fritzi. She recalls,

While I was with Mrs Frank, she often spoke about Otto. They seemed to have a very good marriage. Mrs Frank rarely spoke about her first husband, though she would talk of her lost son many times. He was very artistic and she had many, many photos of him. Mrs Frank told me how unhappy Otto's first marriage had been. He had been forced to marry Edith Holländer and never loved her. Mrs Frank said, 'The only one he really loved was me.' Then she went over to the big photo of Otto she kept in the room, clasped her hands together and said sadly, 'Otto! Why did you leave me?'

As her health worsened, Fritzi's mind began to fail. At the end of 1997 Eva arrived in Basel to take Fritzi to England. She died in London in October 1998, aged ninety-three.

In his will, Otto bequeathed Anne's diaries and other writings to the Dutch government. In November 1980 a notary public from Basel collected them from the bank safe in the city where they had resided ever since Otto emigrated to Switzerland, and presented them to Amsterdam's Institute for War Documentation (NIOD). In 1986, 'to dispel the attacks made upon the book's authenticity coming from hostile circles', NIOD published *The Diaries of Anne Frank: The Critical Edition*. Together with biographical material and the Ministry of Justice's reports testifying to the diary's genuineness, the book included Anne's original diary, her revised version, and the edition published in 1947. Now that Otto's editing could be scrutinized, a backlash against him began. Cynthia Ozick's article 'Who Owns Anne Frank?' appeared in *The New Yorker* on 6 October 1997. Ozick condemned the misrepresentations of Anne and her diary, and held Otto ultimately responsible for the 'shallowly upbeat view' of his daughter and her work:

Again and again, in every conceivable context, he had it as his aim to emphasize 'Anne's idealism', 'Anne's spirit', almost never calling attention to how and why that idealism and spirit were smothered, and unfailingly generalizing the sources of hatred . . . Otto Frank, despite his sufferings in Auschwitz, may have had less in common with his own daughter than he was ready to recognize. As the diary gained publication in country after country, its renown accelerating year by year, he spoke not merely about but for its author – and who, after all, would have a greater right? The surviving father stood in for the dead child, believing that his words would honestly represent hers. He was scarcely entitled to such certainty: fatherhood does not confer surrogacy.

Ozick concludes her piece with a dream of the diary 'burned, vanished, lost – saved from a world that made of it all things, some of them true, while floating lightly over the heavier truth of named and inhabited evil'.

Barbara Epstein (formerly Zimmerman) is furious at such criticism:

Who do these people think they are? They weren't around at the time, they don't know zip about any of it, they didn't know Otto! Those people are so far off the mark with their wild conspiracy theories. It's absolutely appalling. But that's a lot of American Jews for you – they have a real identity problem and have this need for self-aggrandizement. They're all assimilated Jews who have to have some sort of reinforced identity or something. They don't have any troubled personal experience of their own and it torments them. It's maniacal! It all started with Levin, of course. I feel so sorry for the way people talk about Otto now. How they rant about what he did to the diary. Don't any of them understand? This great glorious thing had to be killed in order for that book to be published and Otto's impulses in regard to it are so humane. There's nothing scandalous in it.

Otto Frank undoubtedly did promote the diary in a universal manner, but it seems clear that he did so because he believed it to be the most effective way of propagating understanding and tolerance. He was so traumatized by his own experiences and the loss of his children that whenever anyone approached him enthusiastically about the diary he felt compelled to respond: 'It's my opinion that one should never give up, even in the most extreme circumstances.' He was cautious when asked expressly about Anne's belief – taken out of context by the Hacketts – that 'people are really good at heart', replying, 'My daughter was at an age of great idealism, but I think she didn't mean that. She thought there is some good in every man and I am an optimist too. I try to find the good in every man, but we know how many bad people exist. You can't forgive those who really are murderers. This is going too far.' Everyone wanted (and wants) their own Anne Frank: 'Otto Frank wanted his daughter to teach a universal lesson of tolerance:

and Meyer Levin wanted her to teach Jews how to be good Jews.' Finding a middle ground proved difficult.

One aspect of the 'problems' the diary has faced stems from the timing of its initial publication. It was the first book to bring the attempted annihilation of European Jewry into the public domain. At that time the full scale of the horror remained largely unrecognized, and not until the late 1950s did people begin to refer to 'the Holocaust'. In the Netherlands, where so much Jewish life had been extinguished, the deportations were not discussed. The Eichmann trial in Jerusalem, and the accompanying press coverage, revived interest and broadened understanding among non-Jews. In the 1960s, Louis de Jong, director of NIOD, narrated a series of programmes about the war for Dutch television and Jacob Presser's ground-breaking *Ashes in the Wind: The Destruction of Dutch Jewry* was published to coincide with the twentieth anniversary of the liberation of the Netherlands. Presser's book sold well: 'the time was right; distant but rememberable, and the young of the nation were becoming more inquisitive'. Primo Levi and Elie Wiesel published their accounts of surviving the camps, and, in 1979, NBC's *Holocaust* drama series was watched by over one hundred and twenty million Americans. The show made an impact in Europe as well, and in West Germany especially, where it was seen by many as 'a turning-point in German history'. The Holocaust emerged from a period of neglect, if not denial, to become, in the Western World, 'probably the most talked about and oft-represented event of the twentieth century'.

As the Holocaust flourished as a subject for television, film and books, Otto's 'universal Anne' regained some of her Jewishness, becoming a symbol for the 1.5 million Jewish children who were murdered. She still retains her potency as a universal symbol, nonetheless: Hans Westra, the director of the Anne Frank Stichting, promotes her memory as 'directly related to a concern for preserving freedom and maintaining human rights and a pluralistic and democratic society'. In this sphere, the visitor to the Anne Frank House learns not just about the Holocaust but about 'human rights, discrimination and racism'.

A large proportion of visitors to the Anne Frank House are American and the United States has accounted for a quarter of the diary's twenty million plus sales. When *The Definitive Edition* was published in America in 1995 it remained on the *New York Times'* bestseller list for weeks. The accessibility of Anne and the optimistic slant given to the diary by its earliest dramatizations are the defining factors in these statistics. The Holocaust has been virtually 'adopted' by Americans. The fact that it actually happened in Europe has 'added rather than detracted from its attractiveness to an American audience. It is sufficiently "foreign" and distant over both time and space to be relatively unthreatening'. Steven Spielberg told the press that while filming his Holocaust memorial *Schindler's List* he had become a witness rather than a director, while Bill Clinton implored people to watch the film and Oprah Winfrey announced that doing so had made her 'a better person'.

For the Dutch, the heroine of the Anne Frank story is very much Miep Gies, who represents their wartime ideal. She is the sole survivor of the five helpers (Kugler died in December 1981; Bep Voskuijl-van Wijk in May 1983; and Jan Gies in January 1993) and was appointed a knight of the Order of Oranje-Nassau by Queen Beatrix. Anne Frank's story has enabled older Dutch citizens who were either bystanders or perpetrators in the persecution of the Jews to

alleviate their guilt, and blame the Nazis for having decimated their Jewish population . . . The Anne Frank story suggests to the world: 'Look, we Dutch hid her; the terrible Germans killed her. They were evil and we were virtuous' . . . While the Anne Frank story does point to the Netherlands as the place of refugees, and Dutch sheltering of Jews, it also points to a more murky side of Dutch wartime collaboration with the German occupiers.

Otto admitted to the *Haagse Post* on 3 August 1968 that he gave few interviews in the Netherlands and had to 'hold back' there: 'You know how it is. In the Netherlands I can sense a certain resistance, conscious or unconscious . . . Here they lived through it all. Thousands of people died here . . . Thus, there is a certain feeling: why Anne Frank?'

Otto's friend, Rabbi David Soetendorp, declares:

Otto was a visionary. In the 1940s and 1950s you didn't speak about the Holocaust, but, for him, it was as though his daughter had left him a legacy in which she came back to life. He was a driven man. The last time I saw him was in Amsterdam in the synagogue in 1971 or 1972. He was there for my first service as a Rabbi. For him, for me, and for all Jewish survivors of the Holocaust, Amsterdam has a hollowness at its core. It is a town in a state of bereavement. Although it is vibrant and never sleeps, there is a sense of something missing. What happened there in the war is a scar. Amsterdam's Utrechtsestraat today is full of very good restaurants and design shops, but before the war the houses belonged to Jewish people. My mother would tell me how that street on a Saturday night would be packed with Jewish people singing. It was their entertainment and they delighted in it. All those people are dead now and nothing can replace them.

★

There are two particular criticisms levelled at Otto Frank which merit attention; both arose during the controversy surrounding the existence of the 'missing pages', which are discussed in Appendix 1. The first criticism concerns the amount of money Otto left to his helpers under the terms of his will and the second, his attitude towards Miep and Jan Gies. Because he had been unwilling to use the income generated by the diary and the adaptations from it, Otto left behind a substantial amount of money. Understandably, the main beneficiary of Otto's will was his wife, Fritzi. To her, he bequeathed a sum of 220,000 Swiss francs. He left his sister, Leni, 200,000 Swiss francs, and his brother, Herbert, 10,000 Swiss francs, which would be administered by the Anne Frank-Fonds, since Herbert was never very good at handling his own money. He also named a number of charities which would benefit specifically under the terms of his will. The Anne Frank-Fonds in Basel inherited the copyright to Anne's diaries and all her writings. Otto also charged them with the task of administering the royalties that would accrue from the diaries and the various dramatic adaptations from it. While Fritzi was alive, she would receive 40,000 Swiss francs from the annual royalties, and Leni and Herbert would receive 20,000 Swiss francs each. Anything above that would go to the Anne Frank-Fonds to administer for charities and worthy causes, under supervision of the Swiss Federal Department of the Interior. The Fonds would remain a completely separate organization from the Anne Frank Stichting in the Netherlands, which would continue to maintain the house at 263 Prinsengracht as a museum and to disseminate and educate against racism and prejudice in any form. To those friends who had protected him during the Holocaust, Otto bequeathed fl.10,000 to Miep and Jan Gies and fl.10,000 to Bep Voskuijl.

Cor Suijk, former finance co-ordinator and international director of the Anne Frank Stichting, comments, 'Miep told me that Fritzi was behind it. Otto wanted to leave her more money and originally he had, but Fritzi insisted that he change his will, out of jealousy, Miep felt. She understood it, but that did not make it better. So he left a small amount to each of them, not to show favouritism.' Otto's last will and testament was drawn up in December 1978, replacing an earlier one, but Fritzi's daughter, Eva Schloss, refutes emphatically that it had anything to do with her mother's influence: 'This business with Miep and the money – it's ridiculous, the way that came out. Otto just would not use the money he had at his disposal because he felt it did not belong to him. He was utterly correct in all his dealings. If he had wanted to leave Miep more, he would have done. My mother could not have changed his mind if he had felt differently. He didn't leave Miep much in the end because he felt that the money was not for him and not for her. It was nothing to do with my mother. Mutti liked Miep and admired her. She was upset with Miep when she published her book, but that was because she got some facts wrong there too.' Eva's husband Zvi admits, 'It's true that the money he left Miep was not a lot. And he left his family more. But surely that is understandable? Miep did so much for him, yes, but his family would always come first, especially after his experiences. It was a way of protecting them for the future – and Miep would never need that sort of protection. Otto was a bit silly with money, it's as simple as that. He was old-fashioned and he didn't know the true value of it. It was Anne's money and not his – that was his feeling until the day he died.'

Along with the accusations that Otto had disregarded Miep in his will, there was also the issue of Miep and Jan having to stay in a hotel when they travelled to Switzerland to see Otto and Fritzi, despite Otto having lived with them for several years after the war. Suijk contends, 'They had to pay for the hotel themselves; Jan's pride would never have allowed Otto to pay their bill. Miep was very hurt by the fact they could not stay in Otto's house, small though the space was. If the situation was the same with them, she would have moved heaven and earth to have Otto and Fritzi stay in their home. She thinks it was jealousy again which meant they could not stay there.' Eva Schloss replies to this avowal with her own, 'This thing about the apartment – look, the space that Mutti and Otto had was small. The only place visitors could have slept was in the sitting room. If I went alone, then I stayed there, but that was different. Remember, this was Miep, Jan and their son Paul. Otto would not have wanted that because they wouldn't have been comfortable and it was difficult for them too. So he asked them to stay at a hotel instead – and I am sure he paid their bill. Sure of it. It's wicked to say otherwise.' Cara Wilson, who visited Otto and Fritzi in 1977, confirms, 'Their home was so small, they told me. It was uncomfortable to have guests in such close quarters. They hoped I understood.' The author asked Miep Gies, via Cor Suijk, who had offered to put a list of questions to her on the author's behalf, how she felt about the way in which these two issues had been made public and whether she now regretted having brought them out into the open. The reply came back: 'This is too personal. Miep chooses not to answer.'

Whatever the rights and wrongs of the situation, Miep did benefit, deservedly so, from her help to the Franks and their friends. She has travelled the world, been received by heads of state, received numerous awards and accolades, written a book, had a film made from her life story, and in 1995 accompanied Jon Blair to the podium when he received the Oscar for his documentary *Anne Frank Remembered*. Like many concentration camp survivors, yet very few of the people who tried to help them, Miep Gies has enjoyed 'a greatly heightened public profile' and is treated quite rightly with 'honour, respect, fascination and no small degree of awe'.

On two occasions after 1964, Otto was recorded as saying that they had been betrayed by a Dutch policeman; he told his friend Robert Kempner, who represented him at the Harster trial, that a Dutch policeman had received payment for his information. Otto's stepdaughter Eva recalls, 'Otto wanted to know who had betrayed his family at first, but later, he said he had had enough, after the second trial, he didn't want to know.' Miep also confirms, 'Mr Frank was the only one who could have done something. He chose not to.'

Miep was often asked by reporters and writers over the years if she knew who had betrayed them. She said nothing, but always held firm to her belief that it was not van Maaren. Cor Suijk declares, 'Once I wanted to know something very badly and I kept asking Miep and asking her. Finally she said, "Cor, can you keep a secret?" Very eagerly I answered, "Yes, Miep, I can!" And she smiled and said, "Me too."' In another interview Miep affirmed, 'I am a person who can be silent.'

Miep's close friend Father John Neiman attempted to draw Otto on the subject of the betrayal, but recalls, 'Otto would never talk about that. Anything and everything but not that. Miep also said nothing – for a long time. And then something strange happened. Miep came to America for the Oscars and we were together at author Alison Leslie Gold's house. Out of the blue, Miep said she knew who had betrayed them. She knew. You could have heard a pin drop. I said, "Was it someone Otto knew?" She said, "Yes, it was someone Otto knew." Then I saw her face change and knew that nothing further could be said.'

Tonny Ahlers and his wife divorced in 1985, but continued to live together in Amsterdam until his death. The author visited his widow twice; on the first occasion Mrs Ahlers's attitude was one of surprise. She said then that Otto and her husband had worked together and that she had met Otto herself, her sons too. Asked whether her husband and Otto Frank were friends, she hesitated and then replied that they were. Told that the author had letters in which her husband had written about Otto, she said that was quite possible, but when asked whether she would be willing to speak about the matter further, she declined. When the author visited several months later, Ahlers's widow's reaction was very different; she was openly aggressive. Despite the author making it clear that she was aware that Ahlers had, in 1941, prevented Otto's arrest by the SS, his widow became extremely agitated, and suddenly unleashed a tirade: 'My husband never wrote anything about Otto Frank! Otto Frank was my very best friend – I was the first person he took to see the secret annexe after the war and I have photos of him all over my house! You have no idea what that time was like for us, the war was terrible for us, not just the Jews but for us too. I had Jewish girls working for me all through the war. My husband never betrayed anyone!' Asked then why she was not willing to be interviewed, if she and her husband had helped Jews during the war, Ahlers's widow did not answer, but threatened to call the police. During both visits, the author had not said a word about Ahlers's character – and had made no reference to the betrayal of the Frank family.

Tonny Ahlers died in 2000, at the age of eighty-three. In a strange twist of fate, his death occurred on the anniversary of the Frank family's arrest: 4 August.

Afterword: The Enigma of Tonny Ahlers

'I have to tell you that the idea put forward in your book was wrong. My father did not "probably" betray Otto Frank and his family – he most certainly *did* betray them.' With these words, Tonny Ahlers's son confirmed the suggestion asserted in these pages that his father had managed to evade justice for over half a century for the betrayal at 263 Prinsengracht.

When this book was published in the Netherlands I fully expected someone who had known Tonny Ahlers to come forward and say that he or she had more information about him. What I did not anticipate was that family members would contact my publishers and the press to verify that Ahlers had indeed betrayed the Franks and their friends on 4 August 1944. But that is what happened.

Following the publication of an article in *De Volkskrant*★ about this book, Tonny Ahlers's brother Casper called the newspaper and spoke to journalist Sander van Walsum. He told van Walsum that he had known for many years that his brother was the Franks' betrayer and claimed to have in his possession a candlestick that his brother had taken from the secret annexe. A few days after his telephone call, I accompanied Sander to Cas Ahlers's home in the quiet countryside village of Emmen. Not far away lay Camp Westerbork, where the Franks and their friends were sent to await the train that would take them to Auschwitz and their deaths, save for Otto Frank.

At the age of eighty-two, Cas Ahlers was able to recall a good deal about his childhood and that of his troubled older brother Tonny. Handicapped from birth with polio which left him lame in one leg, Tonny refused to attend school regularly and became even more difficult after his parents divorced in 1928. The seven Ahlers children were split up after a spell in a Salvation Army children's home, though Cas and Tonny were able to remain together through a succession of foster homes. These transfers usually occurred because of something Tonny had done; his behaviour was not only disruptive but also cruel. Cas recalled how his brother waited for the newspapers to be delivered and then, as the man pushed the papers through the letterbox, Tonny grabbed his hands and pulled them back and forth until they were badly grazed on the metal of the opening. 'He liked to hurt

★ Dutch national daily newspaper.

people,' Cas said simply. After two years in Apeldoorn – where Tonny had befriended and protected a local man who believed himself to be God's messenger and was thus ridiculed by the youths in the town – Tonny returned to Amsterdam, where he immediately began making a nuisance of himself among the city's Jewish population.

Substantiating Josef van Poppel's 1945 declaration about Tonny Ahlers's wartime conduct on the Rembrandtsplein,★ Cas Ahlers told us that his brother often went to the square's Café Heck to harass the Jewish clientele who liked to drink coffee there with friends. Tonny was incensed by the presence of these particular customers, who he claimed only ever bought one coffee and made it last all day ('typical Jewish behaviour', he told his family); he made a habit of upsetting the tables and throwing the coffee cups to the ground. Despite this, and Tonny's involvement in the fighting at the Jewish-owned Café Alcazar on Thorbeckeplein, where he hurled chairs through the windows, Cas insisted that his brother was not so much anti-Semitic as that he was seeking to cause trouble and sensation wherever he went. The incident in the Bijenkorf in 1938 and the vandalism of the Herman Heijermans statue were merely further evidence of Tonny's troublemaking, Cas said.

Cas knew about his brother's Nazi sympathies, although he himself spent most of the war working in Bremen, helping to build U-boats. He could never remember Tonny talking about Maarten Kuiper, but knew that he worked with Willi Lages and Aus der Fünten among others. Towards the end of the war, Tonny began telling his family he was working for the resistance, taking clandestine photos of documents in Lages's office with his Minox camera, which he concealed under his coat. He felt no guilt about his earlier actions and expected to sail through the liberation without any difficulties; he had no idea that he would be arrested and imprisoned.

It was only after the war that Cas Ahlers learned there had been 'a relationship – not a friendship, Tonny always called it "business"' between his brother and Otto Frank. He claimed that Tonny had told him personally that he had turned in the Frank family to the Gestapo and had seemed 'proud of the fact'. Cas assumed he had done it for the money and the possessions Tonny had been able to filch from the hiding place. He said that Maarten Kuiper had not made the call after all, that the call came from Tonny himself. He also told us that some time after Otto emigrated from Amsterdam to Basel, Tonny had begun to blackmail him again,

---

★ A popular square in Amsterdam with many cafés and bars.

and received regular, substantial payments from Otto in Switzerland. Cas stated that he had even seen a letter from Otto in which was written, 'The goods have been delivered again' – an apparently bitter reference to the past. The payments, Cas said, continued until Otto Frank's death in 1980.

Cas Ahlers's testimony is problematic on two counts: first, it is based on hearsay and, second, he was clearly confused about certain issues. Cas claimed, for instance, that the Franks had been picked up on the Euterpestraat, which is patently untrue, though a possible explanation for his confusion is that the Franks were taken there immediately after their arrest. On the other hand, as to the statements that substantiate Cas's story, in addition to the candlestick he had already mentioned as having been taken from the Franks (and which he had shown us), Cas recalled having seen Tonny with a brass menorah which also came from the hiding place. In a 1960s interview for French television, Otto mentioned a brass menorah as being amongst the items confiscated by the Gestapo and NSB on the day of the arrest. It has never been found.

Cas Ahlers was not the only member of the family to come forward and affirm that Tonny Ahlers was the betrayer of the eight in hiding at 263 Prinsengracht. Tonny Ahlers's son indirectly contacted my publisher at the end of the week in which the book was published. During our first meeting, Ahlers's son explained, 'I could never have told people voluntarily that my father betrayed Otto Frank, but now that it has been made public, I feel that it's my duty to tell what I know and to prevent any more lies and half-truths going into the papers. I just want to set everything straight, and to get rid of this burden that I've lived with most of my life.'

Born in 1945, just two weeks before his father was arrested, Ahlers's son insists he is not out for revenge, despite the pain his father inflicted upon him and the rest of the family, physically, emotionally and mentally. He is an intelligent man and those who know him attest strongly to his integrity; and he has nothing to gain from admitting that he is the son of the Franks' betrayer. He wishes to remain as anonymous as possible, and hopes that his privacy will be respected. Before he heard his father talking about the betrayal of 4 August 1944, he already knew that he had been a member of the NSB. 'Myself and my brother and sisters suffered terribly because of that. Hardly any of the other children in the neighbourhood would play with us and we were not allowed to have contact with anyone outside the family. Our parents wouldn't allow it, in case something was said. If I came home with a letter from school, my parents wouldn't sign it because someone might recognize the name. There were many children in my class but, as far as they were concerned, I was alone; no one would speak to me because my father had been a Nazi. My first relationship with a girl ended because her father couldn't stomach the idea of her marrying the son of an NSB man. The same thing happened to my sister. We suffered a lot.'

Ahlers's son laughs at the memory of his father's ostensible role as a freelance photographer: 'My father was an amateur in all things. He did everything – all his forms of employment – for a very short length of time. Photopress International, the "company" he set up in 1950, was just a front. He never made any money from his photography, not really. My mother was the one who kept us. She worked very hard, and had her own business dressmaking and that sort of thing. She worked day and night at the sewing machine and the people who lived downstairs from us used to complain about the noise. It's unbelievable that she stuck by my father for so long. He was very violent towards her. Often at the dinner table, if the food displeased him or his mood was bad, he would just pick up the dish and fling it across the room. He lied, he cheated, he didn't do any work. He made himself a hiding place in the small boxroom of our apartment which was meant for storing bicycles. When the police came to the house – which they often did – he would slip in there and then dash out when their backs were turned. And they came to that house often, believe me. My mother stood by him always, and it's my feeling that whatever he did during the war she must have known about it. She never had Jewish girls working for her – it's rubbish! And she told you I met Otto Frank, but I didn't. At least, I was not aware of it, although I know my father told someone close to me that Otto Frank had once been to our house.'

The name Otto Frank cropped up early in Ahlers's son's life. 'Yes, I remember it very clearly. My father suddenly disappeared in 1952. He went to the Koninklijke Nederlandse Stoomboot Maatschappij [Royal Dutch Steamboat Society] and spent two years travelling the world. We were able to follow his progress in the papers, because we could follow the route of the ship. He went everywhere: Australia, Indonesia – he had always loved travelling. Then when he came back, he bought a telephone. I was very excited by this new element in our lives and I remember it was a white telephone that sat on the windowsill. When I was about seven or eight years old, I heard a conversation on that phone. I was in bed one night, listening to the phone ringing. My father picked it up and he was talking. I heard him mention Otto Frank. And then I heard him say, "I got them in [to the hiding place] and I got them out again."'

Soon after his return to Amsterdam, Tonny Ahlers disappeared again: 'That was in 1960 and it followed something dramatic happening in his life, although I don't know what it was. There was suddenly this huge panic; he left and we had to get out of our apartment. Some terrible thing . . . We went to stay with my mother's sister, who had a house near the Overtoom. My brother was in the military then, so it was me, my mother and two little girls. And then one day my father reappeared. It was the end of 1961. All our furniture had been packed up and hidden away. Then when my father came back we suddenly found ourselves moving into this great new apartment in Amsterdam-Osdorp. In those days it was very modern and very nice. But I couldn't stand to be in that house. My brother couldn't either.'

There were other references to Otto Frank over the years, but in 1963 Tonny Ahlers suddenly began to talk about him far more openly: that was when Silberbauer was found and the subject of the betrayal was in newspapers across the world. Ahlers's son remembers his father writing letters about Otto Frank to the authorities in Vienna, and to Silberbauer: 'Yes, I watched him, tapping furiously on his old typewriter. The keys were banging down hard. Those letters were written out of hatred, jealousy and hatred. That was a turning point in our lives. After that, Otto Frank was a subject of daily discussion in our home. My father became obsessed by him. He would talk about him every night before, during and after dinner. He told us about the business he had done during the war with Otto. He said Otto's product was sold in bottles, but in the war they sometimes had to use special paper, the type that holds in water. My father sold this paper to Otto Frank and he got a nice profit from it because he got the price of the contents along with their packaging. I got sick of him talking about Otto Frank and I decided I wasn't going to listen any more and I wasn't going to believe him any more either. That made him crazy, to think he was talking about all this and no one took him seriously, or even listened to him.'

Blackmail and writing accusatory letters were typical of his father, Ahlers's son explains: 'I had my own business in the early 1980s and, unfortunately, the market for our product plummeted and we went bankrupt. My father sent an anonymous letter to the receivers, telling them that myself and my wife had been drug-running. We were stunned. Later on, I found a copy of the letter in my father's house. He had done it, of course. That was how his mind worked: informing, snitching on people, getting the police involved – for nothing. He was always fighting with neighbours over parking spaces and that kind of thing. And he tried repeatedly to blackmail people. He once wrote to the Albert Heijn supermarket chain, saying he was disgusted with their peanut butter and he wanted hundreds of guilders to keep quiet about it. A madman, really.'

I asked Ahlers's son if he knew anything about money his father may have received from Otto Frank after the war. He nodded. 'Well, I didn't know where it came from, just that he had an income he couldn't explain to us. Every month he received the equivalent of a director's salary into a bank account that he kept separate from his usual business account. With the money he was able to buy items he could not normally have bought and we took holidays in places that were very exotic for that time. My father said it was a government benefit on account of his having had polio as a child, but the payments were far too high. He was very proud of this mysterious income, of how large it was. He bought presents for everyone in the family with this money.' His wife agrees: 'That was really very puzzling to us. A friend of my mother told her that he knew Tonny was receiving a lot of money every month from abroad. When we asked this man about it he just told us, "Don't go digging, because a lot of dirt will come out."' In 1980 – the year Otto Frank died – Tonny Ahlers closed his bank account. His lifestyle changed radically; there were no more luxury holidays, no more expensive gifts, and he and his wife were forced to move out of their six-room apartment in Amsterdam-Osdorp into a tiny, rent-assisted flat.

In the last years of his life, Tonny Ahlers became senile and had serious problems with his heart and lungs. His wife, who had vowed never to allow him back into her life after they had divorced in 1985, took care of him. On 4 August 2000, the rest of the family heard that he had died. His son recalls: 'Two of us children went to his funeral – to make sure he was really dead. My mother was there, of course, but we ignored her when she waved to us. I sat at the back, listening to the music playing as the coffin disappeared to be cremated; first "We Shall Overcome" and then "I Did It My Way".' The man who had overshadowed so many lives, and whose brother Cas described as 'an absolute sadist; he could be threatening and charming at the same time', was gone.

His son says, with an ironic laugh, 'And then he comes back from the dead. One night, there he is, on the news, his betrayal of Otto Frank there for everyone to see and hear. But I have to say that it is a relief now to have this out in the open. Of course it was a terrible shock to see his face again, and in such a way, but I've lived with this secret a long time. He did betray the Frank family. I am sure of that. There are still things I can't quite remember, but I know I heard a lot over the years, and I already knew it for myself a long time ago. Now is the time to tell all. Then I can close the door and truly say: "He is dead."'

Did Tonny Ahlers betray the Frank family? The evidence we have at the moment is largely circumstantial, and his relatives have only been able to provide us with oral testimony. These people are witnesses, nonetheless – Ahlers's son in particular – but whether Tonny Ahlers was telling the truth is another matter. His ever-present need to seem important is a factor against him, but it may also be one of the reasons why he informed the Gestapo that there were Jews hiding at 263 Prinsengracht. And although he was indeed a storyteller, his tales always had some basis in truth.

At the time of writing, Tonny Ahlers's son is preparing to confront his father's wartime past head on, to look at his prison records and the files on his collaboration activities himself. He is also hoping to talk to other family members who may know more, to trace the unexplained payments made into his father's bank account and to locate documents that may give us more of an insight into what actually did take place so many years ago. And already, new facts are starting to emerge.

When articles about this book appeared in Germany, a retired journalist named Carole Kleesick contacted me. She interviewed Otto Frank in 1964 for *Die Neue*, the magazine for which she then worked. The assignment was given to her after her colleague, photographer John de Rooy, had spoken to Simon Wiesenthal about the Silberbauer investigation; Weisenthal told de Rooy that he was completely convinced that Otto Frank knew the name of the traitor. Although Kleesick liked and admired Otto Frank, she was puzzled by his attitude towards the matter of the betrayal and recalls, 'He was evasive and, yes, I got the feeling that he knew who the traitor was.'

The most frequent question put to me since this book was published has been: how could Ahlers have known for certain that there was a 'back house' to Otto's business premises? Although it is now known that the Gestapo arrived at 263 Prinsengracht aware that there were Jews in the building but without knowing exactly where they were, Ahlers would have known that there was an annexe to the premises. When he visited Otto in his private office in April 1941, he was actually inside the annexe. Otto Frank's office was on the first floor of that building, and the stairs to the upper floors were clearly visible to Ahlers when he left. But in the last few days, another explanation still has surfaced.

In 1938 and 1939 Tonny Ahlers's mother rented the property at 253 Prinsengracht. Just five doors away from the building where Otto Frank would one day take his family into hiding, her home was strikingly similar to 263 Prinsengracht – complete with the same 'back house'. Therefore, if Ahlers was the traitor, he probably had some idea that Otto Frank had taken his family into hiding in the annexe, without knowing it for certain.

Tonny Ahlers liked to tell people that where he had been 'no grass shall ever grow'. What he did not realize was that his footprints may still be visible upon the scorched earth.

Appendix 1: The Missing Pages of the Diary of Anne Frank

In 2001 *The Diaries of Anne Frank: The Critical Edition* was updated to include five pages from the diary which had never before been published. The pages in question, written on loose sheets, consisted of an introduction to the diary Anne had written on 20 June 1942 and an observation about her parents' marriage, dated 8 February 1944 (B), which Anne had rewritten from her original entry (A). In the winter of 1945, Otto translated the pages into German when he was in the process of sending excerpts from the diary to his family in Switzerland but never sanctioned them for publication.

After Otto's death and the return of Anne's writings to Amsterdam, NIOD set about the task of authenticating and publishing the complete diaries, but ran into difficulties. There were some objections from people who did not wish their full names, or a few personal details, to be made public; this could only be resolved by the use of initials rather than names and explanatory footnotes. The greatest objection, however, came from Otto's widow, Fritzi. She wrote to Father John Neiman, 'I am not at all happy about this book as I think it violates Anne's right of privacy and my husband's intentions.' In another letter to Bep Voskuijl, Fritzi makes her feelings equally plain: 'I want to try and get the director of the Institute to omit certain passages, because I do not consider them fit for publication . . . Anne writes too openly about sexual matters. I don't know whether I'll succeed though, but I hope so.' One of the passages which caused Fritzi concern was the entry dated 8 February 1944 (A), in which Anne discussed her parents' marriage. This was omitted from the published *Critical Edition*, with a footnote explaining the objections to it.

In early 1998 Cor Suijk contacted the Fonds to inform them that he had five original diary pages, which he said had been given to him by Otto Frank. These incorporated Anne's introduction for the diary and her rewritten draft of 8 February 1944 (B). In April 1998 Suijk wrote to Buddy Elias, claiming to know more about the Stichting, Otto Frank and the diary than Hans Westra [director of the Anne Frank Stichting] had in his archive, and declared that the day was coming near when he would present his knowledge. Suijk asserted that Otto had passed the pages to him during the Bundeskriminalamt investigation of the diary's authenticity in 1980, wanting to save himself and Fritzi unpleasant questions.* By handing the

* Details about the Bundeskriminalamt (Federal Criminal Investigation Bureau) investigation can be found in Chapter Seven, *Attacks on the Authenticity of the Diary,* in David Barnouw and Gerrold van der Stroom (eds.), *The Diaries of Anne Frank: The Critical Edition* (London: Viking, 1989) pp.97–98.

pages to Suijk, Otto could legitimately claim to have no further pages in his possession.* When Suijk offered to return the pages, he maintained that Otto put out his hands in a silent way of saying, 'Keep them.' In his 1998 letter to Buddy Elias, Suijk outlined his plans for the diary pages, insisting under Swiss law the right to publish them first in Melissa Muller's biography of Anne Frank. They would also form part of a television documentary pertinent to the book's publication, whose producer intended to give Buddy Elias a prominent role. Once this was achieved, Suijk promised that the Fonds would have the right to copyright.

Suijk had not come forward with the five pages while NIOD were compiling *The Critical Edition,* though this would surely have been the moment to do so when the most extensive inspection of the diary's authenticity was being conducted. The reason he gave for not doing so was the desire to protect Fritzi from being confronted with awkward questions, but he could have informed NIOD about the existence of the pages with the stipulation that they were not for publication; after all, the original version of the entry concerned was omitted at Fritzi's wish. Paradoxically, Suijk was clearly willing for Muller to print them in her book while Fritzi was still alive.

In May 1998 the Anne Frank-Fonds asked Suijk to honour Otto's will by delivering the diary pages to NIOD. Suijk refused on the grounds that because the pages were not in Otto's possession when he died, they were exempt from the clauses in his will and Otto had not wanted them to form part of the diary. In her book, Muller asserts that Otto stipulated in his will that the original diaries, including 324 of the 327 'loose sheets', were to go to NIOD. Otto makes no such distinction; his will states that 'RIOD in Amsterdam will receive all handwritten notes and the photo album of my daughter Anne Frank . . . Whatever other material which has a bearing on Anne Frank and which is still in my possession at my death . . . should be given to the Anne Frank Stichting, in as far as the material is not needed by my wife for continuing the current correspondence.'

In August 1998 the news that there were five previously unpublished pages of Anne's diary broke. The press and public interest in the missing pages was immense, heightened by speculation about what would happen to the pages, since Suijk had declared that he wanted a 'financial sponsor' for the pages before he would release them to NIOD. Initially he was quoted as saying he would donate the money to the Anne Frank Center in the USA,† where he was then working, but when he and the Center parted company he announced his intention to use it instead for his

---

* Suijk was then still working for the Stichting.
† The Anne Frank Center in New York organizes the travelling Anne Frank exhibition and educates against racism and prejudice.

own Holocaust Education Foundation, also based in the USA. Having learned that Muller would be unable to quote the pages in her biography due to disputes over their copyright, Suijk used his platform to attack the Anne Frank-Fonds, whom he accused of squirrelling away millions in Swiss bank accounts. The Fonds did not aid their cause by refusing to be drawn on the subject under pressure from Suijk. Their support of various charities and funding of many anti-racism related projects was largely ignored by a now hostile press.

Buddy Elias, meanwhile, gave a radio interview in which he discussed visits Suijk had made to Otto's house in 1996 and 1997. On one occasion, Fritzi's nurse, Katja Olszewska, had been disturbed by Suijk's interest in reading Otto's will, which lay in a drawer of the writing desk in the 'office'. On another occasion, Suijk appeared with a photocopier. He told Katja he wanted to make copies from the facsimile diary, which consisted of voluminous loose pages and was kept in the house. Katja telephoned Eva Schloss to ascertain whether she should permit Suijk to do so and was told that Suijk had been given permission to copy materials. The Fonds were angry over such affairs, however, and Katja had given statements about both incidents to a lawyer. She also told the author, 'Suijk came here often. Once he asked me if I knew where there were letters, private letters. I said I didn't know.' In June 1998 Suijk wrote an astonishing letter to the executor of Otto's will, in which he enquired which items belonging to Anne were found to be in Otto's possession after his death. He asked to be informed of whatever had been found, in which way any items had been registered, and if an inventory had been made. Exactly why Suijk believed he had the right to be informed of such matters is puzzling.★

The Fonds' attempts to reclaim the pages failed; Suijk was able to hold on to them because he maintained that Otto had given them to him as a gift. He placed the pages with Christie's Auctioneers in New York for one year on the understanding that they would be used to attract donations to his Holocaust Education Foundation, which hoped to raise $1.2 million in funds. The Dutch government bought the pages eventually for $300,000. Initially the press attacked Suijk for his actions, but in the past year or so they have been less antagonistic towards him, particularly in the Netherlands, where the pages are now stored in NIOD's archives.

Public opinion, meanwhile, remains divided. Eva Schloss is vociferous in her reproach:

I'm sure that Otto would never have wanted those pages published. And I don't see that they make such a great difference to the diary. As for the story behind it all – I am sure that Otto gave them to Cor for safe keeping. That is true. But *not* to keep. They were not a gift.

★ The Anne Frank Center, for whom Suijk then worked, does not hold archive material on the Frank family.

He just wanted Cor to take them at that moment so that he was not compromising himself. In May 1980, or around then, Cor visited Otto with the pages and he says that Otto put up his hands in a dismissive gesture. That didn't mean 'They're yours', it meant, 'Don't bother me now.' He was a very sick man at that point and found it hard sometimes to deal with even the smallest things. He wasn't thinking right at that time. And Otto would hate Cor for selling them, he would hate him.★

Laureen Nussbaum, who has written extensively about Anne's diary, disagrees:

Otto did well to get the diary published in the first place. The Dutch wanted us to fade into the background, they weren't interested in us or what the Jewish people had suffered in those years. So Otto should be congratulated for being probably the first to publish a document from the Holocaust, but when it comes to his editing of it, on that issue I feel that he was headstrong and misled people as to the content. Once he had made certain statements about it, he either could not or would not retract and, as a result, those statements have been accepted over the years. And the missing pages add so much. Cor faxed me in early 1998 about them and asked if he could send me copies to translate. This I did, and I kept it secret for as long as he asked. I'm sorry it made such a scandal. In the new *Critical Edition*, Barnouw says nothing about Cor and that is terrible of him. Cor deserves better than that. Without him, there would be no new version and those pages would still be unknown. He kept them back until the time was right, until Fritzi could not be bothered by the journalists who would surely have come banging on her door. I don't think Otto would be upset at their publication either. He made a present of them to Cor, so in effect he said Cor had the right to do with them what he wanted.

There are a number of questions arising from the 'missing pages' affair. In the first place, Suijk claims that Otto removed the pages in 1945 and put them in an envelope, then numbered the remaining pages in sequence as if nothing was missing. The pages must have been removed before Otto's death in 1980, but there is no evidence to confirm that it was in 1945 (or that Otto was the person to number the pages afterwards). The Fonds have a copy of Otto's German translation of the pages from late 1945, making it improbable that Otto secreted the pages at that time; he was clearly unfazed by his family and friends reading the pages then.

In the second place, Anne's diary – including the entries written upon the loose sheets – was examined in 1959 for purposes of establishing its authenticity. Handwriting experts travelled to Basel to inspect her work. What happened to these

★ In the press, Suijk claimed that Otto had given him the pages in May 1980 and he tried to return them several months later, which would be shortly before Otto's death in August 1980.

delicate pages on that occasion? Did Otto entrust them to someone then, as he apparently did with Suijk later? And if so, why did he clearly require the pages to be returned to him then (which he must have done in order to give them to Suijk), while he allowed Suijk to keep them?

In the third place, Otto allowed the handwriting experts to view Anne's original version of the entry in question, yet felt that the revised version was too sensitive for them to scrutinize. However, a comparison of both texts reveals that they are quite startlingly similar, and there is certainly nothing that can be deemed disparaging in the second draft that is not present in the first. In effect, Otto was not concealing anything by retaining Anne's revised entry about his marriage. As for the introduction she wrote, although it is different in substance to other passages in the diary, it contains nothing that could be construed as damaging. In it, Anne writes that no one must get their hands on her diary, but the published diary also included the line, 'I don't intend to show this cardboard-covered notebook to anyone.'

It seems extraordinarily remiss of Otto to have given them to Suijk, the Finance Co-ordinator of the Anne Frank Stichting in 1980, without any form of declaration to confirm that he was making a gift of them to him, to corroborate that they were authentic, and to set out the terms of the bequest (that they could only be released after a certain time). Over the years, Otto had endured many problems with diary-related issues, particularly those involving ownership, rights and fraud. He knew that he had to be absolutely circumspect in such matters, and to have drawn up some sort of attestation about the pages would also have protected the man he apparently trusted more than any living person – let us not forget, if we ever could, that the diary was Otto's life – against accusations of theft and avarice when he decided to sell them, as Suijk eventually did.

In an interview with the Dutch news programme *NOVA* in summer 2000, Suijk pronounced himself certain that Otto would approve of his conduct regarding the hidden pages. Otto advocated Holocaust education, unquestionably, but the answer to whether or not he would have sanctioned selling the remains of his daughter's legacy may be found in an interview he gave not long before his death in August 1980. He explained then that he was writing his will and would bequeath all Anne's writings to NIOD. Asked why he was not pledging them to the Anne Frank Stichting, Otto replied, 'I'm never sure what the Anne Frank Stichting will be one day. What will become of the Stichting in fifty years? Do we know? You just asked about finances. Maybe some time something will happen. What can I know? It's not safe enough for me.' The interviewer pointed out that the pages would be worth a fortune. Otto's response was quiet but confident, 'Yes, but they will be with the government so that they won't be sold. You see?'

Appendix 2: Chronology of the Jewish Persecution in the Netherlands

1940

10 May: Germany invades the Netherlands.

15 May: Surrender of all Dutch forces.

1 July: Jews have to leave the air-raid precaution service.

2 July: Jews excluded from labour drafts to Germany.

31 July: Bans on ritual slaughter (VO 80/1940) effective from 5 August.

20 August: Special regulations on administrative matters (VO 108/1940).

28 August: College of Secretaries-General informally instructed not to appoint, elect or promote anyone of 'Jewish Blood' within the civil service.

6 September: College of Secretaries-General instructed not to appoint any more Jews to the civil service.

13 September: Measures concerning the employment of Jews and others in government service (VO 137/1940).

14 September: Jews banned from various markets in Amsterdam.

20 September: Measures for a survey of non-economic associations and institutions (VO 145/1940).

30 September: Circular to local authorities defining a Jew as anyone with one Jewish grandparent who had been a member of the Jewish community.

5 October: Civil servants forced to sign 'Aryan attestation'.

22 October: Order for the registration of Jewish businesses at the Wirtschaftsprüfstelle (VO 189/1940).

21 November: Circular sent out banning all Jews from holding public office.

December: The creation of the Jewish Co-ordination Commission.

19 December: Bans on Germans working in Jewish households (VO 231/1940).

1941

7 January: The Dutch Cinema Association bans Jews in all cinemas, publicized in daily newspapers on 12 January.

10 January: Compulsory registration of all persons 'wholly or largely of Jewish blood' (VO 6/1941).

1 February: Introduction of *numerus clausus* in education.

5 February: Doctors must declare if they are Jewish.

8 February: WA incite fighting on the Rembrandtplein, Amsterdam.

11 February: Restrictions on Jewish students (VO 27/1941). Decree of Secretary-General of Education, Science and Culture implementing the above decree (VO 28/1941). WA attack on Amsterdam's Jewish Quarter, resulting in the death of Nazi Hendrik Koot.

12 February: German authorities seal off the Jewish Quarter and insist on the establishment of a Jewish Council.

13 February: Amsterdam Joodse Raad (Jewish Council) set up.

19 February: German police raid on Kocos, an ice-cream parlour owned by two Jews. Police attacked.

22–23 February: German reprisal arrests of 425 young men from the Jewish Quarter.

25–26 February: Strike in Amsterdam and beyond in protest at the arrests.

27 February: Decree of the Secretary-General of the Department of Social Affairs on Jewish blood donors.

28 February: Measures against Jewish non-commercial organizations (VO 41/1941).

12 March: Measures for the registration of Jewish businesses and the appointment of Verwalters (VO 48/1941).

31 March: Creation of the Zentralstelle für Jüdische Auswanderung.

2 April: Series of prohibitions of Jews in Haarlem.

11 April: First issue of the *Joodse Weekblad*.

15 April: Instruction by Commissioner-General Rauter to all Jews to hand in their wireless sets on the basis of regulation of 11 February (VO 26/1941).

1 May: Ban on Jewish doctors, apothecaries and translators working for non-Jews. Jews no longer allowed to own wireless sets. Ban on Jews attending stock and commercial exchanges.

6 May: Certain streets in Amsterdam designated 'Jewish Streets'.

15 May: Synagogue in The Hague destroyed by fire. 'Aryanizing' of orchestras.

27 May: Decree on declaration and treatment of agricultural land in Jewish hands (VO 102/1941).

31 May: Jews banned from using swimming baths, public parks and from hiring rooms in certain resorts and coastal localities.

4 June: Freedom of movement for Jews restricted.

11 June: Raids against Jews in Amsterdam.

Mid-June: Jewish lawyers banned from working for non-Jewish clients.

1 August: Ban on Jewish estate agents from working for non-Jews.

8–11 August: Regulations on the handling of Jewish assets and property. Registration of assets with Lippmann-Rosenthal Bank.

1 September: Jewish children forced to attend separate schools (1 October in Amsterdam).

14 September: Raid in Twente area (east Overijssel).

15 September: Signs 'Forbidden for Jews' appear. Jews no longer allowed to visit parks, zoos, cafés, restaurants, hotels, guest houses, theatres, cabarets, cinemas, concerts, libraries and reading rooms (VO 138/1941). Registration of land and property owned by Jews with Lippmann-Rosenthal.

16 September: Travel permits introduced.

22 September: Jews barred from all non-economic organizations and associations.

24 September: Permits made compulsory for the establishment of certain trades and professions.

7–8 October: Raids in the Achterhoek, Arnhem, Apeldoorn and Zwolle.

20 October: Further regulations on the establishment of businesses by Jews (VO 198/1941). Joodse Raad sanctions the creation of a card index of Jews in the Netherlands.

22 October: Jews forced to resign from non-Jewish associations (VO 199/1941), and banned from bridge, dance and tennis clubs from 7 November.

27 October: Germans limit their recognition to Joodse Raad; Jewish Co-ordination Commission forced to disband.

1 November: Jews required to resign from associations with non-Jewish members. Legislation VO 198/1941 used to rescind 1,600 permits for Jews.

3 November: Jewish markets established in Amsterdam.

7 November: Jews banned from travelling or moving house without permission.

10 November: Final dissolution of the Jewish Co-ordination Commission.

5 December: All non-Dutch Jews ordered to register for 'voluntary emigration'.

1942

1 January: Jews not permitted to employ non-Jewish domestic servants.

9 January: Jews banned from public education.

10 January: First Jews from Amsterdam sent to work camps. The Joodse Raad advise those targeted to obey the summons on the grounds that a refusal would lead to trouble for everyone.

17 January: Beginning of the concentration of Jews in Amsterdam with removal of Jewish community from Zaandam.

20 January: Wannsee Conference in Berlin outlines practical measures for the extermination of European Jews.

23 January: Jews banned from using motor cars. Identity cards for Jews to carry a letter 'J'.

9 February: One hundred and fifty stateless Jews from Utrecht moved to Amsterdam and Westerbork.

20 March: Jews forbidden to dispose of furniture or household goods.

25 March: Ban on marriage between Jews and non-Jews. Extra-marital relations to be severely punished.

26 March: First transportation of Jews from occupied Western Europe (Drancy) to Auschwitz.

27 March: Effective introduction of the Nuremberg Laws in the Netherlands.

1 April: Jews banned from marrying in Amsterdam town hall.

24 April: Most Jewish butchers closed down.

3 May: Introduction of the Jewish Star. The fate of Jews in the Netherlands is now sealed for, as the historian Jacob Presser writes, it 'marked them out for slaughter'.

12 May: Jews no longer allowed to have accounts at the Post Office.

21 May: Jews forced to hand in all their assets and possessions valued at more than fl.250 to Lippmann, Rosenthal by 30 June 1942. No longer allowed to hire safety deposit boxes (VO 58/1942).

29 May: Jews prohibited from fishing.

5 June: Total ban on travelling for Jews without prior permission.

11 June: Jews banned from the fish market.

12 June: Jews no longer allowed to buy fruit and vegetables in non-Jewish shops. Bicycles and other transport have to be handed in. All forms of sport forbidden for Jews.

26 June: The Joodse Raad receives notification of the beginning of the deportations.

30 June: Curfew on Jews from 8.00 p.m. Jews no longer allowed to ride bicycles. Jews banned from certain trades and professions. Jews banned from using public transport.

4 July: First call-up notices sent out for 'labour services in Germany'.

6 July: Jews no longer allowed to use telephones or visit non-Jews.

14 July: Raids on Jews in south and central Amsterdam.

15 July: First trainload of Jews leaves Amsterdam. Deportations begin from Westerbork to Auschwitz.

17 July: Jews may only shop between 3.00 p.m. and 5.00 p.m., and are banned altogether from many streets in The Hague and Scheveningen.

25 July: Dutch Prime Minister Gerbrandy urges help for the Jews via a broadcast from London on Radio Oranje.

2 August: Arrest of all Catholic Jews, excluding those in mixed marriages.

6 August: Raid on Jews in south Amsterdam.

9 August: Further raid in south Amsterdam.

August: Series of raids throughout the Netherlands. All Jewish street names changed.

11 September: Registration of those in 'mixed marriages'.

15 September: Jewish students excluded from education.

16 September: First issue of exemption stamps.

2–3 October: Raids against Jewish work camps.

1943

16 January: First Jews arrive in Vught concentration camp.

21 January: Raid on Jewish asylum Het Apeldoornsche Bos.

5 February: Jews banned from sending requests or letters to the German authorities. All of these to be directed via the Joodse Raad.

2 March: Deportations to Sobibor begin.

27 March: Amsterdam population registry attacked and set on fire.

April: All Jews to leave the provinces and be accommodated at Vught.

23 April: Provincial Netherlands declared free of Jews.

5 May: Harster gives the orders for the final phase of Jewish deportations.

15 May: Jews in mixed marriages offered choice of deportation or sterilization.

21 May: Joodse Raad instructed to select 7,000 of its 'exempt' staff for deportation.

26 May: Mass raid in Amsterdam to capture remaining Jews.

20 June: Further mass raids in south and east Amsterdam.

15 July: Rauter gives instructions for raids in the countryside.

29 September: Last major raid in Amsterdam. Joodse Raad wound up.

5 October: Seyss-Inquart gives instructions for the treatment of the legally remaining Jews in the Netherlands.

December: Those in mixed marriages called up for service in work-camps.

1944

16 May: Raids against gypsies and 'asocials'.

5 September: Dolle Dinsdag (Mad Tuesday). NSB leader Mussert orders the evacuation of Dutch National Socialists from the west and centre of the country to the east.

5–6 September: Two large transports of inmates from Vught concentration camp eastwards to Germany.

17 September: Operation Market Garden, the Allied airborne landings around Nijmegen and Arnhem, begins.

1945

5 May: Official liberation of the entire Netherlands.★

★ This table is based upon the one featured in Bob Moore, *Victims and Survivors: The Nazi Persecution of the Jews in the Netherlands 1940–1945* (London: Arnold, 1997), pp.261–267.

Dramatis Personae

Tonny Ahlers NSB and NSNAP member, informant for Kurt Döring, who entered Otto Frank's life in 1941 and was arrested in 1945 for betraying people to the SD, among other charges.

Kermit Bloomgarden Producer of the Hacketts' 1955 stage adaptation of the *Diary*.

Janny Brilleslijper Together with her sister Lin, she became acquainted with the Franks in Westerbork and was with Anne and Margot shortly before their deaths.

Lin Brilleslijper In the summer of 1945, she informed Otto that his children were dead.

Werner Cahn Otto's friend in Amsterdam who tried to find a publisher for the diary in 1945.

Ab Cauvern Otto's friend who helped revise the diary manuscript and passed it on to Jan Romein, which led to the diary's publication in 1947.

Isa Cauvern Wife of Ab, Otto's secretary before the war. Typed up the manuscript of the diary in 1945.

Cheryl Crawford Theatre producer who showed first interest in bringing the diary to the US stage.

Julius Dettman Recipient of the telephone call regarding the hidden Jews at 263 Prinsengracht. He killed himself in 1945.

Kurt Döring Tonny Ahlers's boss at the SD headquarters, and his neighbour (Jan van Eyckstraat 20) from 1943 to 1944.

Anton Dunselman Amsterdam lawyer who was appointed supervisory director of Otto's company in January 1935, remained a close friend after the war.

Buddy (Bernhard) Elias Otto's nephew and now President of the Anne Frank-Fonds in Basel.

Erich Elias Brother-in-law of Otto, married to Leni, and father of Stephan and Buddy. Helped Otto set up the Opekta business in Amsterdam in 1933.

Leni Elias (née **Frank**) Otto's younger sister. Married to Erich Elias and mother of Stephan and Buddy.

Stephan Elias Otto's nephew who died unexpectedly five days after Otto's death in 1980.

Alice Frank (née **Stern**) Otto's mother.

Anne Frank   Otto's youngest daughter who kept the diary that later formed such a large part of Otto's life. Died in Bergen-Belsen aged fifteen.

Edith Frank (née **Holländer**)   Otto's first wife and mother of his two daughters. Died in Auschwitz in 1945.

Fritzi Frank (née **Markovitz**)   Otto's second wife, also a survivor of Auschwitz with her daughter Eva. She lost her first husband and son in the Holocaust. Fritzi died in 1998.

Herbert Frank   Otto's younger brother.

Jean-Michel Frank   Otto's Parisian cousin and celebrated furniture designer. Committed suicide in 1941.

Lottie Frank (née **Witt**)   Otto's sister-in-law, married to his brother Robert.

Margot Frank   Otto's eldest daughter. Died in Bergen-Belsen aged nineteen.

Michael Frank   Otto's father.

Robert Frank   Otto's elder brother.

Jetteke Frijda   Margot's best friend, she remained in contact with Otto after the war and still lives in Amsterdam today.

Jan Gies   Husband of Miep, close friend and helper to the Franks during their years in hiding.

Miep Gies (née **Santrouschitz**)   First employed as a secretary in the Opekta business in 1933, she became one of Otto's most trusted friends and was one of the Franks' helpers during the years in hiding.

Hilde Goldberg (née **Jacobsthal**)   Friend of Margot Frank and neighbour of the Franks in Amsterdam's Rivierenbuurt. She saw Otto often after the war and her emigration to America.

Gabi Goslar   Younger sister of Hanneli Goslar.

Hanneli Goslar   Anne's best friend in Amsterdam since 1933. Otto helped Hanneli and Gabi to emigrate to Switzerland after the war. She and Otto remained close and she lives in Israel today.

Hans Goslar   Father of Hanneli and close friend of Otto. Died in Bergen-Belsen in 1945.

Gezinus Gringhuis   Employed by the Zentralstelle where he worked alongside Tonny Ahlers's closest friend, and was present at the Frank family's arrest on 4 August 1944.

Willem Grootendorst   Employed by the Zentralstelle and present at the Frank family's arrest on 4 August 1944.

Frances (née **Goodrich**) **and Albert Hackett**   Writers of the stage and film adaptations of the *Diary*.

Lammert Hartog   Husband of Lena and assistant warehouseman at 263 Prinsengracht. Heard from Wilhelm van Maaren (see below) that there were Jews in hiding in the building where they worked.

Lena Hartog (née **van Bladeren**)   Wife of one of the warehouse workers at 263 Prinsengracht, she mentioned to another woman, Anna Genot, that she had heard there were people hiding on the premises.

Lillian Hellman   Writer to whom Frances Goodrich and Albert Hackett turned for advice about their adaptation of the *Diary*.

Hendrik van Hoeve   Resistance worker and supplier of groceries to the Franks during the period in hiding. Betrayed for hiding a Jewish couple in his home in 1944, he survived four concentration camps.

Julius Holländer   Otto's brother-in-law, the eldest brother of Edith. Emigrated to America with his brother Walter.

Rosa Holländer (née **Stern**)   Otto's mother-in-law, who lived with the family in Amsterdam from 1939 until her death in January 1942.

Walter Holländer: Otto's brother-in-law, Edith's brother, who was briefly imprisoned in a concentration camp before escaping to America.

Jetje Jansen   Former sales representative for Opekta and wife of Joseph Jansen.

Joseph Jansen   Member of the NSB and former casual employee of Otto who tried to betray him to the SS in 1941.

Garson Kanin   Director of the play whose considerable input omitted almost all references to the fact that the people in hiding were Jews.

Johannes Kleiman   Otto's friend since 1923, employee and helper during the Franks' two years in hiding.

Victor Kugler   Employed by Otto in 1933 as his 'right-hand man' in the Opekta business, and helper during the Franks' two years in hiding.

Maarten Kuiper   Employed by the SD to hunt down Jews, present at the Frank family's arrest on 4 August 1944.

Willi Lages   Wartime head of the Amsterdam Bureau of the Commander of the Security Police and Security Service.

Meyer Levin   Jewish newspaper correspondent and writer who hoped to dramatize the diary for the stage, but was rejected in favour of the Hacketts. Levin pursued a legal battle with Otto for many years.

Rose de Liema   Wife of Sal, she met the Frank family in Westerbork and has written an account of her experiences.

Sal de Liema   One of Otto's Dutch comrades in Westerbork and Auschwitz, he retained contact with 'Papa Frank' after the liberation. Lives in the USA with his wife, Rose.

Wilhelm van Maaren   Warehouseman at 263 Prinsengracht from spring 1943 until his dismissal in 1945. The main suspect in the betrayal investigations, but nothing could be proved against him.

Jacqueline van Maarsen   Anne's best friend from 1941 until the Franks went into hiding, she stayed in contact with Otto after the war and wrote a book about her friendship with Anne.

Joseph Marks   Doubleday Vice-President who was Otto's friend and first suggested opening the secret annexe as a museum.

Myer Mermin   Otto's lawyer during his legal battles with Meyer Levin.

Barbara Mooyart-Doubleday   Original translator of the English language version of the *Diary*.

Gertrud Naumann   Neighbour of the Franks in Frankfurt, who often baby-sat for Margot and Anne. Remained close to Otto after the war and still lives in Frankfurt.

Father John Neiman   Began writing to Otto in the early 1970s and became a confidant of Otto, Fritzi and Miep.

Laureen Nussbaum (née **Klein**)   Margot Frank's friend, and neighbour of the Franks in the Rivierenbuurt, who stayed in contact with Otto after the war and her emigration to America with her husband, Rudi. She has written extensively about the diary.

Edith Oppenheimer   Granddaughter of Otto's mother's cousin. Her grandparents and parents saw the Franks often in Frankfurt.

Gusti van Pels (née **Röttgen**)   Wife of Hermann van Pels. Died in 1945.

Hermann van Pels   Employed by Pectacon since 1938, hid in the secret annexe alongside the Franks and Pfeffer with his wife, Gusti, and son, Peter. Died in Auschwitz in 1944.

Peter van Pels   Son of Hermann and Gusti. Brought Otto food regularly in Auschwitz until he was forced to participate in a death march. Died in Mauthausen in 1945.

Millie Perkins   Portrayed Anne in the George Stevens film of the *Diary*.

Fritz Pfeffer   Dentist friend of the Franks who hid with them in the secret annexe. Died in Neuengamme in 1944.

Lotte Pfeffer (née **Kaletta**)   Wife of Fritz Pfeffer, she had their marriage posthumously recognized after the war. Otto's close friend until the 1950s when the unfair portrayal of her husband in the dramatic adaptations of the *Diary* led her to break off their friendship.

Josef van Poppel   Spy for the Abwehr who employed Ahlers as an agent until Ahlers tried to betray him to the SS.

Frank Price   Head of Doubleday's Paris office, who read the diary in its French translation and eventually recommended it to Doubleday in the USA.

Jan Romein   Author of the very first article about the then unpublished diary, in *Het Parool* in 1946.

Herman Rouwendaal   Abwehr spy who rented a room from Tonny Ahlers on Jan van Eyckstraat from 1943 to 1944.

Emil Rühl   SD official and Tonny Ahlers's neighbour (Jan van Eyckstraat 20) from 1943 to 1944.

Leah Salisbury   The Hacketts' agent.

Judith Salomon (née **de Winter**)   Met the Franks in Westerbork and remained in contact with Otto after the war.

Joseph Schildkraut   Portrayed Otto on stage in 1955 and in the 1959 George Stevens film.

Eva Schloss (née **Geiringer**)   The daughter of Otto's second wife, Fritzi.

Zvi Schloss   Husband of Eva.

Anneliese Schütz   Otto's friend, who helped him translate the diary from Dutch into German in 1945.

SS Oberscharführer Karl Josef Silberbauer   Led the arrest of the Frank family on 4 August 1944, traced by Nazi hunter Simon Wiesenthal in 1963.

Rabbi David Soetendorp   A close friend of Otto, his parents were also in hiding in the Netherlands during the war, together with his brother.

Franzi Spronz   Wife of Joseph, and Fritzi Frank's best friend.

Joseph Spronz   Husband of Franzi, met Otto in Auschwitz. He and Franzi were with Otto the day before he died.

Milly Stanfield   Otto's cousin who lived in London but became his confidante.

George Stevens   Director of the 1959 film *The Diary of Anne Frank*.

Lothar Stielau   Teacher in Germany who accused Otto of the diary being a forgery. Otto fought him in the courts and won his case.

Susan Strasberg   Portrayed Anne in the 1955 stageplay to critical acclaim.

Nathan Straus Jnr (formerly Charles Webster Straus)   Otto's closest friend since university in 1908, offered him a job at his father's department store, Macy's in New York.

Cor Suijk   Former finance director of the Anne Frank Stichting, who sold five pages from Anne's diary to the Dutch government in order to fund his own Holocaust educational work.

Tereska Torres   Wife of Meyer Levin.

Friedrich Christian Viebahn   SD official and Tonny Ahlers's neighbour (Jan van Eyckstraat 20) from 1943 to 1944.

Bep Voskuijl   Employee of Otto Frank since 1937 and helper of the Frank family during the years in hiding.

Johan Voskuijl   Father of Bep, worked for Otto until his illness prevented him from continuing his job. He died in December 1945.

Simon Wiesenthal   Nazi-hunter who located Silberbauer in the 1960s.

Cara Wilson: American girl who began corresponding with Otto and Fritzi in the 1960s and became a friend, visiting them in the 1970s. Some of their letters have been published.

Rootje de Winter Wife of Manuel and mother of Judith, she met the Franks in Westerbork and was present at Edith's death in Auschwitz.

Karel Wolters Lawyer and prosecutor in Amsterdam who oversaw the liquidation of Otto Frank's company Pectacon in 1941. Lived opposite Tonny Ahlers at Jan van Eyckstraat 31.

Barbara Zimmerman (now Epstein) The diary's US editor and Otto's close friend to whom he often turned for advice in business matters connected to the diary.

Glossary

Abwehr Wehrmacht counter-intelligence organization.

Armee Oberkommando German Army High Command in Berlin, headed by Adolf Hitler.

Bureau Nationale Veiligheid Netherlands Bureau of National Security, based in Scheveningen.

Deutsche Revisions- und Treuhand AG German Audit and Trust Company.

Economisch Front Economic Front.

Expositur Department of the Jewish Council responsible for liaison with the German authorities. Headed by Dr Edwin Sluzker, the staff of the Expositur also determined who was eligible for exemption from deportation.

Grüne Polizei The German Ordnungspolizei derived their name (Green Police) from the colour of their uniforms.

Hollandse Schouwburg Also known as the Joodsche Schouwburg, this former theatre was used as a collection point for Jews awaiting deportation to Westerbork, the first stop on the journey to the concentration camps of the east.

Joodse Raad voor Amsterdam The Jewish Council of Amsterdam, established in February 1941 and headed by Abraham Asscher and David Cohen, liaised with the German authorities and passed on the discriminatory decrees to the Jewish community.

Nationaal-Socialistische Beweging (NSB) The Dutch National Socialist Party, led by Anton Mussert.

Nationaal Socialistische Nederlandse Arbeiders Partij (NSNAP) The Dutch National Socialist Workers' Party, whose aim was to reproduce the ideology and operations of the NSDAP in Germany.

Nederlands Beheers Instituut (NBI) Dutch authority in charge of the administration of 'enemy property', property of NSB party members, and property of deported Dutch citizens who had not returned.

Nederlandsch-Duitsche Kultuurgemeenschap Dutch-German Cultural Union.

Nederlands Instituut voor Oorlogsdocumentatie (NIOD, formerly RIOD) Netherlands Institute for War Documentation.

Politieke Opsporings Dienst (POD) Political Criminal Investigations Department of the Dutch police.

Politieke Recherche Afdeling (PRA) Political Investigation Branch of the Dutch police.

Rechtsfront Legal Front.

Referat IVB4 Headed by Adolf Eichmann in Berlin, this department of the Gestapo was responsible for the deportation of European Jews to the annihilation camps. In the Netherlands, the office was based in The Hague and run by Willi Zöpf.

Reichssicherheitshauptamt (RSHA) Reich Security Main Office, controlling intelligence, security and criminal police work.

Schutzstaffel (SS) The NSDAP's security organization, under the command of Heinrich Himmler.

Sicherheitsdienst (SD) The Security and Intelligence Service of the German SS.

Sicherheitspolizei (Sipo) The German security police.

Weerafdeling (WA) Defence section (unarmed) of the Dutch National Socialist movement.

Wehrmacht German armed forces.

Wirtschaftsprüfstelle (BEI) German Bureau of Economic Investigation in the Netherlands.

Zentralstelle für Jüdische Auswanderung The Central Agency for Jewish Emigration. Run by the German Sipo and SD in Amsterdam, charged with the administration of Jewish deportations from the Netherlands.

References

At the decision of the publisher, a general list of sources are given here, but the author has retained all her original footnotes and anyone wishing to ask about a specific quotation or source is welcome to contact the author via the publisher.

Prologue: The Jew Hunters of Amsterdam

UNPUBLISHED SOURCES

Dossier(s) A. Ahlers. Centraal Archief Bijzondere Rechtspleging (CABR), Rijksarchief, Den Haag.

Doc. I., K. Döring. Collection of Nederlands Instituut voor Oorlogsdocumentatie (NIOD).

Dossier K. Döring. CABR.

Dossier G. Gringhuis. CABR.

Dossier W. Grootendorst. CABR.

Victor Kugler, letter, 4 February 1958. Private collection of Buddy Elias (BE), cousin of Anne Frank and President of the Anne Frank-Fonds, Basel.

Doc. I., M. Kuiper. NIOD.

Dossier M. Kuiper. CABR.

Doc. I., W. G. van Maaren. NIOD.

Dossier W. G. van Maaren. CABR.

Doc. I., H. Rouwendaal. NIOD.

Dossier H. Rouwendaal. CABR.

Doc. I., E. Rühl. NIOD.

Dossier E. Rühl. CABR.

Doc. I., K. J. Silberbauer. NIOD.

Dossier F. C. Viebahn. CABR.

Doc. I., K. O. M. Wolters. NIOD.

PUBLISHED SOURCES

Presser, Jacob, *Ashes in the Wind: The Destruction of Dutch Jewry* (London: Souvenir Press, 1968).

Stoutenbeek, Jan and Vigeveno, Paul, *A Guide to Jewish Amsterdam* (Amsterdam: De Haan, 1985).

Press cuttings: Döring, Kuiper, Rouwendaal, Rühl, Viebahn. NIOD.

Chapter 1: Very German

UNPUBLISHED SOURCES

Joan Adler, Straus family historian, email to author, 3 December 1997.

Joan Adler, Straus Family Newsletter: *'Wholedamfam'*, February 1998.

Elias family letters. BE. Note: where letters are too numerous to list individually, I have grouped them together under the relevant archive.

Anne Frank's Baby Book. Archives of the Anne Frank-Fonds, Basel (AFF).

Frank family, letters. BE.

Herbert Frank's private papers. BE.

Margot Frank's Baby Book. AFF.

Otto Frank, letters. Archives of the Anne Frank Stichting, Amsterdam (AFS).

Otto Frank, letter, July 1918. Archives of the Lessing Gymnasium, Frankfurt.

Otto Frank, transcript of tape recording made for a school group, 1970s. AFS.

Otto Frank, interview transcripts of recorded discussion with Arthur Unger, New York, 1977. AFS.

Edith Gordon, email to author, June 2001.

Grossman, Jean Schick, 'The Story Within Her Story' (unpublished manuscript), 5 December 1954. AFS.

Dr Trude K. Holländer, letter to author, March 1997.

Hondius, Dienke, 'The Return'. Unpublished English translation of *Terugkeer: Antisemitisme in Nederland rond de bevrijding* (The Hague: SDU, 1990).

Landau town archives, and the pamphlets *Some Historical Facts About The House* and *Facts Relating To The Jews Of Landau*, available from the Frank-Loeb'sches House.

Sal de Liema, transcript of interview conducted by the Anne Frank Stichting. AFS.

Katja Olszewska, author interview, March 2001.

Milly Stanfield, 'A Talk: Anne and Otto Frank', 22 April 1990. AFS.

Milly Stanfield, letters. AFS.

Milly Stanfield, Memoirs. AFS.

Nathan Straus, letter, 19 April 1957. AFS.

PUBLISHED SOURCES

Anne Frank Stichting, *Anne Frank House: A Museum with a Story* (Amsterdam: Anne Frank Stichting, 1999).

Anne Frank Stichting, *Anne Frank Magazine 1999* (Amsterdam: Anne Frank Stichting, 1999).

Arnold, Hermann, 'Waren es Vorfahren von Anne Frank?', *Tribüne*, 1990.

Barnouw, David and Stroom, Gerrold van der (eds.), *The Diaries of Anne Frank: The Critical Edition* (London: Viking, 1989).

Barnouw, David and Stroom, Gerrold van der (eds.), *De Dagboeken van Anne Frank* (Amsterdam: Bert Bakker, 2001).

Birmingham, Stephen, *Our Crowd: The Great Jewish Families of New York* (New York: Dell Publishing, 1967).

Craig, Gordon A., *Germany 1866–1945* (Oxford: Oxford University Press, 1981).

Ferguson, Niall, *The Pity of War* (London: Penguin, 1998).

Frank, Anne, *Tales from the Secret Annexe* (London: Penguin, 1982).

Fussman, Carl, 'The Woman Who Would Have Saved Anne Frank', *Newsday*, 16 March 1995.

Gilbert, Martin, *The Holocaust: The Jewish Tragedy* (London: Harper Collins, 1987).

Goldhagen, Daniel Jonah, *Hitler's Willing Executioners: Ordinary Germans and the Holocaust* (London: Abacus, 1999).

Middlebrook, Martin and Mary, *The Somme Battlefields* (London: Viking, 1991).

Moynahan, Brian, *The British Century: A Photographic History of the Last Hundred Years* (London: Random House, 1997).

Muller, Melissa, *Anne Frank: The Biography* (New York: Henry Holt, 1998).

Pressler, Mirjam, *The Story of Anne Frank* (London: Macmillan, 1999).

Rürup, Reinhard, *Topography of Terror: Gestapo, SS and Reichssicherheitshauptamt on the 'Prinz-Albrecht-Terrain' A Documentation* (Berlin: Verlag Willmuth Arenhövel, 1989).

Sanchez, Leopold Diego, *Jean-Michel Frank* (Paris: Editions de Regard, 1980).

Schnabel, Ernst, *The Footsteps of Anne Frank* (London: Pan Books, 1976).

Steenmeijer, Anna G. and Frank, Otto (eds.), *A Tribute to Anne Frank* (New York: Doubleday, 1971).

Straus, R. Peter, article in *Moment*, December 1977.

Sulzbach, Herbert, *With The German Guns: Four Years on the Western Front* (London: Leo Cooper, 1998).

Wilson, Cara, *Love, Otto: The Legacy of Anne Frank* (Kansas: Andrews & McMeel, 1995).

Wolzogen, Wolf von, *Anne aus Frankfurt* (Frankfurt: Historical Museum, 1994).

Chapter 2: The Eyes of Our Persecutors

UNPUBLISHED SOURCES

Dossier(s) A. Ahlers. CABR.

Tonny Ahlers, letter, 20 December 1964. Photocopy received from Paul Willem van Maaren.

Tonny Ahlers, letter, 27 December 1963. Doc. I., K. J. Silberbauer. NIOD.

Tonny Ahlers, letter, 15 January 1964. Doc. I., K. J. Silberbauer. NIOD.

Report on Tonny Ahlers, 1964. Doc. I., K. J. Silberbauer. NIOD.

Ahlers's ex-wife, conversation with author, February 2001.

Report of a conversation with Mrs I. Baschwitz, 12 January 1981. NIOD.

Doc. I., K. Döring. NIOD.

Dossier K. Döring. CABR.

Elias family, letters. BE.

Frank family, letters. AFS.

Edith Frank, letter, 1937, in the exhibition *Anne Aus Frankfurt*, Anne Frank Youth Centre, Frankfurt, 1998.

Frank family, letters. BE.

Otto Frank, letter, 27 November 1945. Dossier(s) A. Ahlers. CABR.

Otto Frank, postcard, 1934, in the exhibition *Anne Aus Frankfurt*, Anne Frank Youth Centre, Frankfurt, 1998.

Otto Frank, interview transcripts, Unger. AFS.

Otto Frank, transcript of tape recording made for a school group, 1970s. AFS.

Report of two conversations with J. A. Gies and M. Gies-Santrouschitz, 19 and 27 February 1985. NIOD.

Hilde Goldberg, author interviews, May and June 2001.

Grossman, Jean Schick, 'The Story Within Her Story'. AFS.

Hondius, Dienke, 'The Return'.

Dossier J. M. Jansen. CABR.

Laureen Nussbaum, author interview, May 2001.

Opekta file. NBI archive, Rijksarchief, Den Haag.

Opekta/Pectacon Delivery Book, 1940. AFS.

Hanneli Pick-Goslar, author interview, June 2001.

Doc. I., J. van Poppel. NIOD.

Dossier J. van Poppel. CABR.

Press cuttings J. van Poppel. NIOD.

Doc. I., E. Rühl. NIOD.

Dossier E. Rühl. CABR.

Milly Stanfield, 'A Talk: Anne and Otto Frank', 22 April 1990. AFS.

Lotte Thyes, author interview, March 1998.

Report of a conversation with Bep van Wijk-Voskuijl, 25 February 1981. NIOD.

PUBLISHED SOURCES

Press cuttings, AFS.

Anne Frank Stichting, *Anne Frank House: A Museum with a Story*.

Anne Frank Stichting, *Anne Frank Magazine 2000* (Amsterdam: Anne Frank Stichting, 2000).

Barnouw and Stroom, van der (eds.), *Diaries*.

Brasz, Chaya, *Removing the Yellow Badge: The Struggle for a Jewish Community in the Post-War Netherlands* (Jerusalem: Institute for Research on Dutch Jewry, 1996).

Duke, Juliane, 'Anne Frank Remembered', the *New York Times*, 11 June 1989.

Fussman, 'The Woman Who', *Newsday*.

Gies, Miep and Gold, Alison Leslie, *Anne Frank Remembered* (New York: Bantam Press, 1987).

Grobman, Alex (ed.), *Anne Frank in Historical Perspective: A Teaching Guide* (Los Angeles: Martyrs Memorial and Museum of the Holocaust, 1995).

Last, Dick van Galen and Wolfswinkel, Rolf, *Anne Frank and After: Dutch Holocaust Literature in Historical Perspective* (Amsterdam: Amsterdam University Press, 1996).

'The Living Legacy of Anne Frank,' *Journal*, September 1967.

Miller, Judith, *One by One by One: Facing the Holocaust* (New York: Simon & Schuster, 1990).

Moore, Bob, *Victims and Survivors: The Nazi Persecution of the Jews in the Netherlands 1940–1945* (London: Arnold, 1997).

Muller, *Anne Frank*.

Sanchez, *Jean-Michel Frank*.

Schnabel, *Footsteps*.

Straus, *Moment*.

Wolzogen, *Anne aus Frankfurt*.

Chapter 3: Fac et Spera

UNPUBLISHED SOURCES

Dossier(s) A. Ahlers. CABR.

Tonny Ahlers, letter, 20 December 1964. Photocopy received from Paul Willem van Maaren.

Tonny Ahlers, letter, 27 December 1963. Doc. I., K. J. Silberbauer. NIOD.

Tonny Ahlers, letter, 15 January 1964. Doc. I., K. J. Silberbauer. NIOD.

Report on Tonny Ahlers, 1964. Doc. I., K. J. Silberbauer. NIOD.

Doc. I., K. Döring. NIOD.

Dossier K. Döring. CABR.

Elias family, letters. BE.

Frank family, letters. BE.

Otto Frank, memoir. BE.

Page of testimony written by Miep Gies. AFS.

Doc. I., G. Gringhuis. NIOD.

Dossier G. Gringhuis. CABR.

Dossier W. Grootendorst. CABR.

Grossman, 'The Story Within Her Story'.

Hondius, Dienke, 'The Return'.

Victor Kugler, letter, 4 February 1964. BE.

Doc. I., M. Kuiper. NIOD.

Dossier M. Kuiper. CABR.

Doc. I., W. G. van Maaren. NIOD.

Dossier W. G. van Maaren. CABR.

Father John Neiman, author interview, April 2001.

Laureen Nussbaum, author interview, May 2001.

Dossier Opekta/Pectacon. NIOD.

Doc. I., J. van Poppel. NIOD.

Dossier J. van Poppel. CABR.

Doc. I., H. Rouwendaal. NIOD.

Dossier H. Rouwendaal. CABR.

Doc. I., E. Rühl. NIOD.

Dossier E. Rühl. CABR.

Doc. I., K. J. Silberbauer. NIOD.

Cor Suijk, author interview, April 2001.

Dossier F. C. Viebahn. CABR.

Doc. I., K. O. M. Wolters. NIOD.

PUBLISHED SOURCES

Press cuttings, AFS.

Anissimov, Myriam, *Primo Levi: Tragedy of an Optimist* (New York: Overlook Press, 2000).

Anne Frank Stichting, *Anne Frank House: A Museum with a Story*.

Barnouw and Stroom, van der (eds.), *Diaries*.

Colijn, G. Jan and Littell, Marcia S. (eds.), *The Netherlands and Nazi Genocide* (New York: Edwin Mellen Press, 1992).

Gies and Gold, *Anne Frank Remembered*.

Goldhagen, *Hitler's Willing Executioners*.

Grobman (ed.), *Anne Frank in Historical Perspective*.

Press cuttings, M. Kuiper. NIOD.

Last, van Galen and Wolfswinkel, *Anne Frank and After*.

Maarsen, Jacqueline van, *My Friend Anne Frank* (New York: Vantage Press, 1996).

Miller, *One by One by One*.

Moore, *Victims and Survivors*.

Muller, *Anne Frank*.

Press cuttings J. van Poppel. NIOD.

Presser, *Ashes in the Wind*.

Pressler, *The Story of Anne Frank*.

Press cuttings, H. Rouwendaal. NIOD.

Press cuttings, E. Rühl. NIOD.

Rürup, *Topography of Terror*.
Schnabel, *Footsteps*.
Press cuttings, F. C. Viebahn. NIOD.

Chapter 4: Unforgettable Marks on My Soul

UNPUBLISHED SOURCES

Otto Frank, French television interview, 1960s. Buddy Elias has a copy of the interview on video, but I have been unable to find further details of this broadcast.

Otto Frank, interview transcripts of recorded discussion with Arthur Unger, New York, 1977. AFS.

Frank family, letters. AFS.

Frank family, letters. BE.

Otto Frank, memoir. BE.

Otto Frank, liberation diary 1945. AFS.

Otto Frank, transcript of tape recording made for a school group, 1970s. AFS.

Report of two conversations with J. A. Gies and M. Gies-Santrouschitz in Amsterdam on 19 and 27 February 1985. NIOD.

Grossman, 'The Story Within Her Story'.

Declaration of Dr S. M. Kropveld in dossier *Westerbork–Auschwitz, 3 September 1944*. NIOD.

Sal de Liema, transcript of interview conducted by the Anne Frank Stichting. AFS.

Rose de Liema, unpublished memoir, 'So You Will Remember'. AFS.

Judith Salomon, author interview, May 2001.

Franzi Spronz, author interview, May 2001.

Joseph Spronz, unpublished manuscript, 'Auschwitz Memoirs'. AFS.

Milly Stanfield, letter, undated. AFS.

PUBLISHED SOURCES

Press cuttings, AFS.

Anissimov, *Primo Levi*.

Anne Frank Stichting, *Anne Frank House: A Museum with a Story*.

Blair, Jon, *Anne Frank Remembered*, documentary (BBC2, 6 May 1995).

Cohn, Vera, *The Anti-Defamation League Bulletin: The Day I Met Anne Frank*, undated.

Czech, Danuta, *Auschwitz Chronicle 1939–1945* (New York: Henry Holt, 1990).

Frank, Otto, 'Anne Frank Would Have Been Fifty This Year', *Life*, March 1979.

Friedrich, Otto, *The Kingdom of Auschwitz* (London: Penguin, 1994).

Gilbert, Martin, *Auschwitz and the Allies* (London: Michael Joseph, 1981).

Gilbert, Martin, *Holocaust Journey: Travelling in Search of the Past* (London: Orion, 1997).

Gilbert, *The Holocaust*.

Gutman, Yisrael and Berenbaum, Michael, *Anatomy of Auschwitz Death Camp* (Indiana: Indiana University Press, 1994).

Last, van Galen and Wolfswinkel, *Anne Frank and After*.

Levi, Primo, *If This Is A Man: The Truce* (London: Abacus Books, 1979).

Lindwer, Willy, *The Last Seven Months of Anne Frank* (New York: Pantheon Books, 1991).

Moore, *Victims and Survivors*.

Presser, *Ashes in the Wind*.

Press leaflet for the film *Ein Tagebuch für Anne Frank* (Berlin: VEB Progess Film-Vertrieb, 1959).

Rürup, *Topography of Terror*.

Schloss, Eva and Kent, Evelyn Julia, *Eva's Story* (London: W. H. Allen, 1988).

Schnabel, *Footsteps*.

Shapiro, Eda, 'The Reminiscences of Victor Kugler, the "Mr Kraler" of Anne Frank's Diary', *Yad Vashem Studies*, XIII (Jerusalem: Yad Vashem, 1979).

Todorov, Tzvetan, *Facing The Extreme: Moral Life in the Concentration Camps* (London: Phoenix, 2000).

Wasserstein, Bernard, *Vanishing Diaspora: The Jews in Europe since 1945* (London: Penguin, 1996).

Watertown Daily Times: Holocaust Survivors Recall Their Hell On Earth, 5 February 1995.

Welt am Sonntag: Anne Frank's Vater: Ich will Versohnung, 4 February 1979.

Chapter 5: Everything is Like a Strange Dream

UNPUBLISHED SOURCES

Dossier(s) A. Ahlers. CABR.

Tonny Ahlers, letter, 20 December 1964. Photocopy received from Paul Willem van Maaren.

Tonny Ahlers, letter, 27 December 1963. Doc. I., K. J. Silberbauer. NIOD.

Tonny Ahlers, letter, 15 January 1964. Doc. I., K. J. Silberbauer. NIOD.

Report on Tonny Ahlers, 1964. Doc. I., K. J. Silberbauer. NIOD.

Elias family, letters. BE.

Frank family, letters. AFS.

Frank family, letters. AFS.

Otto Frank, Engagements Diary 1945. AFS.

Otto Frank, interview transcripts, Unger. AFS.

Otto Frank, letter, 27 November 1945. Dossier(s) A. Ahlers. CABR.

Otto Frank, liberation diary, 1945. AFS.

Otto Frank, memoir. BE.

Jack Furth, author interview, April 2001.

Report of a conversation with Miep and Jan Gies, 18 February 1981. NIOD.

Hilde Goldberg, author interview, May 2001.

Doc. I., G. Gringhuis. NIOD.

Dossier G. Gringhuis. CABR.

Dossier W. Grootendorst. CABR.

Holländer family, letters. BE.

Hondius, 'The Return'.

Sal de Liema, letter, 25 July 1945. BE.

Laureen Nussbaum, author interview, May 2001.

Polish Red Cross, declaration regarding Otto Frank's return to the Netherlands, 1945. AFS.

Doc. I., J. van Poppel. NIOD.

Dossier J. van Poppel. CABR.

Press cuttings J. van Poppel. NIOD.

Judith Salomon, author interview, May 2001.

Doc. I., K. J. Silberbauer. NIOD.

Rabbi David Soetendorp, author interview, June 2001.

Milly Stanfield, 'A Talk: Anne and Otto Frank', 22 April 1990. AFS.

PUBLISHED SOURCES

Anissimov, *Primo Levi*.

Anne Frank Stichting, *Anne Frank Magazine 1999*.

Brasz, *Removing the Yellow Badge*.

Enzer, Hyman A. and Solotaroff-Enzer, Sandra (eds.), *Anne Frank: Reflections on her Life and Legacy* (Illinois: University of Illinois Press, 2000).

Fishman, Joel, 'The Jewish Community in the Post-War Netherlands 1944–1975', *Midstream* XXII (1976).

Frank, 'Anne Frank', *Life*.

Gies and Gold, *Anne Frank Remembered*.

Gilbert, *The Holocaust*.

Grobman (ed.), *Anne Frank in Historical Perspective*.

Last, van Galen and Wolfswinkel, *Anne Frank and After*.

Lindwer, Willy, *The Last Seven Months of Anne Frank*.

Maarsen, van, *My Friend*.

Moore, *Victims and Survivors*.

Schnabel, *Footsteps*.

Schloss and Kent, *Eva's Story*.
Wasserstein, *Vanishing Diaspora*.
Wilson, *Love, Otto*.

Chapter 6: This at Least Has Survived

UNPUBLISHED SOURCES

Dossier(s) A. Ahlers. CABR.

Tonny Ahlers, letter, 20 December 1964. Photocopy received from Paul Willem van Maaren.

Tonny Ahlers, letter, 27 December 1963. Doc. I., K. J. Silberbauer. NIOD.

Tonny Ahlers, letter, 15 January 1964. Doc. I., K. J. Silberbauer. NIOD.

Report on Tonny Ahlers, 1964. Doc. I., K. J. Silberbauer. NIOD.

Report of a conversation with Werner Cahn, 12 March 1981. NIOD.

Report of a conversation with Ab Cauvern, 23 January 1981. NIOD.

Doc. I., K. Döring. NIOD.

Dossier K. Döring. CABR.

Elias family, letters. BE.

Barbara Epstein (née Zimmerman), author interview, June 2001.

Frank family, letters. AFS.

Frank family, letters. BE.

Otto Frank, Engagements Diary 1945. AFS.

Otto Frank, Engagements Diary 1947. AFS.

Otto Frank, interview transcripts, Unger. AFS.

Otto Frank, interview transcript. Westinghouse Broadcasting Company Inc, USA, 16 February 1960. AFS.

Otto Frank, letter, 6 January 1947. Private collection of Gertrud Trenz.

Otto Frank, memoir. BE.

Otto Frank, undated document, headed 'Comments'. AFS.

Otto Frank, undated document, headed 'Remarks Regarding Warrant Sent to Me with your Letter of 19 March 1956'. AFS.

Jetteke Frijda, author interview, March 1998.

Miep Gies, letter, 16 July 1949. AFS.

Hilde Goldberg, author interview, May 2001.

Doc. I., G. Gringhuis. NIOD.

Dossier G. Gringhuis. CABR.

Dossier W. Grootendorst. CABR.

Report of a conversation with Rabbi Hammelburg, 23 February 1981. NIOD.

Hondius, 'The Return'.

Dola de Jong, letter to author, March 2001.

David Kessler, letter, 25 March 1951. AFS.

Victor Kugler, letter, 4 February 1958. BE.

Doc. I., M. Kuiper. NIOD.

Dossier M. Kuiper. CABR.

Press cuttings, M. Kuiper. NIOD.

Meyer Levin, letters. AFS.

Doc. I., W. G. van Maaren. NIOD.

Dossier W. G. van Maaren. CABR.

Jacqueline van Maarsen, author interview, February 1998.

Report of a conversation with Mrs R. E. Mengelberg-Draber, 19 February 1981. NIOD.

Barbara Mooyart-Doubleday, author interview, April 2001.

Father John Neiman, author interview, April 2001.

Laureen Nussbaum, author interview, May 2001.

Opekta file. NBI archive, Rijksarchief, Den Haag.

Opekta dossier. NIOD.

Doc. I., J. van Poppel. NIOD.

Dossier J. van Poppel. CABR.

Press cuttings J. van Poppel. NIOD.

Frank Price, letters. AFS.

Reviews of *Anne Frank: The Diary of a Young Girl,* press cuttings. Private collection of Barbara Mooyart-Doubleday.

Doc. I., H. Rouwendaal. NIOD.

Dossier H. Rouwendaal. CABR.

Doc. I., E. Rühl. NIOD.

Dossier E. Rühl. CABR.

Report of a conversation with Annie Romein-Verschoor, undated. NIOD. Eva Schloss, author interview, January and May 1998.

Doc. I., K. J. Silberbauer. NIOD.

Hello Silberberg, letter, July 1947. AFS.

Rabbi David Soetendorp, author interview, June 2001.

Milly Stanfield, 'A Talk: Anne and Otto Frank', 22 April 1990. AFS.

Nathan Straus, letters. AFS.

Nathan Straus, letters. BE.

Gerrold van der Stroom, *Anne Frank and her Diaries*, paper delivered at the Institute of Jewish Studies, University College, London, June 1997.

Barry Sullivan, letters. Private collection of Barbara Mooyart-Doubleday.

Barbara Zimmerman, letters. AFS.

Paul Zsolnay, letter, 6 October 1947. AFS.

PUBLISHED SOURCES

Press cuttings, AFS.

Anne Frank Stichting, *Anne Frank Magazine 2000*.

Barnouw and Stroom, van der (eds.), *Diaries*.

Evans, Martin and Lunn, Kenneth (eds.), *War and Memory in the Twentieth Century* (London: Berg Publishers, 1997).

Farrell, E. C., 'Postscript to a Diary', *Global Magazine*, 1965.

Flanner, Janet, 'Letter from Paris', *New Yorker*, 11 November 1950.

Frank, Anne, *Het Achterhuis* (Amsterdam: Contact, 1947).

Frank, 'Anne Frank', *Life*.

Gies and Gold, *Anne Frank Remembered*.

Gold, Alison Leslie, *Memories of Anne Frank: Reflections of a Childhood Friend* (New York: Scholastic Press, 1997).

Graver, Lawrence, *An Obsession with Anne Frank: Meyer Levin and the Diary* (California: University of California Press, 1995).

Last, van Galen and Wolfswinkel, *Anne Frank and After*.

Levin, Meyer, 'The Restricted Market', *Congress Weekly*, 13 November 1950.

Levin, Meyer, 'The Girl Behind The Secret Door', *New York Times Book Review*, 15 June 1952.

Levin, Meyer, 'Anne Frank: The Diary of a Young Girl', *Congress Weekly*, June 1952.

Maarsen, van, *My Friend*.

Melnick, Ralph, *The Stolen Legacy of Anne Frank: Meyer Levin, Lillian Hellman and the Staging of the Diary* (Connecticut: Yale University Press, 1997).

Miller, *One by One by One*.

Ozick, Cynthia, 'Who Owns Anne Frank?' *New Yorker*, 6 October 1997.

Romein, Jan, 'A Child's Voice', *Het Parool*, 3 April 1945.

Schloss and Kent, *Eva's Story*.

Stocks, Mary, 'The Secret Annexe', *Manchester Guardian*, 28 April 1952.

Wasserstein, *Vanishing Diaspora*.

Wistrich, Robert S., *Anti-Semitism: The Longest Hatred* (London: Methuen, 1991).

Chapter 7: The Question of a Jewish or Non-Jewish Writer

UNPUBLISHED SOURCES

Kermit Bloomgarden, letter, 1 August 1952. AFS.

Cheryl Crawford, letter, 10 September 1952. AFS.

Buddy Elias, author interview, April 2001.

Barbara Epstein, author interview, June 2001.

Calvin L. Fox, letter, 1 November 1955. AFS.

Otto Frank, interview transcripts, Unger. AFS.

Frank family, letters. AFS.

Frank family, letters. BE.

Otto Frank, speech to the US Anne Frank Center, 1959.

Otto Frank, telegram, 18 June 1952. AFS.

Otto Frank, undated document. AFS.

Miep Gies, letter, 10 December 1956. AFS.

Hilde Goldberg, author interview, June 2001.

Ruth Goldberg, letter, 1984. AFS.

Garson Kanin, letter, 3 July 1956. AFS.

David Kessler, letter, 17 June 1953. AFS.

David Kessler, letter, 17 September 1953. AFS.

Meyer Levin, letter, 22 December 1952. AFS.

Joseph Marks, letter, 8 July 1952. AFS.

Lillian Marks, letter to author, May 2001.

Carson McCullers, undated letter. AFS.

Myer Mermin, letter, 28 October 1953. AFS.

Myer Mermin, letter, 11 December 1953. AFS.

Barbara Mooyart-Doubleday, letter, 3 October 1955. AFS.

Father John Neiman, author interview, May 2001.

Laureen Nussbaum, author interview, May 2001.

Frank Price, letter, 19 January 1954. AFS.

Reeves, letter, 19 January 1953. AFS.

Tony van Renterghem, author interview, June 2001.

Joseph Schildkraut, letter, 22 March 1955. AFS.

Eva Schloss, author interview, April 2001.

Zvi Schloss, author interview, April 2001.

Milly Stanfield, letter, undated. AFS.

Helen Straus, letter, 15 January 1953. AFS.

Nathan Straus, letter, 15 January 1953. AFS.

Barry Sullivan, letter, 2 April 1953. AFS.

Tereska Torres, letters. AFS.

Barbara Zimmerman, letters. AFS.

PUBLISHED SOURCES

Press cuttings, AFS.

'Anne Frank's Secret Annexe Awaits The Wrecker's Ball', *Het Vrij Volk*, 23
    November 1955.

Anne Frank Stichting, *Anne Frank House: A Museum with a Story*.

Ariel, 'Testament of Youth', *Huddersfield Weekly Examiner*, October 1954.

Ballif, Algene, *Commentary,* November 1955.

Barnouw and Stroom, van der (eds.), *Diaries.*

Baron, Alexander, *The Jewish Chronicle,* 15 October 1954.

Bundy, June, 'Anne Frank: The Diary of a Young Girl', *Billboard,* 27 September 1952.

Chapman, John, 'Anne Frank Wins Prize', *Sunday News,* 13 May 1956.

Cole, Tim, *Images of the Holocaust: The Myth of the 'Shoah Business'* (London: Gerald Duckworth & Co Ltd, 1999).

Donahue, William Collins and McIsaac, Peter M. (eds.), *German Politics and Society,* (California: Center for German Studies at the University of California Press, 1995), Volume 13, Number 3, Issue 36.

Doneson, Judith E., *The Holocaust in American Film* (New York: The Jewish Publication Society, 1987).

Evans and Lunn, *War and Memory.*

Frank, 'Anne Frank', *Life.*

Frank, Otto, 'Has Germany Forgotten Anne Frank?', *Coronet,* February 1960.

Graver, *An Obsession.*

Hayes, Peter (ed.), *Lessons & Legacies: The Meaning of the Holocaust in a Changing World* (Northwestern University Press, 1991).

Kolb, Bernard, 'Diary Footnotes', *New York Times,* 2 October 1955.

Melnick, *The Stolen Legacy.*

Pepper, William, 'Drama of "Diary" is Nonsectarian', *New York World Telegram and Sun,* January 1956.

St George, Andrew, 'The Diary That Shook A Nation', *Pageant,* July 1958.

Schach, William, 'Diary Into Drama', *Midstream,* June 1956.

Schloss and Kent, *Eva's Story.*

Spetter, Ies, 'Onderduik Pret Broadway', *Vrij Nederland,* 5 November 1955.

Strasberg, Susan, *Bittersweet* (New York: Signet, 1980).

Wolff, Margo H., 'Anne Frank Lives On', *Hadassah Newsletter,* May 1958.

Chapter 8: I Have No Scars Left

UNPUBLISHED SOURCES

Dossier(s) A. Ahlers. CABR.

Tonny Ahlers, letter, 20 December 1964. Photocopy received from Paul Willem van Maaren.

Tonny Ahlers, letter, 27 December 1963. Doc. I., K. J. Silberbauer. NIOD.

Tonny Ahlers, letter, 15 January 1964. Doc. I., K. J. Silberbauer. NIOD.

Report on Tonny Ahlers, 1964. Doc. I., K. J. Silberbauer. NIOD.

Cassette recording of A Memorial Tribute to Otto Frank, October 1980, Anne Frank Center, USA. AFS.

'Peter Dawson', letter, 19 January 1959. BE.

Document: 'Financial Information Regarding The International Anne Frank Youth Centre', 1959. AFS.

Barbara Epstein, author interview, June 2001.

Mel Ferrer, letter, 2 August 1957. BE.

Frank family, letters. AFS.

Frank family, letters. BE.

Fritzi Frank, 'My Life with Otto Frank', memoir, 1980. BE.

Otto Frank, interview transcripts, Unger. AFS.

Miep Gies, letter, 17 April 1960. AFS.

Ruth Goldberg, letter, 1984. AFS.

Frances Goodrich and Albert Hackett, letters. AFS.

Edith Gordon, email to author, June 2001.

Dr Trude K. Holländer, letter to author, 25 March 1998.

Dola de Jong, letter to author, March 2001.

Johannes Kleiman, letter, 18 June 1958. AFS.

Bee Klug, author interview, April 2001.

Irene Lewis, letter, 23 December 1974. AFS.

Doc. I., W. G. van Maaren. NIOD.

Dossier W. G. van Maaren. CABR.

Myer Mermin, letter, 19 January 1959. AFS.

Myer Mermin, list, 29 December 1964. AFS.

Father John Neiman, author interview, April 2001.

Lotte Pfeffer, document, 1957. AFS.

Lotte Pfeffer, letter, 5 September 1956. AFS.

Hanneli Pick-Goslar, author interview, June 2001.

Doc. I., J. van Poppel. NIOD.

Dossier J. van Poppel. CABR.

Press cuttings J. van Poppel. NIOD.

Eleanor Roosevelt, letter, 2 April 1957. AFS.

Eleanor Roosevelt, letter, 22 April 1957. AFS.

Leah Salisbury, letter, 28 January 1964. AFS.

Leah Salisbury, letter, 4 December 1974. AFS.

Henk Salomon, author interview, June 2001.

Judith Salomon, author interview, June 2001.

Eva Schloss, author interview, April 2001.

Zvi Schloss, author interview, April 2001.

Marguerite Scialtiel, letter, 26 August 1957. AFS.

Eda Shapiro, letter, 7 May 1974. AFS.

Doc. I., K. J. Silberbauer. NIOD.

Silberbauer's mother-in-law, letter, 4 December 1963. AFS.

Rabbi David Soetendorp, author interview, June 2001.

Franzi Spronz, author interview, May 2001.

Milly Stanfield, 'A Talk: Anne and Otto Frank', 22 April 1990. AFS.

Anneke Steenmeijer, author interview, June 2001.

Nathan Straus, letter, 19 April 1957. AFS.

Cor Suijk, letter to author, March 2001.

Gertrud Trenz, letter to author, January 2001.

Bep van Wijk-Voskuijl, letter, 1957. AFS.

PUBLISHED SOURCES

Press cuttings, AFS.

Anne Frank Stichting, *Anne Frank Magazine 1998*.

Anne Frank Stichting, *Anne Frank Magazine 1999*.

Anne Frank Stichting, *Anne Frank Magazine 2000*.

Anne Frank Stichting, *The Anne Frank House*, leaflet, 1999.

Anne Frank Stichting, *Anne Frank House: A Museum with a Story*.

Barnouw and Stroom, van der (eds.), *Diaries*.

Donahue and McIsaac (eds.), *German Politics and Society*.

Doneson, *The Holocaust in American Film*.

Enzer and Solotaroff-Enzer (eds.), *Anne Frank: Reflections*.

Evans and Lunn, *War and Memory*.

Farrell, 'Postscript', *Global*.

Frank, 'Has Germany?', *Coronet*.

Graver, *An Obsession*.

Grobman (ed.), *Anne Frank in Historical Perspective*.

Levin, Meyer, 'The Suppressed Anne Frank', *Jewish Week*, 31 August 1980.

Majdalany, 'Anne Frank Was Never Like This', *Daily Mail*, 5 June 1959.

Melnick, *The Stolen Legacy*.

Muller, *Anne Frank*.

New York Times Book Review, 28 September 1997.

'Otto Frank, Father of Anne, Dead at 91', *New York Times*, 21 August 1980.

Paris, Barry, *Audrey Hepburn* (London: Orion Books, 1996).

Press leaflet, *Ein Tagebuch*.

Pressler, *The Story of Anne Frank*.

Steenmeijer and Frank, *A Tribute*.

St George, 'The Diary', *Pageant*.

Strang, Joanne, 'Stevens Relives Anne Frank's Story', *New York Times Magazine*, 3 August 1958.

Straus, *Moment*.

Visser, Anneke, 'Discovery of Letters Written by Man who Hid in Anne Frank's Secret Annexe', *NRC Handlesblad*, 7 November 1987.

Vuur, Willem, 'Anne Frank House in Money Trouble', *Herald Tribune*, 1 April 1971.

Waggoner, Walter H., 'New Yorker Aids Dutch Students', *New York Times*, 26 July 1957.

Wasserstein, *Vanishing Diaspora*.

Wilson, *Love, Otto*.

Windsor, John, 'Duty of Dr Frank', *Guardian*, 15 June 1971.

Epilogue

UNPUBLISHED SOURCES

Ahlers's ex-wife, conversation with author, February 2001.

Bevolkingsregister, Amsterdam.

Barbara Epstein, author interview, June 2001.

Frank family, letters. AFS.

Otto Frank, interview transcripts, Unger. AFS.

Otto Frank, letter, 20 July 1971. AFS.

Barbara Hauptman, essay, 'A Visit to Amsterdam', August 1971. AFS.

Father John Neiman, author interview, May 2001.

Laureen Nussbaum, author interview, May 2001.

Judith Salomon, author interview, June 2001.

Eva Schloss, author interview, April 2001.

Zvi Schloss, author interview, April 2001.

Milly Stanfield, letter, August 1992. AFS.

Cor Suijk, author interview, April 2001.

PUBLISHED SOURCES

Anne Frank Stichting, *Anne Frank Magazine 1998*.

Barnouw and Stroom, van der (eds.), *Diaries*.

Buruma, Ian, 'Anne Frank's Afterlife', *New York Review of Books*, Vol XLV, Number 3, 19 February 1998.

Cole, Tim, *Images of the Holocaust: The Myth of the 'Shoah Business'*.

Colijn, G. Jan and Littell, Marcia S. (eds.), *The Netherlands and Nazi Genocide*.

Kramer, Mimi, 'Spotlight: Encore, Anne Frank', *Vanity Fair*, December 1997.

Last, van Galen and Wolfswinkel, *Anne Frank and After*.

Ozick, 'Who Owns?', *New Yorker*.

Rosenfeld, Alvin H., 'The Americanization of the Holocaust' in *Commentary*, June 1995.

Stern, 21 May 1982.

Wasserstein, *Vanishing Diaspora*.

'Who Killed Anne Frank?' *Hadassah Magazine*, No 7, March 1965.

Wilson, *Love, Otto*.

Bibliography

Books

Anissimov, Myriam, *Primo Levi: Tragedy of an Optimist* (New York: Overlook Press, 2000).

Anne Frank Stichting, *Anne Frank House: A Museum with a Story* (Amsterdam: Anne Frank Stichting, 1999).

Anne Frank Stichting, *Anne Frank 1929–1945* (Heidelberg: Lambert Schneider, 1979).

Barnouw, David and Stroom, Gerrold van der (eds.), *The Diaries of Anne Frank: The Critical Edition* (London: Viking, 1989).

Barnouw, David and Stroom, Gerrold van der (eds.), *De Dagboeken van Anne Frank* (Amsterdam: Bert Bakker, 2001).

Birmingham, Stephen, *Our Crowd: The Great Jewish Families of New York* (New York: Dell Publishing, 1967).

Borowski, Tadeusz, *This Way for the Gas, Ladies and Gentlemen* (London: Penguin, 1983).

Brasz, Chaya, *Removing the Yellow Badge: The Struggle for a Jewish Community in the Post-War Netherlands* (Jerusalem: Institute for Research on Dutch Jewry, 1996).

Cole, Tim, *Images of the Holocaust: The Myth of the 'Shoah Business'* (London: Gerald Duckworth & Co Ltd, 1999).

Colijn, G. Jan and Littell, Marcia S. (eds.), *The Netherlands and Nazi Genocide.* Chapter: Nanda van der Zee, 'The Recurrent Myth of "Dutch Heroism" in the Second World War and Anne Frank as a Symbol' (New York: Edwin Mellen Press, 1992).

Craig, Gordon A., *Germany 1866–1945* (Oxford: Oxford University Press, 1981).

Czech, Danuta, *Auschwitz Chronicle 1939–1945* (New York: Henry Holt, 1990).

Dawidowicz, Lucy S., *The War Against the Jews 1933–1945* (London: Penguin Books, 1987).

Donahue, William Collins and McIsaac, Peter M. (eds.), *German Politics and Society.* Chapter: Alex Sagan, 'An Optimistic Icon: Anne Frank's Canonization in Post-war Culture' (California: Center for German Studies at the University of California Press, 1995), Volume 13, Number 3, Issue 36.

Doneson, Judith E., *The Holocaust in American Film* (New York: Jewish Publication Society, 1987).

Elon, Amos, *Founder: Meyer Amschel Rothschild and his Time* (London: Harper Collins, 1996).

Enzer, Hyman A. and Solotaroff-Enzer, Sandra (eds.), *Anne Frank: Reflections on her Life and Legacy*. Chapters: Bruno Bettelheim, 'The Ignored Lesson of Anne Frank' and Lin Jaldati, 'Bergen Belsen' (Illinois: University of Illinois Press, 2000).

Evans, Martin and Lunn, Kenneth (eds.), *War and Memory in the Twentieth Century*. Chapter: Tony Kushner, 'I Want to go on Living after my Death: The Memory of Anne Frank' (London: Berg Publishers, 1997).

Ferguson, Niall, *The Pity of War* (London: Penguin, 1998).

Fogelman, Eva, *Conscience and Courage: Rescuers of Jews During the Holocaust* (London: Cassel, 1995).

Frank, Anne, *Tales from the Secret Annexe* (London: Penguin, 1982).

Friedrich, Otto, *The Kingdom of Auschwitz* (London: Penguin, 1994).

Gies, Miep and Gold, Alison Leslie, *Anne Frank Remembered* (New York: Bantam Press, 1987).

Gilbert, Martin, *Auschwitz and the Allies* (London: Michael Joseph, 1991).

Gilbert, Martin, *Holocaust Journey: Travelling in Search of the Past* (London: Orion Publishing Group, 1997).

Gilbert, Martin, *The Holocaust: The Jewish Tragedy* (London: Harper Collins, 1987).

Gill, Anton, *The Journey Back from Hell: Conversations with Concentration Camp Survivors* (London: Grafton Books, 1988).

Gold, Alison Leslie, *Memories of Anne Frank: Reflections on a Childhood Friend* (New York: Scholastic Press, 1997).

Goldhagen, Daniel Jonah, *Hitler's Willing Executioners: Ordinary Germans and the Holocaust* (London: Abacus, 1999).

Goodrich, Frances and Hackett, Albert, *The Diary of Anne Frank* (London: Blackie & Son, 1970).

Graver, Lawrence, *An Obsession with Anne Frank: Meyer Levin and the Diary* (California: University of California Press Ltd, 1995).

Grobman, Alex (ed.), *Anne Frank in Historical Perspective: A Teaching Guide*. Chapters: Dienke Hondius, 'A New Perspective on Helpers of Jews during the Holocaust: The Case of Miep and Jan Gies', Elma Verhey, 'Anne Frank's World' and Elma Verhey, 'Anne Frank and the Dutch Myth' (Los Angeles: Martyrs Memorial and Museum of the Holocaust, 1995).

Gutman, Yisrael and Berenbaum, Michael, *Anatomy of Auschwitz Death Camp* (Indiana: Indiana University Press, 1994).

Hayes, Peter (ed.), *Lessons & Legacies: The Meaning of the Holocaust in a Changing World*. Chapter: Alvin H. Rosenfeld, 'Popularization and Memory: The Case of Anne Frank' (Northwestern University Press, 1991).

Hellwig, Joachim and Deicke, Gunther, *Ein Tagebuch für Anne Frank* (Berlin: Verlag der Nation, 1959).

Hillesum, Etty, *Letters from Westerbork* (London: Jonathan Cape, 1986).

Hondius, Dienke, *Terugkeer: Antisemitisme in Nederland rond de bevrijding* (The Hague: SDU, 1990).

Jong, Louis de and Schema, Simon, *The Netherlands and Nazi Germany* (Connecticut: Harvard University Press, 1990).

Kedward, H. R., *Resistance in Vichy France* (Oxford: Oxford University Press, 1978).

Kolb, Eberhard, *Bergen-Belsen from 1943–1945* (Gottingen: Sammlung Vandenhoeck, 1988).

Last, Dick van Galen and Wolfswinkel, Rolf, *Anne Frank and After: Dutch Holocaust Literature in Historical Perspective* (Amsterdam: Amsterdam University Press, 1996).

Levi, Primo, *If This Is A Man: The Truce* (London: Abacus Books, 1979).

Levin, Meyer, *The Obsession* (New York: Simon & Schuster, 1973).

Lindwer, Willy, *The Last Seven Months of Anne Frank* (New York: Pantheon, 1991).

Lipstadt, Deborah, *Denying the Holocaust: The Growing Assault on Truth and Memory* (New York: Free Press, 1993).

Maarsen, Jacqueline van, *My Friend Anne Frank* (New York: Vantage Press, 1996).

Marrus, Michael R., *The Holocaust in History* (London: Penguin Books, 1989).

Melnick, Ralph, *The Stolen Legacy of Anne Frank: Meyer Levin, Lillian Hellman and the Staging of the Diary* (Connecticut: Yale University Press, 1997).

Middlebrook, Martin and Mary, *The Somme Battlefields* (London: Viking, 1991).

Miller, Judith, *One by One by One: Facing the Holocaust* (New York: Simon & Schuster, 1990).

Moore, Bob, *Victims and Survivors: The Nazi Persecution of the Jews in the Netherlands 1940–1945* (London: Arnold, 1997).

Moynahan, Brian, *The British Century: A Photographic History of the Last Hundred Years* (London: Random House, 1997).

Muller, Melissa, *Anne Frank: The Biography* (New York: Henry Holt, 1998).

Paris, Barry, *Audrey Hepburn* (London: Orion Books, 1996).

Presser, Jacob, *Ashes in the Wind: The Destruction of Dutch Jewry* (London: Souvenir Press, 1968).

Pressler, Mirjam, *The Story of Anne Frank* (London: Macmillan, 1999).

Rittner, Carol (ed.), *Anne Frank in the World: Essays and Reflections* (New York: M. E. Sharpe, 1997).

Rürup, Reinhard, *Topography of Terror: Gestapo, SS and Reichssicherheitshauptamt on the 'Prinz-Albrecht-Terrain' A Documentation* (Berlin: Verlag Willmuth Arenhövel, 1989).

Sanchez, Leopold Diego, *Jean-Michel Frank* (Paris: Editions du Regard, 1980).

Schloss, Eva and Kent, Evelyn Julia, *Eva's Story: A Survivor's Tale by the Step-sister of Anne Frank* (London: W. H. Allen, 1988).

Schnabel, Ernst, *The Footsteps of Anne Frank* (London: Pan Books, 1976).

Steenmeijer, Anna G. and Frank, Otto (eds.), *A Tribute to Anne Frank* (New York: Doubleday, 1971).

Stoutenbeek, Jan and Vigeveno, Paul, *A Guide to Jewish Amsterdam* (Amsterdam: De Haan, 1985).

Strasberg, Susan, *Bittersweet* (New York: Signet, 1980).

Sulzbach, Herbert, *With The German Guns: Four Years on the Western Front* (London: Leo Cooper, 1998).

Todorov, Tzvetan, *Facing The Extreme: Moral Life in the Concentration Camps* (London: Phoenix, 2000).

Wasserstein, Bernard, *Vanishing Diaspora: The Jews in Europe since 1945* (London, Penguin, 1996).

Wiesenthal, Simon, *Justice Not Vengeance* (London: Weidenfeld & Nicolson, 1989).

Wilson, Cara, *Love, Otto: The Legacy of Anne Frank* (Kansas: Andrews & McMeel, 1995).

Wistrich, Robert S., *Anti-Semitism: The Longest Hatred* (London: Methuen, 1991).

Young, James E. (ed.), *The Art of Memory: Holocaust Memorials in History* (Munich: Presetel-Verlag, 1994).

Articles and Other Publications

Adler, Joan, Straus Family Newsletter: *'Wholedamfam'*, February 1998.

'Anne Frank's Secret Annexe Awaits The Wrecker's Ball', *Het Vrij Volk*, 23 November 1955.

'Anne Frank Betrayed for Ten Shillings', *Sunday Times*, 5 February 1967.

Anne Frank Stichting, exhibition catalogue in Dutch and English, *Anne Frank in the World 1929–1945* (Amsterdam: Bert Bakker, 1985).

Anne Frank Stichting, exhibition catalogue in Japanese, *Anne Frank in the World* (Amsterdam: Anne Frank Stichting, 1985).

Anne Frank Stichting, exhibition catalogue in English, *Anne Frank: A History for Today* (Amsterdam: Anne Frank Stichting, 1996).

Anne Frank Stichting, *Anne Frank Magazine 1998* (Amsterdam: Anne Frank Stichting, 1998).

Anne Frank Stichting, *Anne Frank Magazine 1999* (Amsterdam: Anne Frank Stichting, 1999).

Anne Frank Stichting, *Anne Frank Magazine 2000* (Amsterdam: Anne Frank Stichting, 2000).

Ariel, 'Testament of Youth', *Huddersfield Weekly Examiner*, October 1954.

Ballif, Algene, *Commentary*, November 1955.

Baron, Alexander, *The Jewish Chronicle*, 15 October 1954.

Bundy, June, 'Anne Frank: The Diary of a Young Girl', *Billboard*, 27 September 1952.

Buruma, Ian, 'Anne Frank's Afterlife', *New York Review of Books*, Vol. XLV, Number 3, 19 February 1998.

Chapman, John, 'Anne Frank Wins Prize', *Sunday News*, 13 May 1956.

Cohn, Vera, *The Anti-Defamation League Bulletin: The Day I Met Anne Frank*, undated.

Duke, Juliane, 'Anne Frank Remembered', *New York Times*, 11 June 1989.

Farrell, E. C., 'Postscript to a Diary', *Global Magazine*, 1965.

Fishman, Joel, 'The Jewish Community in the Post-War Netherlands 1944–1975', *Midstream*, XXII (1976).

Flanner, Janet, 'Letter from Paris', *New Yorker*, 11 November 1950.

Frank, Otto, 'Has Germany Forgotten Anne Frank?', *Coronet*, February 1960.

Frank, Otto, 'Anne Frank Would Have Been Fifty This Year', *Life*, March 1979.

Fussman, Carl, 'The Woman Who Would Have Saved Anne Frank', *Newsday*, 16 March 1995.

Kolb, Bernard, 'Diary Footnotes', *New York Times*, 2 October 1955.

Kramer, Mimi, 'Spotlight: Encore, Anne Frank', *Vanity Fair*, December 1997.

Levin, Meyer, 'The Restricted Market', *Congress Weekly*, 13 November 1950.

Levin, Meyer, 'The Child Behind the Secret Door', *New York Times Book Review*, 15 June 1952.

Levin, Meyer, 'Anne Frank: The Diary of a Young Girl', *Congress Weekly*, June 1952.

Levin, Meyer, 'The Suppressed Anne Frank', *Jewish Week*, 31 August 1980.

'The Living Legacy of Anne Frank', *Journal*, September 1967.

Majdalany, 'Anne Frank Was Never Like This', *Daily Mail*, 5 June 1959.

Mulder, Dirk, *Kamp Westerbork* (Westerbork: Herinneringscentrum Kamp Westerbork, 1991).

New York Times Book Review, 28 September 1997.

'Otto Frank, Father of Anne, Dead at 91', *New York Times*, 21 August 1980.

Ozick, Cynthia, 'Who Owns Anne Frank?', *New Yorker*, 6 October 1997.

Pepper, William, 'Drama of "Diary" is Nonsectarian', *New York World Telegram and Sun*, January 1956.

Press leaflet for the film *Ein Tagebuch für Anne Frank*. Chapter: Lientje Brilleslijper-Jaldati, *Memories of Anne Frank* (Berlin: VEB Progess Film-Vertrieb, 1959).

Puner, Morton, 'The Mission of Otto Frank', *The ADL Bulletin*, April 1959.

Romein, Jan, 'A Child's Voice', *Het Parool*, 3 April 1946.

Rosenfeld, Alvin H., 'The Americanization of the Holocaust' in *Commentary*, June 1995.

St George, Andrew, 'The Diary That Shook A Nation', *Pageant*, July 1958.

Shapiro, Eda, 'The Reminiscences of Victor Kugler, the "Mr Kraler" of Anne Frank's Diary', *Yad Vashem Studies*, XIII (Jerusalem: Yad Vashem, 1979).

Spetter, Ies, 'Onderduik Pret Broadway', *Vrij Nederland*, 5 November 1955.

Stern, 21 May 1982.

Stocks, Mary, 'The Secret Annexe', *Manchester Guardian*, 28 April 1952.

Strang, Joanne, 'Stevens Relives Anne Frank's Story', *New York Times Magazine*, 3 August 1958.

Straus, R. Peter, article in *Moment*, December 1977.

Stroom, Gerrold van der, *Anne Frank and her Diaries*, paper delivered at the Institute of Jewish Studies, University College, London, June 1997.

Visser, Anneke, 'Discovery of Letters Written by Man who Hid in Anne Frank's Secret Annexe', *NRC Handlesblad*, 7 November 1987.

Vuur, Willem, 'Anne Frank House in Money Trouble', *Herald Tribune*, 1 April 1971.

Waggoner, Walter H., 'New Yorker Aids Dutch Students', *New York Times*, 26 July 1957.

Watertown Daily Times: Holocaust Survivors Recall Their Hell On Earth, 5 February 1995.

Welt am Sonntag: Anne Frank's Vater: Ich will Versohnung, 4 February 1979.

'Who Killed Anne Frank?' *Hadassah Magazine*, No 7, March 1965.

Windsor, John, 'Duty of Dr Frank', *Guardian*, 15 June 1971.

Wistrich, Robert S., *Anti-Semitism: The Longest Hatred* (London: Methuen, 1991).

Wolff, Margo H., 'Anne Frank Lives On', *Hadassah Newsletter*, May 1958.

Wolzogen, Wolf von, *Anne aus Frankfurt* (Frankfurt: Historical Museum, 1994).

Unpublished Documents (excluding correspondence)

Ahlers, A. Dossier(s), Centraal Archief Bijzondere Rechtspleging (CABR), Rijksarchief, Den Haag.

Ahlers, A. Report by the Dutch authorities, 1964. Doc. I., K. J. Silberbauer. NIOD.

Baschwitz, Mrs I. Report of a conversation with, 12 January 1981. NIOD.

Cahn, W. Report of a conversation with, 12 March 1981. NIOD.

Cauvern, A. Report of a conversation with, 23 January 1981. NIOD.

Document: 'Financial Information Regarding The International Anne Frank Youth Centre', 1959. AFS.

Döring, K., Doc. I., Collection of Nederlandse Instituut voor Oorlogsdocumentatie (NIOD). Dossier, CABR. Press cuttings, NIOD.

Frank, Anne, Baby Book. Archives of the Anne Frank-Fonds, Basel (AFF).

Frank, Fritzi, 'My Life with Otto Frank', memoir, 1980. Private collection of Buddy Elias (BE).

Frank, Margot, Baby Book. AFF.

Frank, Otto, liberation diary 1945. AFS.

Frank, Otto, Polish Red Cross declaration regarding his return to the Netherlands, 1945. AFS.

Frank, Otto, Engagements Diary 1945. AFS.

Frank, Otto, Engagements Diary 1947. AFS.

Frank, Otto, memoir. BE.

Frank, Otto, interview transcript with Westinghouse Broadcasting Company Inc, USA, 16 February 1960. AFS.

Frank, Otto, transcript of tape recording made for a school group, 1970s. AFS.

Frank, Otto, interview transcripts of recorded discussion with Arthur Unger, New York, 1977.

Frank, Otto, undated document, headed 'Comments'. AFS.

Frank, Otto, undated document, headed 'Remarks Regarding Warrant Sent to Me with your Letter of 19 March 1956'. AFS.

Gies, J. A. and Gies-Santrouschitz, M. Report of two conversations with, 19 and 27 February 1985. NIOD.

Gies, J. A. and Gies-Santrouschitz, M. Report of a conversation with, 18 February 1981. NIOD.

Gies, M., page of testimony written by. AFS.

Gringhuis, G., Dossier, CABR.

Grootendorst, W., Dossier, CABR.

Grossman, Jean Schick, 'The Story Within Her Story' (unpublished manuscript), 5 December 1954.

Hammelburg, Rabbi. Report of a conversation with, 23 February 1981. NIOD.

Hauptman, Barbara, essay, 'A Visit to Amsterdam', August 1971. AFS.

Hondius, Dienke, 'The Return'. Unpublished English translation of *Terugkeer: Antisemitisme in Nederland rond de bevrijding* (The Hague: SDU, 1990).

Jansen, J. M., Dossier, CABR.

Kropveld, Dr S. M. Declaration of, in dossier *Westerbork–Auschwitz, 3 September 1944*. NIOD.

Kuiper, M., Doc. I., NIOD. Dossier, CABR. Press cuttings, NIOD.

Landau town archives, and the pamphlets *Some Historical Facts About The House* and *Facts Relating To The Jews Of Landau*, available from the Frank-Loeb'sches House.

Liema, Rose de, unpublished memoir, 'So You Will Remember'. AFS.

Liema, Sal de, transcript of interview conducted by the Anne Frank Stichting. AFS.

Maaren, W. G. van, Doc. I., NIOD. Dossier, CABR.

Mengelberg-Draber, Mrs R. E. Report of a conversation with, 19 February 1981. NIOD.

Opekta file, NBI archive, Rijksarchief, Den Haag.

Opekta/Pectacon, Dossier, NIOD.

Opekta/Pectacon Delivery Book, 1940. AFS.

Poppel, J. van, Doc. I., NIOD. Dossier, CABR. Press cuttings, NIOD.

Romein-Verschoor, A., Report of a conversation with, undated. NIOD.

Rouwendaal, H., Doc. I., NIOD. Dossier, CABR. Press cuttings, NIOD.

Rühl, E., Doc. I., NIOD. Dossier, CABR. Press cuttings, NIOD.

Silberbauer, K. J., Doc. I., NIOD.

Spronz, Joseph, unpublished manuscript, 'Auschwitz Memoirs'. AFS.

Stanfield, Milly, 'A Talk: Anne and Otto Frank', 22 April 1990. AFS.

Stanfield, Milly, Memoirs. AFS.

Viebahn, F. C., Dossier, CABR. Press cuttings, NIOD.

Wijk-Voskuijl, Bep van. Report of a conversation with, 25 February 1981. NIOD.

Wolters, K. O. M., Doc. I., NIOD.

Index